Narrative as Communication

Theory and History of Literature
Edited by Wlad Godzich and Jochen Schulte-Sasse

For other books in the series, see p. 371

Narrative as Communication

Didier Coste

Foreword by Wlad Godzich

Theory and History of Literature, Volume 64

University of Minnesota Press, Minneapolis

Published by the University of Minnesota Press
2037 University Avenue Southeast, Minneapolis, MN 55414.
Printed in the United States of America.

Library of Congress Catalog Card Number 89-040476
ISBN 0-8166-1719-8
ISBN 0-8166-1720-1 (pbk.)

The Apparition by Gustave Moreau is reproduced here by permission of the Musée Nationaux, Paris.

The University of Minnesota
is an equal-opportunity
educator and employer.

This book is dedicated to Nuria
who has given a name to my
happy ending

Selbst der Styx, der neunfach flieszet,
Schlieszt die wagende nicht aus;
Mächtig raubt sie das Geliebte
Aus des Pluto finsterm Haus.

—Schiller

Contents

Foreword: The Time Machine
Wlad Godzich

When Tzvetan Todorov coined the term "narratology" in 1969 to designate the study of narrative he was responding to the then widespread belief that narrative was particularly amenable to being elevated to the status of an object of knowledge for a new science armed with its own concepts and analytic protocols. He was also responding to the hope, or perhaps more accurately, the desire, to lift all of literary and cultural studies to the dignity of science, a desire that strongly animated French structuralism. Todorov's programmatic enthusiasm seemed warranted then: whereas the previous half-century had been punctuated by occasional studies of the art of the novel, some rare analyses of point of view, and limited disquisitions on narrative organization, the sixties had seen colloquia and conferences, entire issues of journals, significant translations from Russian and Czech in addition to the more common European languages, as well as new publications appearing almost daily, all dealing with narrative. Twenty years later, the graduate student who ventures into this area is faced with an almost intractable bibliography, a wealth of specialized terms, and, in some instances, symbolic notations ranging from the linguistic to the mathematico-logical. For some time now, some of the best minds in the field, notably Gérard Genette and Wallace Martin, have called for a moment of reflection and assessment to determine where we are in relation to all of the theorizing that has passed for narratology, and there prevails a general sense of unease suggestive of unfulfilled expectations.

It is the type of situation that calls for the instinctive reactions of complete dismissal that one finds here and there, or for some project of redemption of a field that has gone astray. Didier Coste's book falls more into the latter mode, although redemption is quite foreign to its idiom. Coste refuses, however, to dismiss all that has been done in narrative theory simply because the expectations that were vested in it have not been fulfilled. They were, in any case, beyond fulfillment, since these expectations represented murky responses to the general situation of humanists in universities undergoing rapid expansion. Coste is far more interested in drawing up an inventory of the analytic tools and concepts that have been elaborated and in showing that they constitute a workable overarching approach to the study of narrative, although not in the terms in which they were originally conceived. In other words, Coste proposes a new framework, that of a theory of communication, for the study of narrative, and he shows in the pages of this book that such an approach enables us to give narrative its due. At first sight, this claim may seem implausible. After all, in the eyes of most students of literature, communication theory is hardly in better shape than narrative theory, and it is therefore unlikely that the grafting of two lame legs on the same body would produce a smooth running animal; yet that is the very challenge that Coste has taken up in the pages that follow.

The narratology that Todorov and countless others in his wake have sought to elaborate represented an extension of the very poetics that was being revived in the sixties as part of a larger, if mostly unconscious, societal project of establishing, and policing, a lasting order. Much of that impulse has remained with us, gaining strength rather than weakening from the various instances of sociopolitical, economic, and cultural disorder that have occurred since. The possibility of such an order presided over by the Hegelian figure of the state rests upon our ability to determine all possible actions, calculate their potential combinations, and analyze their outcome. Individual texts, such as the *Decameron*, can be treated as equivalent to languages whose action grammars are yet to be described. Once we had a large number of such individual descriptive grammars, we could determine the deep structures governing all actions, establish the felicity conditions for their accomplishment, and set proper receptive framework for their interpretation. Even though it represented itself as politically progressive, such a narratology, as indeed all poetics, was in the service of a social engineering administered by an almighty state.

Roland Barthes is a case in point. In *S/Z*, his famous study of narrative in a Balzac short story, Barthes may have sought to separate himself from the hard structuralists by distinguishing between the classical readerly texts that are totalizable, decidable, continuous, and unified, and the writerly texts that are plural and open to the free play of signifiers and of difference, but his continued focus on the elementary action as the basic unit of narrative analysis firmly inscribes him within the narratological project. In his *Maupassant*, which resembles *S/Z* a great deal, Greimas cuts the text up in "segments" that correspond to units of the narrative without explicitly taking up the logic of this segmentation. Barthes, who calls his segments "lexias" and "fragments," is far more conscious of the fact that these are artifices of reading, and he indeed seeks to recoup their artificiality in the service of his opposition between the writerly and the readerly. At stake is the very conception of action as denoted by discourse, for which Barthes invokes the Aristotelian term *prohairesis* (a transcription that stresses the term's etymological meaning). Unlike Greimas, Barthes is not seeking to establish the existence of an all-encompassing and all-deciding structure for his text; nonetheless, he is forced to consider action in ways that are not much different from Greimas's conception of it. He borrows the term *prohairesis* from Aristotle, who invoked it in the context of deliberative discourse to denote the future projection of a course of action, and simplifies its meaning to the rational determination of the result of an action. He recognizes, however, that nothing is more difficult than to arrive at such a determination unless one knows beforehand what the outcome of the entire sequence of actions is going to be. Armed with this knowledge, the analyst reads backward as it were and discards those elements that will prove unproductive, keeping only those that will contribute to the general result. This procedure is tantamount to cheating and makes a mockery of the claim that the determination of the result is a rational one. In point of fact, it is an interested determination based upon a form of privileged knowledge, ex post facto applied to a process that is supposed to be open-ended. Barthes acknowledges this by admitting that the prohairetic sequence is an artifice of reading, but he does not seem to notice what this entails.

He may well have thought of himself as arguing in favor of open-endedness, but in fact he was operating with concepts that require closure. The workings of his prohairetic code project each sequence unto a closed continuum that determines both its identity, by means of the labels that the code bestows upon it, and its place in the narrative continuum. This continuum is thus ruled by a form of purposive necessity, not unlike Kant's nature, that ensures that whatever is left to punctual judgment at the level of the individual prohairetic sequence is ultimately recouped in the service of the whole. Barthes seems to be unaware of the fact that having started from premises inherent to poetics in which the purposiveness of form is a foundational postulate, he inevitably winds up with a teleological conception of the narrative process, even though the movement of the telos can be established only through the intervention of the reader.

This conception of action in which the meaning of the action is determined by its place in the configuration of the whole, as assessed by a reader, lies at the center of all narrative theories. One is strongly tempted to say that it is no accident that this is so, but to yield to this temptation is to blind oneself to the very problem at hand, which is that of the commingling of story and history. The purposive necessity that binds the individual action or fact to the narrative whole finds its counterpart in the conception of history in which what Fredric Jameson calls "otherwise inert chronological and 'linear' data" (*The Political Unconscious*

[1981], 101) are reorganized in the form of Necessity: "why what happened (at first received as 'empirical' fact) had to happen the way it did" (ibid). Narrative analysis has stressed this sense of an inexorable logic working itself out through the course of the narrative. Jameson understands this full well and draws out the consequences: for him, history becomes the experience of necessity, that is, the experience of this inexorable logic. What we experience, however, is not this necessity as the secret meaning of history, for that would reify history, but rather as a narrative category imposing an inexorable form upon events. In other words, Jameson attributes to history the capabilities of an agency on the basis of its narrative properties. This agency is not the traditional Aristotelian or Thomistic one of first or ultimate cause of an action, but rather the shaper of intelligibility.

We have seen that Barthes vests the possibility of this shaping in the reader who "cheats" by bringing to bear upon the course of the text his privileged knowledge of the "outcome" of the text. Jameson knows that in order to make an equivalent claim in relation to history one would have to construct a transcendental position in relation to it, so that Barthes's almighty and immanent reader capable of traveling back and forth across the linearity of narrative time would find its counterpart in an almighty God, or in a principle of rationality, or in the all-powerful state armed with the laws of history. Jameson rejects this totalitarian possibility, the nefarious effects of which have been historically well attested, to posit instead the workings of an immanent principle: that of a form.

In Jameson's conception, history becomes then not only the experience of necessity, but the experience of the fact that necessity is the form of history. One may well suspect at this stage that there has been a transfer of properties from story to history, but the very impulse that led one to want to say that this was no accident earlier attests that it is not so, for Jameson's account rests on the solid Hegelian ground in which the transfer of properties goes from history to story and not the other way around. Narrative, in this conception, inevitably espouses the form of history and thus provides us with cognitive access to the latter's workings. In the formal terms that Jameson invokes, the transfer of properties from history to story is sublated; that is, the metaphor is annulled into its own catachresis, so that empirical readers need not play the role of transcendental readers and still can see the shaping of story by history. The catachresis itself is thus rendered necessary and indeed inscribed in the very process of history. The function of this process becomes apparent: to convert metaphor into catachresis or, in less formal terms, to convert linguistic operations into "natural" agency. Narratology, for its part, must redouble this process by analyzing this "natural" agency back into linguistic operations and thus making the latter appear to be the result of the process of narratological analysis and not of a prior massive catachresis. In Marxian terms one must posit the identity of the dialectics of nature and the dialectics of thought, the dialectics of history and of language.

The point of my retracing this ground is to help us recognize the underlying philosophical assumption of narratology: it is the Parmenidean postulate of Being's manifestation in language and its inverse reciprocal that language states Being. To be sure, this Parmenideanism is quite sophisticated now so that it does not expect that every statement corresponds to a state of being, an expectation that would have made fiction impossible; it now admits that the "stating" of Being takes place at a larger structural level, where story and history are indeed a way of stating or manifesting one another. Again, this should not surprise us inasmuch as this sort of Parmenideanism underlies all of poetics and subtends its dependence on mimesis. And if there is one thing that narratology has taken very seriously it is the mimetic character of narrative representation since it is this foundational belief in mimesis that has permitted the elaboration of the concept of minimal action in the first place. Even the Proppian notion of function partakes of this dependence: the mimetic correspondence is established at the level of the whole tale rather than that of each individual action.

This Parmenideanism manifests itself especially strongly in those studies of narrative that are concerned with the effect of narrative upon its recipients, and thus appear to be moving in the direction of the communicational approach that Coste takes in this book. Such studies typically deal with this problem under the name of identification and provide an account of the reading, or the viewing, process as one in which the narratee finds himself or herself interpellated by the narrative program of the work he or she is receiving, and thus reconstituted into the subject of this narrative program. The working of identification is thus premised on the catachresis of story and history: the reader reads the story and is thus shaped by history.

Identification is indeed the name of the operation by which catachresis takes place since it transfers properties from one term to another and erases the memory of the transfer so that the two terms appear to be identical. In narratological studies of identification this operation is described in terms of cleaved consciousness and of the dilemma facing the reader who is thus faced with two distinct temporal frames corresponding to the before and after of the reading. This dilemma, which corresponds to the modern predicament, has to do with the reader's ability to both remember and forget the past, and to forget and remember the conditions under which he or she has come about in the present. It is no problem for a trope to hold both of these temporal frames within itself since tropes do not inhabit phenomenological time. But as soon as human beings are expected to behave like tropes, and especially as complicated a trope as catachresis (the description of which requires, after all, an anthropomorphized way of talking about language inasmuch as it is mediated through categories of remembrance and forgetting, i.e., categories of human time), we are likely to be facing major difficulties. Identification narratology avoids these difficulties by focusing on the secondary issues of ideological manipulation, for it could not face the fact that it operates on the assumption that human beings are catachretic.

Identification narratology originates in, and subscribes to, the modern project of the Enlightenment. Its interest in narrative stems from the desire to discern between narratives of liberation and narratives of enslavement. It is committed, in other words, to promoting the autonomy of the reading subject. To understand such a subject as catachretic would be tantamount to admitting that this autonomy is heteronomous in origin, and that the function of the claim of autonomy is in fact to occult this constitutive heteronomy. Identification narratology takes such a heteronomy to be the operator of a deprivation of agency for the modern subject who has to be reinstated as capable agent. Curiously enough, this agent then becomes capable of doing what history requires her or him to do, a strange definition of autonomy, though well attested in Western, and especially Christian, thought.

Coste seeks to effect a break with this Parmenidean conception of the relation of language to Being and with the mimetic conception of action to which it has led. He is, however, fully cognizant that earlier attempts to break with Parmenideanism in Western thought have tended to privilege the imaginary and to cancel out the notion of agency. We need to bear in mind that Parmenidean doctrine establishes a set of identity equations between language and Being, that is, between language and reality. It ensures that language can and indeed does function referentially. Any tampering with these identity equations precipitates a crisis of referentiality. In modern times this problem has taken the form of a predicament in which we, as language users and indeed as language-dependent beings, are forced to remember that language is a system of signs that is governed by its own internal economy and by the history of its past usages, and, at the same time, we must forget the artifactualness of language to continue to be able to refer to reality. Modernity is haunted by this nondialectical conjunction of forgetting and remembering, and it has become increasingly aware of its dependency on language. This has proved extremely disturbing to it because one of the foundations of modernity has been the distinction between fact and fiction, a distinction that did not have the same preeminence in premodernity, where it was the distinction between sacred and profane that was paramount. To bear in mind that referentiality is mediated through the workings of language is to make fiction the mode of access to fact, a disturbing notion if one sees fact and fiction as polar opposites. It is this disturbance that catachretic approaches to story and history are meant to dispel, thereby preserving the underlying economy of modernity.

Within the framework of modernity it does appear that anything short of such a catachretic solution would result in the dissolving of another major axis of opposition: that between real and imaginary. Much of the aesthetic activity of the late nineteenth century and of the twentieth has recognized, and sought to accelerate, this dissolution. But this movement toward the imaginary, in modernity's topology, continues to be perceived as that of agential deprivation and thus elicits resistance and opposition, especially in view of the fact that this agential deprivation does not seem to strike at the major forces that shape our lives and our societies. This perception is incorrect, however, since it is grounded in modernity's conception of the imaginary where the latter is opposed to the real and can thus offer nothing but a simulacrum or at best a representation of the real. It must be understood that the dissolution of the opposition between real and imaginary results in a commingling of what the two terms stand for as the ground of their differentiation. And therein lies another consequence of note: the modern opposition between the real and the imaginary further mapped itself over the distinction between the collective and the individual, leading to the notion that all forms of collective imaginary were instances of ideological manipulation or illusion.

This is the new ground upon which Coste seeks to reconceptualize narratology. It is not a grammar of action but part and parcel of a theory of communication where the latter is understood not as the exchange of messages but as the management of this collective imaginary charged with establishing and regulating the conditions of referentiality in the society that shares it. I should hasten to stress that I do mean referentiality and not reference or even referents as is too often assumed to be the case. Coste is quite emphatic on this point himself.

What is the place of narrative in this conception, and what is the function of narratology? Since these are the questions that Coste addresses in this book I will limit myself to one aspect to which I have already alluded: *prohairesis*. As is well known, Aristotle considered narrative as part of the middle genre of rhetoric, that of deliberative discourse. The function of this genre is to prove to the assembled citizens of the city the need for, or indeed the necessity of, a particular course of action that one wishes to see them execute, or conversely, to dissuade them from a given course of action. Deliberative discourse, in other words, leads to action or to its abrogation. It is not, itself, a representation of an action, and is never meant to be a substitute for it. The best way of thinking about it is as enabling (or disabling) action. And this is where *prohairesis* comes in: we have seen earlier that Aristotle used this term to designate the future projection of a course of action. In other words, *prohairesis* has to do with time, with a special mode of representation called "projection," and with action considered as a course, that is, as a flow. The triggering mechanism for all of this is a decision, and decision is indeed the object of deliberative discourse. What we need to understand better is how decision relates to the constitutive features of *prohairesis*.

Aristotle and all subsequent narratologists have recognized that narrative has a special relationship to time. But they have all thought of time as infinite and homogeneous, analyzable in quantifiable moments of "objectively" equal value; such a time is linear, and ultimately absolute, experienced as a curse or at the very least as a predicament. Philosophy, which is concept oriented, has sought a limitless time in which to define them, and has had thus little patience with decisions. Our habits of thought have been built up around concepts, the proper deployment of which requires the suspension of decisions, a deferral of any decision making, since the latter, viewed from the perspective of the essence of the concept, can only mark the concept's submission to temporality's least attractive feature: its limitation of extension. Decisions are profoundly antithetical to philosophy in this respect. They "rush" time. What philosophical reflection seeks to defer indefinitely, a decision concentrates in a point, the moment, the time of decision. And this concentration has fatal consequences, from a philosophical perspective: it does not allow us to judge whether a statement is true—that is, whether it stands for a state of affairs—or whether a concept has found its proper embodiment. In the concentrated time of decision, the true is not separable from the state of affairs it purportedly stands for, and the concept is not distinguishable from the materiality that confronts us. Insofar as representation occurs in the time of decision, and it does, it is always representation for the other and not representation in itself. This is the fundamental reason why a communication approach to narrative has a chance to avoid the pitfalls of the philosophically sounder narratologies. To put it bluntly, we need to recognize that a decision entails that the elements it manages and affects exist in a temporal dimension that is incommensurable with the infinite extension of concepts inhabiting an infinite and homogeneous time.

It would be tempting to interpret this statement as Nietzsche's statements on perspective have been interpreted, that is, as calling for relativism and advocating a pluralism of worldviews. Such an interpretation runs counter to what is most important in a decision: its sense of urgency. When an assembly deliberates upon a course of action, it is precisely because its members have the sense that an inexorable logic is working its way and they perceive the end of this process as inimical to them. The function of the decision is not to calculate the end product of the process but to figure out an escape from it. The decision is not meant to propose an alternate view or a new representation that will coexist peacefully with the older one, but to escape into a new temporal dimension free from as many of the constraints of the old one as possible.

To figure out how to escape involves a double catachresis: first, the historical predicament has to be converted into story so that its full dimension can be apprehended. This involves the projection of a course of action. But this story is then treated as story so that history itself may be arrested: the time frame of the story is easily manipulated, and the function of the decision is to open up a different time, to produce more time where none was otherwise available; and this production of time permits the second catachresis, which does go from story to history, for the new time is one that can be lived. The function of the story, of its telling within the context of deliberative discourse, is thus to fracture philosophical time, to mobilize its rupture in the service of an alternative, one that will be marked by the sense of a beginning.

It is thus not accurate to say that decisions concentrate time; rather, they produce it. Each such production entails a new mode of establishing referentiality, of organizing the time that has been produced by the decision, of inhabiting a time of our own making as opposed to the inhuman time of concepts. Narratology has been in the service of inhuman time; it has occulted the place of decision to concentrate on concepts of action, analyzed into minimal units, linked into inexorable logics attributed to inhuman forces. Such narratologies go hand in hand with a conception of a time ruled by forces beyond our control, and are indeed in the service of such forces. We have all noted at one time or another that epoch of narratologies, the late sixties to the mid-eighties, has been one of limited and uninspired narrative production in the industrialized world. The celebrated success of Latin American novels, and indeed of emergent literatures, contrasted sharply with our Western orientation toward narratology, and frequently left the latter befuddled since this emergent writing refused to fit easily into its concepts. Such emergent writing has been putting into question narratology's methodological presupposition of an infinite and homogeneous time; better, it has been declaring itself incompatible and incommensurable with such a notion. Narratology's unconscious complicity in the assertion of a universal order, which would be that of "our" time, should not lead us, however, to jettison it altogether, for it is far from clear that a narratology that starts with different premises could not produce some time of its own. Such at least has been Didier Coste's courageous wager in this book.

Acknowledgments

Although this book is published as my exclusive effort, the colleagues and students to whom I am indebted are many, Dr. José Ma Fernández Gutiérrez and Professor Alain Verjat, of the Universidad de Tarragona and Universidad Central de Barcelona, respectively, made me realize the insufficiencies of a theory of the novel when they kindly invited me to lecture on this topic in 1979. The "Construction of Meaning Seminars," at Murdoch University (Western Australia) convened by Professor Horst Ruthrof in 1980, helped me to reconsider the questions of narrative economy and didactic meaning that are at the core of my chapters 8 and 10. Professor Wlad Godzich suggested that I write an American version of my work in progress when he saw the first drafts in French in 1981. My senior and graduate students at Murdoch University and at the universities of Pau and Minnesota, among whom Dr. Anthony Pym, Mr. Thierry Mézailles, and Mr. Ronald Judy were some of the most dedicated to theoretical reflection, engaged in vivid discussions of important problems, such as those of quantitative narrative and ergative transformations, also often pursued with my friend and colleague Jean Caminade. The actual writing and revision of the final version of the book would not have been possible without the generous Visiting Professorships I was offered in the French and Italian Department of Louisiana State University, Baton Rouge, in 1986, and in the departments of Comparative Literature and French and Italian of the University of Minnesota in 1987. I wish to express my sincere gratitude to Terry Cochran, Senior Editor at the University of Minnesota Press, and to Professor Jochen Schulte-Sasse, also of the University of Minnesota, for their insistence that I develop the historical aspect of my research. Professor Tom Conley kindly photographed the thirty frames of *The Quiet Man* that illustrate my discussion of kinetic narrative. Finally, Ms. Mary Byers is to be thanked for her handling of the hard job into which my Latin carelessness turned the copyediting of this text.

D.C.
Pau, Bâton Rouge, Calaceite, Minneapolis
September 1985 – June 1987

Narrative as Communication

Chapter 1
The Nature and Purpose
of Narratology

In the Preface to his *Recent Theories of Narrative* (1986), Wallace Martin does not hesitate to write: "When translations from French, German and Russian are added to the writings of English and American theorists, the only alternative to few books on narrative in general might appear to be none at all."[1] And J. A. Berthoud, in his in-depth critique of Jameson, "Narrative and Ideology" (1985), states, "The attempt to construct a narrative grammar to account for our capacity to recognize and discuss plots or stories extractable from narrative texts has been thoroughly discredited."[2] These two statements should certainly be qualified. Is it true that the early structuralist project of a general narratology was never carried out? Or is it that many unfulfilled promises have disqualified it? And in what sense: as reductive or intuitive and unscientific, as nonsystematic or oversystematic?

The need for a new or renewed narratology that would use all the analytic tools (linguistic, rhetorical, epistemological) developed in the last twenty years in the context of changing technologies and little-changed social relations, makes itself felt even more urgently than it did in the supposedly optimistic and expansionist 1960s. Political, scientific, and moral discourses that were openly normative are being replaced by powerful narrative machines such as soap operas and the successive findings of commissions of inquiry; "deconstruction," in its more popular versions, and poststructuralism in general are misunderstood as antihistorical enterprises like their predecessors, as if the denunciation of a godlike subject, always already there, jeopardized a critical consciousness of human beings in time. The surge of a "New Historicism," with all its age-old illusions of presentness of the past and pastness of the present, as well as the reduction by the general public and many sociologists and cultural commentators of literature, film, and other art forms to their sole narrative aspects, also calls for a radical rethinking of a "science of narratology" grown stale with the epigones of the European literati who gave it its credentials.

It is not reassuring to read in a major journal like *Poétique*, a recent article entitled "De l'obstination narratologique," which engages in obscure terminological quibbles and pretends to break new theoretical ground simply by defending Gérard Genette against the whole world, including himself.[3] At a time when some narratologies tend to become extremely esoteric and express themselves in a nondiscursive sign language made of symbols, equations, and self-contained diagrams, while others sell the same old summaries and paraphrases of "works of fiction" under a new coat of paint, it seems necessary to consider simultaneously a radical revision and redefinition of the scope and method of study of narrative. This is what I attempt in this book, in the framework of an explicit general theory of social communication of which the production and exchange of narrative meaning, the production and exchange of aesthetic value and their occasional combination are three important but not exhaustive instances.

The Preconditions of a Narratology

I shall first of all list several of the constraints under which this research was begun and the resulting demands and claims I have had to make in order to respond to them, if possible, by a profitable, nonmechanical, emancipating course of action.

1. This book is not about narrative in general; it is about narrative *communication* in general. Narrative has no substance. The word "narrative" is basically an adjective, not a substantive. Although I shall use it sometimes to mean "narrative text" or even, loosely, "narrativity," one should never be misled to think that there is a body of *texts* that share enough special features to be called "narrative in general," or that narrativity exists independently from an act of communication that actualizes a message as bearing narrative meaning, whatever the final function, if any, of this feature of the message.

I contend that all the human sciences are sciences of communication—or of its failure, which amounts to the same thing. But, even though the human sciences use narrative discourse liberally in their respective metadiscourses, it does not follow that either communication or metadiscourses on it are all narrative. *An act of communication is narrative whenever and only when imparting a transitive view of the world is the effect of the message produced.*

The study of narrative communication will encompass (1) the processes by which narrative messages are formed and (2) the functions of such messages, the uses to which they are put. The first item includes the behavior and motivations of the human actors involved, the materials used, the rules and codes abided by, and the forms and structures of the mediating means shaped in the process, that is, the "narrative texts." The second item involves the production of value, the individual and collective effects of the messages *qua* narrative, their further transformations into messages of other kinds (injunctive, didactic, lyrical, etc.).

2. A message is narrative not because of the way in which it is conveyed (its "mode," in Genette's terminology), but because it has narrative meaning. A message is not conveyed, properly speaking, since it is the "point" of an act of communication as seen by the observer of this act; the message is, in other words, the meaningfulness that is turned by the participants and witnesses of the act of communication into evidence that this act has taken place. The narrative message, the tale told, is not therefore a "content"; it is not contained within a text. Meaning is meant; it is measured; it is understood; someone places it above him- or herself to stand under it. I measure meaning in order to measure myself. Meaning is the standard of my being; narrative meaning is the standard of my (our) being as mortal (more on this later in this chapter).

3. Since I am writing, or speaking, every piece of knowledge and belief I can acquire and impart, even when it is addressed from myself to myself, formed by the myselves, will be verbal. I can only know, here, within language; I can only know verbalized objects. Narrative communication, however, does not necessarily take a verbal form—not until it becomes an object of knowledge. But verbal narrative communication will be privileged in this study (a) because it presents itself, truthfully or not, as a ready-made object of (verbal) knowledge, as prepared to be known, and it even gives the illusion of knowing itself (thus saving us the difficulty of saying about it anything else than what it "really" says); and (b) because we can play with it and play it as we are trying to know it. In fact, my attempt to know it is a mild transformation, a game of slight disguises, perhaps a digestion à la Valéry, not a destruction. I can show the transformation without violently separating myself from my object, I can seduce it and cheat it without feeling guilty. I then learn that this is not true, but I learn it from its own practice, without being too unfaithful to it.

4. Narratology is the scientific study of narrative communication. It is the study neither of events and actions nor of the verbal mode of signifying such events and actions. Events and actions may have logical structures that will be accounted for by theories of time, action, and the physical world. But narratology has an anthropological scope: it is concerned with the production, transmission, and exchange of information on change and simulacra of change. Verbal discourse takes place in "time," in compulsory succession, but this succession of signifiers does not have to present its signifieds as successive in the world of reference any more than a still in a film indicates that a landscape lasts five minutes. Conversely, the alphabetical list of subscribers in Baton Rouge to the Southern

Bell Telephone Company will not signify change when read at a speed of one hundred names per minute any more than it would at ten names per minute. Discourse certainly *is* transformation in many respects; it is the result of some transformations and a material for others, like most human activities, but discourse does not *mean* what it *is*, even when it tries to suggest precisely this or shows what it is made of. Logos is not muthos.[4] I cannot narrate my talking as I am talking, not just this one; I can only narrate some absent talking, some talking already done, as good as dead, or in project, as good as unborn. Action is not knowable to narratology until it is presented (supposed to be absent, as it is signified and referred to), and acts of discourse are no different from other acts in this respect, except that confusion between enunciation and the enunciated is often possible, and sought by the actors of communication.

5. Narratology wants to catch communication in the act, but it can only catch it, at each stage, as reported in pretext, text, interpretation, cotext, peritext, intertext, context (texts of the milieu), apparatus, gloss, and commentary, answers and their interrogations, and so on. Narratology, like other sciences of communication, thus has as its task the construction of models that should permit the open textualization of the operations that take place between all these reports, showing their continuity and their character of transforms of one another. Narratology, if it succeeds, will tell the standard tale of what happens, for example, between the first time someone began: "Once upon a time . . . " and the latest jokes cracked in the academic community about research projects on TV series. This standard tale is a model in the three senses of the word: descriptive, explicative, and normative. But it can never be told in full and it cannot be found as such in any of its actualizations. An operational model is the horizon of theorization.

Theory, according to the *Grand Robert* French dictionary, is a "methodical and organized intellectual construction, hypothetical (at least in some of its parts) and synthetic." "Methodical" implies "purposeful"; "intellectual" implies (together with "synthetic") a certain degree of abstraction, such that several instances of the phenomenon investigated will fit the same structure and, as a result, comparative verification would eventually be possible. "Hypothetical" means that a theory entirely confirmed by experience would cease to be a theory. The value of a theory is essentially heuristic: a theory is a system of interrogation whose object cannot be given once and for all; it is characterized by the objects it accommodates and unifies, in quantity and quality, and the strategies it uses for this purpose.

A theory should be finite and open at any moment of its life, but theories show two equally dangerous tendencies: to avoid the threats of change and competition, some of them seek to accommodate an unlimited number of objects, extending their territories to the point of showing their failure through a display of self-proclaimed power (they eliminate from "reality," as irrelevant, the objects that would maintain their hypothetical character); others cling desperately to some very limited set of objects that they increasingly narrow down in order to possess it, to become identified with its possession and not be disturbed in the fortress of their singular enjoyment. Theories of the first type become theories of the world and, soon after, theories of themselves (theologies). Theories of the second type become theories of the particular and, as a result, nontheories. Terry Eagleton has sharply characterized these two tendencies in the realm of literary theory.[5]

A theory should always be conscious of its *own* operations, without turning them into its *object*. A metatheory itself cannot have its own operations for its object. Consciousness serves the theorist in two ways: if I am aware of what I am doing, I can do it deliberately and, in this case, I can experiment without scruples. The present book is the trace of a process of theorization that is, I hope, explicit enough to give the choice of weapons—even against me—to the combative reader.

6. But why has this object been chosen at a time when there are so many books on "narrative" and so few that aspire to deal with it "in general"? I could invoke opportunity, but I am not sure reception will grant this claim; utility, but I am afraid this work will seem "difficult" at first sight to the average undergraduate student, since it raises many more questions than it can answer, and undesirable to a number of colleagues because it again complicates problems that had been simplified, trimmed, or reduced by other authors (fictionality is no longer as limpid as pragmatics had painted it; character, an embarrassing guest, makes its return; syntax is now multitiered, etc.). I could invoke my past research on narrative texts, genres, and concepts, but then, why this buildup, this inflation that has finally required book-length expansion and reformulation?

I shall plainly say that my choice is overdetermined: personal, "biographical" factors have played the role of Necessity in the matter. If they are meaningful—and we must see them as such when we place them in an explanatory slot of our argument—their personal character is exclusive of any idiosyncratic specificity as much as of all direct generalization. Personal motivations should be considered as metaphors of collective constraints, sometimes in the guise of their antiphrases.

After three "novels", a play, and an autobiographical diary that never satisfied the usual conditions of narrativity (I could not and probably would not "do it correctly"), I have written and published virtually nothing but lyrical poetry for the last fifteen years, although I have never abandoned *in mente* a vast narrative prose project based on the progressive unification of fragmentary scenes and anecdotes. Nevertheless, I read comparatively little poetry and great quantities of romance. It is as if I needed the satisfactions of narrative communication without taking full responsibility for it, in the falsely passive position of the consumer, or yet in the safe impermanence of conversation: I am wont to "tell my life" at the dinner table. What is it, then, that causes a demand for narrative on my part while it prevents me from committing myself to the production of narrative? Is it the special kind of intelligibility of narrative, which is reputed to be so different from that of the lyrical? In narrative as such, there would be nothing deeper to understand than the mere concatenation of facts: things happen, they happen because other things happened, this is all. In the lyrical as such, there would be something hidden and mysterious to understand, but the quality of the secret, and not its content, is the intelligible goal. Who could believe, however, that mankind has been practical enough, from the earliest beginnings of historical cultures at least, to care incessantly about which things happen, how and why? Is there not another reason, more fundamental perhaps, to tell tales, for example, that what we do care about is that things can *happen?* And does not language hide what it names and name what it hides? After much reflection, I have come up with a very banal pair of hypotheses: the theme of the lyrical is absence or need; but narrative names death—death is the theme of narrative and the referent of its paradox.

A Tale of the Paradoxes of Telling

Most theories of narrative take for granted the philosophical—epistemological and metaphysical—dimensions of their object; they are content with the undemonstrated idea of the universality of narrative for their self-justification. Other theories, like that of Paul Ricoeur,[6] which springs from a philosophical concern for human temporal experience and its figuration, subordinate narrative communication and its study to the requirements of some powerful undercurrent that traverses historically (socially) situated individuals and makes even more difficult the observation of particular historically (socially) functional acts of communication. I think that, in order to avoid these two dangers, any philosophical reflection about narrative must specify its position, a limited argumentative distance, to narrative itself, and must always be attentive to its own conditions of development. Our approach to the narrative paradox—whose trap always threatens to close back on theoretical discourse in the process of its own narration—will try to respect these conditions.

Narrative communication adds a third, complicating, story (level) to the two basic paradoxes that characterize all human expression, both in autosubjective and in intersubjective communication.

The first is the paradox of IDENTITY. As long as I write ∃A, in which the existential quantifier simply marks the textual awareness of writing A, there seems to be no problem at all with language as a symbolic system. At the ontological level ("There is A"), language does not say anything more or less than what it is paid to say, and it cannot be contradicted or found at fault: "There is A" is always true. But as soon as I try to ask a question about A ("What is A?") and answer: "A = A," my troubles begin. Admittedly, the idea of equivalence is helpful in many cases; it is quite true that one A is worth another, that is, if there are at least two A's. But I should not pursue this line of thought very far, lest the same eluded question arise again: if "There are two A's" is to be true, I must ensure that each of them is an A. "Identity," "identification," in bureaucratic jargon as well as in standard speech, are the signifiers (sers) of individuality, particularity, unique- ness: "Jack is Jack, I am myself." That which is one and single, how can it be the same? To write "$A = A$" (which, in any case, cannot be true of the signifiers on the page, one being to the left of the symbol of identity, and the other to the right), I must make "A" stand for something such that "$\exists A_{sed}$" is true, for example; "me." I must compare myself with myself, which is not possible unless I am divisible into two parts that have at least this difference: that they do not occupy the same space, if they can be examined side by side. I must posit "$A \neq A$" — which is false — as true, in order to ascertain whether $A = A$. Identity cannot be thought; the subject can only think itself, not as itself, but as the end product of the never- exhausted differences between x and all the (other) possibles.

The second paradox is the paradox of ENUNCIATION. As soon as I utter any- thing, my existence is symbolically transferred into what I have uttered. That is, not my whole existence, but whatever part of it is relevant to the act of communi- cation concerned (which, from the point of view of this act, amounts to the same thing). Either the subject of enunciation is entirely in the enunciated, and then there is no one to say what is said, no enunciation and no communication; or else (at least some part of) the subject of enunciation is not in the enunciated, and then there is someone to say something; but this someone remains unsaid, and what is said is not him or his: I cannot express myself. Nobody ever does. But then, to whom am I listening?

The NARRATIVE PARADOX, often banalized as that of the "same-but-different," could seem at first sight to result from an erroneous approach to narrative dis- course, an "implication of simultaneity and stasis . . . , [an] implicitly spatial modeling of a temporal form," as Peter Brooks puts it.[7] But narrative discourse is not any more or less "temporal" *as a form* than, say, descriptive discourse or nonfigurative music. Narrative discourse is the discourse that elicits thinking about the passage of time or, if you prefer, that treats time as one-directional at the level of the signified. Narrative communication thinks the subject in flowing time, embracing before and after simultaneously, comparing, bringing together in the diegetic "present of reference" (not the present of enunciation) two proposi- tions of opposite signs. In order to understand "X has changed," I have to accept that X remains X whether p or $-p$ is true about it. In its hard version, the narra- tive paradox was well formulated by Todorov:

> Rather than a "coin with two faces," [transformation] is an operation in
> two directions: it affirms at once resemblance and difference; it puts
> time into motion and suspends it, in a single movement.[8]

In a more nuanced vision, narrative turns out to be infested by yet another paradox that is the corollary of the one described earlier: if narrative tries to comply with logic, it affirms change while saying at the same time that it is *not important*; the subject remains, if not perfectly intact, at least untouched in its essential being, less changed than unchanged at the end of the transformation, or then "it is no longer itself," which is strictly meaningless, since it implies either one of these two formulas: "A $\neq$ $-$A" (a tautology), "A $=$ $-$A" (a contradiction in terms), or both. The *narrative paradox*, in any of its forms, is cumulative with the *paradox of identity* and the *paradox of enunciation*, although some rhetorical devices, such as preterition, and certain syntactic structures can collapse them into a single surface realization.

The narrative paradox, against all appearances, does not hamper narrative communication or make it impossible. It is, on the contrary, at once its prime mover, its *raison d'être* and its most illuminating specific feature, just like the other two paradoxes cast the brightest (blinding) light on the inner motivation of all communication, that is, a challenge to the *doxa*—the corpus of the other's belief, where my word has no place yet, is as yet disbelieved. With the narrative paradox, either it is "impossible" (untrue) to say "I was born" and "I shall die," "I was not" and "I shall not be," or birth and death, beginning and ending are not *really* important: the paradox promises eternal life or at least the eternal existence of our essence, the eternal soul is its product, unless our inability to *think* rupture, the discontinuity of being, manifested in the narrative paradox, is itself the consequence of linguistic structures informed by a belief in our eternity stronger than any evidence of the contrary. Anyhow, this belief and this paradox, this belief and the phenomenon of narrative communication are coextensive in our cultures. Narrative communication is a constant denial of death, in the ordinary and in the Freudian sense at the same time: it affirms underground that which it denies aboveground and vice versa.

Narrative is a chronomachy with a double bind and a double strategy; it lives in time and tries to cancel it and make each of its moments profitable and enjoyable; it is the pimp of time and it has to keep it pure in order to sell it. One manifestation of this utilitarian *schizê* was well expressed by Peter Brooks, commenting on Lacan:

> Narrative is . . . condemned to *saying* other than what it would mean, spinning out its movement toward a meaning that would be the end of movement.[9]

This should allow us to rewrite as follows a statement made in the preface of the same book:

Narrative is one of the large systems of $\begin{cases} \text{understanding} \\ \text{misunderstanding} \end{cases}$ that we use

in our negotiations with reality, specifically, in the case of narrative,
with the problems of temporality. (p. xi)

In this process of negotiation or palaver, narrative names death; it gives death all
the names of the Creation (all those in language). It calls it departure (and arrival),
end (and beginning), movement (and immobility), action (and passion), pain (and
relief); it is the greatest factory of litotes for death, of allusions to death, of
metaphors of death, and so on. Narrative keeps the idea of death constantly in
front of us. With narrative, day after day, we get used to death; it is the greatest
school of resignation and, indeed, of fatalism, as it is the greatest school of
optimism — since bad things can change too, at least for a time. Narrative takes
place in the two nights of Friday and Saturday, at the borders of repose and action.[10] And when, like Gilgamesh and Marcel Proust, we have engraved our
whole long story on a stone, we *can*, at long last, lie in the tomb and be ourselves
no more, as we had so long wanted and not wanted. It is in this sense that narrative
also names (human) life and, beyond its therapeutic power, can make room for
practical information, geared for survival; in this sense so-called natural narratives, legends, and historical narratives are not functionally very different.

Narratology is not only one of the best ways of understanding the individual
perception of mortality and its consequences. It is also an approach to the anthropological dimension of societies, institutions, religions, and rites. All these
constructions of social-memory-made-law are at the outer frontier of narrative
discourse, the many negatives of its structure, the discourses that pretend to arrest
it by inscribing it and thus be equal to it in every point; but, answering the calls
of time stroke by stroke, they reproduce its beat and become the stuff of history.

A truly general narratology or, as is the case here, its patchy and sketchy evocation, should therefore be a first step toward the more ambitious but more *realistic* project of a comparative historical narratology that would examine differen-
tially the functions of narrative communication and the respective systems of
forms and genres in historically defined human societies. The reduction of the
scope of literature to "fiction" by twentieth-century schools, universities, critics,
and publishers, and their frequent conflation of all varieties of fiction into "the
novel" are certainly symptomatic of our present uneasiness and disenchantment
about narratives of progress rather than a manifestation of narrative euphoria.
They render the hermeneutic task of a comparative narratology more difficult and
more alluring than ever: this is not a paradox.

The design of a general theory of narrative communication, as presented in
this book, certainly stretches the competence of the lonely scholar beyond its natural limitations; the wider project could be carried out only by well-prepared in-
terdisciplinary teams, for years to come. Since I am neither a professional philos-
opher, linguist, or historian, nor a jack-of-all-trades, my sole ambitions will be
to alert as many users of narratology as possible to the ideological, political, and

ethical implications of the interpretive schemata on which they rely, and perhaps provide a few new critical tools to improve the yields of some present crises: the crisis of literary theory, the crisis of history, the crisis of the concept of modernity.

What we are dealing with, I suspect, is a phenomenon more complex and less mechanical than it is usually pictured, the phenomenon of the commodification of interpretation as one more cultural product: the substitution of the system of fashion for the dialectics of history that becomes another good to trade, whether as waste or as a sacralized object of worship. On the one hand, complex methods and insightful approaches are discarded without being given an opportunity for self-reexamination and before their techniques can be mastered by an entire generation of intellectuals; on the other, these same methods are still at work during several-score years on the periphery of the sites of theoretical production. But for this reason they are no longer explicit hypotheses; they become "attitudes," undiscussed shameful presuppositions rooted in silence and acting underground (in the next section of this chapter I hope to show that structuralist concepts of narrative, with all their contradictions, are still operative on both sides of the debate between metahistorians and classical historians). The main thrust of a communicational narratology should not bear, therefore, on an eclectic or syncretic reconstruction of the field dismantled by the system of fashion, nor can we dream of a *tabula rasa* when the commensals need their pick of almost everything on the table for a balanced diet. This means that we shall consider all existing narratologies as works in progress, as unfinished and perfectible as ours will be, not as long-buried mummies whose treasures can be unearthed at a risk to our health: the *living* contradictions, the active errors of these narratologies must be made part of their teachings, if they are not to become a heavy legacy.

A theory is always a model; a model cannot be purely descriptive, or better, scientific description is always somehow normative. This generally unacknowledged feature of the structuralist and reception theory enterprises became particularly salient when they were forced to meet from the mid 1970s onward and their conflicting norms began to clash within each theoretical construct. Such an encounter of a stative description of "narrative texts" with the apparently dynamic tale of their actualization in the history of communication was bound to manifest a paradox of telling embodied in theoretical discourse, which is not essentially different from the narrative paradox itself. I have made suggestions elsewhere[11] for a critique of Wolfgang Iser's *Act of Reading* along these lines. Because Gerald Prince's more recent *Narratology* (1982) is one of the very rare attempts to offer a personal comprehensive survey since Barthes's "Introduction to the Structural Analysis of Narrative" (1966), I shall use it as a case in point, with all due respect to his exceptional combination of ingenuity and systematicness.

In his Introduction Prince proposes a set of complementary definitions:

1. Narrative, indeed universal and infinitely varied, may be defined as the representation of real or fictive events and situations in a time sequence.
2. With narratives . . . we can speak of temporal sequence not only at the representational level but also at the represented level [i.e., "in the world referred to"].
3. Narrative is the representation of at least two real or fictive events or situations in a time sequence, neither of which presupposes or entails the other.
4. Narratology is the study of the form and functioning of narrative.
5. Narratology examines what all narratives have in common — narratively speaking — and what allows them to be narratively different."[12]

I shall discuss in some detail points 1–3 in my chapter 2, from a linguistic/semantic approach to narrative discourse. My concern here is with the philosophical assumptions underlying the set of definitions and their possible conflict with the theory of communication that subtends another part of Prince's work.

We can infer that the following affirmations are all necessarily true premises of the preceding definitional set, if each of its elements holds true on its own:

6. Narrative represents.
7. Narrative is successive at the "representational" level; that is narrative enunciation is successive.
8. Narrative is constituted not by implication but by collocation.
9. Narrative, whatever else it may be, has or is both form and "functioning."
10. All narratives have something in common *qua* narratives.
11. Individual narratives or groups of narratives also share (structural?) characteristics that let them manifest their narrativity differently.

Let us now see some of the consequences, either optional or necessary, of these premises, which are not explicitly derived in the definitional set:

12. Narrative occurs *after* the events and situations in the world referred to; it is of the past, it has a retrospective thrust.
13. Narrative is conveyed by semiotically successive vehicles or media; the form of expression of narrative is homologous to its form of content.
14. *Dispositio* rules over *elocutio* in narrative (like succession over embedding in the world referred to, considered under the aspect of linear time).

15. Narrative as form is distinct from narrative as process, but there are constant relations between form and meaning.
16. Narrative diversity is a consequence of the combinatorial possibilities offered by narrative form and process.

Items 6–16 taken together clearly confirm a fairly conventional hierarchy, not essentially different from that involved in the modern reinterpretations of the Aristotelian tradition:

17. The world (or worlds) out there has priority over its rendition, and especially its verbalization.
18. The nature and structure of time have a unity: its universality in different cultures, its identity in the represented and the representational; such a concept of time has priority over narrative understanding.
19. The law of narrative meaning is the law of the text, not that of the communication situation; the law of the text is the law of time; the law of time is that of the world out there.

After all this, we can be somewhat surprised to read in Prince:

Reading [also] depends on the reader. . . . In the first place, and even though the questions I ask while reading are—to a certain extent, at least—constrained by the text since they must be somewhat relevant to it, we must remember that the set of possible questions is very large, especially beyond the level of individual sentences and their denotational meaning, and that I am the one who, in the final analysis, decides which questions to ask and which not to ask. Given a narrative text, for instance, I may tend to ask questions pertaining above all to the way in which some of the activities recounted combine into larger activities; or I may decide to focus on elements in the text which constitute enigmas to be solved and look for the solution to these enigmas; or else, I may attempt to find out whether certain elements in the world of the narrated function symbolically. (p. 129)

It is as if the "reader" were suddenly granted a good measure of freedom as an afterthought, a concession not so much to the parallel constraints of the communication situation as to "myself," a free-willing, freewheeling, preconstituted subject. The empirical, "actual" reader seems to be released from certain textual strictures in counterpart for his competence. In fact, Prince's subsequent discussion casts some doubt on the origin of this newly acquired arbitrariness; the reading, sense-making subject will appear again as determined by circumstantial factors; his erring will no longer be a blessing, and the authority of the text soon takes over again:

> Of course, should we attempt to define the narrative legibility of a narrative text, we would be particularly concerned with how well the text lends itself to narratively relevant operations. (p. 133)

The temporary liberation of the receiver was only peripheral to the formation of narrative meaning with regards to which the "narrative text" and, behind it, the successiveness and eventuality of a naturally narrative world remain paramount.

Contrary to the poetics of (lyrical) poetry, narratology maintains an overtly incestuous relationship with theories of action; it lives in the shade of the concepts of history that prevail in our cultures, and it is always about to impinge on the strategic programs and games of power of various socioeconomic groups. It redefines on its own terms, explaining or disguising them, the formative or enslaving exchanges that obtain between "history" and its subjects and objects.

Precisely for this reason we should be wary of narratologies that purport to be "pure" grammars or "simple" catalogs of logical options; we should distrust those that are ever ready to dive into the secret glamour of "deep structures" and jump to large-scale constructions that they alone are able to uncover, while neglecting the shared evidence of "superficial rhetoric."

Some theorists of intellectual history, like Dominick LaCapra, rightly insist on the textual stuff of history; LaCapra tries to apply a psychoanalytic model of transference to the reading transaction and the subsequent construction of reality,[13] but he is still mainly concerned with the inscription of "macroplots" in the sense given to "plot" by Peter Brooks and does not sufficiently take into account the negotiation of narrative and other meanings at the level of stylistic structures and their analysis. Richard T. Vann notes in an article just published at the time of completing this book that "Mink displayed a consistent skepticism towards schematizing efforts directed towards narrative, whether in the style of Northrop Frye or Vladimir Propp; he had, as it were, passed straight into post-structuralism."[14] I am not sure that this is a consciously ironic evaluation, but it should be: if the prefix "post-" has any sense, there is no shortcut into "poststructuralism" without passing through it and pushing it to its limits. American historians and metahistorians alike seem to remain largely ignorant of French, Dutch, German, and Israeli narratological research in the last twenty-five years, and as a result an undiscussed *proto*structuralist narratological *doxa* is unknowingly at work in their writings. The "linguistic turn" has not yet been taken. I contend that instead of paying lip service to linguistics, we should force it, at all levels of analysis, to contribute as much as it can to our elucidation of what it is to make transitive sense of our experience.

The Day History Ran out of Time

I hope to show in this section that the present controversy of metahistory would be reduced to humbler proportions if we took into account its outdated narratological presuppositions. I also intend to demonstrate that various types of more or less "unorthodox" Marxism of the day will not become nimbler than those of yesterday until they are able to (re)think critically their narratological foundations. In fact, the crisis of "history" and the crisis of Marxist thought ("historical materialism") are closely linked by the narratological weaknesses that plague these two theological sites. They both provide pressing arguments for an alternative communicational narratology.

The Narrative Outlay of Human Experience

Let us recall the main claims of metahistory set forth by Hayden White in a series of essays written between 1966 and 1976, and collected in 1978 under the title *Tropics of Discourse*.

In the opening essay, "The Burden of History," White points out that the tactics used by historians for many years to defend their activity against the combined critiques of scientists and artists, a "Fabian" tactics of occupation of the middle ground, have become inefficient:

> The expulsion of history from the first rank of the sciences would not
> be quite so unnerving if a good deal of twentieth-century literature did
> not manifest a hostility toward the historical consciousness even more
> marked than anything found in the scientific thought of our time.[15]

He goes on to argue that, instead of adopting a paranoid attitude, historians should become aware that they have nobody but themselves to blame for this state of affairs; they have become blocked at some middle point between the apex of the discipline and the present:

> When historians claim that history is a combination of science and art,
> they generally mean that it is a combination of *late-nineteenth-century*
> social science and *mid-nineteenth-century* art. That is to say, they seem
> to be aspiring to little more than a synthesis of modes of analysis and
> expression that have their antiquity alone to commend them. (p. 43)

Historians should "take seriously the kinds of questions that the art and the science of [*their*] own time demand that [they] ask of the materials [they] have chosen to study" (p. 41). This is not only a tactic to assuage the critique leveled at the profession; since the task of the historian is future oriented, it is "a moral charge to free men from the burden of history" (p. 49). The means to achieve such an ambitious result is inevitably "interpretation," which is always already involved in the construction of historical narrative, through its selection and arrangement of facts:

> In fact, by a specific arrangement of the events reported in the docu-
> ments, and without offense to the truth value of the facts selected, a

given sequence of events can be emplotted in a number of different ways. (p. 61)

The responsibility of the historian consists in choosing one of the basic "pre-generic plot-structures" classified by Frye, in order to "transform a chronicle of events into a 'history' comprehended by its readers as a 'story of a particular kind' " (p. 62). The choice of "emplotment," which is free to the extent that no historical sequence of events is intrinsically comic, tragic, romantic, etcetera, is essentially a rhetorical operation, placed under a dominant metaphor. Historical narrative itself can be spoken of as an extended metaphor:

As a symbolic structure, [it] does not *reproduce* the events it describes; it tells us in what direction to think about the events and charges our thought about the events with different emotional valences. [Historical narratives] succeed in endowing sets of past events, over and above whatever comprehension they provide by appeal to putative causal laws, by exploiting the metaphorical similarities between sets of real events and the conventional structures of our fictions. (p. 91)

We recognize here all the characteristics of narrative in general that were implied by Prince's narratology (propositions 6–19), notably the logical priority of chronologically sequential events over their "description" or representation, an imperialism of the written text whose "form" is now as significant and authoritative as all the individual events recounted, and a reader treated like a student who will be taught for his own good, whether he wants it or not. It is never asked which needs and interests will be served by historiography so that it can (is allowed to) fulfill at the same time its educative mission. Is our "need" of historical narratives born with the species and with each of us, and, if so, how is it possible to escape Lévi-Strauss's conclusions that history is a (substitute for) mythical discourse? Or is this desire induced under special social circumstances that have to do with the structure of power and its modes of symbolization, and, if so, how are we rewarded for reading history and thinking in terms of historical narratives? Some confusions are noteworthy; on the other hand, Louis O. Mink's "strategy to create perplexity about the concept of narrative"[16] manages to do just that without bringing any clear answer as to its shape and functions. We would perhaps help to reject some of the objections that unfortunately invalidate in their wake the refreshing oppositional claims of metahistory, if we could outline the major areas in which these confusions occur. They are all linked together.

1. Chronicle and narrative. Mink's defense and illustration of the interpretive power of historical narratives similar in form and genre to those known as fiction rely on a basic distinction between narrative and chronicle that is, in my opinion, fallacious:

> While objectivity is conceivable for a cumulative *chronicle*, it cannot
> really be translated into terms of narrative history (and in general the
> belief in historical objectivity fails to distinguish between narrative and
> chronicle, which has no form other than that of chronology and no rela-
> tions among events other than temporal relations). . . .
>   . . . The model of logical conjunction . . . is not a model of narra-
> tive form at all. It is rather a model of *chronicle*. Logical conjunction
> serves well enough as a representation of the only ordering relation of
> chronicles, which is " . . . and then . . . and then . . . and
> then . . . (pp. 143, 144)

It is impossible to determine what an actual narrative is or should be by contrasting it with a "pure" chronicle, which is as "purely" imaginary as a unicorn but
much less satisfactory for a logically inclined mind. An event is something that
comes (out) to be, that is extracted from a continuous background—time as
linear—thus creating a discontinuity in time because this something has no existence before or after. Nothing can be perceived (meant) as an event unless it is
the site of a change of sign, as we shall see. As present, as a point in time, an
event has an oxymoronic structure: p is both true and not true of A, so that A
answers to two contradictory descriptions at this point. The narrative utterance
that signifies an event is the device by which we make time responsible for the
contradiction; actually, time is the name we give to the inferred cause of all contradictions of this sort. Chronology, the discourse of time, is an answer to the apparent invalidation of the principle of noncontradiction by our confusing experience of change. This answer, logically motivated, is fundamentally different
from that of myth, magic, or poetry, all of which seek to efface the contradiction
instead of explaining it. If chronology is first of all a serialization of events so
understood, a grid constituted by the hypothesis of a regular distribution of certain events (astronomical, for example), relations among events in chronology
are always already logical *qua* temporal; the model of the chronicle is an incessant
combination of logical conjunction and logical disjunction, and it is also the
model of narrative communication, unless we mean by it mythic communication,
a prechronological form of communication, or one that does away with the principle of noncontradiction.

   2. Metaphor and narrative structure. White, who explicitly borrows from
Frye his types of "emplotment," is led to become more Fryian than Frye and to
reject "Frye's distinction between (undisplaced) myths, fiction, and such forms
of direct prose discourse as historiography."[17] He also draws a distinction between two basic types of processes of interpretation, one being analytic, paradigmatic, and lexical-like, and the other synthetic and syntactic; the former divides,
dissociates, and generates ever smaller "specific" or rather singular objects: units;
the latter aggregates, associates, and generates ever larger objects: unities. These
two processes themselves, dependent as they are on the prevalent pair of oppo-

sites in structural linguistics and poetics, are viewed with paradigmatic, not syntactic, lenses, so that their opposition requires the intervention of a mediator, which will be tropology, an imperialist branch of rhetoric. Where interpretive meaning is equated with the imposition of syntax over scatterbrained paradigms (but this imposition is feared as "reductive" and mechanicist if it is metonymic, "representative" and integrative if it is synecdochic, and skeptical or cynical under the auspices of irony), you can only call the "anarchist" displacement, the freedom provided by metaphor, to the rescue — that is, if you accept a tropological model of signification limited to four tropes. I cannot discuss here the various problems there are with a tropological model inasmuch as it collapses transportation with transformation without questioning how and why this conflation can take place, but, in any case, within such a model, narrative would be a fifth trope. It does not present A as a part of B like synecdoche, A as a part of A + B in denotational simultaneity like metonymy, A as actually −A like irony, or A as being simultaneously B and not-B like metaphor and simile, but A as being both A and −A like an oxymoron; the only difference between narrative and oxymoron is a rationalization: according to narrative, A can be both A and −A because of time, which separates the field of validity of the two propositions at all points but one, the point that we call the site or date of an event, or yet, by metonymy, an event. The confusion between metaphor or metonym and narrative is quite understandable, but they are condensations in the minds of historiographers and philosophers of history, which a proper narratology should be able to explain or decondense, allowing a conscious choice of narrative technique on their part.

3. *Event and Fact — Signification and reference.* These last two closely related confusions, endemic in representational narratologies, have their worst effects in the philosophy of history.

Let us reread a sentence already quoted:

> In *fact*, by a specific arrangement of the *events* reported in the documents, and without offense to the truth value of the *facts* selected, a given sequence of *events* can be emplotted in a number of different ways. (italics mine)

The only thing clear is that the lexemes "event" and "fact" are interchangeable to a certain extent, as quasi synonyms in the Discourse of History. The word "facts" seems to have been intercalated here between "events" and "events" to avoid excessive repetition; but "fact" could not be replaced by "event" in the metalinguistic expression "in fact," which belongs to a series of quasi synonyms including "indeed" and "in truth," and the collocation of each occurrence of "events" and "facts" in the sentence is revealing. "Events" appears in the grammatical role of complementing "arrangement" and "sequence"; "facts" as the complement of "truth value." In the absence of a definition, genitive noun phrases of this type have a semantic effect of mutual determination: "events" are items susceptible of being arranged and found in sequences; arrangements are activities pertinent for events; sequences may — to say the least — be made up of events, they can work as indexes to the presence of events. But "facts" can be the locus of truth-value; maybe they can produce it or contain it, or the assignment of a truth-value is what transforms something into a fact. This occurs when facts are selected — because they are selected or in spite of this selection? An arrangement in turn is "specific," particular, of a kind, whereas a sequence is "given"; it is a datum, presumably a piece of reality like facts are reputed to be. As a result of this semantic haze, "events" and "facts" are definitely the same and not the same.

They are the same insofar as historiography cannot renounce its aspiration to a truth-value grounded in representation, iconic rather than symbolic: popular history exemplified by Alain Decaux on French television is a caricature of this feature because it manifests it hyperbolically. They are also the same insofar as "past" facts need to have occurred and be completed, per-fect; they can only be presented as events, entailing the permanence of a concept of "past actuality" as a story, untold or already told and later recited — it does not really matter.

"Events" and "facts" are not the same in the sense that truth is static if you want to escape relativism; facts are the warrantors of truth if they are always already there, not dynamic and fluctuating but anchored at their own point in time. An almost caricatural example of this attitude is offered by Stephen Greenblatt in his review of Judith Brown's *Immodest Acts: The Life of a Lesbian Nun in Renaissance Italy*. Greenblatt tells of being approached by a *New York Times* reporter who wanted to know whether it was news that there was a lesbian nun in Renaissance Italy:

> I tried to explain that there was something inherently misguided about the question. . . . In what sense is there any continuity between lesbian nuns in late 20th-century America and the strange, lonely figure of Benedetta Carlini? . . . Those who wrote in the late Middle Ages and the Renaissance about sexual acts between a man and a man or a woman and a woman did not regard those acts as evidence of a psychological orientation, a personality disorder, a habitual object choice, a condition of sexual "inversion." . . . If we are to understand this very different structure of sexuality, we must learn to suspend or rather to historicise our own cultural constructions.[18]

Foucault, among others, is invoked to condemn any form of historical report that would make the past relevant to the present; the past, according to Greenblatt, should be protected against interventions, even lexical, on our part, that would make it speak a language that was not its own, and in this case the language of the past is apparently that of "those who wrote" — essentially theologians. "Understanding" the past, according to this view, is to impersonate it by assuming the very voice of the censorship that silenced minorities, "deviants," and so on: the "possessed." But perhaps "censorship" is too modern a concept to apply it to the seventeenth century. Perhaps Greenblatt should write his review in Elizabethan English. Such "respect" for the past has a function, though: it lets it speak only a language of repression that we must abstain from translating into terms that would make it address our potential rebellion against all forms of oppression, and if it sacralizes "uninterpreted facts," it is precisely because there *is* a continuity of action informed by our knowledge and our forgetfulness, because we are thus taught to sacralize that-which-is (which is not so different). On the other hand, truth-value can be produced only in a discourse that is of *this* time, always new, always becoming. The form of truth, which is its truth, is that of an event; historiography must emplot true static facts as dynamic events in order to communicate a dynamic truth. This is at least consistent with the "extended metaphor" view of historical narrative, if it is not with the dichotomy between past and present that founds all historical (re)writing.

P. H. Nowell-Smith, in a brilliant article, argues for the purely epistemological character of the concept of fact and maintains that it is not logically acceptable to ask or answer questions like "What is the nature of a fact?" as if it were some independent entity; that the word "fact" is used in an idiomatic fashion that prohibits separate analysis in statements like "It is a fact that . . . " And that "fact" makes sense only in terms of oppositions like those of fact versus fiction, fact versus opinion, and fact versus interpretation. He goes on to show that "since . . . documents are the only data (*données*) from which an historian can start and by reference to which everything he tells us must be substantiated, it is natural that we should come to identify documents with facts,"[19] and he concludes: "Facts exist nowhere and nowhen. And this is not because they are timeless entities not located in space, but because they are not entities at all" (p. 323). A philological approach to "fact" and "event" would perhaps lead to more manageable, if less provocative, inferences. "Fact," as it is more obvious in the Romance languages (*fait, hecho*, etc.) but nonetheless true in English, is the substantivized past or passive participle of a verb (*facere*) that means "to make'; it is thus "made" (up or not), fabricated. The subject of this verb remains generally, but not necessarily, hidden, and the participle, like the verb itself, requires at least an implicit agent to make sense: what is done is done, and what is made was made by someone; moreover, there are no future facts. "Event," from *eventus*, is the substantivized "past," but not passive, participle of *evenire*, to "come out"; neither *evenire* nor "come out" is transitive. Neither can function in the passive voice; moreover, they are essentially impersonal verbs like "it rains." Things that happen are happenings; things that eventuate are events; and there are future events because an ergative, let alone a causal, relation does not need to be established for events to eventuate. The historical notion of "fact" results from the double confusion of causal with ergative relations and reference with signification, so that "data" are preauthored in the real, in a real that is both past and present, present in a material document or monument, past insofar as these objects are traces; they stand for their own origin.

The dominant narratological notion of "event" results from similar productive errors: since many of our languages do not let their verbs loose in discourse without an express father figure of a subject ("*it* rains," "*il* pleut," "*something* moves," "*God* willing," etc.), this interested formal constraint of signification manifested in the person, if not in a pronoun, is projected onto the world of reference as an actual causality, so that the ultimate cause of all events is "reality," without predication, not time/tense within.

We could well ponder Michel de Certeau's magnificently lucid analysis:

> That which gives credit [*accrédite*] is always ultimately power, since it functions as a warranty of real, in the same way as gold capital validates banknotes and paper money. This reason which brings the discourse of representation toward power is more fundamental than psychological and political motivations.[20]

That "the representation of historical realities is a means of camouflaging the actual conditions of its production" (p. 24) is even more flagrant in the works of "classical," traditional historians than in those of the metahistorians.

4. *Past actuality.* It is this whole notion, wrongly used as the last stronghold of common sense against absolute relativism, that cries out to be dismantled by a new narratology.

I must quote extensively from Leon Pompa's answer to the metahistorians at an important conference on the philosophy of history (Ottawa, 1980):

> I shall [argue] for a version of the traditional view that meaning is something that belongs to past actuality in and of itself and that it is the function of the historical narrative to establish this meaning rather than to impose it on the past. . . .
>
> The metahistorian . . . contrives to suggest that reality, or the way things are, is a meaningless content to which, through the structuring relations that the narrative form brings to it, meaning can be given. But what justification could there be for this identification of reality with some bare, unstructured experience? . . .
>
> The metahistorian cannot avoid conceding that certain events or occurrences in the past had a certain significance for past agents and that therefore it is a fact that the human past contains at least that sort of significance in and of itself. . . .
>
> If [my] arguments are correct and if we want also to maintain that narrative accounts are an adequate vehicle for the expression of historical knowledge we must be prepared to take the reality of the historical past more seriously than the metahistorian and allow that it includes everything that constitutes a possible object of knowledge for the historian *qua* historian. This is not, of course, to deny that historical

agents may have knowledge, but it is to insist that it will count as historical only when it conforms to the standards of historical knowledge accepted by a current generation of historians. For to accept anything less than this would be to deprive historiography of too much for it to count as a proper form of knowledge for those who possess it.[21]

"Past actuality" is an authentic semantic maze. According to *Webster's Collegiate Dictionary*, "actuality" means (1) "the quality or state of being actual" and (2) "something that is actual"; and "actual," on top of being an obsolete synonym of "active," has three main acceptances: (2a) "existing in act and not merely potentially," (2b) "existing in fact or reality," (3) "existing or occurring at the time," which is akin to "coeval," "simultaneous," and "contemporary" in English, *contemporain* and *actuel* in French (where "the time" considered is the present), and *coetáneo* and *actual* in Spanish. The six possible combinations play in strikingly different fashions with the scope of "past" and can go as far as reversing or canceling the hierarchy in the adjective↔substantive relation. "Past actuality" could thus be, among many other possibilities, a quality of existing in act that is no longer actual, something that existed in fact or reality and no longer exists, something that was coeval with itself but is no longer so (a combination of tautology and nonsense), the past as real, the past in act and not merely in potentiality, and so on. Indeed, if we take the context into account, we realize that "actuality" is some sort of agent, since meaning "belongs" to it, unless this word is taken metaphorically in the sense of "having its usual place somewhere," in which case "actuality" could be a spatially determined object. But, at the same time, if the "meaning" concerned is not "established" before a historical narrative is developed, "past actuality" has an essential feature, its intrinsic meaning, which exists only in a potential state, not in act. And if "past" is an adjective, and "actuality" can be qualified temporally—without which the adjective relation would not obtain—then we must ask, "For whom, for which observer is this actuality past?" If it is past for us, it is no longer actual in senses 2a and 3, and if it is not past for us, it could not be past for those who experienced it, unless their time is not in the same universe as ours and we cannot say anything about it, or time is oriented "backwards." The syntagm "past actuality," in summary, is either a nebula of semantico-logical incompatibilities or a *petitio principii* stating that something called the past is forever real in the past because it was once real, without stipulating the conditions of access to *that* world of the agent making the claim in *this* world; or even, and more probably, it is a mixture of nebula and *petitio principii*, giving the bewildering illusion of depth because sense seems to be multiplied by contamination, analogy, and metonymy, even when the claims of resemblance and congruence are spurious.

A similar fallacy mars Pompa's third argument: the significance of past events for those who experienced them is either not a past event for us, and if so it does not qualify for historicity, or it is a past event for us and qualifies for historicity but, if this is true, it is a different past event from those events that elicited significance for those who experienced it, and the significance of these two kinds of events and their relation has to be established by and for us, so that there is again no meaning that belongs to the past "in and of itself."

Pompa's second argument, like many others in his paper, seems convincing at first sight because it displays the seduction of the *reductio ad absurdum*, but it has its common disadvantage: it is self-defeating. If the metahistorians suggested that "reality is a meaningless content" (whatever this means), which, by the way, they do not, they would certainly be wrong, because this would presuppose that there can be such a thing as "unstructured experience." Classical historians are thus obliged to accept that "to experience anything in a cognizable way is to experience it in relation to other things, as part of one process and not another, as an instance of one kind of thing and not another, and so on" (p. 148). Pompa is thus inadvertently saying that experience is informed by language in its combined paradigmatic and syntagmatic dimensions, but, since he subconsciously equates language with narrative or considers narrative to be a language — the most advanced and meaningful of all languages — he includes processualizing and instancing in the basic operations of the linguistic information of human experience. Therefore the metahistorians should be all the more right to say that they assign meaning to facts by arranging them into a narrative: they are just imitating, reproducing in writing the most fundamental step of all cognizance. Needless to say, I believe that Pompa's argument is wrong for a better reason than that it is self-defeating and that the metahistorians are also wrong for a different reason from that suggested by Pompa: our narratology is based on the specificity of narrative meaning, which is only one of the many types of meaning mediated by language, on the transactive, communicational nature of all meaning, and on the separation between narrative successiveness and linguistic successiveness.

Finally we cannot but be struck by the accumulation of metaphors of property and currency and a lexicon of power in Pompa's fourth argument: "accounts," "take," "allow," "have," "count," "conform," "accept," "deprive," "proper," "possess." Historical knowledge is presented as capital exploited by its legitimate owners and the value of its "expression" as that of a commodity that increases the power of those who sell it. The capital counts as such because it is owned by the right owners who valorize it, and the same owners also determine who is allowed to own this capital: themselves. Except that legitimation takes place explicitly in the present and is only secretly subtended by the constant tradition of the object (with cumulated gains and without loss), it is hard to see a difference between this and the attitude of Henri-Irénée Marrou, for example:

History exists . . . ; we only have to acknowledge the existence of our object, which is this sector of human culture exploited by a specialized corps of technicians, the order of historians; our datum is the practice recognized as valid by the competent specialists. The reality of such a datum cannot be doubted: it is quite certain that the corps of historians possesses a lively methodological tradition. . . .

History differs from its falsifications or its clones [*ses sosies*], by this character of reality that permeates all its being.[22]

I am not trying to say that there is *no* difference between the ultraliberal position of the metahistorians who let the burden of narrative interpretation rest on the individual historiographer and the corporatist assurance of the conservative large-scale traditionalists, or between them and the Marxist tradition of historical materialism, but the differences are relatively minor because the narratological credo is largely shared and not much questioned; it is not even conscious in most cases.

I am confident that most historians and philosophers of history have never realized that they cling to a Cratylian concept of narrative discourse, whether the essence of events motivates the form of this discourse or whether it is this discourse that gives shape to transitive reality. The separation between past and present that motivates their activity and the continuities and discontinuities that they seek to establish between pasts, and past and present, are all preempted by the Cratylian separation *and* homology of a language and its nonverbal referent. To treat a text produced in the past as a "document" means precisely to deverbalize it, to destroy it as a text.

Contemporary Marxism, therefore, when it no longer abides by the rules of a mechanistic "explanation" or reconstruction of historical narrative, is at pains to formulate any but virtually atemporal deconstructive frames of reflection. Most of us will remember that we never reached the contemporary period in our history programs at school because the teachers would run out of time; it is the whole Discourse of History that now seems to have run out time quite some time ago. Will a new narratology help to reinstate it?

A Picture of Marxism Facing the Loss of the Ur-narrative

Philippe Ariès remarked many years ago that a conservative public would discuss more willingly the Marxist view of history, because it is systematic, than those concepts of history that distrust generalizations and question the supposedly constant features of humankind and its cultures.[23] Ariès, a fervent political reactionary by his royalist ubringing and his initial commitment to the "Francisque," meant to attack Marxism in this statement. He had a vested interest in believing that "nothing can be more wrong than the idea of continuous progress, perpetual evolution" and that "history with an arrow does not exist" (p. 16), in order to sustain his hope that particular communities anchored in tradition could somehow break up the uniform mass of "average type" and world hegemonies characteristic of the modern world. History had to become a "science of differences" and thus reduce any possible large-scale syntax of events to the paradigmatic couplings of a European mythology. It may seem strange that, perhaps under pressure from emergent oppositional groups such as women, blacks, and "southern" nations, seen as objective allies of the proletariat and/or petit bourgeois intelligentsia, similar ambitions have been internalized by a vast sector of contemporary Western Marxists and are seriously beginning to trouble their critical method at the core together with its narrative presentation. Fredric Jameson's attempt to rethink "narrative as a socially symbolic act" and its curious contradictions will be best apprehended with these conflicting interests in mind, such that the desirability of alliance politics (not only in the United States) pleads simultaneously for a utopian theoretic retotalization and for apparent concessions to various "decentering" ideological elaborations that displace the centers of telling from their traditional discursive sites without removing it from the Judeo-Christian *logos* in its European attire.

Jameson states in his preface that his "specific critical and interpretive task [is] to restructure the problematics of ideology, of the unconscious and of desire, of representation, of history, and of cultural production, around the all-informing process of *narrative*," which he takes to be "the central function or *instance* of the human mind."[24] Since the argument is begged (or rather there is no argument about the validity of a task undertaken from within Marxism, the "untranscendable position" "which, in the form of dialectic, affirms a primacy of theory which is at one and the same time a recognition of the primacy of History itself" [pp. 13–14], one could be tempted to adopt Jameson's proclaimed attitude to the alien text and treat his own writings "as the always-already-read," which indeed they often seem to be, in spite and because of their intricacy, not just because they have been so widely commented on in America and abroad. In view of the verve and nerve with which Jameson's "impressive" book seems to have energized several of his reviewers, it would be even easier to apply "metacommentary" to *The Political Unconscious* and give it the role of the absent center of some further reflections. Notwithstanding the probable elegance of the game, I prefer to dispense with it on the evidence that Jameson is more provocative than thought-provoking even for his harshest critics, as if his argumentative technique had been all too successful in limiting the debate to a well-rehearsed set of problems. Instead, on the face and faith of his own profession of faith, I shall bluntly address a single question that can be put in slightly different terms, depending on one's hierarchy of theoretical-methodological priorities: How does Jameson define "narrative"? Or, how does he construe narrative into an object? Or even, to what extent is the concept of narrative operational in his remodeling of ideological analysis? An appropriate answer should also be able to explain my resistance to Jameson's enterprise, if boredom is a symptom of resistance, and perhaps change it into a vivacious interest.

We are unfortunately forced to adopt a double strategy, due to Jameson's peculiar combination of emphatic proclamation with lateral thinking and his proclivity to confusion in the guise of cannibalizing other (non-Marxist) approaches: on the one hand, we have to look for express statements about narrative, on the other, we must also make inferences from utterances in which the paradigmatic position of the concept is not evident. The initial impression that "narrative" is everywhere and nowhere in particular, as for the early Barthes and some of his followers or for Greimas and his epigones, may thus be both confirmed and qualified as we read on.

It is posited in the first place both that there is one and a single adventure of mankind, a long, difficult march from a realm of necessity to a realm of freedom, and that the "*mystery* of the cultural past" is worth recovering and encovering for the purpose of overcoming obstacles encountered on the said march. The word used to designate this retrieval is curiously evocative of (compulsive?) repetition: "This mystery can be reenacted only if the human adventure is one; . . . These matters can recover their original urgency for us only if they are retold within the unity of a single great collective story" (p. 19). Since necessity is both of the past and of the present, it should certainly be at work in this undertaking; Jameson insists that any belief in the existence of islands of freedom "is only to stengthen the grip of Necessity," but then it is not clear how necessity combines positively with anticipation, which plays the role of a liberation drive, unless it is by the magical action of some immanent dialectic that automatically generates contrary forces:

> [These matters must be] grasped as vital episodes in a single vast un-
> finished plot; . . . It is in detecting the traces of that uninterrupted
> narrative, in restoring to the surface of the text the repressed and buried
> reality of this fundamental history, that the doctrine of a political un-
> conscious finds its function and its necessity. (p. 20)

Narrative = reality = history. All three are perceived as a master plot. All four are unfinished. It must be in the sense of an incomplete actualization, but this still poses a serious problem for the validity of the present enunciation of the master plot, unless plot *and* reality are conceived as the constitutive rules of possible worlds, not as contents of an actual world, which contradicts the idea, expressed elsewhere, that reality makes itself felt in the form of necessity. But the key problem here is the "uninterrupted" character of a narrative whose future is not actualized and whose past is only textualized in a scanty, impoverished, and fragmentary fashion. Where is the grand narrative "uninterrupted"? There are two possible answers: (1) in a past that is *not* a text and (2) in a text that, from now on, will be uninterrupted. I think Jameson in fact gives these two answers, which are complementary and solidary in his theory in that the past must not *be* a textualized narrative, if the Marxist theorist is to have a *raison d'être*: writing forever into its lacunae. The function of the textualizing-transcoding-narrativizing of the Marxist theorist-critic-historian remains, as it was for Althusser and Macherey, that of unmasking the false (aesthetic) unity of the cultural text in order to start healing the hidden wound. The cultural text has abscesses that must be cut open and that will need permanent medical attention (contrary to the opinion of the deconstructionists, who believe in natural cure after they have shattered the bones of the patient [my free translation of Jameson's p. 56]). Anyway, even this far from idyllic vision of therapeutic harassment does not solve the question of the span of the "uninterrupted" character of the fundamental narrative: is it eternal, having no beginning and no end, or then, when does it begin, when will it finish? We find that an eternal narrative is difficult to conceive, and, moreover, it would look too much like God. Jameson adheres to the belief that a story must have a beginning and an ending; the result, which conforms to standard Marxist eschatology, is a bizarrely asymmetric boundary: the narrative begins with mankind, mankind is defined by its role of supreme, if dislocated, character in this adventure (story), but adventure and story will finish before it does, and mankind will not be fully realized until the conclusion of the story. This leaves us with a jobless hero at the same time as the individual characters of the collective saga dissolve and become united in the classless society.

A narrative, it is implied, needs human characters (its archetype is the epic or the novel); the only true narrative has collective characters who come disguised as individuals to all particular narratives (except perhaps the best—Marxist— historical narratives, like *The Communist Manifesto*). Now, who is the author, sender, narrator, or other enunciator of the Ur-narrative? I have been unable to find an unambiguous or even a noncontradictory answer in Jameson's book. We could say that, insofar as the human species tells its story through each individual, humankind is uninterruptedly writing and rewriting its autobiography; or maybe it does so by fits and starts from the standpoint of determined moments in time which involve a sequential projection and retrojection: "Individual period formulations always secretly imply or project narratives or 'stories'—narrative representations—of the historical sequence in which such individual periods take their place and from which they derive their significance" (p. 28). We can see, by the way, that, in Jameson's perspective, sense will be narrative or will not exist; meaning itself is sequential, is oriented along linear time and consequently occupies on it a place, a vector, which has duration. Reciprocally, time is narrative. On the other hand, we can also derive from their collocation/coordination in several sentences that "text" (in spite of its holes and hollows), "representation," "interpretation," and "narrative" (in spite of its holistic character) are essentially one and the same thing: "the ultimate ground of narrative and textual production" (p. 32); "the problem of representation . . . is essentially a narrative problem" (p. 49); "the study of cultural or literary texts, or in other words, essentially of narratives" (p. 61). This hegemony of narrative coupled with the deficiencies of

all existing partial narratives, reechoes into confusion on the question of author-
ship of the narrative, which is at times also attributed to the Marxist hermeneut
and the self-transparent class or party whose universal interests he lucidly inter-
prets. This is done thanks to the notion of "master code," which duplicates and
supplements that of master plot:

> The construction of a historical totality necessarily involves the isolation
> and the privileging of one of the elements *within* that totality . . . such
> that the element in question becomes a master code or "inner essence"
> capable of explicating the other elements or features of the "whole" in
> question . . .
> But in the Marxian system, only a collective unity—whether that of a
> particular class, the proletariat, or of its "organ of consciousness," the
> revolutionary party—can achieve this transparency; the individual sub-
> ject is always positioned within the social totality. (pp. 28, 283)

Some striking contradictions are motivated by an anxious quest of legitimacy,
even more irrepressible than the self-praise of the conservative historians: an
American Marxist like Jameson is in the uncomfortable position of having to
justify himself vis-à-vis the academic "superstructure" that supports him as a token opponent *and* the oppressed from whose standpoint he is supposed to denounce late capitalist superstructures (hence too his fetishism of blue-collar work,
which I mention in chapter 8):

> Insofar as the idea of textual production helps us break the reifying
> habit of thinking of a given narrative as an object, or as a static struc-
> ture, its effect has been positive. . . .
> We will suggest that such semantic enrichment and enlargement of
> the inert givens and materials of a particular text must take place within
> three concentric frameworks. . . .
> One does not have to argue the reality of history: necessity . . .
> does that for us. That history—Althusser's "absent cause," Lacan's
> "Real"—is *not* a text, for it is fundamentally non-narrative and non-
> representational. (pp. 45, 75, 82)

History, which is "fundamentally" nontextual, or nontextual *ab origine*, if "fundamental" means something, must be "retextualized" to become accessible.
"Given" narratives (who "gives" them to whom?) must be understood as
processes, not as objects, but they are inert until they are rewritten.

Jameson's treatment of the issues of rhetorical and generic models, the last that
I shall address here, is equally disappointing, but more revealing of his underlying narratology than some other imbroglios, presumably because they welcome
normativity. Although "an ideal of realism [remains] in one form or another the
central model of Marxist aesthetics as a narrative discourse which unites the experience of daily life with a properly cognitive, mapping, or well-nigh "scientific"

perspective" (p. 104)—a formulation that disconcertingly mixes time with topography—the genres/tropes of "allegory" and "utopia" are the mode(l)s of emplotment successively favored in the book. There is definitely an element of fashion in the recent revitalization of allegory; after metaphor was overexploited in the 1960's, it had to be laid to rest for a while, and Hayden White's shift of allegiance in his later writings is significant in this respect.[25] But the choice of this new model is also heavily overdetermined. First of all, it is certainly motivated by its very ambiguity and its poor theorization; many people, such as Samuel Levin, still see it as a variety of extended metaphor, and since extended metaphor (*métaphore filée*) is often associated with narrative sequences and scenes, in the novel and in lyrical poetry as well, it serves to blur several distinctions at once: between metaphor and metonymy, figurality and narrativity, narrative and didactic significance. Moreover, as I shall show later, it is wrongly confused with personification, which facilitates its role of narrative impersonator. Second, allegory, which is (after the literal) the second level of interpretation in medieval hermeneutics, offers not only a practical and much needed transition to the moral and anagogic (totalizing) levels of interpretation, but it eases some traffic problems along the "two-way street" where Christian and Marxist thought meet, according to Jameson. The only problem is that transit on such a busy thoroughfare must be difficult for other "progressive" vehicles. This is in part the reason to give the last word to utopia, which fulfills more than one function: for those who are not too finicky, it can easily pass for a twin sister of allegory, which it is not, and for a cousin of the parable, the legend, and the exemplum, which it is even less. At the same time, it is a less distasteful way of "coming to terms" with these resurgent anarchist trends that seem to worry Jameson seriously, than to condemn them radically in the name of totalization, and a generous concession to the idealist-leftist hopes bequeathed by the Frankfurt school—Bloch and Marcuse in particular—through the "ideas of May '68," on some revolutionary parties and individuals who have now come of age. More interestingly for the narratologist, we should note two key features shared by allegory and utopia: they are teleological narratives; they are "caused" retrospectively by their goal, a final cause; and the key event in their presented world takes place after the end of the narration, breaking by the postponement of its advent the frightening symmetry of birth and death. To this extent they are, like autobiography, powerful defense mechanisms against what all true narrative utterance shows and conceals in the same gesture.

Unlike the metahistorians, Jameson is obsessed with causation. So much so that he accepts, for different purposes all three causal systems analyzed by Althusser: the theory of the "absent cause," which is the one Althusser goes by; mechanical causality, which "retains a purely local validity" in "our particularly fallen [reified] social reality";[26] and "expressive causality," which remains the only way of answering the question; "What does it mean?" This fierce insistence on causality, at both ends of the narrative and in its avatars too, is surely symptomatic of the unacknowledged loss of the securing Ur-narrative that it tries in vain to repair by an endlessly repeated ritual denial. I would suggest three more *productive* ways—*pace* the *ouvriériste* academic—of accomplishing the work of mourning: the lyrical way of elegy, epitaph, or *tombeau*, on which Jameson touches at times, but which he represses, obviously because he cannot see the narrative element in it; celebrating the sacrifice of God on a regular basis, like a number of abandoned Marxists, Garaudy, for example, have done before him; traveling to new theoretical grounds to forget the loss, like John Frow in his *Marxism and Literary History*. But the worst of it all is that the lost "object" was not even an "object" or what it pretended to be, namely, a "proper narrative"; it was not an object because it was that magnified mirror image of the missing self that represented all "value" before value could be exchanged, before a subject of sorts could be constituted in a relatively autonomous sphere and become the subject of his own narrative. And it was not a "proper" narrative because it was an uninterrupted continuum, while, as I will show, narrative discourse, the discourse of uncaused change at its primary, nontransactive level, means the breaking up of the temporal continuum, this radical heterogeneity of "before" and "after" that causal transactive discourse (the discourse of early science) and the cycle of renewed myth make desperate efforts to dissimulate better, each in its own manner.

Finally, I want to stress that the loss of the Ur-narrative has left scars on all contemporary forms of Marxism, including the most "avant-garde," such as Frow's vast critical and metacritical system, which would deserve a better title than the one given his book. In fact, his only explicitly programmatic chapter, "For a Literary History," however illuminating it may be in many respects, with the stress correctly placed on our dependence on notions of oppositional innovation inherited from the romantic and postromantic (modernist) avant-gardes, and the present impossibility of thinking a "postmodernity" ("Until our historical space is totally altered, there can be no 'beyond' of modernism which would not *thereby* be a moment of it"),[27] still lacks a general narratological base that would question the very possibility of writing a literary history and *thus* make it possible. The negative and positive actions of narrative predication: the simultaneous affirmation and negation of the identity of the semantic theme or the grammatical subject, are not to be opposed or balanced; they *are* a formally balanced account, *en partie double*, which at one and the same time take the act of a necessarily imbalanced operation and symbolically cancel it. Thus, if "the history of the formation of the canon is something like a crystallization of the regimes of valuation which have governed this process,"[28] the devaluation of the texts excluded from the canon in the process is qualitatively and quantitatively much greater. The valuation of "masterworks" and the formation of a body of "classics" is relatively homogeneous, at least in a short synchrony, while the devaluation of "nonliterature," "infraliterature," "paraliterature," "popular literature," and other "junk", together with the debunking of former classics, is extremely varied in its processes and official purposes. Moreover, valuation is acquired at the expense of an immense devastation of general literacy; it requires a huge destruction and the shedding of much blood and tears on the part of the repressed and oppressed subcultures, just as capitalist accumulation and Western welfare have been and are still acquired through the exploitation, disruption and uprooting of entire civilizations. This history of exclusion has yet to be written, but, for this, we must become fully aware of what any narrative represses as it manifests it symbolically and symptomatically. We must become conscious participants in narrative communication, constituted as narrative agents by this very participation, although the narrative in which we partake, of which we are the subjects, need not be the one proposed by the text transacted in the act of communication *or* history as a narrative. The construction of narrative meaning and the protonarrative semantic matter of narratogenic texts, it can now be demonstrated conclusively, both depend on the conjunction and disjunction, "under" and about the communicative act, of particular discursive formations that constitute its milieu.

Chapter 2
The Structure and Formation of Narrative Meaning

The several negative definitions of narratology I have given resulted from the mapping of the field proposed early in chapter 1: "(1) the processes by which narrative messages are formed and (2) the functions of such messages". It should be clear, however, that these two areas represent analytic moments that, considered separately, would be relatively uninteresting. Neither should narratology include in its premises any simple one-way relation between point (1) and (2), which would foreclose the constitution of its object into an instance and/or an image of communication in general. The processes of formation of narrative messages do not determine unilaterally and unequivocally the functions of such messages any more than these processes are dictated teleologically by preexisting functions (informative, imaginative, instrumental, etc.). The many intricate correlations (positive and negative, of homology and contrast, junction and disjunction) between process and function are here supposed to form a third system in which motivation has as great a part as causation. Trying to grasp, describe, and interpret this system is the ultimate goal of narratology, which an inevitably progressive itinerary from (1) to (2), as in this book, cannot accurately reflect. The book could certainly not be published one way and then back to front again as it was written, but the reader would be wise to use it in *fort/da* style. A similar remark is valid for the structure of the present chapter, the relations between individual narrative utterances and macronarrative significance through textual communication being of mutual determination, motivation and figuration.

When Roland Barthes announced in his ill-fated "Introduction à l'analyse structurale des récits" (1966) that the study of "narrative form" was a legitimate concern of early structuralism (*le structuralisme naissant*), he confused a number of very different, sometimes incompatible, claims in the same programmatic gesture. (A close reading reveals numerous terminological superpositions and semantic slippages, from *récit* to *récits*, *structure* to *structures*, and vice versa, between matter, manner, vehicle, support, and form, etc.) We need to proceed deductively, he says, and construct a descriptive model in the first place, because there are too many narratives, narrative is everywhere; linguistics will be our model because it was the first site of development of the structural method. But "model," in this second sentence, means the methodological *imitandum* needed to construct a "model of narrative." Is it not a fortunate coincidence, then, that narrative (*le récit*) is itself, like *le discours* in general, three things at the same time: a language (*la langue générale du récit*), the "message of another language, superior to the language of the linguists,"[1] and "a long sentence" (*une grande phrase*)?[2] Even this sweeping proclamation is only a springboard for another, even bolder claim: the "identity between language [*le langage*] and literature." Since a miracle always happens twice—at least—the "levels of meaning" in the narrative model or the narrative text(?) happen to coincide with the necessary distinction between "levels of analysis," which "are operations," a correspondence never questioned as a possible effect of projection.

This would-be seminal paper, full of brilliant intuitions and coarse paralogisms, tried to survey and synthesize theories and methods of analysis that were soon to be dropped by Barthes himself in *S/Z*. Together with Todorov's *Grammaire du Décaméron* and some other highly reductive formalizations like those of Jean-Claude Coquet,[3] it has been constantly used as evidence of the automatic failure of linguistic approaches to the narrative phenomenon. I propose instead to show the necessity and productivity of such an approach (lexico-grammatical in essence) within the framework of a theory of social communication of which Michael Halliday and Michel Foucault would be, separately, major exponents.

Even for a Whorfian, and a fortiori in Saussurian linguistics, "narrative" could not be considered a "language," for two reasons: it is manifested through many and perhaps all natural verbal languages as well as a vast array of other semiotic systems or "languages" in the extended sense of the word: the motion picture, the comic, photography, painting and drawing, mime and music, and so on, while all these languages can also do, in parallel, something else than narrate, function as the media of meanings other than narrative; and second, there are plenty of things that "narrative" cannot do, at least directly, such as giving orders, making requests, asserting existence, settling claims and providing definitions, things that are common functions of all languages. It is not even possible to say that "narrative" is a *register* in the Hallidayan sense, if "a register is a 'diatypic variety' of language 'according to the use,' what you are speaking (at the time), determined by what you are doing (nature of social activity being engaged in) and expressing diversity of social process (social division of labour)."[4] "Narrative" would simply be closer to "register" than to "dialect," if the former is a "way of saying different things," while the latter is a "variety of language according to the user," "a way of saying the same things" (ibid.). On the other hand, it is highly confusing to treat "narrative" as a "genre" on the same plane as poetry, the fable, the sermon, the manifesto, or the minutes of a meeting, since it can occur in any of these genres and it must in a number of them; in other words, narrative meaning can or must arise in any number of genres so determined, which are genres of texts. "Narrative," therefore, is a kind of meaning that occurs at a level of *parole* or "discourse" inferior to text: at the level of *utterance* (*énoncé*).

Our first task must be to determine the specificity of the narrative utterance in language: How does it arise in relation to utterances that elicit other kinds of meaning? Does it have logical constituents, parameters, and rules of validity? Does narrative meaning have a particular locus in the utterance, admitting that an utterance has a structure similar to that of the sentence? Consequently, is the formation of narrative meaning subjected to particular lexico-grammatical rules in natural languages? And finally, how do narrative utterances combine or compete with other utterances? With what effects? This first series of questions will be subsumed under the notion of narrative *d*iscourse (small *d*).

But, obviously, narrative meaning, or its expansion into significance, is not confined in practice to individual utterances; it is a phenomenon that cuts across the whole range of units of social communication and their corresponding codes. We find it again at the other end of the spectrum, informing, shaping, characterizing, or distorting vast networks of actual and potential texts ("actual" texts being always also potential as far as the actualization of their significance is concerned), at a level best understood through its vicinity with Foucault's "discursive formations", which I will call for my part that of *D*iscourses (capital *D*):

> In the case of being able to describe, between a certain number of utterances, such a system of dispersion, in the case of being able to describe a regularity (an order, correlations, positions and functionings, transformations) between objects, we shall say conventionally that we are dealing with a *discursive formation*. . . . We shall call *formation rules* the conditions to which the elements of this distribution [*répartition*] (objects, modalities of enunciation, concepts, thematic choices) are submitted. . . .
>
> Discursive relations do not characterize the language used by the discourse or the circumstances in which it is displayed, but discourse itself as a practice. . . . We discover not a configuration or a form, but a set of *rules* that are immanent to a practice and define it in its specificity.[5]

The reader will see in chapter 8 that I am suspicious both of Halliday's notion of addressing a text as a sort of potlatch and of Foucault's wishful effort to eliminate the subject, since one does not take sufficiently into account the *labor* of discourse production and the bounds it creates or reinforces between all the parties to the act of communication, and the other dehumanizes this labor or renders it metaphorical insofar as it is carried out by discourse itself. But what is important is that we have now three main levels of analysis (not full-fledged objects, but analytic moments or landings) that will refine and complicate a model of communication and crisscross the positions and roles defined within this model: a dominantly *instrumental* level of *utterances*, a nonneutral communicational medium whose genre will be determined by a structure of distinctive, necessarily present minimal units; a dominantly *reified* level of (whole) *texts*, characterized by coherences, such as the dominance of a type of utterances, the unity — individual, choral, or dialogic — of enunciation, and linguistic-semantic or thematic homologies functioning as starters of aesthetization and moralization; and a dominantly *sacralized* level of more or less rigid or fluid *Discourses* through which cultural uniformity, cultural and historical rifts, and social stratification are manifested. Themes mediate between discourses and texts, genres between texts and Discourses and the institutions between Discourses and time or "reality" or need or desire or whatever requires the stabilization of knowledge, the regulation of exchange.

The Structure of Narrative Utterances

Event and Narrative Meaning

The narrative meaning of an utterance is essentially bound to its predicative configuration. The standard utterance of a kind of discourse will be called its minimal unit. Hence the following propositions:

1. *narrative discourse is the genre of discourse whose minimal unit, the NARRATEME, (re)presents an EVENT;*
2. *an EVENT is a comparison between two states of a single entity separate in time and differing by at least one feature other than their temporal situation.*

The notion of event requires the following conditions:

a) the taking into account of a temporal axis
b) the division of this axis into separate moments
c) the recognition of the identity of an entity (a nounlike signified to which certain semantic features are attached) on either side of the dividing cesura of the temporal axis
d) the acknowledgment of a difference on the plane of a feature on either side of the above-mentioned boundary.

The preceding diagram crudely visualizes the "deep" structure of an event that we could call "rise in the price of a pound of beef."

All things being equal in other respects (the notions of beef and meat, the avoirdupois system, the monetary system, etc.), a feature of entity A, considered as relevant to the communication situation (here the relevant feature is the price per pound expressed in dollars), has changed, which can be rewritten:

$$price\ A_2 \neq price\ A_1$$

or, even better:

$$price\ A_1 \neq price\ A_2\ (price\ A_1 \neq \$5)$$
$$price\ A_2 \neq price\ A_1\ (price\ A_2 \neq \$4)$$

The comparison *contains two symmetrical negations.*

Many consequences can be drawn from this analysis, of which I shall mention only two at this stage:

1. An event can be (re)presented by means other than linguistic.
2. The successiveness involved in the narrateme is different from that of the medium in which it is expressed, if the latter is naturally successive—an important distinction often overlooked by narratologists.[6]

Most plastic works of art arrange their signs in such a way that they can and should be perceived simultaneously by the receiver capable of correctly constructing the intended message (i.e. competent and willing to construe such an intention). A painting of "The Rape of the Sabines" is composed simultaneously of fierce warriors, voluptuous women, terrified and disheveled, prancing steeds, dust and blood (i.e., first of all, of the corresponding spots of color on the painted canvas). But a painting depicting the beheading of Saint John the Baptist,[7] in which we see the saint with his head on his shoulders and, next to him, the *same* head cut off and lying on a dish, *must* be interpreted by *breaking up* the perceptive simultaneity. The same remark applies to an ancient copy of *The Fall of Icarus* by Pieter Brueghel, in which there coexists an Icarus flying high with an Icarus drowning in the sea. In these two cases we can see that broken simultaneity depends on the acceptation of identity between the two heads of John the Baptist or the two figures of Icarus: *there is no narrative discourse without (actual or implied) repetition.*

Gravure tirée de l'édition princeps de Héro et Léandre *(Venise. Alde. 1494).*

Hæc Herûs antiquæ domicilia· hæ turris
Reliquiæ.proditrix hic pendebat lucerna.
Cómuneɋ; amboshoc habet fepulchrum ,núc quoɋ;
De illo inuido conquerentes uento ·

Clamabat tumidis audax Leander.i undis,
Parcite dú propo.mergite dú redeo.

Σηςὸ̀
Seftuś

Αβυδὸς
Abydus

Gravure tirée de l'édition princeps de Héro et Léandre *(Venise. Alde. 1494).*

"In spite of the text, they will not be buried, but detained in the incompleteness of the fall and the duality of dying."

But this repetition must not be interpreted as duplication, and this depends on the code activated during the act of communication. If there is any uncertainty about the code, ambiguity (hesitation) may appear between event and nonevent: thus the spatial coexistence of the three legs of the bronze statue *Femme au bain* by Ipousteguy (Chicago Art Institute) can be read as an event ("the woman has moved') or as a nonevent (a monster, a goddess, a fantastic creature). In any case, this type of internal repetition or semantic anaphora of the subject with a variant—whether "similant" or "mutant," to use Ricardou's terminology[8]— distinguishes the signified "event" from simple perceptual successiveness (examination of a fresco, visit of a monument, etc.) and from mere decorative recurrence (the patterns of a frame).

In the linguistic text too, far from being confused with the obligatory successiveness of language, the narrateme should detach itself and contrast with the background of the medium. It is not enough to say that language is successive on the level of enunciation and the narrateme on the level of utterance, or that there may be a different ordering on these two levels, the relationship between the two orderings being arbitrary in principle. In fact, narrative successiveness is internal to one specific utterance (the narrateme) and thus presents itself on the surface as a temporal condensation, a reduction to the instant, to simultaneity, of data that take time to be perceived (realm of cognition) as well as to fulfill themselves (realm of the presented world).

The Meaning of Narrative Meaning

An excursus is necessary to clarify notions of signification and reference, time, tense, and order associated with the production of narrative meaning and differentiate them from those presupposed by other authors.

My approach has several similarities with Gerald Prince's *Grammar of Stories* and his later *Narratology*. Like Prince, I initially rely on the consensual recognition of what constitutes or does not constitute narrative. But, in spite of a common search for minimal units, our frames of study are somewhat at variance thereafter.

In the first place, I avoid speaking of the semantic "content" of an utterance, because it seems to imply some degree of immanent actuality of meaning in the utterance, a materiality that relies on representation as reproduction, on constantly being in touch with a nonverbal world of objects. Narrativity is, in my opinion, completely indifferent to "reference" (in the specialized sense of a bridge between words and things). The possibility condition of meaning in descriptive and narrative utterances, which comes with a semantic investment of lexico-syntactic structures, is simply the *possibility* of reference to some possible world in which the utterance could be logically true. This is why the narrative character of an utterance is independent of the "meaningfulness" of individual noun phrases (NPs) involved in the utterance.

The butcher has become a baker
Bonaparte has become Napoleon
The snark has become a boojum

are equally well-formed narratemes, with a shared kernel signified = "change"; whereas

*Bonaparte has become Bonaparte

is not correctly formed because there is a patent contradiction between "unchanged set" signified by the two identical NPs and change signified by the verb. On the contrary, if there was a world that respected the principle of biunivocity of language, and containing snarks and boojums, nothing other than an additional rule could prevent snarks from becoming boojums.

"Then followed a torrent of laughter and cheers" (Lewis Carroll).

With many linguists, Prince calls "event" 'any part of [a] story which can be expressed by a sentence"[9] in the Chomskyan sense: "(1) *A man laughs* would represent one event since it is the transform of a single elementary string; (2) *The man said the boy laughed* would also represent one event since it is not derived from two discrete elementary strings," (pp. 17–18). This also implies that there are "stative events" ("when they constitute a state").[10] I disagree on this use of "event" as well as on the interpretation of unit in the two examples given: Chomskyan syntax and the semantic idea of units of content—or signified—appear incompatible in this case. The syntactic condition of existence of a sentence is $\overset{S}{\underset{NP \diagdown VP}{\diagup}}$ the structure; the semantic condition of existence of an utterance is the compossibility of sets of semes within this utterance. The dimensions of *minimal* units are also different: syntactically speaking, *The man said the boy laughed* forms one S; but semantically, it contains two obviously separate strings: "man says (something)" and "boy laughs," just like *The boy laughed, then the man spoke*, which is one of the possible paraphrases. If we deal with narrativeness as a phenomenon of meaning, semantic analysis must be our primary method of analysis.[11]

We should also see how philosophically and epistemically important it is to choose one model of narrateme rather than another. When Prince writes:

No sentence expressing one event and only one can ever represent a story . . . , no story is constituted by a single event and . . . a minimal story consists of more than one event.[12]

Narrative is the representation of at least two real or fictive events or situations in a time sequence, neither of which presupposes or entails the other,[13] he not only insists, rightly, on the semantically synthetic character of the narrative utterance, if "events" can be stative as well as active in his terminology; he also takes at face value the junctive effect of narrative, thus concealing or repressing disjunction, discontinuity, rupture, the breach of identity, the irreversible inversion of sign that fascinated Foucault:

> For history in its classical form, discontinuity was at the same time the given and the unthinkable. [It] has now become one of the fundamental elements of historical analysis, where it plays a triple role. It constitutes, first of all, a deliberate operation on the part of the historian. . . . It is also the result of his description, for what he undertakes to discover are the limits of a process, the point of inflection of a curve, the inversion of a regulating movement, the boundaries of an oscillation, the threshold of a functioning, the moment of destabilization of a circular causality. It is finally the concept that our work ceaselessly specifies.[14]

The choice of a linguistic model is overdetermined by one's attitude to transitivity, fear or hope, reality principle or pleasure principle, need or desire, conservation wish or conquest and expansion impulse — all asymmetrical pairs — and it conditions to a large extent the hermeneutics of narrative texts. It is a major link between the apprehension and use of discourse and our negotiations with Discourses.

Narrative discourse is often associated with "action" or "making," if not with causality. In Greimassian semiotics, the notion of "narrative program," which I shall use in a different sense (see chapter 7) presents some similarities with my narrateme: "The narrative program . . . is an elementary syntagm of surface narrative syntax, consisting in an utterance of 'making' [faire] that rules an utterance of state. . . . The narrative program should be understood as a change of state, effected by any subject S_1 and bearing on any subject S_2 whatsoever."[15] This is, in my perspective, a correct — although not transformational — definition of transactive narratemes, but not of nontransactive narratemes (narratemes of simple "becoming"), unless we demand that any change necessarily implies an external agent of change, an S_1 different from S_2, but, even in this case and discarding the fact that the demand in question is unscientific in view of the modern theories of biophysical systems, for example, we could be left with a different classification of some key utterances. "Years passed," a nonnarrative utterance for Greimas, is for me a narrateme because the date has changed (e.g., "It was 1946, then it was 1964"), and for Genette because it is often a substitute for the utterance of other events presented under the narrative mode ("The characters grew older," etc.).

Reading other theorists, we must already face some major difficulties concerning temporal axis, succession, duration, and tense.

Traugott and Pratt:

> Narration is essentially a way of linguistically representing past experience, whether real or imagined. The basic characteristic of narrative discourse is that the order in which it presents events is the order in which those events are claimed to have occurred in time.[16]

These ideas, however shocking they may seem, are still so pervasive that they require a detailed critique. I shall consider them one by one.

The first statement implies that experience is prior to discourse, not only logically but also temporally. It would be delightful to indulge in an egg-and-chicken digression about discourse shaping experience or experience shaping discourse, but I shall resist the temptation. Let me simply argue that "past experience" is pleonastic if there is no such thing as present or future experience, and that it does not make sense if there is not present or future experience of it as memory to account for its pastness; but, in this case, which discourse will represent present and future experience? Moreover, the distinction between "real and imagined experience" would be useless if all experience was equally past: "imagined experience" is experience that proves either to a second subject or at a later time not to have taken place at time T_1 in a particular universe called "real" (see chapter 4). There is no way out of this dilemma.

Traugott and Pratt's basic idea is that narration is an a posteriori report, whatever it reports. My basic ideas are that narrative discourse condenses time and, in its sucessive linguistic and kinetic media, represents successive difference—difference in time—by nonsuccessive means, as far as it can. The arbitrariness of the linguistic sign is closely linked with the paradigmatic principle also in that discourse (or *parole*) functions, at least in part, in contrast with the features of language. Similarly the actualization of a code, a genre, or a model in practice is also a distortion and a potential opposition. Only a "second-degree," rhetorical process such as the introduction of iconic features will attempt to make a statement signify again in conformity with a mechanical mimesis, a certified copy of perceptions. Thus, when we have a linguistic account of:

$$(\text{snark}) \rightarrow (\text{snark}) \rightarrow (\text{boojum}),$$

the normal technique is not to say, "There was a snark, the snark was a snark, then the snark was no longer a snark, then there was no longer a snark, but there was a boojum instead," but, "The snark has become a boojum." The analytic paraphrase or development will be perceived by the receiver as protracted, less narrative than the condensed utterance; it will be perceived as an explanatory and evaluative comment rather than a "natural" manner of making a long story long. Narrative discourse denotes difference in time, that is, difference between two or more states of affairs indexed with a distinct temporal situation, whether these situations are all past regarding the time of enunciation or another time of reference, or whether one is past and another present or future, or whether yet they are all future, and so forth. "In 1988 the GNP will grow 2.5 percent" is just as narrative as "Caesar died in 44 B.C." and more so than "The potted plant was dying."

It follows from the same principles that linguistic narrative discourse has little or nothing to do with the order of the events presented or with "causal order," unless we imagine an "analytic" language in which phrastic syntax is primarily ordered temporally—whatever it would mean—and which would be devoid of any temporal markers other than this syntactic order, that is, a language without tenses, temporal adjectives, adverbs, prepositions, and so on. Then, instead of saying, "I'll go to sleep after dinner and I'll dream about our last afternoon together," one would be obliged to "follow the order of events" and say, "It is now [if this at least was allowed!], I spend time with you, I have dinner, it is dark, I sleep, I dream about you and me." Moreover, many natural languages make it either impossible or indifferent to "follow the order of events" at the phrastic level. " 'Get rich!' says PM to crowd at electoral meeting" is not any more or any less narrative than "There was an electoral meeting, a crowd came, the PM said to them: 'Get rich!' "

These elementary considerations lead us to other problems related to time and the narrateme.

What are the principal characteristics of temporal coordinates necessary for the sense effect of "event" to be achieved?

The answer that comes to mind immediately, namely, that this time must be linear (single track) and irreversible, is not fully satisfactory if we agree that many narratemes can hardly be considered under a purely propositional value. I will show in chapter 7 that some modalizations are analyzable in terms of juxtaposed predicates sharing the same subject, but this cannot be said of the linguistic possible, and especially of the linguistic unreal in the past:[17] "Had he not come back that night, the house would have burned." This utterance contains at first sight two correlated sets of statements based on the same propositional set, but of opposite signs:

Propositional Set: [$\pm$] (He come back) + [$\pm$] (House burn).
Modalized Set 1: (He did not come back) + (The house burned).
Modalized Set 2: (He came back) + (The house did not burn).

The actual utterance considered posits Modalized Set 1 as negated (untrue) in order to claim Modalized Set 2 as factual (positive). This does not mean that Set 1 has no existence in time or that it is to be situated in a time different from that of Set 2; in fact, its temporal situation is exactly the same as that of Set 2, and it differs from it only on the plane of its truth or mode of existence. Hypothetical, interrogative utterances, for instance, do not alter the *directionality* of the temporal axis; they simply require it to branch out into parallel streams in order to flow simultaneously through different planes of existence.

On the other hand, it is moot whether an event can occur at all in reversible or cyclical time. We should note that statements like "They were all happy together again" are often accompanied by "as if nothing had happened" (in Spanish: "como si tal cosa"). There is some measure of mutual dependence between linear time and event, time does not *pass* unless it is *broken* by events (as food needs to be broken in order to be digested). Time is only perceptible (and acceptable) thanks to its discontinuity brought about by events that presuppose in turn a linear temporal continuum. Reversible time, on the contrary, would be typified by the undifferentiated recurrence of "events," that is, by the identity of features before and after, thus canceling change, defined as the main seme of "event." In reversible time, "Bonaparte becomes Bonaparte," but he never becomes Napoleon. This question is vital for the interpretation of myth and mythic reference. It is also involved in the process of significance of narrative genres, like the ballad, which combine the forceful repetition of signifiers with a reduced slot for formal and semantic alteration (see chapter 9), or in those that combine procedures of synchronic explication, like stylistic embedding, *mise en abyme*, and so on, with a progression dictated by desire (examples in the fantastic).

Tense, as I have suggested, is no key to the narrative character of an utterance, nor is mood. Narrative predication can be found in French, for example, in any tense form from the *passé surcomposé* to the future, and these tenses do not show a simple and direct relationship with temporal referentiation. In other words, they are not directly and automatically bound to a particular situation of the event on the temporal axis, whatever T_0 is chosen in a text. Science fiction, fantasy, and utopian narratives are generally written in the past tenses, while the future tenses are sometimes dominant in ancient history lectures (see chapter 7).

If the aorist, even in French, in no way plays the leading role that Anne Banfield, following Barthes, is ready to give it,[18] does this mean that tense forms have no part in the construction of narrative meaning? Although we may not accept the lists established by H. Weinrich[19] or the psychological value attributed by him to two tense groups, his notions of commentative and narrative tenses still hold some interest, because the theoretical existence of such a dichotomy in the background is the precondition for a rhetoric of tense, for tropic effects of all sorts (hyperbolic, euphemistic, etc.) that would be impossible without the contrastive basis of supposedly standard usage. In this respect, on the textual scale, "obstinately recurrent features" such as tense frequency (e. g., the quantitative dominance of the imperfect and its group of tenses) are just as much the necessary background for tense shifts pointing to an event, as they are the expression of a rule of tense usage; Weinrich shows it very well in his chapter 5, particularly about the -ing form in Hemingway's short story "Indian Camp." These reflections on tense will lead many of us to suspect that the signified "event" or "change" is not so much a question of lexical content or tense used, as of presentational breaking off from the cotext, often signaled by a tense *shift*. Let us compare these two French utterances:

1. "Il acheta une propriété, il oublia la ville et les cercles, il se maria, il eut des enfants, enfin il vivait."
2. "Il travaillait dur, il plaisait à ses supérieurs, il montait en grade, enfin il vécut."

In both, opposite tense shifts foreground the same predicate, to be read as bearer of event.[20]

The first examples of narratemes given here leave us in doubt as to the instantaneous or progressive character of "change" in "event." Can an event have duration, can it last? Our irreflexive tendency would be to answer no, like those who let themselves be guided by the imperfect/perfect dichotomy to determine the narrative or nonnarrative nature of a text. But, if an event has no duration, takes literally no time, how does it occur in time? The paradox of becoming will be less threatening if we introduce notions of temporal frame and temporal measuring. Let us compare:

1. The price of petrol will rise three cents per gallon as of midnight today.
2. The price of petrol keeps rising over the years.
3. After constant rises in the last decade, the price of petrol has dropped sharply in 1986.

In item 1 the maximum temporal extension of the period considered is two days (the price will rise "between today and tomorrow") but the temporal count unit is the hour or even the minute (at one to twelve, the price will still be x, but at one minute past twelve, it will already be x + .03). In item 2 the temporal frame is very vague, and the relation of the rise to this frame is a fuzzy coincidence. In item 3 the temporal frame, counted in years (a total of ten or eleven, depending on whether T_0 is situated at the beginning or at the end of 1986, marking the end of the constant trend period), permits a clear cut between a long period and a short, different, new one: "in 1986." We can see that the meaning effect of "event" is strongest in (1), still clearly perceptible in (3), and weakest in (2) where there is no obligatory cut on the temporal axis, but only arbitrary points of observation, probably coinciding with the temporal count unit of the year, used in the utterance, which forms in turn as many minitemporal frames: when change is coextensive with the temporal frame, it characterizes the continuity of a period and thus tends to be perceived as a *state* of things in spite of the lexical meaning of the predicate expressed in the utterance. On the other hand, a change so "fast" that it is not seen as a destabilization process taking some time is "unbelievable," "baffling," it upsets the temporal coordinates themselves, without which difference in or along time cannot be perceived: death destroys time and the possibility of change; the life of death is eternal.

Finally, we must return to a logical and philosophical remark on the (c) and (d) conditions of event listed on page 36.

McCawley,[21] following Thomason,[22] shows that the nontrivial use of the = predicate can be explained only by its exploitation in A = B, and that this exploitation in turn is possible only if A and B are treated as classes or sets (such that one or more B's can belong to the class of A's): "Identity plays a role in the analysis of many semantically complex words." Now, identity across time, being the precondition of the signified "change," whichever of the following forms it may take—"Bonaparte becomes Napoleon," "Bonaparte becomes himself," "Bonaparte remains Bonaparte"—presupposes that individual noun phrases (NPs) are treated as classes or sets of features. The predicate of change (or nonchange) plays the trick of selecting one or more variants, while forcefully maintaining one or more constants due to its *conjunctive* effect. This is why, in surface expressions, "Bonaparte becomes himself" is grammatical, but "Bonaparte becomes" is not. In a narrateme, the conjunctive property of the predicate of change is associated with the continuum of time, so that time, also uniting what it separates, is somehow conquered or redeemed. Linguistic narrative is a device to blur contradictions by means of a bifocalization of description. This will become salient with the transformational-generative use we propose to make of Kress and Hodge's schema of predicates.[23]

A Transformational Model of the Kinds of Predication

Although it has been invaluable in the development of the theoretical model presented in these pages, Kress and Hodge's classification in its original form (next page) relies heavily on intuitive categories and gives no explanation of the transformational mechanisms that allow a speaker to shift from an equative to an attributive, say, without changing the denotative meaning of the utterance (e.g., "John is president" → "John has the leadership"). Some of the finer categories too are the consequence of rampant psychologism and moral-metaphysical dichotomies. The underlying bias should have been elicited, and some examples are far from convincing: why is "John liked the picture" transactive and "Mary looked at the picture" nontransactive? Paraphrases show that the dividing line is thin, if it is to be found at all: "The picture pleased John"; "The picture drew Mary's attention." Why is "look at" mental? How would we classify "stare at" or "see" in this schema? Moreover, is there only one type of equative? Finally, the role of shifters and syntactic order has been neglected, when they are essential to frame the

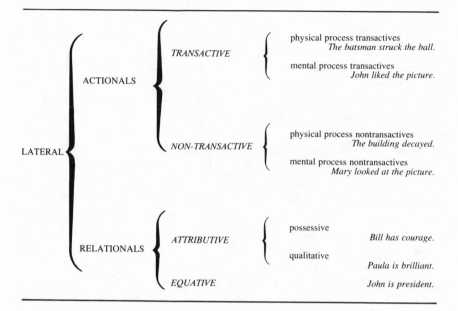

domains in which an equative or an attributive relationship, for example, can be detected. Compare:

1. "John is president."
2. "John is the president."
3. "This John is the president."
4. "The president is John."

It is quite clear that the = sign in the "deep" (simplified) structure (John = President) has a different value in each case and that, for instance, (1) is easily transformed into "John has (the) leadership," and (4) into "The group has John for its president," two *inverse* possessive relationships. (1) has the potential to turn John into a bearer of power, and (4) into an instrument of power.

At this stage, instead of refining the classification, we have tried to rationalize it and complete it vertically, so that it would yield some basic transformational rules that we might test on all sorts of predicates.

The Model and Its Interpretation

Here, in condensed form, is the result of my work:

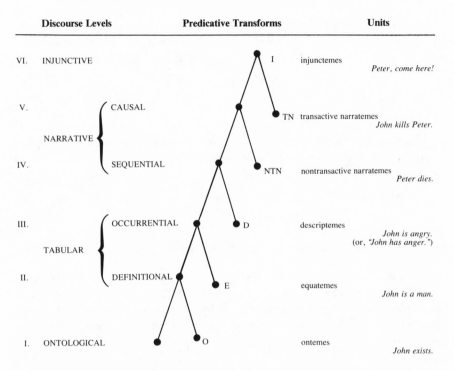

Discourse Levels	Predicative Transforms	Units

VI. INJUNCTIVE — I — injunctemes — *Peter, come here!*

V. CAUSAL — TN — transactive narratemes — *John kills Peter.*

NARRATIVE

IV. SEQUENTIAL — NTN — nontransactive narratemes — *Peter dies.*

III. OCCURRENTIAL — D — descriptemes — *John is angry.* (or, *"John has anger."*)

TABULAR

II. DEFINITIONAL — E — equatemes — *John is a man.*

I. ONTOLOGICAL — O — ontemes — *John exists.*

Notes on this model

The patience and attention of the reader are kindly requested for a slightly technical discussion that forms the substratum of many textual analyses in this book.

1. The ontological predicate ∃x ("x is," or better, "There is at least an x") is (posited as) unanalyzable. One cannot predicate less about any NP, and one must predicate first its existence in some possible universe of discourse in order to say anything about it.

2. Ideally, all other predicates should be the synthesis of a pair of immediately inferior (simpler) predicates. Thus "John is a man" joins into one sentence "John is" and "a man is," so that, within this utterance, the domains of "John" and "a man" are coextensive. The semantic synthesis effected by the equateme corresponds formally to the application of a deletion rule: the verb "is" is found only once in "John is a man"; it is used with a triple function: as ∃ John, ∃ man, and John = man. It results from this that "two-place" predicates at the definitional level, like "John is Peter's brother," pose a problem of complexity and possible asymmetry that we shall also find, only worsened, at other, upper levels. It is not sufficient to analyze "John is Peter's brother" into ∃ John, ∃ Peter, ∃ brother, and apply a deletion rule, if we want to fall back on the same initial utterance. It is

not enough either to add a rule of introduction of conjunction, since this could yield: "John and Peter are brothers," which is not contradictory but has a different domain. In fact, we are obliged to follow two distinct lines of analysis:

> . . . the ontological reduction already evoked
> . . . this sequence: "Peter has brother, John is him" (that brother that Peter has),

and we find that such a definitional utterance contains another unit (descriptive or attributive) of a higher level. The explanation lies in an implied subordination or embedding of the type:

> "John is the one who has Peter for brother."

or:

> "John is the one whom Peter has for brother."

3. At levels IV and V, those of special interest for us, we should note that:
a) Nontransactive narratemes are analyzable into two descriptemes opposed as contraries and of opposite temporal "signs" or directions: "Peter dies" results from the semantic fusion of "Peter was alive" and "Peter will not be alive."

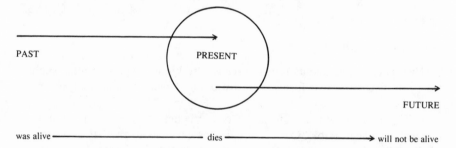

T_0 or the present of the event is situated at the shared point of departure of the truth-value of the two descriptemes, that is, at the moment when both contraries are true (or neither is).

b) Transactive narratemes (TNs) are easily analyzed into two nontransactive narratemes (NTNs). "John kills Peter" results from the combination of "John becomes a murderer" with "Peter becomes dead," each of these NTNs being decomposable in turn into the corresponding pairs of descriptemes as above. While at the NTN or sequential level, the temporal validities of the two lower units (D's) are only joined at their point of departure, the respective temporal validities of the component NTNs of a TN coincide completely: John becomes a murderer *as* Peter becomes dead, and vice versa. The expression of causality is an effect of *com*plication; *ex*plication finds its origin in coincidence. Since explication (or decomposition or analysis) is always necessary, even if it is not conscious, for the comprehension of narratemes (the eventual production of narrative meaning), any narrateme, and consequently all narrative discourse, including causal discourse, questions causality as much as it states or suggests it. An attorney defending a criminal case will use this well-known device to dissociate verbally the death of the victim from the gesture of the murderer; the defending attorney analyzes the prosecutor's claim that "X shot Y dead" into an unfortunate coincidence between "X shot" and "Y died."

A possible narrateme like any other predicate requires that the receiver first of all explicate (develop) it into its coincident (coincided, collapsed, or amalgamated) parts. But then the receiver has a choice between various lines of behavior: (1) not move from there if he resists believing in causality (at TN level) or change (at NTN level); (2) operate a systematic detransformation (identical or similar to the transformation that has permitted the textual formation of the narrative utterance) and stop at this point, thus achieving what we could consider a mechanically successful act of narrative communication; (3) go on transforming (analyzing) and detransforming (synthesizing) ad libitum or endlessly, which is likely to be the case when the utterance is not acceptable to the receiver, as typically happens in mourning: "He's dead → He was alive yesterday / I won't see him any more → He's dead → He was alive yesterday," and so on; (4) operate "illegal," additional, or parasitic transformations on one or more of the components resulting from the initial analysis (further analyses down to the ontological level, dissolving and scattering more elaborate meanings, are one possibility; ergative substitutions are another; all of them are characteristic of literary and especially modern literary readings that claim complete freedom or an extreme plurality of interpretations); (5) operate higher-level syntheses that are not explicitly demanded by the text for the sake of its semantic concretization: this is what will usually happen when didactic meaning is sought beyond merely narrative meaning (see chapter 10).

4. The injunctive level poses a special problem because of its great complexity: it combines a predicative and an ergative transformation (a change of subject: the addressee is to transform the signified action into a performative), and its second element (the "content of the order," so to speak) may apparently belong to either level V or level IV.

5. Time appears (although not oriented) as early as level III. Causality (nonverbal) appears at level V. It is important to realize that our model is like a flight of stairs; its step-by-step discontinuity makes it functional, but there are many ways in which contiguous steps can be grouped, depending on various conceptual criteria. For example, levels I-III together group all the "predicates of state" and levels IV-VI all the "predicates of change"; occurrential and sequential discourses have in common that they make use of some temporal coordinates without necessarily inferring any form of causality. These considerations will have to be borne in mind to understand discursive displacements in surface structures and their ef-

fects. The fact that *narrative discourse is at least two-tiered* is particularly noteworthy, since it gives a special *flexibility* (and often a high degree of ambiguity) to the narrative construction of meaning and the functions of narrative genres at large.

Practical and Functional Problems

A narrateme is an utterance that contains an actional predicate (transactive or nontransactive).

Is this rudimentary definition sufficient, even in the framework of a fairly complex transformational model of predication, to embark immediately on the great narratemic hunt that should allow us to differentiate tales (shorthand for "narrative texts" or texts through which narrative significance obtains) from other texts? Before we rush to "apply" the definition and the model, there are four more nagging questions to be asked. The question of explicit and implied or virtual narratemes pertains rather to the general problem of the dominance or not of narrative discourse in a text, to be treated in the last section of this chapter. The three other questions raised by the confrontation of classroom practice with my own research will be examined briefly now.

A. How do we identify a predicate, and what are the effects of *functional translations*, or grammatical class transformations, the surface realizations of a function pertaining to one grammatical class through a member of another class? In the present context, this concerns particularly all the guises in which a verb function may appear in actual surface structures, but also nonverb-based sentences, and possible pseudoverbs (transforms of other grammatical classes). I shall take two examples:

   1. What a man!

This nonverb-based sentence can be paraphrased as "This man is ↑q x," where ↑q is an augmentative such as "very" or "so" (possibly amplifying a reductive factor such as "little," in depreciatory irony), and x is an adjective provided by the verbal or nonverbal context (as in direct oral communication). Such sentences present no special difficulty other than their relative context-bound indeterminacy. Their discursive status will depend on that of the most adequate paraphrase we can find: "What a man!" will usually turn out to be occurrential or definitional.

   2. Love overpowered my soul.

Love is always a noun transform of the verb "to love"; in the context of Dante's writings, the noun "soul" also appears as the result of a nominalization, but it gathers together several verbs such as "to feel," "to will," "to desire," and "to think." For the sake of simplicity, I shall neglect this factor. Any nominalized verb loses the marks of person and tense that it would show in its conjugated form; these marks can be replaced to a certain extent by possessive adjectives, a genitive, or anaphoric possessive pronouns (for person), and by temporal deictic adjectives, pronouns, or adverbs (for tense). "My soul" is thus a substitute for "I feel" or "I desire," but without the tense-mark substitutes that adjectives such as "old," "new," or "eternal" would provide. "Love" lacks person mark as well. So that reverse translation yields:

    2a. "(x love) overpowered (I feel)."

In such a case, cursory reading will automatically feed in the missing information by contamination: since sentence 2 contains one tense (a preterit) and one person mark (a first person), this will give:

    $2a_1$. "(I loved) overpowered (I felt)."

But cursory reading can be completely wrong, and, at any rate, it reduces the ambiguities that give, together with a much wider potential domain, its affective value to the sentence. Compare:

    $2a_2$. "(We loved) overpowered (I feel)."

Nominalizations tend to make narrative analysis difficult (they are generally meant to do just that), because both tense *and* person are useful indexes of the discursive status of predicates. However, nominalizations are a complicating factor mainly because they can produce excess predication, as in sentence 2a, at least at an intermediate stage of explication. In order to make good sense of sentence 2 and not interpret it abusively as an essentially metalingual statement, as sentence 2a and its variants would suggest, we must realize that, if "love" and "soul" are disguised verbs, the surface structure verb "overpowered" is also a transform, the result of the complementary translation of an adjective, necessary to bear the minimal tense marker—an index of narrativity too—and give grammaticality to the sentence, which could now be reexplicated as follows:

    2b. "I felt that (x love) strong."

This is not the place to analyze all the semantic and semiotic effects of the transformation of a nontransactive (at least not obviously transactive) structure like that of sentence 2b into the transactive structure of sentence 2, and Dante does it in his own way;[24] but let us observe that transformational predicative analysis demands a description of deep and embedded *semantic* structures without which these effects would go unnoticed and remain indescribable, or describable only in an impressionistic manner.

B. Are there displacements of discursive levels other than those related to grammatical class translations, and how do they work? I shall take one example to start with:

3. The rainbow bent over the village.

Verbs of motion such as "go" ("on," "over," "under," etc.), "rise," "fall," "follow," "turn," "bend," and "stretch" are commonly used to describe contour, line, shape, and extension of static objects. In many cases, as in sentence 3, it would even be difficult or awkward to look for another word completely exempt from motion or action; compare:

3a. The rainbow formed a curve over the village

and

3b. The shape of the rainbow was a curve over the village.

It remains that a verb such as "arch" would reduce considerably the actional charge:

3c. The rainbow arched over the village.

And, if we imagine a personification of the rainbow as young and beautiful Iris (not necessarily an athlete, though), "bend" would certainly be more appropriate than "arch":

3d. Iris bent over the village.

This only confirms our interpretive guess about the "figurative" use of verbs of motion: it is linked with an anthropomorphic or, by extension, an animate view of nature and things, and closely related to the projection of the perceiving/describing subject onto the object of perception. These verbs are traces of frames; the corresponding utterances are clearly subjective in that they inscribe the subject's "point" of view or, better, his style of viewing ("subject" does not necessarily mean the sender, but one or more human or quasi-human entities involved in the communication situation). The subject's eyes rise, "describe" a curve, then "fall" again to follow the shape of the rainbow: "bent over" accounts for this motion, this physical process, at the same time as it "describes" the shape of the rainbow; it communicates the shape through a parallel experience of the decoder of the utterance, giving him directives on how to use his "mind's eyes" and his body to "figure out" the rainbow.

This almost pragmatic approach to "translated" predicates will be very fruitful if we can see that sentence 3 is actually composed of two "deep" utterances fused into one:

3e$_1$. The rainbow (over the village) has an arching shape (*occurrential D*).

3e$_2$. The eyes of the viewer describe a curvilinear movement (over the village) (*sequential NTN*).

Sentence 3, in fact, joins not only two different types of predicates but two different subjects. Generally speaking, we find that *predicative tropes* like the one described here are indissociable from ergative transformations; they are a privileged point of encounter between noun phrase (NP) grammar and verb phrase (VP) grammar, as well as an attempt to bridge the discontinuity between the steps of the stairlike predicative transformational system.

Let us now compare three utterances that are possible paraphrases of each other in conversational usage:

4a. He appears and disappears.

4b. Now I see him, now I don't.

4c. Now he is here, now he is not.

C. Our third question asks: is the model proposed not only transformational in a descriptive sense, but actually generative in the sense that it would be a reliable guide to produce well-formed utterances (narrative, for example)? To try and answer this question, three elements ought to be taken into consideration.

First, NP grammar and VP grammar constantly collaborate for the production of discourse in natural languages. A VP grammar does not suffice to generate grammatical utterances of any kind, even though the constructions of narrative and didactic meanings—our main concern in this book—are more dependent on predicative than themic components. It is also apparent that a transformational grammar of NPs is much more difficult to elaborate than that of VPs; relations between NPs would be more distributional than integrative.

Second, in my present perspective, utterances that take the form of complex sentences are generated from other utterances and sentences, not from microcomponents like individual semes or valences. Therefore, to analyze an injuncteme into its component actional discursemes, or a nontransactive narrateme into its component descriptemes, is as good a way of generating utterances as it is to build a nontransactive narrateme from a pair of descriptemes. On the other hand, the results of analysis on a large number of utterances do provide a few highly reliable constructive rules. Let us take some examples of nontransactive narratemes and descriptemes for this purpose.

1. Peter dies.

2. Marcel becomes a writer.

3. Marcel has become a writer (overnight).

4. A snark becomes a boojum.
5.* Bonaparte becomes Bonaparte.

The analysis of these various utterances into their component descriptemes gives:

1a. Peter was alive + Peter will not be alive.
2a. Marcel was not a writer + Marcel will be a writer.
3a. Marcel was not a writer + Marcel is a writer.
4a. A snark was a snark + A snark will be a boojum.
5a. *Bonaparte was not Bonaparte + Bonaparte will be Bonaparte.

On top of the general rules already indicated, some more specific constraints can be ascertained to build a nontransactive narrateme from a pair of descriptemes. When they are all combined, they come close to ensuring that the utterance produced will conform to the actual strictures of surface structures in natural language. Let us list some of the most obvious of these specific rules:

Rule 1. The subject NPs of the component descriptemes must be identical; this same subject occurs only once in each descripteme.

Rule 2. The VPs of the component descriptemes are copula based; these copula-based VP's must be transformed into a single verb-based VP.

Rule 3. There is a time-scale gap between the tenses of the VPs of the component descriptemes; the tense of the VP of the resulting nontransactive narrateme, whenever it can be marked adequately, will be intermediate on the time scale between the two original tenses.

Rule 4. In order to construct a grammatical nontransactive narrateme, both original descriptemes selected must be themselves grammatical (i.e., logically valid in some possible world W and in some universe of belief U).

Third, "understanding" narrative involves synthesis (reconstruction according to rules, of deconstructed narratemes), but also very often the construction of narratemes not textualized in their canonical forms, such as those proposed in the form of parallel descriptemes or associable NTNs, like the pieces of a jigsaw puzzle. All the receivers who make narrative sense out of such texts are assumed to follow complex sets of generative rules, but empirically, intuitively, or out of sheer habit, just as in the conversational practice of language. Nobody will claim that these operations are fully conscious, but it is the theorist's task to formulate normally tacit rules as explicitly as possible in order to understand the nature of narrative, that is, to understand what we do when we understand narratively.

The Trial of the Text

The text chosen is the beginning of *Palomita torcaz* (*Turtle dove*), a novel by Rafael Pérez y Pérez:

> The numerous travelers who crossed almost uninterruptedly the dazzling region of the Levant, commonly known as the "Costa del Sol," would often cast an inquisitive glance at the circular tower that rose toward the Mediterranean, capping a certain granitic promontory and calling to mind the well-known inspired lines of Núñez de Arce:
>
> > Adorning of a river mouth
> > the dangerous and narrow entrance
> > on a promontory of the coast
> > beaten night and day by the sea
> > there rises gigantic and dark
> > a high circular tower
> > that a king ordered to be built
> > in the guise of a bastion
> > to defend the shore
> > against the threats of the sea.
>
> It was a stern, strong, rather heavy, massive building, evocative of pirates, fantastic and adventurous epics.
>
> In the past it had only some narrow, well-dissimulated holes for all ventilation and light; they opened in that huge wall, several feet thick, behind which the onlooker could imagine catching a glimpse of the tanned face and disheveled beard of some Christian soldier. It was perhaps for its lack of windows that the tower had received its nickname from the neighboring peasants: they called this refuge of the coastal garrison "the blind tower," and the name remained.
>
> Now, obviously, the Blind Tower had windows; windows in Gothic style, with finely designed arches, which bore artistic stained glass; but this addition was recent and due to the present owner of the historic property.[25]

The first predications with human subjects ("to cross," "to know" = call or name, "to cast" a glance, "to wonder") could be interpreted as events, being actional, if they gave evidence of a before and an after separable by analysis, but the frequentative aspect implies on the contrary the identity of the contents of all the moments into which the temporal axis could be divided: the frequentative reduces to a minimum the internal difference of the actional predication by placing the stress on the identity of its own repetition (in a widened frame); in fact, it potentially transforms the actional predication into a "state" (a single relational predication). This may be expressed superficially not only by frequentative auxiliaries like *soler* in Spanish, "used to" (although it manifests the completion of the series), "would," and "will" in English, or by frequentative adverbs ("often") and other quantifiers ("many"), but even by the Spanish turn *"estar* + gerund" and the English turn "be + -ing," in spite of their mainly processive value.

The other verbs, which have an inanimate for their subject (the tower), are on the whole false actionals ("rise," "cap," adorn"): their temporal denotation is coextensive with the existence of the subject, but two of them, which are adjectivized to different degrees ("calling to mind" and "evocative") deserve special attention; understanding them involves introducing an *additional* subject, a human one, and splitting up the predicate into a dual deep structure: "someone sees the tower / someone remembers." These two predications are actional; they could form two narratemes, but the surface realization that conjugates them ("the tower calls to mind," or, especially, "the evocative tower") conceals these narratemes and finally cancels their narrativity by imposing the frequentative aspect on them. It is interesting to note that these hidden or obliterated narratemes are related to the production of the text through the role of the narrator.

Up to "adventurous," the text therefore contains only one fully realized narrateme: "a king ordered [the tower] to be built," which attributes an origin, a cause to the existence of the tower but, in doing this, only fills in the logical blanks created by its existence: if there was a tower, it had surely been built by someone! The aforementioned narrateme partly answers the questions "how?" (by the modality of "ordering to") and "by whom?" (= a king), thus giving legitimacy to the tower, so to speak; but the position of the same narrateme within a subordinate clause, itself situated in a formally and stylistically isolated quotation (italics + verse + archaism), confers on it a threefold indirect relationship to the rest of the text. Authority is as powerful as it is remote.

What happens afterward is all the more interesting: "In the past it did not have other openings . . . / In our time, it had windows." We are offered successively two relational (possessive) predicates, the first marked by a negative sign, the second not; in other words, we have the loose pieces of a narrateme that could read: "the tower acquired [or rather: 'had acquired'] windows." But the search for causes according to the code of common sense implies that a figural activation of the tower takes place and suggests the following further transformation: "someone had given windows to [or: 'cut windows into'] the tower." This expectation is actually fulfilled by the text as soon as possible, when it determines the human subject to a certain extent ("the present owner of the historic property") and modalizes the action in various ways, especially on the temporal plane ("recently"). But all this is done without letting the real subject of the action reemerge in the surface grammar role of subject; we have instead a causal complement of the passive voice structure: "was due to."

The stepping into narrative, analyzed through the first narratemes in the text and their particular features, reveals a technique of writing that stubbornly conceals its own production by not uttering the subject of enunciation. The narrator of *Palomita torcaz* remains in hiding for a while; we can barely catch a stealthy glimpse of him or guess his presence under disguises (people, travelers, someone, the inspired poet of the past, the tower itself as a container full of stories . . .). This inversion of roles can be seen again in, and reinforces itself through, that of the roles of animate and inanimate in the presented world (the tower/the owner). The two-way displacement of narrative and infranarrative discursemes contributes heavily to the game of hide-and-seek played by the narrator: everything is, on the surface, as if the human actors were by-products, subjected to nonhuman actants (the "landscape"). And the landscape itself, as I have shown elsewhere,[26] is the material counterpart, witness and warrantor of tradition, the semisocialized presence of God on earth.

It is now becoming clear that the semiotics of discourse, particularly when it is actualized on a macrotextual scale rather than in artificially isolated "individual" utterances, offers remarkable insights into the politics of Discourses. Narrative grammars that neglect surface structures are blind to these "screens," which can be made to reveal what they hide by manifesting it too obviously, if we just take care to push them *au pied du mur, au pied de la lettre*, into the last bastions of their evidence. In this effort, which will be mine throughout this book, we will be greatly assisted by the determination of narrative significance, which occurs at the scale of the complex communicative act that we synecdochically call a text.

The question is, when do we call a text *a narrative?* The ready answer: when narrative discourse plays a dominant or key role in it. In other words: what linguistic and other elements do we combine, how and in relation to what parameters do we combine them to produce narrative significance from a text and to encode narrative significance into a text?

From Narrateme to Narrative Significance

What is it, for narrative discourse, to dominate? How do we decide that it does? How do we make it dominate? The value of this dominance constitutes all the difficulty and interest of the question.

First of all, a distinction must be drawn between *quantitative* and qualitative or *hierarchic* dominance.

Quantitative Narrative

A Day in the Life of Nancy
Nancy gets up very early in the morning. She wakes up the children, gets their breakfast ready, then she drives to the mall in the blue Chevy. When she returns, she does the washing, cleans the house, and has some lunch. Early in the afternoon, she mows the lawn, studies

recipes in a magazine, and tends the pets, two dogs and three cats. As
soon as the kids are back from school, she prepares dinner for the
whole family. At around eight o'clock, she watches TV for a while with
her husband, then they rest together in their queen-size bed with a comfortable new spring mattress, tired but happy. Just before she goes to
sleep she thinks that, only a few days away now, there will be the great
adventure of the holiday on the beach with all the loved ones.

This is a text that we could find, with few modifications, in a variety of contexts
such as the letters of an au pair or in a middle school composition. Making it up
as an example, I have been careful to set a determined temporal frame (the period
of twenty-four hours this text shares with classical French tragedy) and a clear
temporal vector oriented from the immediate past to the near future. Of nineteen
surface predicates, eighteen are actional, and a fair number are transactive.
"Nancy" is the sole subject of fourteen out of eighteen actional predicates, her
identity through the whole period presented being well marked by constant
pronominal anaphora. In brief, "A Day in the Life of Nancy" is a text in which
narrative discourse is quantitatively dominant in the appropriate frame to confer
spatiotemporal and thematic coherence on the whole.

What is it then that leaves us with the uneasy, almost bitter feeling that we have
been cheated of a "real" narrative, that nothing really happens in Nancy's world?
Is it the sheer banality of Nancy and her boring life? (But then, what is banality?)
Or is it some "formal" feature we have not considered yet? Comparative analysis
could help discover it.

Let us rewrite the text, adding a precise setting in historical time and geographic space (date and place) and putting all the verbs in the past. The text will
now read something like this:

On May 4, 1985, at her home in Baton Rouge, Louisiana, Nancy got
up very early in the morning. She woke up the children . . . she
thought that, only a few days away now, there would be the great adventure of the holiday on the beach at Biloxi with all the loved ones."

We note some improvement in the narrative effect: the precise date and place
seem to indicate that, at different dates and in different places, before or after that
May 4, Nancy's life may have been or become different. For instance, on December 19, 1975, she was still a high school student, it was a Saturday after an end-of-
term party with her friends, she got up late, her mother served her breakfast, and
so on. And/or again, on July 20, 1985, after the terrible accident on Interstate
I10, she woke up a widow in the hospital at Hammond. There appears a *virtual
narrateme* such as: "Nancy's life had changed"; or, "Nancy's life would change."
Yet the discontent of narrative fans with our new text is not alleviated, since the
new text *does not require* the contextual extension we have carried out in order
to produce the macronarrateme "Nancy's life changed." Moreover, even after the

extension, the conclusion is merely optional; it depends whether we include the semantic content of the frame in the data used to process the predicative content of the text itself. We could very legitimately concentrate on the probability that "on May 4, 1985 (*as on any other day during all those years*), Nancy got up early in the morning," and so on. The "day in the life of Nancy" would then be a "typical" day negating any change on its horizon; its textualization would have an iterative value. The other option, which proposes a narrative program—not full-fledged narrative significance—does so by comparing two *states of affairs* and joining them into a macronarrateme through the generative process of higher-level predication synthesis.

One of these states of affairs is presented in the text, which can be validly interpreted as descriptive or even definitional, yielding the following interpretive summaries:

1 (Occurrential). A day in the life of Nancy happens to be ordinary.

2 (Definitional). Nancy is an ordinary lower-middle-class housewife.

And one of the following teachings, depending on the ideological context and communicative situation:

3a (Injunctive). Do the same as Nancy, she is happy.

3b (Injunctive). Do not act like Nancy, she is stupid.

The narrative (causal and sequential) levels are now skipped as an unessential pretext, a disguise perhaps: we have been dealing with a pseudonarrative.

In fact, we are now able to understand the formal cause of our initial disappointment on attempting to construct narrative significance. The title of the "story" consists of three nouns: "a day," "the life," and "Nancy"; individually or combined, they are supposed to act as subjects of all or a majority of predicates in the text, like "United States" in *A History of the United States*. In this case, though, the presented "day" does nothing but elapse, it offers a narrative vector that remains void of particularity. Since it is indeterminate, "the life" is presumably made up of a multitude of such days, all identical to each other and identical to many "other" days in many "other" lives. Banality is formal otherness negated by actual similarity (nothing is more banal than fashionable clothes). "The life" is reduced to a synchronic signified by the representative character of "a day" in it.

We have here what Danièle Chatelain, after Genette, calls "an iterative narrative in its primary, 'not concretized' state composed of . . . 'invariant features' ". Indeed, this kind of text, it is acknowledged, is not really a narrative; it produces an effect of "nonnarrative dryness."[27] Finally, Nancy is equated with her (non)life, since her consciousness is reduced to the bare minimum: just enough to identify herself with what she does or rather repeats "mechanically." The lack of "deep" or remote causality, the lack of "distance" and alternatives in the text, is figured and produced by the iconic value of a mechanically repetitive syntax in surface structure: "She does this, then she does that, then she does something else . . . " This repetition restates in sequential form the multiple embedding of temporal and other quantitatively definable frames in the presented world: thirty days in twelve months of so many years, in so many lives in so many provincial towns of so many countries, like a cross section of a set of Russian nesting dolls.

Repetition, we have said, is as necessary to the rise of narrative meaning as is variation, but repetition is the zero degree of structure; the very accumulation of micronarratemes can defeat the purpose of narrative significance, if it is, as Barthes once said, to "overcome [*triompher de*] repetition and found the model of a becoming."[28] Something similar happens even with the dispersion and multiplication of incidents that we find in Joyce's *Ulysses* and in *The Recognitions* as well as in Sartre's *Age of Reason*. Curiously and interestingly, the linguist Carl Bache associates this quasi-aspectual feature of (certain) quantitatively narrative texts with what he terms "the fictional mode of description":

> there is no concrete distance between the situation expressed and the reader. The semiperformative nature of the verb forms in this mode makes the reader witness the situation from beginning to end and hence experience all the phases with equal or almost equal weight: the beginning, the process/activity, and the terminal point.[29]

Quantitative "pseudonarrative," though never actualized in a pure form, is not just a scholastic case made up for the sake of demonstration. It is well represented in many genres and styles of narration, "literary" or not,[30] even when it is not as obvious as with the fate of dear Nancy or the scene with Charlie Chaplin turning bolts on the assembly line. Iterative and frequentative repetitions of micronarratemes play a decisive role in adventure stories, westerns, and travelogues, as well as in the traditional epic, where the hero is a character who can "do it," not just once but three times and many more and once again. The picaresque, the fairy tale, the romance, the dreamwork, the Fantastic, the parable, the legend, as well as the journalistic *fait divers* and the realist novel all partake of pseudonarrative and repetitive more than rhythmic structures, each for its own purpose and with its own generic variations. Quantitative narrative, whatever its thematic input, is a means of generalizing a nonnarrative significance. It can be that "strange things do happen quite often" (but "if strange things happen so often, nothing *is* strange anymore"), so that defamiliarization is turned into its opposite, or a meek assent to the given. "The more things seem to happen, the less things actually change" (in France we know only too well that successive educational reforms are the only way to maintain the status quo).

Quantitative narrative can be served by and generally goes with one of two opposite configurations of characters. We can have a vast display of "people" who are, in the end, "all the same," samples of a type, although they seem to be superficially different, like women for a misogynist (this is the "ship of fools" type, often encountered in comedy and satire). Or it can be a single radiating character whose dealings with the presented world are repetitive, so that the a priori unity assigned to the subject is eventually matched by the unity of the world that mirrors it, or vice versa, through a process of efficient ambiguity and indeterminacy. Autobiography and neorealist narrative offer frequent illustrations of this phenomenon, with repetitive events, structures, and relations echoing world closure at the same time as they generate narrative closure by exhaustion. Certain historiographic styles could also be analyzed in this light.

Thus, in "slice of life" neorealist narratives like *Saturday Night and Sunday Morning*, by Alan Sillitoe, *Storia d'amore*, by Giorgio Bassani, or works by López Salinas, Vaillant, and others, the subplots are only embryonic, if they exist at all. At each point of narrative "development," the plot can be represented by a simple series of "and" hyphens radiating from the protagonist. In Sillitoe's novel: Arthur and Brenda, Arthur and work, Arthur and money, Arthur and Fred, and so on. Complicating relations between the peripheral items are weak and few in number, there are hardly any significant or deviant accessory narratives branching out from them. These stories do not cover an extensive historical period in their temporal core, or even the entire lives of their respective protagonists; they are not centered on one particular dramatic event affecting these lives or the corresponding period, like a detective story or a conversion story. If there is such an event, it has to be reabsorbed in the texture of repetition. But these narratives are also, to a certain extent, biographical fictions, in the sense that the prenarrative period is covered by flashbacks, and the postnarrative period by a final prolepsis into an implied or sometimes explicit future of the narrative past: it is made clear to us that the world and the feast continue along the lines reached in conclusion, in a profoundly eventless, daily eventful, unchanging way. At the end of both *Storia d'amore* and *Saturday Night*, although the framed periods of fictional story time are only about fifteen years and one year, respectively, we need not worry about the protagonists' lives any longer, the key "narrative" transformation has taken place, and it is the negation of the possibility of actual change. A potentially narrative kernel has been eventually transformed into a nonnarrative kernel.

Hierarchic Narrative

Childhood III
In the [wood], there is a bird; [its] song stops you and makes you
blush.
There is a clock that does not strike.
There is a gully with a nest of white beasts.

There is a cathedral that goes down and a lake that rises.
There is a little carriage abandoned in the thicket, or which, adorned with ribbons,
goes racing down the path.
There is a company of little [comedians] in costumes, glimpsed on the road across the
edge of the wood.
There is finally, when [one] is hungry and thirsty, someone who chases you away.[31]

This text seems to take virtually all possible steps to dispel any impression of narrativity. The title, without shifter, epithet, or complement, remains sufficiently indeterminate to avoid suggesting a relevant temporal frame or a particular human subject who would indirectly provide it, like "a day" and "Nancy" could do in the earlier text. All the surface segments of the text are uniformly introduced by "In the wood, there is" (= the wood contains). Depending on the more or less permanent nature of the content and its relationship to the container, but regardless of lexical filling out, we should only have a choice between an occurrential and a definitional interpretation of each assertion, hence of the whole text.

The deictic effect of the definite article "the" ("In the wood") and the relation of the indefinite article "a" ("a bird") to it make us rapidly opt for a series of descriptemes: a creature belonging to the class of birds is in a particular forest, the forest in question, specified by its forthcoming content and its relation to one or more subjects. All the other predicates are grammatically subordinate to and semantically framed by "In the wood, there is . . . " For example, in the first verse, the wood contains a bird that sings (a song) that stops you. Most of these subordinate predicates, moreover, are not transactive. And, even when they are actually or virtually actional, this semantic value is partly defeated by modality, connotation, and the retroaction of dubious reference on signification:

- a clock does not strike = negated action
- white animals are in a nest in a gully = not actional
- a cathedral goes down
⎫
⎬ = topsy-turvy world → metaphor
- a lake goes up
⎭
- a little carriage [was] ⎧ abandoned
⎨   ⎫ = transactive, but subject absent
⎩   ⎬ and action in indeterminate past
                    decorated ⎭
- or which goes racing = possible alternative between narrative of the
                                              past and of the present.

Only six predicates have human subjects, and two of these ("you stop" and "you leave") result from logical entailments. One of the subjects is omitted ("seen on the road": by whom?); the five other subjects are pronominal: "you" (three times), "one" (once), and "someone" (once). These pronouns are not directly referentiated to the semantic content of a noun in the text. Actually, the only such possible referentiation is an anaphora of "child" from the general title of the group of poems, "Childhood," to the three "yous" in the text. The lack of determination, as Nathaniel Wing noted,[32] makes the subject dependent on the semantic content of the predicates in each occurrence, so that a coherent narrative—a narrative of the self—becomes all but impossible.

Nevertheless, I shall argue that this text is hierarchically narrative in that both the surface and the deep predicates that afford its unity are narrative; the quest for narrative significance is the first satisfied and the most rewarding. In fact, paradigmatic coupling opposes and joins the first and the last actional (transactive) predicates, which are semantically symmetrical, into a proper narrative sequence that reads as follows:

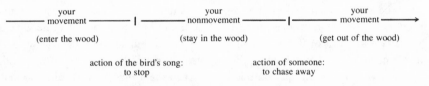

We should also be alert to the parallel transformation of the NP "you." In the first two narratemes in which it was involved ("a song stops you," "a song makes you blush"), the pronoun, as I have said, has no clear antecedent; it can designate anyone, but the communication situation will make it point particularly at the receiver of the text, the other of the poetic "I" or "voice of the text." In the last narrateme, "you" does have an immediate logical and grammatical antecedent: "one (who is hungry and thirsty)." If "one" and "you" represent the same agent in the first and the last sentence, we can say that this agent was not hungry or thirsty at the beginning of the text, but has *become* so by the end of the text, presumably as a participant in the presented world, during his or her stay in the wood: this would amount to introducing a third narrateme between A_1 and A_2. However, even if the reader in the beginning has accepted wholeheartedly projecting "himself" onto the (child?)-subject who entered the wood, stopped, and blushed, nothing forces him in the end to feel hungry and thirsty, either physically or spiritually, so that it is no longer a narrative but an ergative transformation that has taken place. Instead of becoming hungry, "you" has become another: the narrator or just any child, any human being. We now discover that the poem is a metaphorical cuckoo's nest: the only bird whose song is likely to make one blush.

Regarding the relations between inscribed speaker and inscribed reader/hearer, there are really three possible scenarios: (1) the receiver has become identical with the sender; (2) the receiver is replaced by the sender as subject and object of the actions—so that, in an apparent paradox, the former is excluded from the "subject matter" of the text, just like the latter is driven away from the wood that contains all the presented world; (3) the receiver and the sender have always been identical, or they have at least shared the same attributes and circumstances—the first "you" represented already an indefinite "one," an undifferentiated subject serving as an example to test a fictional hypothesis —but then the text provokes, reveals, and confirms the very process of identification that is reputed, at the same time, to be superfluous. The embedding of narrative transformation within the descriptive frame of "the wood" therefore does not subordinate narrative to description. Even though it is contradictory, ambiguous, tense, and full of incompatible elements, description offers here the conditions of possibility of a narrative whose incompatibilities are the real problem.

Even stripped of almost all its attributes—abandoned, orphaned—the subject remains the empty center of a textual space figured as described space, because it is necessarily generated by the autonomous dynamics of narrative, appointed to be its bearer. (Laurent Jenny had the same kind of intuition when he gave a "narrative" analysis of Baudelaire's second "Spleen," but he was unable to support his claim by other than vaguely philosophical considerations.)[33] In "Childhood, II," family relations already outlined that semivacant place: the young mother, the cousin, the young brother, the old people (grandparents) forming a circle around the "little dead girl" (or boy—gender definition is not important; ambiguity, indeterminacy, or rather neutrality is the point: to be neither male nor female, neither dead nor alive). The "cousin's carriage" of "Childhood, II" becomes the "abandoned little carriage (a "miscarried" baby's pram?) of "Childhood, III"; "abandoned" characterizes the child that "Je" would rather like to be in "Childhood, IV." Cradle and tomb are confused, presence is the rest of absence, as in the successful elegy. But Rimbaud seizes everywhere the narrative moment par excellence, reduced, condensed into the point when "I" is both A and B, neither A nor B.

Not all hierarchical narratives follow the pattern of "Childhood, III." A much less complex invitation to construct narrative is extended by texts that "juxtapose" descriptive sequences (tableaux, idylls) incompatible in the same point in time, but which can be reconciled by succession on the narrated time vector. On the scale of a long poem or even a novel, the process is still grossly the same as the reconciliation by narrative synthesis of antithetical descriptive utterances:

A, "Marcel is not a writer," versus B, "Marcel is a writer," → "Marcel has become a writer" (without ceasing to be [called] Marcel) between time T_1 when A was true and time T_2 when B is true.

The totalizing overarching macronarrateme is fully provided by the work of the reader, micronarratemes tend to be scarce at sentence level, and individual sequences will lack express overarching narratemes. I have indeed analyzed an autobiographical construct of this type, whose author is close to the *nouveau roman* school,[34] and similar trends can sometimes be observed in the self-portrait (e.g., *Roland Barthes* by Roland Barthes; see also *Miroirs d'encre* by Michel Beaujour); but this is actually an extreme pole of the narrative construction of meaning, which is hardly ever found in its pure form.

Most narratives combine the quantitative and hierarchical modes of dominance of narrative discourse, complement the one with the other, make the one pass for the other, and so on, instead of dissociating them. This is probably why the not so obvious communion of the two modes was taken for granted until recently. In fact, novelists and other tellers were much less naive about it than the critics themselves; the example of Henry James will undoubtedly show how, for the classical novelist, such deliberate confusion could be a way of mastering a kind of significance that was not entirely narrative because it was not ultimately so.

Combined Dominance: **In the Cage**

Once upon a time there was a girl who slaved in a post-office "cage" in the corner of Cocker's grocery shop in Mayfair, a district of London. The impoverished, almost Dickensian, girl, who works to support herself and her old mother and is engaged to a dignified shop assistant, Mr. Mudge (a cross, you will observe, between mug and fudge), sees many elegant customers who spend fortunes on telegrams, many of them coded, to their friends, mistresses, and lovers. Captain Philip Everard and Cissy (Lady Bradeen) are one of these extramarital, semi-secret couples. The girl (I use Daphne Du Maurier's terminology) takes a particular interest in them, especially the Captain, whose house she passes on purpose every night after work, on her way home. Mrs. Jordan, a parson's widow who does floral arrangements for the aristocracy, suggests to the girl that she leave the post office to share the profits of her flourishing business, and Mr. Mudge, in preparation for their marriage, is waiting for her to move to the district where he works. But the girl indulges with such a thrill, with such intimate pleasure in her brushes with the gentry that she cannot make up her mind to leave Cocker's for the time being. One day she meets Everard on his doorstep, and they have a long conversation seated on a bench in the park. In September, she goes on a short holiday to Bournemouth with her mother and Mr. Mudge, who has just arranged to rent a little house so that the mother can live with them after they are married. The girl wants some more time. The Captain is in great trouble. She helps him check that a telegram to Cissy, which had been intercepted, did not contain compromising evidence. Sometime later, Mrs. Jordan invites her to her shabby place: the widow is going to marry not Lord Rye but his butler, Mr.

Drake, who will now work in Everard's and Cissy's house (the latter's husband has died). The girl will soon settle down with Mr. Mudge.

This summary could easily give the impression that we are dealing with a conventional comedy of manners. Actually there is a small number of characters, a smaller number "on stage" (directly presented by the general narratorial voice in the presented setting) at any one time, and still fewer foregrounded. Only four locations are used: Cocker's grocery and post office, passim; Captain Everard's street and the park nearby, once; Mrs. Jordan's lodgings "in the region of Maida Vale," once; and Bournemouth, once. It could come as a surprise, were it not for the name of the author, that this simple story takes some 140 pages to tell.[35] But maybe it is not a "story" (= a narrative) after all? Could we not say that James gave us a descriptive figuration of the lowest petit-bourgeois class and its vision of the elegant, futile, and somewhat corrupt London gentry, together with a thorough psychological account of the heroine's mental contents? The occurrential and definitional discourses would then be dominant, both quantitatively and hierarchically. But it is not so, although tabular discourses compete mildly with narrative on the hierarchic scale of dominance: we have here a regular, undoubtedly well-formed narrative.

The technique of "psychonarration" is virtually the only manner of presenting consciousness in the novella. Its overbearing attitude obfuscates the few bouts of quoted monologue to the point of subordinating them completely and securing exclusive legitimacy. Dorrit Cohn remarks that "psycho-narration has almost unlimited temporal flexibility. It can as readily summarize an inner development over a long period of time as it can render the flow of successive thoughts and feelings, or expand and elaborate a mental instant."[36] And, "Psycho-narration often renders, in a narrator's knowing words, what a character 'knows' without knowing how to put it into words" (p. 46). In other words and with a less directly representational interest in mind, I would say that psychonarration, in conformity with Jamesian techniques of mastery, is a "diegetic" technique (in Genette's sense) that is exactly meant to give narrative discourse hegemony over the text, with as few threats of disruption as possible. It reduces the volume of other discourses and, at the same time, transforms into collaboration their potentially competitive role. Psychonarration, by the same token, makes for the quantitative expansion of narrative discourse at the expense of the "unsaid." This is evident from beginning to end in *The Cage*:

> It had occurred to her early that in her position — that of a young person spending, in framed and wired confinement, the life of a guinea-pig or a magpie — she should know a great many persons without their recognizing the acquaintance.[37]

Lasting belief and conjecture, caught at the retrospected moment of their initial formation, are thus shifted from the realm of states, properties of being, to that of events (coming into and out of being): states seem to be always on reprieve between event and event. In the passage quoted, the social position, condition, or state of the character is accordingly bracketed between dashes; this device provides an iconic bonus by figuring materially the "framed and wired confinement" of the cage, while reversing at the same time its discursive location, if action can only be exceptional and sterile for a character in this position. Event-making retrospection apparently respects, in phrastic syntax, the "order of events': first, she thinks, then she knows people, then they do not recognize; but homologous linearity is a trap, both for the character (it bears the mark of excessive, uncritical rationalization) and for the naive reader who has already lost his or her bearings without knowing it. What is the point of reference of "early," a "subjective" temporal adverb? When is the "now" of the character, and when the "now" of the narrator?

Multiple temporal anchoring facilitates a certain eventfulness of the text where there should be only boring uniformity, but it will turn out to appear as a seductive device of time itself. On the scale of the novella as a whole, on the other hand, alternate embedding of the "cage" in the ever wider worlds of Cocker's, Mayfair, and London, and of these wider worlds within "the cage," is the adequate means for generating narrative suspense; both spaces are structured with their respective narrative programs in view: "inner" events or consciousness events for the cage, outer or social events for the wider worlds, but this structural mirroring will also turn out to be a false symmetry:

A policeman, while she remained, strolled past her; then, going his way a little further and half lost in the atmosphere, paused and watched her. But she was quite unaware—she was full of her thoughts. They were too numerous to find a place just here, but two of the number may at least be mentioned. One of these was that, decidedly, her little home must be not for the next month, but for next week; the other, which came indeed as she resumed her walk and went her way, was that it was strange such a matter should be at last settled for her by Mr Drake. (p. 507)

The ironic reversal of positions of observation, from believing herself to be the watchful spider at the center of high society amorous intrigues, to be watched unaware by that derisory figure of authority, an ordinary bobby in the fog (with the metaphorically dimmed vision entailed on both sides by the weather conditions), could be a perfect ending if only the character's defeat with regard to her social and emotional-sexual ambitions doubled as a defeat of narrative discourse. But it does not: the last two "thoughts" in the text are events like the very first one. They do not even recur, they occur; one is a forceful conclusion resulting ("decidedly") from a long deliberation—time is ripe for it; the other, associated with resumed physical movement, is a new reflection on the strangeness of things that irons out, in the guise of the "ways of Providence," the humiliation of error, illusion, and false expectations, and takes over as mild humor the irony of which "she," the character, is the victim. Narrative closure, here, does not stop narrative, it takes place within it, thus confirming once more the lack of "autonomy" of the protagonist with regard to the narrator, the world narrated, and the other characters. Her persistent lack of name had obviously served this eventual purpose throughout the novella: what else could "our young friend" do but what the narrator and his accomplices held in store for her? "She" could only *be* what was happening to her; "the betrothed of Mr. Mudge" would not, in the end, marry Captain Everard. "What's in a name?" it is usual to ask, but that which is in not naming may well be in particular the increased supremacy of verb grammar in the construction of meaning and, therefore, an additional incentive to narrative imperialism.

Solutions of compromise between the two modes of dominance of narrative discourse—also most common in historiography—turn out to work as their combination and reinforcement in favor of undisputed narrative significance. Symmetrically, in other texts and genres, the suppression of narrative dominance, when nonnarrative discourses and Discourses struggle for supremacy over a text, tends to attack narrative discourse both quantitatively and qualitatively, in its organizing and explanatory force with regard to the text as a whole. But narrative significance, even in this novella, is never alone or absolutely final: the superimposition of a macronarrateme over accumulated events also erases their diversity; they will have been "much ado about nothing," in James's pessimistic vision, or so many minor signifiers of a grand historical design, in a Christian or a Marxist vision. It is in this sense that Barthes once said that "narrative is, in the end, nothing but the language of Destiny." Unfortunately, Destiny can only say one thing, which is a nonnarrative tautology: "I am myself," ever present when something happens.

We may wonder whether the aestheticization of narrative is a combat against this nonnarrativeness of narrative itself, or whether it contributes to it by siding with the lyrical or manifesting the return of repressed myth.

Chapter 3
Narrative and Verbal Art:
Literariness in Communication

So-called literary narrative is, at least in modern times and in urban, industrial societies, one of the grand categories of narrative communication, so central indeed, as we have already noted, that it has come to obfuscate the study and relevance of narrativeness in other semiotic systems, for example, film, television, advertising, photography, and drama, and appears as a model or a key antagonist for historiography, philosophy, and scientific Discourses. We must therefore try to determine the specific weight and implication of the concept "literary" in phrases like "literary narrative" and "literary work of art"; in other words, we have to come to grips with the "literariness" of literary communication. We shall proceed in three partly successive, partly overlapping phases that correspond to so many questions: Are there, in our contemporary cognate cultures, and perhaps in others too, standard practices that could characterize literary communication in general? How do such practices affect, distort, encroach on, react against, or contribute to implement the separate dynamics of narrative communication (see also chapter 8)? And finally, does a particular type of significance arise at the intersection of narrative and literariness? Chapter 4 will be dedicated to this last question; we shall deal with the other two here.

Formalist views still prevail, consciously or not, in many literary groups and critical schools. The protracted "crisis of art," the hasty succession and rapid demise of isms and avant garde movements, the new role of academia as a refuge for literati and writers, all contribute to the relative stability of these ideas in a rather wide sector of the "liberal arts." Since the word "literariness" is mentally associated with its Russian origin, *literaturnost*, it will be useful to begin with a discussion of formalist, neoformalist, and similar aesthetic options, as exemplified by Jan Mukarovsky's *Aesthetic Function, Norm and Value as Social Facts* (1936)[1] and Roman Jakobson's famous paper: "Linguistics and Poetics" (1960).[2] The steps will be as follows: (1) the explication of a new diagram of the literary sphere of exchange as deferred, mediated, and phantasmatic communication, stressing that the elusiveness of the message is above all a factor of proliferation of meanings and the institutional network needed to disseminate them and control their dissemination; (2) the development of a working definition of literariness, with a cluster of rules of "reception"—more or less programmed by "the text"— designed to make certain elaborate communicative acts possible, rewarding, in the context of our modern cultures; and (3) a concise description of some operations commonly involved in the literary construction of meaning and value, with an evocation of the possible consequences of their combination with the narrative construction of meaning and value.

A Critique of Noncommunicative and Self-Oriented Notions of Literature

Mukarovsky's book is rich, complex, full of perceptive detours, and therefore difficult to summarize, if one wants to do it justice. However, taking into account the "noetic" approach chosen by Mukarovsky, it does not seem unfair to round up some key words and try to determine their fate in the work considered. Let us start with the lexical material of the title.

Not quite unexpectedly, but in a highly symptomatic fashion, the word "aesthetic" is and remains an adjective, an adjunct ever in need of substantive support, once the noun "beauty" has been relegated to the gallery of outmoded allegories. This is not always true of value-bearing general lexemes: "erotic" has not been left in a void by the devaluation or defunction of "love"; "Eros" and "eroticism" have on the contrary acquired new dimensions and a more positive image; in French, *le politique, le poétique,* and *la poétique* have recently joined a well-furnished store of nominalizations. Not so with "aesthetic," however; "aesthetics" remains a marginal philosophical discipline or a pretentious substitute for cosmetics; "aestheticism" is effete, definitely pejorative. As a result, the change in grammatical status of "aesthetic" from the first to the last page of Mukarovsky's book, is like the forceful product, neological in essence, of the whole enterprise:

> The *aesthetic function* occupies an important position in the life of individuals and society as a whole. . . .
> Thus the *aesthetic realm,* i.e., the realm of the aesthetic function, norm, and value, is broadly distributed over the entire area of human affairs, and it is an important and many-sided agent of life practice. . . .

All these aspects, and many others, are embraced by *the aesthetic*, particularly in its highest manifestation, art. (pp. 1, 96)

The word "aesthetic" never receives a definition for itself, it is progressively associated with various nouns (function, value, pleasure, etc.). The validity of such associations is supposedly established by an appeal to contrastive experience, so that a vast territory is cut out for "aesthetic" from other domains of action and perception; "aesthetic" comes to be both all-embracing and quite distinct, insofar as it is a modality able to affect any area of life. This universal character of "the aesthetic" thus enlarges the scope of the concept almost to the point of sacralization, but at the same time it fails to give it a content that would justify more than a fleeting substantivation. This solid role is in fact fulfilled by the concept of "art," the "highest manifestation" of the aesthetic.

The tension between territorialization and modalism, or, if you prefer, between an intrinsic and an epiphenomenal view of "aesthetic," persists throughout Mukarovsky's book, despite his reiterated denegations; for example, on page 5:

In separating the aesthetic from the extra-aesthetic . . . we must always bear in mind that we are not dealing with precisely defined and mutually exclusive areas. Both are in constant, mutual contact which can be described as a dialectical antinomy.

It is easy to observe that this spatial demarcation of the semantic field, opposing an aesthetic area to all the rest, instead of being an incentive to examine the contradistinctive output of a number of pairs of opposites, at once privileges the aesthetic area and makes it virtually impossible to circumscribe. The same is true of art within the area of the aesthetic function: the definition of art—where the aesthetic function is "felt as fundamental . . . while dominance by another function is considered as a violation of the normal condition"[3]—relies on the consensus of a particular, historically defined society or a social group within it. Mukarovsky, let us hasten to stress, does not mean that art is exempt or deprived of any other function, but these other functions, all subsumed under the term "communicative" (of which even the "symbolic," for instance, is merely a variant), are either parasitic or ancillary when we regard art *qua* art, which is the only manner of making it appear. "Emotional language," he writes, "often *supplies* poetry with formal devices" (p. 91). A note against Bally's notion of poetry warns us that poetry is a "self-referential" phenomenon, and later we are told that the portrait "oscillates between communicative and *self-centered* functions" (p. 11). Moreover, although it is a natural proclivity of human productive activities to try to save their validity thanks to the substitution of the aesthetic function for some other vanished function, there follows a diatribe against the perversion of turn-of-the-century crafts and architecture that sought to become full-fledged "decorative arts." In short, the dominance of the aesthetic function, contrary to the function itself, belongs somewhere in particular, and it should not trespass certain boundaries at the risk of becoming ridiculous. Although art is not "a closed territory," its own twisting on itself or self-orientation, its Ouroboros shape, is more fitting whenever the "communicative function" is already out of the way because no practical, utilitarian purpose, such as persuasion, truth telling, shelter, or exaltation of social institutions, is directly involved in its production.

The aesthetic function develops and relates *as a whole* to objects ("aspects of reality") placed outside its scope. The aesthetic function has the property of *isolating* objects, focusing attention on them, so that valuation and the resulting value are essential parts of the aesthetic attitude. Nevertheless, value is not taken here as something arising from exchange and/or entering into a process of exchange; it is pure use value: "We accept the teleological definition of value as the ability of something to assist in the attainment of some goal" (p. 25). Aesthetic pleasure is the only goal named. The goal is set by an *individual* whose relation to the object of evaluation is socially mediated only by the fact that he cannot ignore, even when he rejects it, the socially established aesthetic norm. For Mukarovsky, the aesthetic relation (e.g., the literary or poetic relation to a linguistic text) is the private specification of and reaction to certain sociological and anthropological determinants. Art, primarily conceived as the "reification" of the aesthetic function, as Jakobson would put it,[4] is pure spectacle, a spectacle without communication, which mirrors itself: the aesthetic attitude construes its object into a datum. The material artifact combines extra-aesthetic factors into the single unifying property of acquiring a potential aesthetic value; in this, it is strikingly similar, I would say, to male adult genital sexuality, which, according to Freudian theory, absorbs, resorbs, and transforms all partial sexual drives for the purpose of self-reproduction.

But the work of art

> . . . releases every one of the [remaining values] from direct contact with a corresponding life-value. It brings an entire assembly of values contained in the work as a dynamic whole into contact with a total system of those values which form the motive power of the life practice of the perceiving collective.[5]

This is not idealistic "disinterestedness" or "art for art's sake," but the holistic segregation of the work of art from its environment is even more imperialist here in that it erects it into a valuable and valid global alternative; it turns it into the single other of all remaining life practices in a one-to-one dialogue. What, you will ask, is a noncommunicative interlocutor? Mukarovsky does little to disentangle the paradox or make it fruitful. The few elements for an answer are contained in his approach of fictionality understood as a combination of indirection (a "figurative tie with realities which are vitally important to the perceiver"; p. 75) and abstraction or retraction. One can imagine that the focus on "form," the structure of the system of signs within the work, extends its applicability through the power of analogy.

Jakobson will include parallelisms and the rhetoric of grammar in the basic makeup of the "poetic function." The structural coherence of the work of art, its tension between fulfillment and infringement of the aesthetic norm, or between a deconstruction of norms and an offer of future norms, confer on it a significance that can be compared, equated, or contrasted with that of existential experience filtered by memory and interpretation. These factors act as a technique of distancing, with the double meaning it has for the Frankfort school thinkers: a synthetic reduction to intelligibility, on the one hand, and quasi-formalist *ostranenie* or power of estrangement of both the work of art itself and the real, on the other hand. It remains that the aesthetic attitude suggested is basically voyeuristic, not participative: its selection of the work of art, isolated by the act of evaluation, mirrors the metaphorical election of a single subject with a single point of view, however socially determined this subject may be. Aesthetic contemplation provides a solitary ecstasy before the mirror of the self.

Jakobson's "Closing Statements" were so influential in the 1960s and early 1970s, so often discussed, explained, and applied,[6] that a general critique of the paper can now be easily summarized, allowing us to concentrate on its aesthetic and literary ideology.

The first problem with Jakobson's model of verbal communication is that the point from which communication is observed remains unclear. If it is observed from inside, the addresser and the addressee cannot be embraced in the same look, we would have to choose between identification with the one or the other, and, if it is observed from outside, a third party, the OBSERVER or analyst, must be introduced to construe the MESSAGE conveyed by the act of communication. The second problem is the nature of the MESSAGE, which is never defined: if it is the result of the combination of the five other factors, the position of MESSAGE between contact and context, on the vertical axis of the diagram, can hardly be understood. The third problem, as in formalist theory generally, is the ambiguity, not to say the utter vagueness, of the notion of "orientation":[7] for example, "Orientation toward the ADDRESSEE, the CONATIVE function, finds its purest grammatical expression in the vocative and imperative."[8] If an act of communication is fundamentally the transmission of a message from A to B, only the message is "oriented" toward B, or then the whole act of communication is; any other possibility should be rejected as illogical and confusing. We can barely guess that "orientation" is actually taken by Jakobson in the sense of tendency, stress, thrust, or emphasis, rather than direction or bearings; the first statement about the POETIC function would confirm this view:

We have brought up all the six factors involved in verbal communication except the MESSAGE itself. The set [*Einstellung*] toward the MESSAGE as such, focus on the MESSAGE for its own sake is the POETIC function of language. (p. 356).

Self-orientation, whatever it means, or the orientation of x (the act of communication?) toward the message itself—in other words, a narcissistic view of a personified act or concept—is all we get in lieu of a working definition. In fact, it is significant that the dynamics of communication breaks down or is forgotten when Jakobson intends to deal with the POETIC function of language. It is also significant that (1) although the sphere of the POETIC function should not be reduced to poetry, poetry *is* its most typical example and the study of the poetic function of poetry remains the essential linguistic object of investigation, and (2) the linguistic study of poetry is the first and only one that obliges Jakobson to take the notion of text into account (even though the poetic "work" is named instead).

We remember that "Tut! Tut! said McGinty" (p. 354) suffices to exemplify the EXPRESSIVE function, but the famous axiom *"The poetic function projects the principle of equivalence from the axis of selection into the axis of combination.* Equivalence is promoted to the rank of constitutive process of the sequence" (p. 358), forces the linguist to consider the metaphrastic dimension of discourse and the notions of textual unity and congruence that had been forgotten until then. The so-called POETIC function allows Jakobson to envisage the "principle of repetition" in discourse and the "conversion of the message into something that lasts" (p. 371). Unfortunately, he does not reinvest this acknowledgment of a fundamental characteristic of texts in general into the study of other functions of language: it is up to us to carry out this task and propose a new model of communication.

It can be safely assumed that Jakobson's late article was so widely publicized because, written in English and soon translated into French, it coincided with the fast rise of structuralism and the academic institutionalization of general linguistics in the 1960s. But it did little more than crystallize old tensions and oscillations of the formalist movement by building a whole model of linguistic communication in order to enshrine in it a "noncommunicative" or minimally communicative act of linguistic production, a text-centered oasis in a message-based theory. The autotelic notion of poetry and, by extension, literature, was nothing new; in a 1921 article, Jakobson himself already gave this answer to the question "What is poetry?": "an utterance oriented toward the mode of expression [and] governed by immanent laws,"[9] while, in his *Literary Theory: A Poetics* of 1925, Tomashevsky also insisted on the "orientation toward expression" of artistic language and its relegation of the communicative function to the background.

The foregrounding and opacification of "expression" for its own sake were not undisputed, however, among the formalists, despite Jakobson's efforts to dismiss the divergence from Sklovsky as a mere misunderstanding of the latter's position by his readers (see the 1965 preface to *Théorie de la littérature*).[10] The doctrine of "making *things* strange" as the principal function of literary or artistic *devices* was not limited by Sklovsky to a renovation and a renewed prominence or an increased visibility of *signs*, or a displacement of interest toward the texture of the work. As Victor Erlich accurately noted, the idea of the struggle of art against the automatization of perception *in life* was one widely shared with the surrealists, Cocteau, and T. S. Eliot, without proven contact between these poets and the Russian formalists. The aspiration to restore a fresh, sometimes childlike vision of things blurred by routine, was also a legacy of early romanticism: "And he beholds the moon, and hush'd at once / Suspends his sobs, and laughs most silently";[11] it belonged to a quest of origin and originality just as much as it affirmed the primacy of the means of expression over intelligibility. For the formalists, the repeatability of the work of art actually meant its fixedness, the possibility of identical reproduction of its reception, its monumentality, the noncontingency of its effects and, correlatively, the impossibility of imitating it: the work of art is created once and for all, its singularity is its independence from the circumstances of reception, or rather the authority with which it is endowed to dictate a situation of (non)communication that will be ever the same.

The constant affirmation of the autonomy of the work of art is the main point. Whether its aloofness and inimitableness are linked with self-closure of the object on itself, or with its prismatic radiation over the world vision of its receivers, is only a secondary option. It is not surprising that formalism was born in Russia in a period of intense, if superficial, modernization to which it presented a dual, rather astute response: on the one hand, it tried to build a dike around art in order to resist the onslaught of the age of mechanical reproduction, like the Parnassians and symbolists had already done in the past; on the other hand, formalism justified the territorialization of this protected reserve by making it the object of modern scientific examination: a theory of language and, to a much lesser extent, the sociology of the conditions of production (to the exclusion of psychology, a dangerously subjective exercise whose scientific status was still in doubt). It is hardly surprising, too, that formalism was taken up in the Western world from the 1950s to the 1970s, thanks to the dissemination of its tenets by many exiled scholars from Eastern Europe, although the motor of its expansion was perhaps somewhat different, more narrowly academic (the fast development of tertiary education combined with a need to counteract the pressures of the hard sciences, which wanted to increase their share of resources and power at the expense of the humanities). A similar phenomenon can be observed now with the rather artificial interest of a fair number of theorists in artificial intelligence. I do not ask that the literary and aesthetic profession commit suicide, but it would certainly do them no harm to become aware of the historical determinants and the possible side effects of their survival strategies. Is it so difficult to get rid of rampant, defensive theories of incommunication without rejecting the rich heritage of structural linguistics and poetics?

Instead of pining for the "lofty" character of verbal art, our aim should be to investigate its constant participation in other registers of communication and the participation of these other modes in it, not only as a dialectical struggle, but as competition, collaboration, and complicity. Narrative is a privileged field to observe these multiple relations of exchange, substitution, impersonation, critique, contamination, and solidarity. If the object of literary science is literariness, as the object of narratology is narrativity, literariness, however, is nothing else than a *modality* of communication, with the same basic properties as any other act of communication: all communication fosters individualization and foments particularism and limited dissent at the same time as it promotes socialization, limited assent, and conformism. Literary communication is contingent, transitive, transactive, and unfixed. Contrary to Tomashevsky's opinion, literature is not an autonomous, fixed language.[12] The literary message is probably quite the opposite, especially in modern times: more open, fluctuating, undecidable, and outward-turned than many others; this could well be one reason for the endearing, enduring, "transhistoric" character of many literary and artistic texts.

For the purpose of keeping literariness open, that is, alive, we should pinpoint a number of operations facilitated or encouraged by certain texts in certain situations, which enable the participants in the communicative acts mediated by these texts to produce complex meanings and values exchangeable in a distinct fashion. I hope the following model of communication will help us to achieve this goal.

A Model for (artistic) Communication

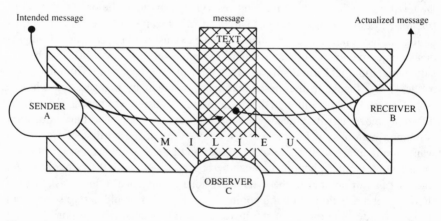

Three-role General Model.

Explications and Remarks

1. The model describes situations of monologic enunciation only; dialogic enunciation as inscribed in TEXTs will be studied in Chapter 6.

2. The only thing that can be literally and physically transmitted from a SENDER to a RECEIVER is a TEXT, in the restricted sense of a recordable set of (meaningful) signals (phonemes, graphemes, pictures, etc., arranged in a certain order). This TEXT may be the main or sometimes the only trace of an act of communication between A and B. When recorded (printed, on tape, or simply memorized), it is the most easily observable part of the act of communication for a third party. It is indeed what makes the existence of a third party possible, or, in other words, the third party (not the SENDER or the RECEIVER) is a function of the TEXT; if telepathy, a MESSAGE communication, or TEXTless communication existed, it would be unknowable, indescribable.

3. The TEXT can also be seen as the plane of intersection of *langue* and *parole* or, better, the weaving together of *milieu* and *expression* (symbolized in the diagram by crosshatching).

4. The factor CONTACT, according to Jakobson, could be split up into two elements: physical channel and psychological connection. The introduction of TEXT in our diagram shows that these two elements have in fact nothing in common. The first (sound vibrations carried by the air, light waves reflected on a surface, etc.) is the *material* substance of the TEXT itself, which makes it reproducible or not and observable to a variable number of third parties. The second element is not different from the mental structures shared by the SENDER and the RECEIVER, hence it is part of the MILIEU at large.

5. SENDER, RECEIVER and OBSERVER are taken here not as physical beings or complex fictional characters but as actantial roles required by the statement "An object is transmitted." He who utters this statement is the OBSERVER. It does not matter whether the same "actor," say, Jeff Smith, also sent the TEXT a moment before or has also received it—which he has necessarily done to some extent, if he is able to say, "An object is transmitted."

6. The production of a TEXT and its transmission require a material support, which may or may not coincide with the vehicle and the physical channel, and *space*, that is, a distance across which transport can take place, with its corollary: temporal delay. But they also require the intervention of "immaterial" factors that come to be partly actualized materially in the TEXT and mentally in the MESSAGE, on the occasion of each particular act of communication. These factors are rules combined into CODES, structures combined into SYSTEMS, needs or desires combined into dynamic MOTIVATIONS, and past acts of communication whose traces are combined into a CONTEXT. All four sets of factors combine to form the MILIEU.

We shall credit the MILIEU with some degree of permanence or stability, while its specification by a very precise, temporally determined configuration of circumstances is the COMMUNICATION SITUATION (*stricto sensu*) of the act considered. The MILIEU is the locus of the conditions of possibility of TEXT and MESSAGE, and the interpretant of the TEXT as a complex sign, carrier of a possible MESSAGE; but the production of the TEXT manifests a particular communication situation that, by definition, can never be repeated. Insofar as it is recordable and intelligible for human communities, the TEXT will then, on each new transmission (e.g., readings), be engaged into new situations of communication that will modify its MESSAGE. The very presence of the TEXT as a valuable object in the MILIEU will contribute to generate new situations and even new acts of communication. Art, literature, proverbs, popular tales, and other "cultural goods" are typical instances of such patrimonial TEXTS, whose "life" or rules and opportunities for further transmission and transaction are largely regulated by social institutions and codes of behavior. They are also the most usual objects of "transversal communication" (discussed later).

7. A is part and parcel of the MILIEU, to the extent of his (its) being determined by it, but he is also distinct from it (from its previous state) to the extent that the circumstances that make him A, rather than C or X, at time T, are an always unique life experience, a uniquely condensed life history orienting his energies toward a certain modification of his environment (or a contribution to its perpetuation, which amounts to the same thing from our present perspective). Exactly the same statement can be made about B or C; when A feels the need to act on his MILIEU, one of the means is to manifest it to B, trying to modify B, deterring him from showing hostility or enlisting him (it) on A's side, and so forth, by an act of communication directed to him: we say that a MESSAGE is *intended* by A. To convey this message, A encodes it into a TEXT: a linguistic utterance, a photograph, a gesture, a musical tune, or a sequence of torch flashes. Whoever comes into contact with this TEXT, undertakes to decode it and considers himself to be addressed by A in one way or another, plays the role of a RECEIVER, and *actualizes* the intended MESSAGE.

Whoever undertakes to decode the TEXT, that is, actualize a MESSAGE from it, although he considers or pretends he is not the intended RECEIVER B — not addressed to by A — is an OBSERVER C of the act of communication. C combines the intended MESSAGE and the actualized MESSAGE into the hypostatized "MESSAGE of the communicative act," here represented by "[MESSAGE]," which is a derived potential TEXT (e.g., the exegesis, the paraphrase, the summary, the translation, or hermeneutic commentary of a poem). In the second case — the "as-if-it-were-not-meant-for-me," distancing attitude of a RECEIVER — the same *actor* may and usually will reincorporate the [MESSAGE] or part of it into the actualized MESSAGE.

Such return trips between actantial roles B and C are characteristic of the behavior of the literary critic vis-à-vis a published TEXT, since critics are readers too. When the critic communicates his interpretations, conclusions, and value judgments to others, he becomes another A (let us call him or her A_2) producer of a new TEXT T_2 and sender of [MESSAGE]$_1$ as intended MESSAGE of his TEXT T_2. In relation to TEXT T_1 and the "initial" communicative act (between A_1 and B_1), this new act of communication can be called "transversal," which leads us to the next diagram.

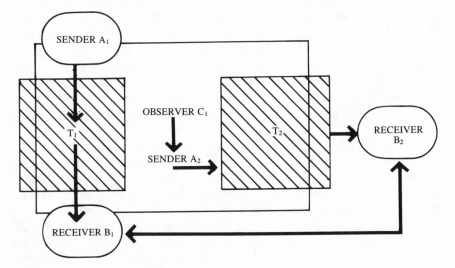

A Model for Critical or "Secondary" Discourse.

8. Adopting the role of OBSERVER is an obligatory precondition for the production of new TEXTS on the transversal axis. This remark is conducive to a complicating insight about the production of *all* texts, insofar as they all occur after an apprenticeship of language and Discourses (dialects and registers) contained in the MILIEU from which their signifying elements and rules of organization have been selected: SENDER A_1 produced T_1 only after such an apprenticeship, that is, after fulfilling the actantial role of OBSERVER in relation to $T-$ ($T-1$, $T-2$, $T-n$) bound acts of communication in a regressive series, so that, in relation to these texts, the supposedly "initial" act of communication, centered on T_1, may also be considered to be transversal.

9. The acting slot of the RECEIVER B_2 in transversal communication can be filled by any actor who has at one time actually filled the receiving position B_1 regarding T_1 or who can construe his being in this position. Thus the audience of the critic, commentator, or teacher of literature typically includes himself as reader or spectator of T_1, other early readers, future readers, the author of T_1 as reader of his own TEXT, and so on. (But the author *qua* author cannot be effectively addressed by the critic.)

10. For any OBSERVER C_2 of the twofold system of the preceding diagram, the act of communication that relates A_1 to B_1 through T_1 will be called "vertical" because it implies the authority of A_1 over T_1 and, through it, over B_1, a hierarchical superiority conferred by the precedence of initiative: any B_1 finds T_1 already there and ascribes it to a prior A_1. On the contrary, A_2, as an ex-C_1 and B_1, must at least *pretend* to embody a position of equality vis-à-vis his RECEIVER B_2. A_2 thus contests the hierarchy of vertical communication at the same time as he in fact founds a new substitutive or alternative hierarchy and assumes some or all of the authority of A_1 over T_1. Nevertheless, a distinction should be drawn between genres of transversal communication in which the assumption of authority is the dominant gesture (like paraphrases, summaries, interpretive, and evaluative commentaries, as well as some forms of translation), and quotation, allusion, and parody, on the other hand, in which the power strategy of A_2 is more likely to remain ambivalent: at once an assumption and a subordinate acknowledgment of authority. [13]

11. The alleged relative fixity of "artistic texts," particularly in cultures of the written and printed word, tape recordings, and printed films (something that may change with the high erasability and correctability of computer data bases), should be understood not as a factor of reproducibility of some initial act of communication through T_1, but rather as a factor of multiplication of similar acts, each of them being equally initial or noninitial in relation to the state of the MILIEU in which it occurs, unique in terms of its particular communicative situation, and, still more decisively, as the precondition of the indeterminate proliferation of transversal communication through T_2-type TEXTS.

These TEXTS tend to encircle completely the "famous" TEXT, the "masterwork," create a special new MILIEU for it, and even generate a sufficient image of it when it is lost or never "existed." Nathalie Sarraute's novel *Les Fruits d'or* is an excellent illustration of this phenomenon. Anyone who has tried to take a fresh look at *Hamlet, Don Quixote, Remembrance of Things Past, The Waste Land*, or *Citizen Kane* will know what I mean: it is sometimes virtually impossible to *see* a text through the veiling maze of the transversal apparatus. I would even risk suggesting that the so-called autonomy of the work of art is an uncontrolled illusion generated by the socially dictated "choice" of a corpus of preselected, preinterpreted, hyperabundantly commented "masterworks," artificially isolated from other manifestations of social Discourses by their private apparatuses acting as bodyguards. In the framework of the conventional elitist view of the "literary work of art," for example, any commentary, any writing-about thus contributes to perform the isolating task that is supposed to characterize the aesthetic attitude, although it is also and perhaps mainly a projection of the institutional exegetic and evaluative functions of the scholar onto the role of the reader and the TEXT itself that has been elected object of the "critical" transaction.

Unfortunately, the only way to denounce the illusion that consolidates the power of scholars and agents of transmission (often under the pretext of defending the oppositional institution of literature) is to practice metacriticism and metatheory as I am doing at present: one thus seems to try to assume and subsume the whole jackpot of power involved in vertical and transversal communication alike by inaugurating a new axis, transversal to the transversal axis.

12. As we shall see later, particularly in chapter 8, the deferred, delayed, distant character of vertical literary communication, reinforced by the development of the transversal network, contributes to the idealization, abstraction, and generalization of aesthetic values in two different ways. In view of the relative indeterminacy of the identity of the intended RECEIVER, delimited only by the inscription in the TEXT of his virtual competence under varying reception circumstances, the empirical reader can never coincide with the ideal reader.[14] At the time of TEXT production, this coincidence tends to be postponed, projected into a future in which textual predictions will have been fulfilled and people changed and formed or informed by the TEXT; the awareness of writing for posterity is the shape this phenomenon takes in the writer's mind and normative theories of literary production. When years have elapsed, in counterpart, new generations of readers and critics tend to feel that they have lost the adequate conditions of reception and that the reader contemporary of TEXT production has taken away the secret of competent appreciation with himself into the grave.[15] Truly corrrect reception is hanging in a void and will be eventually returned to the TEXT that "points at itself": we are back to the "self-oriented" MESSAGE that justifies our fictitiously humble readings.

Toward an Operational Definition of Literariness

Let me insist one last time that the use of the notion of "literariness" does not amount on my part to a quest for the "*differentia specifica* of verbal art in relation to other kinds of discourse"[16] or of the "*intrinsic linguistic properties* of a text which make it a poem."[17] On the contrary, and even though there are undeniably texts composed to provoke the exercise of literariness, I see literariness as an interactive and intersubjective, transportable process that can remotivate itself through ever new texts and across the varied, changing landscape offered by a never completely fixed, forever inexhaustible milieu. If the notion of literariness aimed at replacing that of literature, it would soon become no less misleading. Literariness will simply be dissociated from literature inasmuch as we consider the latter as an institution and a corpus of texts demarcated by methods belonging to empirical sociology. This entails that a definition of "literariness" cannot rely on *any* of the criteria used to define "literature" in the modern cultural history to which "literature" belongs. Here are some of the criteria to be dismissed:

1. *Self-reference*, already amply discussed here.

2. Literature as *canon*, or the historicist, relativist concept. According to it, if we want to know what literature actually *is*, it is sufficient to consult witnesses or documents about it: literature would be what, in any determined period, one used to call literature. I will make three logical objections to fight this view.

a) There exist texts that have reached us from past eras or remote civilizations about which we know very little and cannot document anything like "literary reception." Consider *The Epic of Gilgamesh*: is it impossible or illegitimate to read it now as literature? Or, if we do, does any text ever received in this fashion qualify for the dignity of belonging to literature?

b) Since every "determined period" or era is the result of a synchronic cut practiced within a diachrony, how is one to determine the limits of a period before such criteria can be used, as in particular, the concepts of art and literature, supposing they are recoverable?

c) The historicist concept is based on the inter- and intralinguistic translatability of transversal communication documents (a translation seen as part-to-part lexical equivalence), that is to say on the assumption of the same universals from which historicism wants, as a rule, to rid itself. If witness A writes that X is the artistic expression of national truth and, consequently, texts x_1 to x_n are *Dichtung*, while witness B, in some other culture, writes that Y is a false statement in which the rich and famous revel and, consequently, texts y_1 to y_n are *concetti*, how can I say that we are dealing with two conceptions of Z ($=$ literature), unless I have established from my present point of view and sociocultural situation, that Z should, for any reason, include X and Y, or unless I have built a general structural system of analogies between networks of systems of signs and values, analogies that were not relevant or even perceptible to the witnesses invoked?

3. Literature as *intrinsic aesthetic quality* (bearer of beauty in the works, not in the eye of the beholder). Such is the presupposition of the disappointed reader who exclaims, "This book is too bad, this is not literature", or that of the scholars who classify a corpus into categories of major and minor pieces, gold and silver poets, high, para-, and infraliterature, and so on. These people thus express their personal experience of being unable to construe certain texts into aesthetic objects, frustrated of a particular pleasure or reward. Can one place one's trust in the pleasure capacity of empirical readers? And, should the answer be yes, which such readers? All of them? Or a statistical average? Or those on whom the Establishment has conferred certain duties, responsibilities, and honors? Moreover, how could I, how could any reasonable individual at once base a key concept on the experience of pleasure and deny his own experience, which may be grossly at variance with those most common in his cultural group or peer group, in order to abide by the (reported) experience of others?

4. Literature as the bearer of *figurality*. Its high degree in literary texts could be determined either at the level of stylistic microstructures or at the macrostructural level (thematic isotopies, argument, macronarrative structures, etc.), or yet

by the cohesive homology of these two levels. Unfortunately it is easy to substantiate that many texts that integrate social Discourses not recognized as literary by most people, and literary norm givers in particular, are equally or more figural than "literary" discourse, at whatever level it is analyzed: political propaganda (*langue de bois*), commercial advertising, military puns, amorous conversation, domestic quarrels, and computer technology jargon are just a few obvious examples. Anyhow, who is able and entitled to determine a generally valid scale of figurality, and beyond what threshold on this farfetched scale would literature automatically make its appearance?

5. Literature as *fiction*, or the playful or imaginative criterion. If literature is defined as that activity that defines life as its other, only self-proclaimed literature would hold true. If literature is an inoffensive game, Oulipo tricks would be more literary than Greek tragedies, and those who fight for artistic freedom of expression at the cost of their lives would be really wasting their time. Is the difference between a Platonic dialogue and the discursive account of a chess match a merely quantitative one on a combinatory gauge? If literature is fiction opposed to reality or deviant from it, where is the text of reality with which it can be compared, and/or what constitutes the literariness of Michelet's *Histoire de France*, Samuel Pepys's or Anne Frank's diaries, and Truman Capote's *In Cold Blood*? (See chapter 4.)

Any combination of the preceding criteria could do nothing to save their individual paralogisms; it would only add them up and render their mutual exclusion more tangible.

There cannot be any entirely textualized constituent of literariness. Whence the following collection of propositions.

Definitions

1. *The literariness of a text is the situational, unique, or partly repeated product or by-product of acts of communication that the text mediates and motivates.*

2. *Literariness consists in the application by a reader, or by a group of readers placed in a particular situation, of a special regime of reading to a text*, in response to the solicitation, inscribed or not in the text concerned, of its producer and/or the relevant cultural institutions, and the cognitive and emotive output thereof.[18]

3. The literary regime of reading is, like any other regime that discriminates valuable meanings and functions on the background of postenunciatory indeterminacy, *a variable but not arbitrary collection of potential operations* able to be performed on a text or a collection of texts in the framework of a milieu or cultural constellation, and compatible with the psychological makeup of the receiver or receivers.

4. *The repertoire of operations able to be performed on texts is neither closed nor uniform*. The label "literary" applied to a regime of reading thus inevitably implies an ideological, normative stance anchored in what we perceive as "the present," or its synchronized extensions and ramifications into the diachronic, dynamic texture of cultural practices.

5. To each of these reading operations, *there normally correspond in the reception milieu of the text* (but not necessarily in its production milieu) *particular strategies and techniques of encoding, as well as special materials available to encoders*. Thus a text written in a "dead" language cannot be read *as such*, but only after a de facto preliminary translation; the same is true of a text that manipulates thematic material censured in its reception milieu, like pornography in an integrist religious community, or sentimental love in a group of radical Marxist linguists. Pornography in America is rendered legible by its "immorality," which, since an amoral regime is not available, places it under a moral regime of interpretation and commentary.

This position reverses the traditional view of a passive, submissive decoding, which can hardly stand, even at the level of primary semantic concretization (the determination of what a text is about or talks of), and tentatively introduces the following ideas: (a) *the texts of the past adapt to the conditions of production of new texts in their milieu of reception*, rather than vice versa (it is these new conditions that, in the final analysis, elicit new meanings from old texts); thus the Christian myth is denarrativized by liturgical repetition and renarrativized by the theology of liberation; (b) *textual stability is virtually as relative as that of the messages to be induced from the texts*, even when the substance of expression seems to remain unchanged.

6. Since literariness is neither a specific function of language nor the result of the presence in a text of a dominant function (e.g., the Jakobsonian POETIC function, hardly distinguishable from the METALINGUAL), it consists of: (a) *the activation and productive transformation of the nondominant functions of an act of discourse, whatever functions of it cannot be dominant in the reception milieu* (e.g., the POLEMIC or AGONISTIC function, if the milieu represses it, stressing consensus, or the CONSENSUAL function, if the milieu is ideologically shattered; see chapter 6, the final section); (b) *the complexification of the mutual relations between the functions* (e.g., an ironic reversibility between the EXPRESSIVE and POLEMIC functions); (c) *experimental de- and recontextualizations of the act of discourse concerned* (the question asked being; "What would this mean, if it did not occur here and now, if it was about something else, or if the speaker addressed somebody else under different circumstances?").

Examples are given in the next section with our description of some current operations of literary reading, (see also chapters 4, 9 and 10).

Operations of Literariness

These operations can be divided into three major groups, depending on whether they bear mainly on the signifier, the signified, or reference. All of them modify the treatment given the same linguistic elements in other types of readings.

The function and effect of these operations are uniformly to *increase* the communicative value of the text that mediates the act of discourse considered.

The first group is more closely associated with the reception of formally hypercoded texts like poetry in verse, and also with thematically and structurally hypercoded texts like those belonging to formulaic genres. The second group applies to all classes of texts, but more forcefully in certain aesthetic contexts than others. The third group (described in chapter 4) is more commonly tagged to narrative and, accessorily, descriptive and conative discourses (probably due to local and functional contamination).

The Hypersemanticization of Signifiers

This collection of operations challenges the "insignificance" of signifiers and takes a secondary profit (semantic and sensual-emotive) from their materiality, their disposition, their individual and systemic relations with the corresponding signifieds in language and discourse.

To this effect they can break up the unity of signifying units, contest their groupings in the surface realization of the text, "project the principle of equivalence from the axis of selection onto the axis of combination," to quote Jakobson, or, in other words, subvert the supposed independence of lexis and syntax; they can contest the arbitrariness of the sign by remotivating it in a Cratylian fashion, or even explode and expose the false neutrality of codes and conventions that have been naturalized or banalized by common, dominant usage (this is an aspect of formalist "defamiliarization").

These very numerous operations are difficult to classify; we shall simply enumerate a few types related to various aspects of the substance of expression and interferences between different semiotic or sensory systems.

Phonetisms create interferences between the oral and written substances of expression; they play with the oral substance; they establish additional correlations between sound and meaning. For instance, one can isolate from a text and pair or group together the words that represent exceptions to the rules of pronunciation of the language (e.g., foreign words, strange proper names), or homophones, which are spelled differently, and homographs, which are pronounced differently (e.g., rhymes "for the ear" in the first case, and series like [tear] and [tear], [wind] and [wind], in the second case). Alliterations, assonances, but also dissonances, hiatuses, cacophonies, tongue-tying collocations, and so forth, can be treated in the same manner.

One can let diction be ruled exclusively or primarily by meter, contrastive length of vowels, stressed and unstressed syllables, and so on, to the exclusion of apparent, semantically induced rhythm. "Musical" diction, as often in prayer or opera singing, will produce anacoluthons or other striking anomalies at the syntactic level. We can transform the suggested expressive value of a text by trying many different intonations, accents, and tempos, and thus exploit a sound-related semantic potential by impersonating different speakers and interpretations. We can also defeat expectations by blurring and "unmarking" vocally a text that is strongly marked, dissimulating rhymes and other parallelisms, reducing pauses, or using a "flat" diction and an unvarying, mechanical tempo. Texts in verse, but also rhythmic prose, lend themselves particularly well to these operations, as do all texts that inscribe a strong oral transmission program; but other texts meant to be read silently can also be acted on by reading them aloud.

Graphisms produce interferences and correlations similar to those previously mentioned, but use the written substance and play with it. For example, the superposition of iconic value on the conventional value of signs and symbols by onomatopoeia at the phonetic level, which overmotivates and saturates the signification process of certain words, may be complemented or substituted by a similar phenomenon at the graphic level; we shall call it "graphopoeia", for want of a better term. If words that include tall, thin consonants are perceived as appropriate for designating sharp, thin, elongated objects, like [file] and [flute] do, or words made of low wide rounded letters to designate shapeless viscous substances, like [marrow] does, then the text that contains such signifiers sees its evocative, representational capability enhanced by features of the substance of expression that are in fact purely random in language, not manifestations of an underlying iconic system (cf. [filter], [arrow]). Phallic [i]'s and other similar "psychoanalytic" readings *au pied de la lettre*, like Julia Kristeva's commentary of the poem "Prose pour des Esseintes" by Mallarmé, are typical hypersemanticizations of graphic and phonic signifiers.[19]

One can also isolate from a text words that constitute exceptions to orthographic or morphological rules (irregular plurals, feminines or conjugations, rare declensions) and read their sequential combination across the text, or assign narrative or argumentative meaning to mnemotechnical texts, crosswords, or other texts composed on graphic bases for nonsemantic purposes, like Mérimée's dictation, grammatical examples, or morphological lists: "men, women, oxen, brethren." Adorned, spatially redistributed letters as in bri , calligrammatic writing, and concrete poetry are other textual markers that invite us to engage into similar procedures, as we also tend to do when we read a text in original or facsimile handwriting.

Materialisms are readings that rely on factors such as the quality, thickness, and colors of the paper support, the color of the ink used, the weight, size, and binding of a volume, the shape of the pages, the size of the print, the margin width, and so on. Boris Vian bet on these effects when he published a limited edition of *L'Automne à Pékin* on "infamous paper" (*papier ignoble*, i.e., toilet paper). We all know that a printed text is "not the same" in typed or photocopied form, or on microform (if it is read literarily). Sartre gives striking examples of his early materialisms in his childhood autobiography, *Words*: "Corneille was a big reddish fellow, a bit rough, with leather on his back and a smell of glue about him."[20]

Materialisms, in turn, as well as phonetisms and graphisms, can become instruments of further operations of synaesthesia or *synaesthetisms*, which apply "parasitic" intersemiotic codes or repertoires of correspondences to the reading or the aural reception of a text. Once "A is black, E white, I red, U green and O blue," poems become a "symphony of colors" or, why not, a picture of fresh perfumes.

All of the preceding operations are, to varying degrees, normally applied to the reading of poetry (verse, in particular), which differs traditionally from prose by numerous markers (rhyme, meter, rhythm, spatial divisions of the text, use of capital letters, or calligraphy in certain cultures) that encourage these practices. From the standpoint of the production and transmission of texts, poetry encodes, inscribes, and stresses the corresponding operations. Those described have the common aim and/or effect of semanticizing (rendering meaningful) features of the text that would otherwise pass unperceived or even be, in certain situations, obstacles, noises, stumbling blocks for communication. The literary regime does not limit itself to practicing certain operations rather than others, and it always shares each of the specific operations with one or more other regimes: let us think of the "I Like Ike" slogan, verbal advertising for consumer goods and holiday resorts on roadside billboards, words in paintings, rhymes in proverbs for weather forecasting, syllabic redundancy in baby talk, and so forth. The literary regime dictates the choice of operations, orients their action, *and* valorizes their results in a certain fashion.

Hypersemanticization operations are rarely isolated from other classes of operations; they are rather coordinated with or instrumentally bound to them, which is logical, since they straddle several levels of the reality of language, from the substance of expression in which they are rooted, to the sensory (e.g., visual) projection of mental images and the constitution of conceptual clusters. They can thus give rise to polysemy and etymologisms, or even play a catalytic role in the application of fictional reference. The frequency and distribution of the selected signifiers in related social Discourses (history, science, mundane or popular conversation) will be criteria for the demarcation of "fictional domains," together with the greater or lesser adequacy of the signifiers thus semanticized within the narrative or thematic structures of the text tentatively situated in the corresponding Discursive universes.

The previously described operations play a significant role in the fictionalization of narrative through *onomastics*, either in a punctual or in a systemic way.

Due to phonetisms, for example, proper names cease to function (if they ever do) as "rigid designators": the actual, "real-life" event of the marriage of Miss Day to Mr. Knight, or of a Señorita Albajar to Señor Altarriba, will appear to all but their families and intimate friends as a "fiction." We will say that "reality overtakes fiction" on the latter's own ground, while relatives and friends are people who suppress the semanticization of the correlated signifiers of proper names doubling as signifiers of generic words that belong to exemplary pairs of opposites. Literary reading relishes a certain Cratylism of names that the Discourse of history does not corroborate and even energetically repudiates: for a de Gaulle or a d'Estaing, how many "insignificant" Gambettas, Pompidous, and Mitterrands?

Even in "literary" texts, however, the hypersemanticization of signifiers may have adverse or perverse effects. It can foment parallel networks of characters, symbols, and actions that will compete with the primary concretized narrative meaning and propose one or more diverging, auxiliary, marginal narrative or descriptive programs, or even resist the narrativity of the text altogether by substituting static, equative networks for it. This may be due, notably, to the fact that homophonic and homographic series, like rhymes, correspond to patterns of development of the language and logico-semantic classes that are either antipathetic to the "logic of narrative" or poorer in combinatory power, not fine enough to contribute to it. Symmetrical compositional devices tend to have these effects. Onomastic palindromes like [Pip] or [Ada], can serve a supposedly "circular" structure of the narratives where they recur, but they can also induce a "circular" reading when it is not fully warranted by other indexes, and conceal the possibility of a "linear" or "teleological" reading that should also be considered. D'Arlincourt, in his preface to *Ismalie* (1828), pondered for several pages the fascinating problem of the conflict between the regularity of verse and narrative interest, based on chance and mobility. He has a mysterious adviser say to him:

> Do not write in alexandrine, regular verse. . . . Harmony is dominant in it; the argument becomes accessory. Avoid the vicious style that sacrifices thoughts to words and enthusiasm to symmetry. Since your action must be strong, lively, and touching, shun the ambitious style that would throw you back entirely into declamatory and rigid majesty. (p. lvii)

In fact, disharmony, a more or less random scattering of words on the page, the unleashed violence of the signifier, when "wild lines of words [cross] the sheets of paper obeying only their own furor,"[21] is likely to achieve almost the same effect as marching regiments of decasyllables in Cowper or alexandrine verse in Péguy: the "struggle of / word-design //, against / word-syntax" (ibid.). (See also the discussion of drama in chapter 9.)

Some narratives use coded markers to call for an intensive semanticization of signifiers (as in the limerick and certain children's tales), while others do not invoke it and even try to forbid it. Other texts yet, like Balzac's *Sarrasine*, remain half open to these operations without offering them a particulalrly favorable ground. Proust, on the other hand, largely builds on them both the metafictional and the realist strains of *La Recherche*.[22]

Finally, we should note that such operations, like spontaneous "free association" in the dreamwork, are often carried out at a subliminal level of consciousness (whether or not they proceed from the same level in the sender's mind), which makes them all the more efficient on affective responses, empathy or aversion, and the corresponding rewards in the form of aesthetic/erotic pleasure. At the same time, this feature will commonly constitute a disorganizing factor for narrative, where it struggles against temporal frames and temporal irreversibility. When it is inscribed in texts that purport to be narratively concretized (e.g., surrealist "novels," *Nadja, Sur le fleuve Amour, Aurora*), it gives them a standstill or oneirically agitated quality and may prevent the concretization of the *story*. This is also true of many *Nouveau Roman* and metafictional novels (e.g., *Lieux-dits*, by Jean Ricardou, *Take It or Leave It*, by Raymond Federman) in which metalingual utterances and allusions constantly draw the reader's attention to spatial rather than temporal materials and organization, problems of "filling" rather than feeling and "flux." As Federman puts it:

> I can't mess around too much to tell you more about literature because I have to report now the next episode unload that part of the story that comes next and how as soon as he arrived in New York immediately he called Marylin he called her just outside the Lincoln tunnel.

Active Polysemy

I shall not develop this aspect in great detail, since it has been explored fairly often by major poeticians, particularly in the study of poetry (Empson's *Seven Types of Ambiguity*), and has received a great deal, perhaps an excessive amount, of attention in recent years. Literary polysemy begs for terminological clarification more than for exemplification and illustration. The latter is made superfluous by the consecration of the plural, writerly, fragmentary, contradictory, undecidable open text by Barthes, Eco, and many more contemporary theorists in the protracted wake of symbolism, postsymbolism, cubism, surrealism, and the *nouveau roman* among other modernist movements and schools, sometimes indirectly indebted to the baroque and early German romanticism.

The following four pairs of opposites must be briefly considered:

- passive and active polysemy
- polysemy and homonymy

- denotative and connotative polysemy
- lexical and syntactic polysemy.

A. In general semantics, polysemy is an exception, symmetrical and inverse of synonymy, to the rule of biunivocality that characterizes the linguistic code in principle (one signified only for each signifier, one signifier only for each signified); it is then the phenomenon by which, within the scope of the same code, one signifier is used for more then one signified: certain lexemes, for example, have different meanings, depending on contexts (whatever is meant by this last word). Thus, according to the *Diccionario de la Real Academia*, the Spanish lexeme [*arco*] (⁻ [bow]) may have the following signifieds: "(1) a portion of a curved line, (2) weapon made with a thin bar of steel, wood, or other elastic material, with the ends held together by a string or band, so that it forms a curve and is used to throw arrows." For one lexeme in language there may coexist one or more etymological meanings, primary and derived meanings, literal and figurative meanings, special and extended meanings, and so forth. In this *passive* aspect, polysemy is a problem of lexical choice and collocation on the part of the speaker, and a problem of context-tied selection of signifieds (i.e., "reduction") for the receiver. It is a general communicative problem, of no *special* concern for literary communication.

Now, in the framework of literariness, there are at least two types of *active* or activated polysemy. I shall call them "free" and "textual," respectively.[23]

Literary polysemy is the procedure used to activate the plurality of potential signifieds attached to a single signifier.

In fact, any plurality of signifieds that remains part of the definitively discarded possibilities of the linguistic code is not relevant to univocally intended text encoding or decoding. This is what happens in scientific, technological, and legal communication. If I read the printed "tips" for the best handling of a machine or gadget, in which [the valve] seems to be able to designate two different parts, the sign is indeed denotatively polysemic (= ring, or = hole?), but the act of communication will not be successfully completed until I have made the right, efficient choice in context and *forgotten* the other possible *denotata*; I must stop the "noise" made by polysemy in the information process. The opposite is true of the literary regime of reading.

This *does not mean* that literariness forbids monosemic reduction in general or in proportion to the aesthetic output of the text (its "pleasure"): this idea would amount to the equation of literariness with obscurity and limit the interpretive freedom of the reader just as drastically as classical aesthetics.

Literariness, although it does not necessarily hinder monosemic reduction, takes stock of the traces of this reduction (and the corresponding preliminary exploration of polysemy) as an integral part of the act of communication and therefore of the actualized MESSAGE.

When I consider literarily the utterance "El arco iris apareció sobre el valle" (The rainbow made its appearance above the valley), I do choose between the *denotata* "portion of a curve" and "weapon," but I can retain a trace of this reduction by preserving as a connotation the signified "weapon" rejected as denotation; it will play the role of an adjective, with either its straight literal or a metaphorical value (e.g., the *threatening* rainbow). We should observe that, as action movies demonstrate, a weapon is double-edged: it can protect us as much as it can jeopardize our security. But we may find that the context does not even warrant keeping the idea of weapon as a connotation; in this case, we will reject it and retain the traces of this further reduction as an additional, weaker connotation (= connotative neutrality or "absence of connotation"), more or less in this form: "the rainbow, neither protective nor threatening, made its appearance." I have just described an example of *free* polysemy.

Catherine Kerbrat-Orecchioni calls "textual polysemy" the instances in which the very structure of the text forbids a final monosemic reduction, that is, *when this reduction would prevent the receiver from actualizing a message or would severely mutilate the message actualized.* These cases obviously include rhetorical figures like syllepsis, antanaclasis, anagram, paragram, and metaphor in absentia. In "Brûlé de plus de feux que je n'en allumai," we must retain the two signifieds "housefire" and "amorous passion" if we want to make sense of the sentence at all. Francesco Orlando has shown how the contradiction in the signifieds of [monster] (= something exhibited but which cannot or should not be seen and thus becomes invisible) informs the whole significance of Racine's *Phèdre*.[24] Other tropes, as well as nontropic figures of construction, such as anaphoras, cataphoras, and epistrophes of the signifier, may have the same effect.

B. With polysemy, the *same* signifier may bear two or more meanings, while, with homonymy, *apparently identical* signifiers bear different meanings. This distinction would be uninteresting, were it not for the fact that the main criterion taken into account by lexicographers is historical, etymological. Are [port] (= harbor) and [port] (= Portuguese wine) the same lexeme? They both come from the Latin *portus*, but the second through a metonymic derivation from the name of the city of Oporto. According to John Lyons:

> The native speaker is generally unaware of the etymology of the words
> he uses and his interpretation of them is unaffected (except when he is
> being pedantic or exploiting certain aspects of their etymology for
> stylistic purposes) by whatever knowledge of their historical derivation
> he may happen to possess.[25]

This little-studied operation, which I shall call *etymologism*, projects a narrative over a definitional discourse, the axis of combination over the axis of selection, particularly in the case of semantic *archaism*, which gives a quality of "depth" to text significance. Active semantic neology or *neosemy* is less frequent, but it fulfills a similar defamiliarizing purpose through another adventitious narrative. In fact, the diachronic dimension of language may serve both to solve and to create polysemic puzzles, at once to challenge the novelty of events in the presented world and narrativize a static presented world.

C. Beside denotative polysemy — with the connotative effects of reduction already mentioned — literariness can also involve the activation of *connotative* polysemy. If a character in a novel or a play addresses a companion using the word "man" or the word "mate," these words, which would at best connote familiarity in an everyday conversational context (American and Australian, respectively), will now display a wide spectrum of connotations, among them the Americanness and possibly the blackness of one speaker, the Australianness of the other, a "low" sociocultural register, voluntarily populist or acquired by education, fraternity and/or male chauvinism and/or abusive complicity and/or latent homosexuality, and so forth. The inscription of dialects and regiolects, such as a measure of "Walloon" or "joual" in a Belgian or a Canadian narrative, of Catalan in a Castilian novel set in Barcelona, or the partial Africanization of Ahmadou Kourouma's social satire and Hampaté Bâ's picaresque tale, often contributes more to polysemic enrichment than to realistic effects of verisimilitude.

The scope of literary polysemy is in no way restricted to the lexical components of the text. It can bear on *phrastic and metaphrastic syntax*, as any reading of Mallarmé or Wallace Stevens would show, on narrative syntax, on the articulation of social Discourses with grammatical discourses, on thematic isotopies (see Greimas's work on myth, however incomplete), and so on. Its activation at these last four levels is essential in order to recognize and accept or fail to recognize and reject textual unity and coherence, which in turn provide the framework of literary significance, didactic meanings, and aesthetic judgment. Polysemy, through the ambiguous interplay of the different functions of characters and forces (see chapter 5), also contributes to formulate narrative enigmas, give a content to narrative suspense, defer information, and justify its deferral. A narratogenous or protonarrative situation can always be considered as a polysemic utterance.

D. If a narrative persona has given every sign of heroism for a long time, but one of its actions is suddenly ambivalent enough to make it suspicious, subsequent evidence that will clear it of all suspicion obliges us to perform a monosemic reduction of the action in point, but this reduction, just like the polysemy it reduces at the appointed time, remains an integral part of the message: our hero is no longer just that; he becomes an "unfairly suspected hero," he is worth more than before. This is exactly what happens, in the *Princess of Clèves*, to Mme. de Clèves's image in the eyes of her husband, and to Nemours's image in the eyes of the princess; M. de Clèves and the princess are separately inscribed readers who are meant to influence the virtual reader of the novel in the same way. On a more abstract or more general level (at that of the maxim), their actions and the correlative repeated reduction of polysemy are redundant devices for imposing a single truth. The same thing, with an opposite lesson taught, happens in the classical detective story of the Agatha Christie type; in such narratives, the polysemy of all the characters involved during the period of investigation holds one common factor: potential guilt, expressed by the condition of "suspect." All the characters are "alleged" criminals until a number of them, or all but one or two, are cleared by the findings of the detective; but even then their innocence remains marred by the tainting light that was cast on them for a long time, showing how easily they could have been or become murderers. Indeed, novels like *Murder on the Orient Express, The Murder of Roger Ackroyd,* and *Curtain* all but draw this very conclusion by letting the verdict fall on every character in the first case, on the storyteller in the second, on the detective in the third. The device is akin to and often combined with that of *fixations,* which consists in a converging repetition of information from different sources.

However, polysemy may also, like hypersemanticization, play a deconstructive role in narrative, particularly when it extends beyond the semantic content of events and details of characterization, to the spatiotemporal parameters and the identity of the agents, and/or when it is prolonged to the end of an "open work." The repeated sentence "Il est maintenant six heures" in *Jealousy,* when we do not know the date and whether it is six in the morning or six at night, linguistic as well as disturbing visual syllepses in the work of Robbe-Grillet, multiple disguises and misinterpretations in the comedy of errors, the ambiguity of "reality" and "representation" in a novel like *The Magus,* by John Fowles, in Corneille's *Illusion comique,* or in a whole sector of the fantastic (e.g., *The Turn of the Screw*), all these that can pass at first for generators of suspense may also be the cause of its removal: if everything is and remains possible, anything goes and nothing is ever certain; this apparent tautology is the sign of an early foreclosure of narrative meaning. The teaching of (re)presentation is, in this case, identical with that of the world (re)presented, but neither has changed since the beginning; their *constant* meaning is that there is little meaning or there are too many meanings: we can *never* be sure.

Literariness is nothing but a vast and complex *modalizing system* that characterizes a sector of linguistic communication. But its similarities, structural and functional, with other sectors of communication that use different semiotic channels and sensory media under other spatiotemporal parameters, link it with painting, film, music, and architecture, almost in proportion with the specific resources that contribute to each. Verbal art is not any more magic than the other arts and communicative crafts: it does not transform words, sentences, signs, and referents into something else, it does not prevent all the Discourses, techniques, and (re)presentations it involves from continuing to relate to their "original" Discursive, technical, and figurative universes—usually labeled "life"—also just as if they had not entered the realm of literariness. Defensive views of art and exaggerated idealistic claims have the disastrous effect of making classical, "mimetic," and traditionalist aesthetic practices, as well as propagandistic, "utilitarian" notions of art appear more "realistic" and less regressive than they actually are.

We should always remember too that communication does not occur without a text, nor does it occur within a text, but about it, across it, or at its periphery. We textualize to communicate; we remember and we also forget texts in order to communicate better; we disseminate some texts and withhold others as we try to communicate, and our texts bear many marks of the radiating dispersion, truncated performance and mitigated, haphazard successes of communication, but pray we never glory in communicating or pretending to for the sole purpose of objectifying our fears into an illusory self-contained, self-sufficient, autarchic text that would be the last mirror of a subject defeated and yet "lord of his own cottage."

Chapter 4
A Manmade Universe? or,
The Question of Fictionality

The few aspects of the verbal message discussed in chapters 2 and 3 were dependent on the structure of utterances and thus related to sign structure. Without indulging in the absurd wager of trying to isolate this structure from the many systems in which it happens to be produced, recognized, transformed, and exchanged as such, we have treated the sign thus far as if it were self-contained: we had not posited the possibility, let alone the necessity of an external space, a world without sign systems at large. At the new stage we are reaching now, the question is not one of origin or even beginnings; I do not care to speculate on metaphysical problems like the precedence of sign systems or that of pragmatic universes. Yet we feel the urge to ask no longer how signs are formed and relate to each other, but also how they relate to what-is-not-them, if they do at all: What is it that signs try to do to their other? And what do they seem to reveal that this other does to them?

One may at least wonder whether signs and sign systems have a function other than self-maintenance, reproduction, and expansion. If we accept as a temporary working assumption that it may be so, we shall call "reference" this outward perspective from the sign. The key premise in the present chapter is a question: how can we profit by the spatial metaphor contained in the representation of sign systems as limited by some kind of boundary? If they enclose items, processes, and rules within themselves, they must postulate the existence of an outside space, containing and determined by systems and nonsystems of something else than just signs. What are the consequences of this postulation? The premise is interrogative and wishful, hence the probability that we shall find reference itself to be, in the end, anything but affirmative and constative.

Reference is a matter of purpose and motivation: it concerns us. Reference, in desire, points to what we want; in struggle and fear, to what stops us from getting what we want; in powerlessness, to ways of transforming our desires. If the subject is anything or anywhere, it appears at referential crossings. Reference has to do with multiplicity (empirical aspects of being, beyond conceptual unity), potential changes and shifts. Artistic communication, which emphasizes and values semantic wandering, also tends to enhance referential instability and turn it into an asset, a proud claim of identity, while many other types of communication consider such mobility to be a hindrance. Moreover, narrative communication on its own, whether artistic or not, seems to show a special vocation for making its utterances refer severally rather than singly.

As we know, the formalist current denied reference or made efforts to curtail it, as if it were a kind of moral vulgarism. On the other hand, the return of reference, like the return of the subject after and against deconstructionist philosophies, appears in many cases to serve at best traditional humanist values, if not conservative theses according to which artists have a duty to "the real" because they are indebted to it, or, in fact, a duty to the dominant culture because they belong to a corporation that supports it. Our way to shun this insidious but insistent rhetoric will be to place the rhetoric of reference at the center of our inquiry.

Our starting point will be an operational analysis of presentational techniques in two passages from Stendhal's novels *Le Rouge et le noir* and *Lucien Leuwen*.

First Prize: Meet the Character of Your Choice

The little town of Verrières can pass for one of the nicest in Franche-Comté.

In the first sentence of *Le Rouge et le noir*,[1] the Franche-Comté province or region, although it in no way necessarily pertains to mnemonic traces of our "real life" (= nonbookish) experience, belongs in its own right to a set of Discourses including history, geography, sociology, and folklore, which give it a compulsory place within their signifying systems in which, on the contrary, they would not take Oz or Never-never Land, for example. These Discourses, because they share the property of ascertaining and authentifying the objects they mention, will be called *certifying* Discourses. In other words, they are socially endowed with the authority required to establish the "reality" or "unreality" of the designatum of each item introduced in their lexicon. Franche-Comté is part of the certified content of the relevant encyclopedia of Stendhal's reader; this encyclopedia, like any organized archive of human knowledge, provides in turn to Franche-Comté the detail of its semantic content, with its precise headings (area, economic data, historic background, monuments, climate, population) and a unique metasememe (since Franche-Comté is a proper name). Whether the headings are followed with a considerable amount of "correct" detail in the actual reader's encyclopedia is not a priori relevant. What is important is that the network of Discourses that occupy the milieu has these slots ready to be filled, and the metasememe is unique in the sense that a semantic rule prohibits two definitions contradictory in any respect from being at all valid with regards to the lexeme Franche-Comté considered at once in its diachronic and synchronic dimensions.

It is noteworthy that this approach goes decidedly against the Kripkean theory of proper names as "rigid designators." According to Pavel, Kripke thus

. . . describes the structure of the relationship between that linguistic label and its bearer. Once attached to a being, a proper name refers to it, regardless of the possible changes in properties this being undergoes and *a fortiori* regardless of the changes in our knowledge of them."[2]

In our present perspective, contrary to Kripke's and Pavel's hypotheses, no priority is conceded either to "beings" or "names," since it is the link between them that is constitutive of both "beings" and "names" *qua* beings and names. The distinction between a structural and a historical aspect of naming is invalid in such a semantic perspective, since the structure is itself historical: the categories under which semantic contents (pieces of meaning) can be attributed are determined by and constitutive of the milieu without which no signification or designation could take place. Any attempt to separate pure reference (reference to an empty "being") from its semantic bases is thus idealistic and futile. The "label" theory of names is unable to account for pronominal and other anaphoras, since the new act of naming ("attaching" a name) involved in anaphora would be severed from all the previous acts of naming the "same" entity and forbid the very construction of identity without which textual coherence is impossible: Kripke's theory entails paralogically that "Napoleon," "Bonaparte," and "the emperor" refer to three different "beings" whose avatars are without effect on their individuation; "Bonaparte" and "Buonaparte," or "Lille" and "Rijsel" would also designate different beings whose only essential characteristic would be to bear such labels. The adoption of a three-tiered theory of "designation," without skipping the semic level, has, as we shall see, decisive consequences on the understanding of fictionality.

Back to our text, "the little town of Verrières," with which we met first in the order of reading, seemed to answer the question of identity/naming involved, retrospectively at least, in the title of the chapter ("A Little Town"); but, at the same time, it appears as a fuzzy semantic cluster whose functional credibility relies above all on the neutrality or relative indeterminacy of a *typical* French toponym. Its credit is of a concessive nature: although no town by this name is a necessary part of the reader's encyclopedia, we cannot see why there should not exist at least one town by this name in Franche-Comté (Georgetown, Jackson, or Oxford would be perceived in a similar fashion by the American reader of an Ameri-

can novel). The suspension of unbelief expressed by a "Why not?" is amply rewarded when we open the index of a French atlas: not only does Verrières exist,
but *they* exist; there are *two* in Franche-Comté and others in various regions. Unfortunately, this excess of being is rendered more embarrassing by a lack of adequate semantic content: not one of the localities called Verrières seems to qualify
for the status of "little town," in the French sense; they are mere villages. The
scholars who have investigated Stendhal's sources readily acknowledge that Verrières in *Le Rouge* bears no other resemblance than its name to any Verrières certified by geographic and historical dictionaries.

In short, Franche-Comté "exists," Verrières "exists," but there is no "little
town of Verrières *in* Franche-Comté," in spite of the semantic filling out and increasing specification displayed by the text on the plane of signification: on this
plane, the little town evoked is not simply *any* little town, but a concrete and precise little town, situated in a particular province, and which may reasonably be
considered as one of the prettiest in the area. On the plane of reference *to certifying Discourses*, we end up with an *erroneous* utterance. In the supreme interest
of coherence, contextual meaning, and the "deeper truth" expected from the text
as rewards for our investment in its reading, we must seek another type of reference for the signified "Verrières": we shall say that, according to its imaginary
reference, Verrières has no other existence than that lent to it by the enunciator
of the text; this enunciator offers to share such reference with the reader as a felicity condition of the act of communication in which we have engaged on beginning
to read.

Due to this referential transformation, Verrières ceases to be the name of a
"real" town and becomes the designator of an ideal model, a kind or type constructed for and under particular circumstances of communication. Nevertheless
our pains – and our joys – do not come to an end at that: if an imaginary little town
of Verrières is not very disturbing after all (it does not compete with certified Verrières that would be very important in our encyclopedias), an imaginary Franche-
Comté is much more difficult to accept. Franche-Comté resists its referential contamination by Verrières, although the latter is denotatively placed in the former's
semantic comprehension by the same demand that makes us seek textual consistency in the first place. Franche-Comté is too well documented by the certifying Discourses; it withstands the onslaught of the aberrant Verrières with a large
measure of success, encysts it, and we return again, temporarily, to dominant
"real" reference. Now it is the name [Verrières] that will be contested: hence all
the comments to the effect that Verrières is "actually" Dôle or some other town
attested by the certifying encyclopedia. Confronted with this aporia or dilemma
whose dynamics is all too unsettling (much more than any fixedness), we tend to
prefer a translation through a theory of "keys" or pseudonyms. The same frightened reaction to the vertigo of referential duplicity will produce such statements
as: "Berthet is the true Julien Sorel."[3] We should note that, in this case, the secon-

dary transformation of textual utterances produces a new narrative deployment of reading beyond the level at which primary narrative meaning and story are constructed, and the secondary narrative is the cause of interpretive irreversibility, which results in Julien Sorel's not being the true Berthet.

This to-and-fro, in-and-out game between imaginary and real reference beginning with the first line of the text, pursued, repeated, and amplified all along the labyrinth of reading, is what makes Stendhalian *fiction* and determines the specific compass of novelistic communication. Fictionality and its compass will be our constant pursuit through the following analyses.

The initial pages of *Le Rouge* are known to make use of the focalization artifact called "the traveler" (see chapter 5) as the bearer of expositional descriptive discourse. Although the device, reminiscent of traditional story-telling techniques, was far from being new at the time and has been often imitated since, its particular setting deserves all our attention. Roger Pearson has recently demonstrated how a progressive transition toward "narrative tense" (*temps de l'histoire*) in the narrator's utterances combines with the equally progressive introduction of compensatory direct discourse, in the present tense, to "maintain the liminal illusion that character, narrator, and reader coexist at the same time and in one place."[4] In other words, Stendhal provides an apparently coherent set of coordinates for the plane of (re)presentation on which the play of reference(s) can take place. We are now going to examine the respective roles of the three agents outlined by Pearson in the variable design of referential combination.

First of all, the famous "traveler" is not presented textually from the beginning; he appears as a kind of by-product of descriptive discourse, as the result of a substantivating transformation or transgression, a partial cataphoric translation that resubjectifies the subject of enunciation by duplicating it into the subject of certain utterances. The "traveler" is not abruptly stuck either, as an afterthought, in a series of utterances that would have grown wild, unfathered, before it makes its appearance, as if the author and the reader suddenly discovered that such utterances had always wanted a master, a cause, an origin.[5] In fact, the anonymity, the blurring of inscribed communicational roles is never complete, even in the beginning. The words "can pass for," in the first sentence, constitute an indirect offer of transaction to the reader, because they lack an attributive or agential complement: the reader may decide that the appearance is true or that it is deceptive (as it will be suggested later: "this little town which *seemed* so pretty to you").[6] These words do not conceal the prototextual presence of an addresser with whom the values at stake must be negotiated. The "onlooking idea" (*idée regardante*, in Guillaume's terminology) is ever present; it is going to circumscribe little by little the place of a nameable subject and uses a full array of devices for this purpose, of which I shall mention only a few: relative quantifiers ("a large number"), comparatives and superlatives implying a mobile observer-cum-enunciator ("one of the nicest," "the least folds"), appreciation formulas or others involving special parameters of observation or preempting possible false deductions ("*as early as* the first frosts of October," "sawmills, *nevertheless*, are not the source of the town's wealth"), or yet the systematic predicative translation that narrativizes the description of the site ("Its white houses . . . *stretch* on the slope of a hill . . . "; "Snow *starts to cover* the crests as early as . . . "; "A torrent *rushes*,"; etc.).

There are, moreover, two pronominal forerunners of the "traveler," two indefinite "ones" (*on*) between which a subtle kind of skidding takes place, announcing many more such lateral moves in the future:

> It is to the factory of painted cloth called Mulhouse cloth that we are indebted [*que l'on doit*] for the general well-being.
> As soon as you penetrate the town, you feel dizzy [*on est étourdi*] with the din.

If the first *on* is literally or even metonymically indebted like the population of Verrières, he(?) must be very close to them, well acquainted with them—he could even be one of them, an inhabitant of the town; he is understood at first as a virtually collective subject, a "we" like the one who acts as mouthpiece for the city in *The Plague*, for instance. The second *on*, on the other hand, appears from the start as a foreigner who discovers the town of Verrières—so that he can bring a fresh, unbiased vision of it—surprised by certain sights, but likely to misinterpret other aspects that the first *on*, familiar with Verrikres, was bound to know and read correctly. The words *en apparence* ("apparently") occur twice in the same short paragraph: "une machine bruyante et terrible en apparence," "ce travail, si rude en apparence," before undergoing some lexical and semantic variations ("on trouve même, au premier aspect," "une maison d'assez belle apparence"). The narrator, who should not be taken in by appearances and knows better, on the one side, and the *on*, on the other, could thus become completely dissociated, the latter being rather a textual embodiment of the reader, were it not for the first, however little noticeable occurrence of a *je* in the idiom "je ne sais combien," literally confessing ignorance, and for the striking homology between the positional separation of the two *on* regarding the presented world, and the dialogic source of information at the end of the third paragraph:

> If the traveler asks, when he enters Verrières . . . , someone will answer [*on lui répond*].

Dialogism is now explicit, but Verrières does not become any more transparent, in spite of its name. The ambi- and multivalence of *on* continues: he (they?) successively "feels" the limitations of M. de Rênal, informs the traveler, and builds a parapet. From now on, the controlling actant of narration (the Σ narrator, or ΣN) will be strongly textualized, notably through its addresses to the reader: "You can bet one hundred to one" ("il y a cent à parier contre un").

In chapter 2, the narrator is concretized for the first time into an expressive "I":

> How many times, thinking of Parisian ballrooms left behind the day before, with my chest pressed against those large blocks of stone of a beautiful, bluish grey, have my eyes plunged into the valley of the Doubs!

No doubt, despite its physically constituted interiority, its resonance, this "I" is also assimilated to the traveler, because they share the same spatial situation, so that another superior, more distant, and more embracing instance will be needed to take under its rule such an "I" already too committed to the presented world by its explicit textualization. Beyond a certain level of complexity, the successive splitting up of the narrating instance becomes mechanical and compulsive. The upstream flight from the presented world becomes a repeated turning of the screw as fascinating as the pendular alternation of "real" versus imaginary reference.

> Mme. de Chasteller walked across the salon without seeing Leuwen. It was capital. If this good-looking young man had had a little talent, he would have succeeded in making her declare her love for him and promise that she would welcome him every day of her life. . . .
>
> If he had appeared the day before, Mme. de Chasteller had made a decision: she would have asked him to visit her, from now on, only once a week. She was still under the influence of terror. . . .
>
> The sound of the voice in which he uttered this word: *eh bien*, the most consummate Don Juan might not have found it, but there was no talent in Leuwen; it was the impulse of nature, naturalness. this simple word of Leuwen's changed everything. . . .
>
> He was soon mad with joy, which prevented him from realizing how young and naive he was still.[7]

Assumption making is seen by some theorists as the essence of all "fiction," since it allows us to consider and test different situations in worlds ruled by laws similar to those we already know, or identical situations in worlds ruled by other laws. On other occasions, it is treated as a somewhat primitive form of metafiction. When we read the preceding passages attentively, we realize that these two ideas, which contain some truth, are not sufficiently conclusive by themselves and should be submitted to more careful scrutiny.

Assumption making elicits from the immediate generative background of the text the presence of an authority and a sensitivity able actively to modify the rules of the game that had started to inform horizons of expectation, processes of identification and experimental, tentative "contracts." On the other hand, it stresses the arbitrariness of the selection of events and information conveyed in language. We are dealing here with this category of "all the events that *do not* happen but nonetheless appear in the narrative text" which Gerald Prince refers to as the "disnarrated" or, in French, *dénarré*:

> . . . alethic expressions of possibility or impossibility, deontic expressions of prohibition, epistemic expressions of ignorance, ontological expressions of nonexistence, imagined worlds, desired worlds, or intended worlds, (unfulfilled) expectations, (unwarranted) beliefs, (failed) attempts, (crushed) hopes, suppositions and false calculations, errors and lies, and so forth.[8]

Even more generally, this is the work of negativity in narration, of which it is curious to note that it "helps define a narrator"[9] better than affirmation. The "interventions," open enunciation, and metalepses of Sterne-Tristram in *Tristram Shandy* and Gide-Bernard in *The Counterfeiters* insist on the fragility of textualized characters and events, on their nature of paper characters and paper events. But the *Diktat* of the enunciator who proclaims his unlimited power is not without ambiguity and dangers of its own: it tends to subordinate the acceptance of narrative situations by the reader to the seductive force of this enunciator. Factors such as stylistic fashion, descriptive systems, starters of intertextual networks, and other shifters of aestheticization can condition the reader's response to the offer of narrative meaning. In a sense, assumption making reduces the *necessity* of narrative concatenation; making unknown riches glitter in the distance, it could encourage the ephemeral satisfactions of fantasy rather than a dialogic balance between the principle of reality and that of pleasure when prevision and actuality are equally serious.

But, at least as used by Stendhal, this device does not have a one-way action; it not only opens vistas in the walls of that-which-is and that-which-can-be, it also closes any doors to the paths and gardens of "otherwise" that the reader might have tried to cross unguided. Narrative possibilities thus textualized are given a semblance of viability only to be crushed under the stamp of assertion: "But it wasn't like this." Fictional narrative seems to acquire the same factual rigidity, the same irreversibility that is characteristic of history and events in our own lives, particularly when we hold a tragic view of these "realia." In the presented world, as in the world of experience, things are the way they are *and* not any other way. Lucien had no talent, and therefore Mme. de Chasteller did not confess that she loved him then, but this same lack of talent is the other face of the sincerity and naïveté that later touches Mme. de Chasteller's heart and stops her from forbidding Lucien's frequent visits. If Lucien had talent, he would not be Lucien but, maybe, Julien . . . Assumption making circumscribes a place for reality in the presented world and the textual stuff: something else could be written, but it was not, or it was, but on the mode of a negative summary. This is a technique of

preterition, which can well serve what reception aesthetics has rather inade-
quately called the "referential illusion."

Assumption making is a technique with a high rhetorical potential, common
among narrative genres, argumentative genres, and the essay. One of its obvious
effects is redundancy; the propositional content of the predicate in question is
necessarily repeated: "If X had been −X instead of X, he would have done −a
instead of doing a, but he was not −X, so he did a, and p, not −p, is true." As
Gerald Prince puts it,

> [The disnarrated] institutes an antimodel in terms of which the text
> defines itself and indicates the aesthetics it develops and espouses, the
> audience it represents and aspires to, the matters, topics, and configura-
> tions this audience takes to be tellable.[10]

Propositional redundancy is a factor of text coherence and contributes to an increased solidarity among those who partake in the communication situation, but,
at the same time, it underscores the nonnarrative or antinarrative aspects of communication by playing with the status of the predicate in a nonchronological way.
More important, assumption making reveals the true nature of fictionality, which
is not only a comparison between two or more modes of reference for the same
signification, but a competition between them. Where there is representation,
fictionality is thus, as we shall see, the condition of formation of the Real.

Polyreference and *Comparatio*

> Fiction and reality relate in such a way that one serves as horizon for
> the other: the world appears as the horizon of fiction, and fiction as that
> of the world.[11]

A large sector of the theoretical research that seeks to characterize the phenomenon of textualization (thematization, presentation) of items not warranted by certifying Discourses (history, science, etc.) is still conditioned and plagued by this
lame binary opposition that conceals several others. If we take "reality" as the supporting term, the opposition equates fiction with "unreality": a fiction is something
that has no material existence, that does not have the properties of a thing, or even
has no existence at all, whereas reality is something and everything that "exists."
If we take "fiction" as the supporting term, the opposition equates reality with
"nonfiction": a reality is something that does not bear imitation, that is *not* part
of a set of possibilities; reality is, in a sense, the impossible par excellence. The
underlying ontology is so simplistic that it verges on absurdity, as it seeks to compare terms that are predefined as incomparable ("fiction and reality have nothing
in common"). But it is interesting to detect another symptom of paralogism
manifested in the ignorance of the semantic weight and potential of the terms used.

"Fiction" is derived from *fictus*, the past participle of *fingere*: to feign. Its suffix, like that of action, reflection, or abortion, classifies it originally among actional substantives. Like many other substantives of this sort, it has come to denote the result of the action too, but an actional quality remains, at least as a connotation. "Reality," on the other hand, is derived from *res*, thing, through the adjective "real"; it signifies, not an action or its result, but the constitutive property of that which is a thing (= "thingness"). Etymologically, then, "fiction" signifies something like: "Someone simulates = acts on something" (and thus, presumably, on others), whereas "reality" says; "Something has the quality of a thing." How can you relate these two terms, dissimilar as they are? Or, rather, how is it that they are related by usage?

The missing link, barely implied here, but which makes itself felt more clearly in other parts of the Discourse on fiction, is the common denominator of notions such as imitation, representation, substitution, and simulation. Fiction is an imitation of reality, not its reproduction; reality reproduced is another reality of the same order, dependent on the initial reality. But, if fiction means "feigning" in the framework of imitation-representation, it is an unfaithful or untrue imitation, it is deceptive, it substitutes one simulacrum for another, a third object for a second: this third object is a lie because it is pretended to be the same as reality, or reality itself, while the second confessed its nature of imitation-representation. The fundamental ambiguities of "fiction" (action-enunciation or product-enunciated, an homage to reality or its mockery, functional simulation, or deception, etc.) are revealing about the difficulty of thinking representation and sources of further confusions. But "reality" is not less ambiguous, unless we forget that "things" have only two ways of reaching us, superposed in a logical hierarchy constantly disturbed by culture and experience. We perceive things or their simulacra and *analoga*: to re-present is to produce an effect on the receiver similar in some respect to that produced by the perception of the thing; to reproduce is to produce an identical effect. (Let us observe that "reproduction," of works of art, for instance, has been so frequently used for "imitation" or copy that a new word, "multiple," has had to be coined to mean actual reproduction or, in Benjamin's terms, "mechanical reproduction.") A (re)presenting world is always unactual with regards to the (re)presented world, since (re)presentation is constitutive of the distant actuality of the latter at the expense of the former, but a reproduced world is unauthentic because it is actual.

This semantic excursus was necessary to clear the ground for a new start. Let it be understood that my use of the terms "fiction," "fictionality," "real," "reality," "imaginary," and so on, in the following discussion, is self-defined insofar as (1) I am trying to break away from the sterile philosophical polemics about the "value of fiction" and the "truth of beautiful lies" that have burdened semiotic and sociocritical research for too long, and (2) my use of the concepts seeks to be operational; that is, I want to name and describe operations involved in communication, not define and pinpoint essences. These operations are seen in terms of action, process, and result or effect, but, in order not to triplicate the whole terminology, I have generally condensed the three aspects under a single word, hoping that the aspect discussed at any one time will be readily identified by the reader.

Fictionality concerns a semiotic level that is not that of the relation of signification proper (signifier ↔ signified), but that of reference (signified ↔ referent). By the act and process of referentiation, an information-as-signified is linked with, tied to, or situated in a set of spatiotemporal parameters that constitute the "frame" of the utterance. Reference is the relation established by referentiation in all its forms and complexities.

There are three main types of referentiation, depending on the position of the frame in relation to the textual unit considered. DEIXIS is referentiation to an extratextual Discourse, which will be in general, in a delayed telecommunication, an anonymous but highly codified constellation of texts, actual and potential (*doxa* or common sense, founding myths, history, science, law, . . .). ANAPHORA and CATAPHORA make up intratextual referentiation, from one utterance or group of utterances to another within the same textual unit, whatever its size. INTERTEXTUALITY is referentiation from within one text that integrates some part of another, to this second text or part of it; typical forms of initiation of such a textual network are quotation, allusion, erudite "reference," and stylistic imitation.

Referentiation is the operation by which signifieds belonging to different textual areas are related. Reference is to referentiation what significance is to signification, the result of a process of globalization.

Fictional reference is the operation that leads to a compromise formation between conflicting references.

Doreen Maitre's claim that "[fictional worlds of fantasy] function by bringing together disparate fields of discourse"[12] can thus be generalized. Fictional reference resembles polysemy structurally in that it activates a latent plurality and makes it efficient instead of trying to get rid of it, but it is not an aspect of polysemy because it concerns the fate of the same signification in different universes of discourse and universes of belief. The point needs to be illustrated. When I write:

> La nuit chaude Aurore coule autour de toi
> Lente comme miel autour d'une abeille morte[13]

> [The warm night Aurora flows around you
> Slow like honey flows around a dead bee]

the word "Aurora" is polysemic insofar as it can mean "dawn" (morn, daybreak, sunrise) or a woman bearing (or not) this first name. Now, whether you choose one of these signifieds or the other, or choose not to choose between them, each of them is polyreferential: Are you going to use the signified [woman] as working in a world that you hold as "real" (your own or that of the author, for example) or in a world that you hold as unreal (the worlds of dream, mythological personifications, symbolist "symbols," etc.)? Are you going to use the signified "dawn" in the "context" of your own experience of sunrise, in Nebraska or New Mexico maybe, of my supposed experience of sunrise, in Catalonia, Sydney, or Paris, or in that of a collective, transhistoric notion in which the cliché of rosy-fingered morn would reconcile the two signifieds proposed? "Woman" and "dawn" belong a priori to the same universe of discourse, but the woman *you* have known or imagined by the name of Aurora and the woman I have known by this name on a certain night of March 1983 do *not* belong to the same universes of discourse and belief; one exists in English as the projection of your desire (for instance), and the other exists as a mnemonic image — aural, visual, olfactory, and tactile — verbalized in Spanish (for instance).

Connotation is not unrelated to polyreference, but it should not be confused with it: it can be either a starter of polyreference or its trace, the shadow cast by it, at the level of signification, but it remains on a different plane, or rather in a different space, like the two-dimensional projection on a plane of a three-dimensional solid. If the rest of the poem quoted from, or your contextual knowledge of my biography, leads you to discard the mythological reference of [Aurora], for example, because the character appears to make more sense as a gypsy woman from Valencia, you may still retain a classical connotation of the name; conversely, the classical connotation of the name, strengthened by the mellifluent notation applicable to poetic language, etc., may trigger off the mythological reference that will compete with the world of contemporary Spain.

FICTIONALITY is the result of fictional reference (one of its possible results). *Fictional reference takes place in the framework of comparatio*, or, more precisely, *it is a COMPARATIVE POLYREFERENCE*. The signified is referred not to a single "object" but to at least two different objects belonging to worlds ruled by different laws of truth, value, and relevance.

In our contemporary Western cultures, one of the basic worlds of reference is posited as IMAGINARY and another as REAL.

Consequently, without taking into account, for the time being, possible consequences for utterances originated in a text submitted to the literary regime of reading, we suggest that a set of worlds may presently include, for any reader-receiver, at least two subsets of the following types:

"A," whose items have the property p_1 of existing independently of the idea that the reader-receiver may form of them, and the property p_2 of existing independently of their being named or mentioned in any text

("Nobody speaks of it,; nobody thinks of it, it is nonetheless true that 'it exists' or that 'it is true' ");
"B," whose items have the properties $-p_1$ of existing only if the reader-receiver forms some idea of them, and $-p_2$ of existing only inasmuch as they are textualized or textualizable.

We shall provisionally call an A-type possible world "real" and a B-type world "imaginary." The insertion of a signified in an A-type world of reference will be a reference to a world considered as real, or, in abbreviation, "real reference." The insertion of a signified in a B-type world of reference will be called "imaginary reference."

In the following discussion and for all practical applications, we should not forget that, however definitionally discrete A and B may seem at the level of analytic premises, they lie much closer in a concrete communication situation like that which allows a reader-receiver to infer a world of messages MW from a textualized world TW. Indeed, any textualized item satisfies $-p_2$ and any item integrated in the production of MW also satisfies $-p_1$, so that p_1 and p_2 cannot be evidenced for the very reason that communication takes place. Rather curiously, it is the assumption of the real that appears as an unprovable — and unfalsifiable — action of the mind, as an act of faith unsupported by the most basic laws of communication. Real reference seems to operate fully under a double illusion: when the text manages to be forgotten (or tolerates it) and the reader-receiver is acted on by a *doxa* that he cannot manipulate or criticize.

Moreover, there are numerous cases of (limited) accessibility between A-type and B-type worlds. Let me list three examples:

1. A character like Julien Sorel, whom I refer to an imaginary possible world (he exists only through Stendhal's text and inasmuch as this text is read and understood), utters about our experiential world assertions that are relevant to it and verifiable or falsifiable in it, that is, referentiable to a world held as real; for example, "I shall be famous in the twentieth century."
2. An anonymous and unknown person existing in the A-type world A_x constructs a B-type world B_y: this world, imaginary for the person in question or in relation to his or her situation, still belongs to A_x for me, since the unknown person really imagines something I do not know.
3. A B-type world, textualized or textualizable (a corpus of law, utopia, or prophecy) at time T_1 can become, in a later state of the system, the description of society A_1, which exists even if I do not know that it does or ignore its structures and its laws.

These phenomena of limited accessibility are characteristic sources of the fallacies of past actuality and the historicist interpretation examined in chapter 1.

But, in order to simplify the first steps of the demonstration, I shall deal with A-type and B-type worlds within MW (at present, the world of referential concretization of a narrative act of communication) as if they were just potentially overlapping—for the purpose of comparison—not possibly embedded in each other, as they seem to be in the cases outlined in the preceding list. Chapter 6 (on enunciation) will clarify one of the origins of such embeddings.

Before we can confront the theory with any actual act of narrative communication, we must stress the scope and importance of *comparatio*, middleman and midwife of fictional (poly)reference, and define it better than the intuitive empirical approach of "the little town of Verrières" had permitted us to do.

Even holistic pragmatic views of fictionality imply a comparative relation, between two illocutionary modes in general. For them "the writer puts out imitation speech acts *as if* they were being performed by someone."[14] This formulation is grossly inadequate, to the point of contradiction per se, and Thomas Pavel has successfully argued that "the distinction between pretended and genuine acts often becomes blurred in relation to fiction,"[15] but it remains significative of the deepest core of fictionality, which rarely escapes the attention of even the most obtuse philosophers.

I use the Latin word *comparatio* for two reasons: first, to distinguish the general principle of a mental activity from the mere "figure of speech by proximity [*par rapprochement*]" called comparison or simile; second, to evoke by paronomasia the French word *comparution*, appearance before a court of justice, usually as a result of summoning (*citation*), since *comparatio* brings forth referents together. For Fontanier, *comparatio* is the very principle of all thought, the operation on which judgment rests: judgment consists in sanctioning, positively or negatively, the comprehension suggested by *comparatio*. One or more judgments, corresponding to as many clauses, are grouped into a thought, single or complex, which corresponds to a sentence:

> In comparing [a *substantive* idea and a *concrete* idea], we see whether there is conformity, or, in other words, coexistence between them; whether the concrete idea exists in the substantive idea, is part of it, is an element of it; and consequently, whether it has to be affirmed or negated.[16]

Fontanier is not quite sure of the spatial representation of compatibility between ideas; the space in which the initial comparative connection, the predicative relation takes place, is naturally variable in extension because it tends to be confused with referential space, governed by "things" or "extants," not signs. Fontanier's grammar is already implicitly transformational, but it has a strong ontological foundation: the only real verb for him is "to be," so that all predicates are definitional or explicative in essence. *Comparatio*, as the general principle of an approach of being through the manipulation of ideas, is unfortunately dissociated from the structurally similar principle of the operations that modalize expression, seen as subjective interferences guided less by truth than by pragmatic considerations. But it would be possible and rewarding to follow the manifestations of *comparatio* from the analytic moment of predication, through simple tropes right up to some of the most ambitious types of *dispositio* on a large textual scale. We would then realize that it is active in at least five phases of verbal communication, whose responding equivalents are found at both ends of the enunciation-reception chain: comparison of signifiers with signifieds, of signifieds between them, of signifieds with referents, of referents between them, and of figures between them. Hypersemanticization, narrative discourse and polysemy, referentiation, polyreference, and textual significance could all be described as transformations prepared by the corresponding operations of *comparatio*.

Comparatio is the driving force behind a large number of figures: the tropes by resemblance or metaphors, metaphoric syllepsis, the so-called figures of speech (personification, allegory, subjectivation, allegorism, and mythologism), comparison *stricto sensu*, antithesis and parallel; litote and antiphrasis could be added to this list without distortion. Antithesis and syllepsis are particularly interesting for understanding the construction of narrative meaning (much more than metonymy, even granted the semantic relevance of contiguity, which is not obvious). "Antithesis opposes two objects to each other, as considered in one common respect, or an object to itself, as considered in two contrary respects."[17]

One can note, first of all, that *a narrateme results from the particular kind of comparison or antithesis of an object with itself, which spans a temporal break or caesura.* Barthes writes in *S/Z* that "antithesis is a wall without a doorway. Leaping this wall is a transgression. . . . a breaching of the Wall . . . produces a catastrophe: there is an explosive shock, a paradigmatic conflagration."[18] The conflagration, I believe, can take two different forms: the permanent fusion or mutual embedding of opposites (the oxymoron), stable instability, unvarying imbalance, which is the poetic (lyric) solution,[19] or narrative metamorphosis, the figure of change in time. Fontanier, had he not systematically avoided narrative or reduced it to description, would have been able to explain it in the conceptual framework of his own rhetoric. Syllepses and other figures such as antanaclasis (which is to syllepsis what simile is to metaphor) also describe the status of the subject of a narrative predication—which is and is not, in the total time span considered, that which is propositionally predicated of it. But they are also the typical forms of articulation between the symbolic and proairetic codes (in Barthes's terminology) or, if you prefer, between narrative and symbolic syntaxes (see chapter 7, in the third section).

All of the preceding figures or groups of figures are associated with a group of notions variously labeled resemblance, conformity, analogy, similarity, dissimilarity, and difference, but, across the whole spectrum, it is impossible not to recognize the constant recourse to a *comparandum*, a "concrete" point of comparison (in Fontanier's sense). What varies from one group of figures to another is, more than the scope of the figures ("in one word" or more, etc.), the mode of operation of *comparatio* in relation to *comparandum* and the nature of the *marker* of this *comparatio*. In metaphor, metaphorical syllepsis and parallel, resemblance and difference are supposed to preexist the production of the figure, but it is not clear whether they are properties of the signs or of the referents. In figures of fictional expression, resemblance is artificial; it is an effect of the figure itself. In comparison, it is already there but as if it were not, and it is produced, but as if naturally. Comparison and antithesis have a heuristic or maieutic function; they combine novelty and accuracy, just like fictional worlds do when they are considered by their theorists as "a special case of the more general phenomenon of *innovative thought*."[20] Only in comparison, it seems, does there exist a specific, lexically present marker that plays a syntactic role, while in antithesis and parallel, this marker consists of (1) the meaning of the syntagms brought together, and (2) the syntactic relation of these syntagms. In all other figures, *comparatio* is prompted by the obligation for the receiver to make a semantic or a referential choice and/or attempt a semic displacement on the paradigmatic axis. Metaphoric syllepsis, once again, is special in the sense that this last, implicit type of marker combines with another corresponding to the syntactic role of the figure. Thus there are syntactic markers, paradigmatic markers, and combined markers, but also implicit and explicit markers, and some more evident than others in both categories.

The neoclassical rhetoric of Fontanier is an almost complete toolbox for disassembling the machinery of fictional polyreference in order to understand the subtle diversity of its workings and effects, including the pathological aspects of its uses. But, in order not to be overwhelmed by the magnitude of the task, we should provisionally take into account a limited number of variables, for example, the structure of the *comparandum*, the quality and efficiency of the marker of *comparatio*, and a binary set of possible worlds of reference. Thus, in our early example, "The little town of Verrières can pass for one of the nicest in Franche-Comté," the relevant types are "imaginary reference" and "real reference"; the *comparandum* is "presence of names in the Discourse of geography"; and the marker of comparison is implicit and combined. *Comparatio* can treat the *comparandum* (point of comparison, in respect to which references are compared and their validity tested) either as a bipolar axis on which all or certain relative degrees are possible, or as a paradigm strictly ruled by the incompatibility of the terms related in binary opposition. For example, the existence or nonexistence of a city in a particular nation, in modern geographical Discourse, is a question that can only be answered by yes or no, but the historicity of "Christ" or that of a remark or a joke made by a political leader at a private reunion can be almost infinitely nuanced. Double reference or polyreference, on the other hand, is a matter of *truth-value of the propositions considered in the relevant possible worlds*. Since this operation takes place in a comparative frame work, its terms, in any case, are not mutually exclusive a priori; they can only become so as it results from a choice informed by *comparatio*.

As we use it here, the notion of possible world has its recent origin in logical semantics, from which it started to be transferred to literary semantics about a decade ago by various authors, among them Thomas Pavel[21] and Lubomir Doležel, who writes:

> As far as literary theory is concerned, the main interest of the seman-
> tics of possible worlds lies in the fact that it offers a solution to the
> problem of fictional reference [*référence fictive*]. Since reference is the
> main function of the sign, that is the relation between sign and the
> world [*le rapport du signe au monde*], we must necessarily assign an
> area of reference to literature as a semiotic system. The semantics of
> possible worlds provides this area by its affirmation that the sign refers
> to a multiplicity of possible worlds rather than to one only, namely, the
> present real world [*le monde actuel*].[22]

Nevertheless, we must understand that the plurality of possible worlds of refer-ence is *not* the consequence of the structure of literary texts or a sheer by-product of the *literary* regime of reception, it is simply a fact of all complex acts of com-munication that is enhanced and maintained active longer in an artistic regime than in others: we could repeat about polyreference the same observations already made about polysemy.

Possible worlds are not arbitrary clusters of items, unless they are so defined. They are rule governed and their mutual relations are basically of three types: *identity or nonidentity of their domains*, a criterion of "alternativity" or function by which a certain set of items or "population" is assigned to each world; sym-metrical or asymmetrical *accessibility* (for instance, a world to come is in princi-ple accessible from a present world, but not vice versa); *copossibility* or not of worlds having the same relation to the "world of reference," that is, in this sense, the "real world," for example. If we take the utterance: "Once upon a time there was a king called Goody; everybody loved him because he was good," this utter-ance can be true in several worlds defined according to their domains: in W_1 where p_1 (p_1 = there is only one king), in W_2 where p_2 is true (p_2 = there are several kings), in W_3 where p_3 is true (p_3 = everybody is a king), but not in W_4 where p_4 is the case (p_4 = nobody is king). Similarly, it is acceptable in worlds where one person only is good, where several people are good, and where every-body is good, although the relevance or informativeness of the statement decreases, but not in a world where p_8 = nobody is good. Worlds where p_4 and

p_8 are true can certainly be conceived, but they are not compatible with the MW in which "There was a good king" can be true. A world where Franche-Comté is an actual province and one where Verrières is a little town of Franche-Comté or Ernest-Jean Sarrasine is the only son of a lawyer of Franche-Comté and the grandson of a farmer of Saint-Dié[23] are not copossible, although the latter is accessible from the former. But the population of signifiers of a dream world and that of a scientific world can be identical, although the rules of organization and the motivations and signifieds of these signifiers may be different, as Freud demonstrated about the famous injection dream.[24] Mutually translatable languages would be worlds with identical populations of signifieds, symmetrical accessibility, and copossibility with regards to the "real world" at large.

We can now rewrite the last part of our definition as follows: *Fictional polyreference relates identical signifieds to at least two different possible worlds*. This operation is not always successful, but fictional reception consists in attempting it.

Genres of Fictionality

Why is fictional reference generally attempted by the receiver in narrative communication? There are two kinds of answers to this question: some will show the profits derived from the operation, as we are going to attempt, while others envisage deep — perhaps transhistoric — anthropological motivations.

In narrative communication the present is most elusive and the nonpresent is necessarily split into halves related to each other in binary opposition (past and future). The criteria of discrimination between past and future are not as simple as they seem to be; they would be simple without memory or prospective imagination, in which case, there would be no past or future. The discrimination proliferates into intricate sets of rules that govern past and future like discrete possible worlds: the interferences between tense, mood, and voice systems in many languages bear witness to the complexity and efficiency of these rules of which grammar has become the repository. This discrimination can be seen as a model for that between otherwise defined possible worlds. Narrative communication must bring together and compare past and future worlds in order to manifest *and* cancel their difference by thrusting to the foreground the *comparanda* they share.

It is said that narrative is of the past, but I am not even sure that this makes sense. The argument that science fiction stories are written in the past tenses although they refer to a world that lies ahead of us, if it lies anywhere, is at best a weak one. True, we read, in an "Editor's note" at the beginning of Gene Roddenberry's *Star Trek*, "Clearly, public respect for Starfleet would have been seriously imperiled by anything reminiscent of the horrors that grew out of the politicizing of behavior control implants and which led to the bloody Mind Control

Revolts of 2043–7,"[25] but the ever-spreading use of the future and immediate future tenses in historical Discourse would be a complete aberration if we did not have a better principle of explanation than the intrinsic time bias of narrative. "[In the Italy of 1918] this double failure is going to pave the way to Fascism"[26] makes perfect sense because the treatment of time by narrative discourse is necessarily metaleptic (the enunciator inscribes in the verb tense a deliberate position between a before and an after that permits the construction of narrative meaning). Similarly, Roddenberry's past 2043 is past not only in relation to events presented in *Star Trek* but also, like these events themselves, in relation to the temporal center of interest of science fiction, which is *absolutely* future (with regards to *any* present, ours or that of all events depicted). Nevertheless, granting that narrative communication requires more consistent mnemonic exercises than some other types and that it tends to dress up in the trappings of Memory, mother of the Muses, even when it makes a mockery of her, it will be very legitimately obsessed with problems of verification and experimentation whose solution will be sought in polyreference, by default of existential authentification.

If the fundamental matrix of narrative communication is bio- and phylographic, as I have suggested, the displacement of reference from world to world is—as in the dreamwork—a crucial condition for the return of the repressed.[27] A "purely" imaginary reference would drag us away toward the high-risk zone of solipsism, and a "purely" real reference would lead us toward the equally dangerous zone of a world without a tomorrow. We have to move back and forth between imaginary and real reference so that the sun may rise again and be at once the same as yesteryear and another, never seen before.

These considerations do not entail that fictionality manifest itself about all narratogenic texts with the same intensity or the same success under all circumstances. Besides referential valences and the more or less textualized markers of *comparatio*, there are cultural factors in the reception situation, as well as intersubjective and subjective factors (idiosyncratic or not) that influence the fictionalization process in such a way that it can never be exactly the same twice. Imaginary reference is the corollary of fantasy and creativity, the madwomen in the house, and, if this style of reference is informed by early childhood experience and subsequent storical developments that no two individuals can share in their totality (see the conflict of interpretations between the Goytisolo brothers), it will logically appear as a domain of infinite variation. But neither are the features of the Real World (the world held as real) diachronically constant and uniform throughout a given society: two or more Reals are often competing for supremacy or exclusive acceptance, or they are sometimes loosely juxtaposed, as in vast sectors of the contemporary Western world. Our societies are economically and strategically anti-Christian and legally agnostic, which does not prevent them from favouring religiosity in a large "cultural" and aesthetic sector, including sexual morality, advertising, and propriety in public speech.

With all these reservations in mind, it is still possible and useful to determine *genres of fictionality*, that is, types and models of text-bound polyreference that form more or less durable categories of the mind and empower narrative communication for extra- or supranarrative functions and goals (see chapter 10). In order to present a systematic, intelligible construction, I have been led to make some drastic simplifications and some very bold assumptions.

1. The space of (contemporary) fictionality is crossed by two axes, one on which directives of *comparatio* can be located according to their status, scope, and force, and another that extends on one side toward the final reign of imaginary reference (or at least a disambiguation of polyreference to its advantage) and, on the other side, toward the final reign of real reference.

2. The space of fictionality is theoretically saturated; although some of the positions determined by the combination of parameters may be repressed while a few others play a leading role in a particular state of the milieu, each genre of fictionality works in association with and contradistinction to all the others, whether or not they are effectively actualized in the milieu; for example, the realist genre of fictionality should always be seen as a habitual opponent and exceptional, unexpected ally of the marvelous, even if the marvelous is or seems to be virtually banned from the milieu, and realism is not the same when the marvelous coexists with it in the milieu or when it is an outcast.

As I lack space to carry out a thorough study of each genre and I can tackle just three examples in some detail, a diagram and two lists of rankings will be presented instead. In the diagram, the farther one goes to the left of the vertical median, the closer one gets to an exclusive resolution of polyreference in favor of the Imaginary, and the farther one moves to the right, the closer one comes to the exclusive domination of the Real. Yet no act of narrative communication can ever reach either of these poles. Imaginary and Real monoreferences are poles of attraction and poles of repulsion at the same time. In a milieu like that of late twentieth-century American higher education, so-called ungrammatical utterances, like "green ideas sleep furiously," or those that violate the principle of noncontradiction, will have a strong tendency to be referred to an imaginary possible world, but there will always remain some traces of Real reference, because both the Establishment and its critics need to disturb rationality. Let us then consider seriously the truth-value of "Me white mothers was a black man," or, "Not one of the ten people killed in the accident was injured."

On the vertical axis, the upward vector takes us closer to perpetual, compulsory, exacerbated *comparatio*, and the downward vector leads tendentially to a total prohibition of *comparatio*, but neither of these goals is eventually reached. What happens in the lower sectors of the diagram is that we compare against the grain, against instructions given by the text in relation to the milieu: *comparatio* tends to be scamped, ephemeral, and partial due to the sanctions that await us if we persist (not only our enjoyment but our very comprehension of the text can be cut short). In the higher regions of the diagram, by contrast, the productivity of the act of communication will be reduced if we do not compare on and on, as thoroughly as possible. The point of intersection of the IR and CϵC∞ axes, the point of origin of all vectors is the locus of an ideal neutrality and indeterminacy where Imaginary and Real references would be balanced and limited and *comparatio* dialectically carried out. It should be evident that this point, like the poles mentioned before, has only a virtual existence and cannot be mathematically located in relation to any actual act of communication or any such act in relation to it; geometric figuration, here, is no more than a practical device to give visual cogency to an abstract mental configuration.

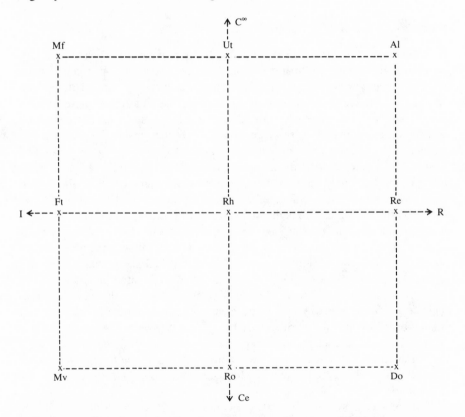

In the two lists that order the nine genres as a function of first one parameter and then the other, 1, 0, and −1 express not actual quantities or status in the linguistic sense but relative values: 1 is a tendency toward the maximum possible in the system, −1 toward the minimum, and 0 a supposed average. Combined fractional, intermediate values like 0.5 or −0.5 would permit us to multiply the genres at will and more precisely describe actual operations of polyreference and their effects. Rehearsal, therefore, despite its central position in the diagram, is not, in principle, a special problem.

GENRES	C	R		GENRES	R	C
Marvelous (Mv)	-1	1		Marvelous (Mv)	-1	-1
Romantic (Ro)	-1	0		Fantastic (Ft)	-1	0
Documentary (Do)	-1	1		Metafiction (Mf)	-1	1
Fantastic (Ft)	0	-1		Romantic (Ro)	0	-1
Rehearsal (Rh)	0	0		Rehearsal (Rh)	0	0
Realism (Re)	0	1		Utopia (Ut)	0	0
Metafiction (Mf)	1	-1		Documentary (Do)	1	-1
Utopia (Ut)	1	0		Realism (Re)	1	0
Allegory (Al)	1	1		Allegory (Al)	1	1

Some Remarks on the Diagram and Listings

1. *Names and realism.* As I said earlier, the kind of narrative text that literary historians will usually call "realist" makes a particuliar use of proper names. Such texts embed as *designata* the signifieds of names not attested by the certifying Discourses (or attested with different *designata*) in those of attested names that do not change contents, except for this "detail" foregrounded in the narrative concerned (e.g., "Verrières in Franche-Comté"). Or they make attested and not-attested names coexist in an attested semantic space, like José Fago and Zumalacarregui in the *episodio nacional* number 21 by Benito Pérez Galdós. The result is approximately the same, since this structure signifies: "José Fago lived in a world characterized, among other relevant features, by the actions of rebel General Zumalacarregui." Yet the realist text is not the only one that uses proper names in similar fashion; name-induced realist and documentary subsystems, for example, may compete with others in any textual unit. Although the proper name should not be held as a "rigid designator," its deictic and intertextual powers are greater than those of most other words; it activates referentiation and reference more promptly because of the relative weakness of its paradigmatic location, which excludes pure antonymy, and because it is not polysemous in the sense that other words are, having in principle, although not always, a one-to-one relation with its signified. French theorists in particular[28] have recently dedicated a great deal of attention to various aspects of onomastics and toponymy in narrative.[29] The influence of Proust's own concern for names has probably been considerable, if not determinant.[30]

"The reference system (the text, the collection of texts) to which the proper name belongs, represents its truth," wrote Charles Grivel.[31] But what is this system, when I refer fictionally? It is not unimportant that it is always double or rather dual, whatever the "text," whatever the size of the "collection of texts" considered (text-induced possible worlds). Emma Bovary is the product of Flaubert's and my own imagination (composition); the name denotes a character who has no birth certificate and whom nobody has ever physically known, but "she" is (named) as if she had been known, a Galatea for any Pygmalion. "She" has become a model, a stereotype and a prototype for future visions of living and dead women, almost a common name; yet this model could not be "embodied" so perfectly by any other than "herself," had she but existed: I attempt her reference through the gadgets of the Real (historical documents and monuments), I oscillate between Imaginary and Real reference; I compare them; I always return, however reluctantly, to the Imaginary (the reference discussed here is not that of the novel *Madame Bovary*, but that of the character; also for Joan of Arc in the novel *Jeanne d'Arc*, by Joseph Delteil, and so on). I shall never undertake to meet Madame Bovary anywhere else than in my mind, I can only play with her reality.

2. *Of "historical" resemblance.* But what of Napoleon in Victor Hugo, in Stendhal? And Joan of Arc, in Delteil, in my readings of Delteil? We stole her from history, chronicles, testimonials, archives, thus rendering her worth cheating and elusive like a Mona Lisa. We attempt imaginary reference on her actions ("let us suppose for a moment that she did not exist, or that she never left Domrémy") and almost succeed; we oscillate between imaginary and real reference; we compare them: Joan of Arc, born in Domrémy and burned at the stake, was more or less seductive, more or less virginal, and so on, than Delteil's, Dreyer's, Chapelain's, or Bresson's Joans of Arc; we probably return more often to the Real, to the texts of the scribes. In Jensen's *Gradiva*, in contrast, it is the lack of documentation about the "historical" Gradiva that makes Norbert Hanold opt finally for Zoe Bertgang. With Madame Bovary as with Joan of Arc, every turn of reference is only provisionally final; the oscillation between the two types of references remains interminable in principle. *Fictional reference explores and deepens the irreducible gap of resemblance between a referent posited as real and a referent posited as imaginary.*

3. *Impediments to comparatio.* Neither Madame Bovary nor Joan of Arc, at least in the texts mentioned, flies over the mountains or changes into a plastic plesiosaurus. They share enough features with our set descriptions of people we know "existentially" and characters employed by certifying Discourses, to promote prolonged *comparatio*. But when we read:

> The studio ceiling was thirty feet high, but each leap brought the dancers nearer to it.
> It became their obvious intention to kiss the ceiling.
> They kissed it.
> And then, neutralizing gravity with love and pure will, they remained suspended in air inches below the ceiling, and they kissed each other for a long, long time.[32]

it is clear that our comparatist activity is at the same time necessary and severely handicapped. It is necessary to appreciate the hyperbolic ability of the dancers, which would not be extraordinary at all in a world of very light, twenty-feet-tall people; but it is also repressed, for fear that the reader's "suspension of disbelief" does not stretch far enough to accept, in any world, the neutralization of physical laws such as gravity — said to apply *there* — by "love and pure will." The genre of fictionality of the passage quoted can be situated for the present-day reader somewhere between the marvelous and the fantastic.

In fact, *comparatio* can never be canceled out; real and imaginary references can only be practiced in relation to each other. If there were no *comparatio*, there would be no reference at all, and, without the horizon of reference, the signification process would also lose its *raison d'être*, the text would revert to gibberish for the receiver. When *comparatio* is difficult or prohibited by the text or the milieu, its results are modified in curious, unexpected ways. The documentary (e.g., "nonfiction" novels and "true stories") provides all the means of comparison and verification, like most modern historiography, so that the reader will *not* have to carry out this task freely by himself. Realist authors and film producers often state — either by irony or preterition — that "any resemblance between the characters and events described in this work and actual persons or real facts, is purely coincidental." This warning is meant to stimulate curiosity; it has become so much a typical sign of the *roman à clefs* that it has worn out to the point of discouraging *comparatio* when real reference readily presents itself, and supporting it when it is least obvious. But there are some genres, such as metafiction, utopia, and allegory, that cannot function without intensive *comparatio*, because their finality is highly didactic and conative: the receiver must *train* to apply their teachings in his real world, following the cognitive principles of experimental science or those of Pascal's wager.

Three Brief Examples

Gregor Samsa, the protagonist of Kafka's *Metamorphosis* is (like?) an insect, but the marker of *comparatio* lies in the work of the semes that permit us to utter without unacceptable contradiction the apparent oxymoron: "The man Gregor Samsa, formerly a traveling salesman, is an insect." The so-called myth of metamorphosis, even with the drastic modifications it incurs in Kafka, appears as the transparently narrative means of making mutually inaccessible worlds coexist on the same communicational continuum without revolutionizing the reference systems that apply respectively to the before and the after. Narrative records the opposition of these systems and solves the problem of their persistence by its own "magic," courtesy of the very moment of change, abandoned exclusively to imaginary reference. A resemblance, after all, is nothing but a shared difference: the monstrous son of Don Jerónimo, in José Donoso's *Obscene Bird of Night*, cannot resemble the monsters by whom he is exclusively surrounded, because he cannot differ *with them* from other human beings. Comparison can only take place outside, and the outside, in this textual world, is rejected to an ever-increasing distance, behind ever-thicker walls: its sign is buried deeper and deeper inside. In fact, the process of totalization that is inseparable from the construction of thematic and aesthetic coherence must always face the risk of becoming totalitarian.

The story of Hervas, in Potocki's *Avadoro*, reminds us that narrative meaning is also destructive and serves to smash—perhaps in the name of a higher necessity, but that is not the point here—the fortress of referential security that each work tends to build at its periphery by solidifying and stratifying its own encyclopedia (self-provided "context"). After fifteen years and forty-five thousand hours of work, Hervas had completed his *summa* in Madrid; before leaving for a holiday in his birthplace, he has the one hundred volumes bound and classifies them side by side on the same shelf, "from the first, which was Universal Grammar, to the hundredth, which was Analysis."[33] On his return he discovers that hungry rats, which never visited his foodless house before, have played havoc with the whole collection. After fainting at this sight, he soon marries his nurse. His son tells the story:

> I was born, and my mother survived only a few hours to that of my
> birth. Hervas had never known love or friendship except by a definition
> of these two emotions that he had placed in his sixty-seventh volume.
> The loss of his wife proved to him that he was made to feel friendship
> and love; it overwhelmed him more than the loss of his hundred tomes
> *in octavo* eaten away by the rats. (p. 249)

Rehearsal is perhaps, of all the genres of fictionality, the one that fights most tenaciously against referential closure and fixation, but does it succeed?

Rehearsal

> The work of Marguerite Duras obliges us to venture into sensuality, the
> immediacy of the never-seen *déjà connu*, to swim timidly, delightfully
> in a Ganges that has flowed on our doorstep ever since the geography
> books of our childhood. . . . We swim in a Ganges whose origin,
> length, and picturesque scenery we can at last forget, remembering only
> its water, constantly flowing here, about our reading body; and your
> body reading silently with me, beside the words too, to which sense
> and nonsense are almost equally spared.[34]

How difficult it is, from now on, to speak a language definitely other than this one, which has become (forever!) ours with Duras. She has cut chatter to the quick, leaving ever-wider patches of silence instead, so wide indeed that they are invisible, and the clearing points to a forest in the distance. I do not need to show it to you, you can see the rye field, the room where Tatiana stands naked, wrapped in her hair, the park, the dining room where the hands of Isabelle Granger's friend have not finished clearing the table, and the black car of the Chinese lover. It takes no effort to repeat after Duras; but paraphrase, parody, pastiche, and recitation keep us away from the true dynamics of this world of communication, satisfy us with its mere tinsel. Without an analysis of Duras's method of reference, we soon find ourselves back among the order and balance of the perfect moment that Lol V. Stein laboriously rebuilds to exclude herself from it.

"Lol V. Stein was born here at S. Thala." "Lol V. Stein" sounds American because of the middle initial, but "S. Thala" is not formed like the name of any city in the world. S. Thala, consequently, cannot be *here* for any person within a Discourse of Reality; it is formed like an anthroponym. Lol V. Stein was born, remains born "here" in a nonplace/person. Realizable, referable to the Real, she is born in an imaginary world; the deictic "here" drives us with her into universal liminality (a threshold, a margin, the edge of nowhere in guise of now-here):

> The essence of liminality is to be found in its release from normal constraints, making possible the deconstruction of the "uninteresting" constructions of common sense . . . into cultural units which may be reconstructed in novel ways. . . . Liminality is the domain of the "interesting" or of "uncommon sense."[35]

It thus shows the same productive ambiguity as formalist defamiliarization, but inscribes it *ex officio* in social Discourse rather than attributing it to individual aesthetic constructions.

"Lol V. Stein was born here at S. Thala. . . . She has a brother, nine years older than her—I have not known him—he is said to live in Paris."[36] S. Thala and Paris coexist in the world of the enunciator. For this enunciator, S. Thala is here and Paris elsewhere. Since I cannot accept the truth of the utterance under real reference, I could consider selecting Paris or Minneapolis as *my* "here." But Paris does not, in principle, fulfill the requirements of imaginary reference, and it is juxtaposed with S. Thala in the same group of utterances. The text adduces motivations for a comparison of referential goals, but the comparison, literally, does not lead anywhere; we cannot do better than state the noncompetitive existence in the enunciator's world, of what is present (but not attested) and what is attested (but not present). If opposite referential orientations are not antagonistic, there is little probability that one will eventually supplant the other. This is a world where the possible is present and S. Thala is its capital. The genre of this world in which the not-yet-present is repeated as if it were already here, a world of short-circuited cataphora, is *rehearsal*. Lol V. Stein, retrospectively, is no longer a good candidate for American citizenship, or even a Judeo-Hispanic-German, but neither is she a creature from nowhere. Prospectively, she joins the company of Jean Bedford, Pierre Beugner, Tatiana Karl, and Jacques Hold, in whose cosmopolitanism the Imaginary and the Real hold hands over a margin of irresolution: the characters do not meet or make acquaintance, they always already recognize one another.

Rehearsal works on the not-yetness and the already-gone-byness of the present. This mode of unpresentation jumps over itself to become the "memory of the future" (and prevision of the past). Not for this only does it have an oxymoronic structure, since, more radically, it presents, actualizes all the nonpresent that it discovers in the present. And the oxymoronic structure—a factor of "poetic" awareness—threatens to pave the way for a mystique:

She is beautiful. It is invisible.
Does she know it?
—No, no.
The voice dies away toward the door of the forest.
Nobody answers. It is the same sharp, almost brutal voice.[37]

Let us consider commonsense beauty, in which we have little faith: this is the visible. A beauty that is seen, ruled by light, framed, denied (defiled), and outlined, is pure text, equal to what is said and thought of it: imaginary. Let us get rid of the beholder: "it is invisible." Beauty now exists in an absolute sphere: Reality (independent from the idea that we can form of it). Reality motivates the Discourses of Reality; they seek it and aim at it. But what difference is there then, between a nonexperimental, or even a nonexperiential, nonexistential, subjectless Reality, and the subjectless Discourse that the subject of the dream proffers to himself without addressing himself, that is, imaginary self-communication? The oxymoron turns the back-and-forth movement of polyreference into a spiral so fast that it abolishes the perception of movement. Reference itself becomes invisible, unconscious, or impeded, and its default can hinder retroactively the process of signification. Nevertheless, the oxymoron may be more apparent than real at the second turn of the screw: the "door of the forest" does not necessarily imply that inside *is* outside, but that inside is the outside of outside, the other of the other. Here we find again the creative negation of negation that does not confuse times but rather places itself always ahead of the time flow.

In *Détruire dit-elle*, Max Thor teaches history, the history "of the future," he says, which is about nothing ("I have forgotten all knowledge"), and many of his students fall asleep in the classroom. But he encounters Alissa, the mad girl, the forerunner who was, is, and always will be eighteen. There is no reason to speak of intemporality, of the destruction of the temporal framework of narrative. In fact, the history of the future is a world of reference in which Imaginary and Real remain distinct, but they overlap much more than in the present or in the past. Scientific prevision refers through the Discourses of Reality, libidinal prevision through those of the Imaginary. But if prevision is a program of action built on and with uncertainty, which seeks to retain in actuality the pleasure of the possible, then it is formed on the threshold of the two modes of reference; it gains its credit from the shuttle service it offers in their space of intersection. Thus there is still narrative meaning because the universal is found in each moment, and one single scene is exemplary of all stories. This story takes place here, at S. Thala:

> Beyond the dike, another town, far beyond, inaccessible, another town, blue in color, which becomes spotted with electric lights. And then, other towns, more and more towns: the same ones.[38]

Cities of the interior. Elsewhere exists, but it is concealed here, it is so evident that it dazzles us. What happens here is universal, not because it happens everywhere, but because it is unique, uniquely the other of otherness. Here, then, has always been elsewhere, but we did not know it. Rehearsal is not the fantastic, which unsettles our here and now, nor the marvelous, which negates it. Rehearsal refuses to forget the possibility of that which is and, in its curious fashion, it narrativizes any ontic assertion: "Mother death" or "the disease of death" presides. Death becomes operative to change each moment and each being into itself. Being here, which was, as a given, the worst impediment to being, becomes the means and aim of movement and change, the adequate response to the until now invisible lack of being of every being. (We recognize, in passing, ideological motives that Ernst Bloch and the Frankfurt school have made familiar.) The music that arrives victoriously at the end of *Détruire*, breaking down all obstacles, is a fugue. The oxymoron of rehearsal struggles in the embrace of temporality, forces it to give its best and penetrates as a conqueror and a discoverer deep into this alienated heart of darkness, which the certifying Discourses of Reality impose on us. The quest of truth is substituted for by the interminable exploration of the forest of ignorance; there is no *return* to order, because there has never been any order here, governed as here has been by the disorder of Law.

Although rehearsal shows certain structural affinities with other communicational practices such as the mystic orison, magic realism,[39] and *Creacionismo* (Huidobro's doctrine of poetry), to name a few, it differs from them because it is based on the generative power of unlimited negativity, initiated in modern art by Mallarmé and Duchamp, a power that has become available only when the death of God was no longer a loss or a model of loss. Rehearsal reverses completely the mystic position of Saint Teresa, for example:

> Entonces vaya enhorabuena: dichosa tal pérdida que es para gozar más de lo que nos parece se pierde; porque entonces . . . el alma . . . goza de lo que no pudiera también gozar, si no fuera perdiéndose a sí, para, como digo, más ganarse.[40]

> [Lo then, oh joy: Lucky such a loss that is to enjoy more that which we seem to lose; for then . . . the soul enjoys that which it could not enjoy so much, if it were not losing itself in order, as I have said, to gain itself better.]

Nevertheless rehearsal manipulates the *Logos* in such a way, pushes it so to its limits that it is bound to trust it as it deconstructs it. Metafiction puts forward a different attitude in this respect, but we can wonder how far it can try the patience of language without being knocked back into place, that is, into banality.

Metafiction

Metafiction will not be taken here in the limited sense of American avant-garde literature integrated by such figures as Barth, Barthelme, Brautigan, and Coover, who have won increasing acceptance lately and would deserve more extensive studies than those that currently exist.[41] Nor shall I take it in the sense of all the manifestations of "self-reflexivity" whatsoever to be found in narrative texts, manifestations that have been rather thoroughly and sometimes tediously explored, particularly in France since the 1960s[42] under the influence of formalist ideology and a common deviation of structuralism. I wish to avoid the simplistic monosemic reduction of Wallace Stevens's famous phrase "Poetry is the subject of the poem," which can by no means signify "Literature is the object of narrative."

Let us call metafiction the *system of polyreference that incites us textually to raise polyreference to the power of 2 or more*. An intratextual commentary, either seemingly literal or figural (metaphorical, ironical, etc.) compares the scope and truth-value of the assertions of the text as referred to different possible worlds. Or yet some intertextual device makes separate textual units work as commentaries of each other in this respect. Naturally, the commentary in its turn at once evokes or actualizes alternate texts and constitutes a new object of polyreference. Whether or not the text thematizes this second operation in its turn, the spiral of the textualization of fictionality has received the impulse that allows us to prolong it with all the prolixity we are able to invest in the game. It is still widely believed that this accumulation of strata of fictionality causes the reader to lose sight of "referentiality" (that is, in a partisan sense, real reference) altogether, probably because this belief provides an easy argument to all those who want modern (and baroque) art to be nonmimetic, nonrepresentational, turned inward, and so on, either to extol it or to loathe it. While Jean Ricardou pitted the adventure of narrative against the narrative of adventure and the life of the text against the text of life,[43] Xavier Rubert de Ventós, in 1963, regretted that, in the artistic film, "the expression *of* the picture [was] replacing expression *by* the picture."[44] Nevertheless, later semiotic and phenomenological studies of the metafictional process have since conclusively proved that metafiction, far from being at the service of art for art's sake, pure, gratuitous art, and similar ideals of the ivory tower, holds a critical power of its own.[45] Its provisionally final preference for imaginary reference is the symbol of this critical standpoint, after due consideration has been given, not once but several times, to the effects of real reference.

One of the key devices of metafiction in *Tristram Shandy* is digression; it functions as a "self-generative mechanism" because it is reputed to be incompatible with a well-told, straightforward story and, in particular, with the imitation of the supposedly consecutive, "linear" disposition of human life required by the art of biography. Digression, then, needs to be justified or pardoned: the narrator must repeatedly plead for its relevance, its productivity, the many pleasures it affords, and each of these speeches in defense of digression is at the same time a new digression and the source of others. In the first chapters of volume 1, the narrator begs the reader's patience, for appearing to be "somewhat sparing of [his] narrative on [his] first setting out," since he has "undertaken, you see, to write not only [his] life, but [his] opinions also."[46] The narrator pretends that he accepts a clear-cut division between narrative, on the one hand, and other discourses such as exposition, description, and commentary, on the other, which can become trying in the long run. But, by chapter 22, it has become clear that the diversity of discourse genres is not to be incriminated alone for digression; any anecdote may be as digressive as a description or a philosophical dissertation, if its "point"[47] does not relate easily to the core narrative, the story of Tristram Shandy, Gentleman, him*self*. Then the interpretation of digression takes a new twist:

> For in this long digression which I was accidentally led into . . . there is a master stroke of digressive skill. . . . That though my digressions are all fair . . . yet I constantly take care to order affairs so, that my main business does not stand still in my absence.
> . . . By this contrivance the machinery of my work is of a species by itself; two contrary motions are introduced into it, and reconciled, which were thought to be at variance with each other. In a word, my work is digressive, and it is progressive too, — and at the same time.
> . . . Digressions, incontestably, are the sunshine; — they are the life, the soul of reading.[48]

The resemblance between these considerations and Todorov's reflections on narrative quoted earlier, that "[transformation] is an operation in two directions: it affirms at once resemblance and difference; it puts time into motion and suspends it, in a single movement," is striking. Digression is for Tristram what transformation is for Tzvetan. If digression is, first of all, a distancing artifact, a device that creates semiotic distances ("millions of miles into the very heart of the planetary system") between sequences of the same text, it is also — in form as well as in content — the model of the various analytic operations by which signifier and signified, signified and referent will be unstuck, the "arbitrariness of the sign" and the arbitrariness of reference discovered and put to work. But digression itself is polysemous and polyreferential. It means the "absence" of the writer-protagonist and the presence of another enunciator and another object: in secondary digressions, the enunciated enunciator and the act of writing. In his absence as written, Tristram is "present" in action; digression, referred to the Imaginary through a bold metaphoric leap, becomes a sign of life, an excursus between the nothingness that was before and the nothingness that will be after. By the same token it is reinterpreted, in real reference, as the "life of reading": "Take [digressions] out of this book, for instance, – you might as well take the book along with them; – one cold eternal winter would reign in every page of it" (ibid., p. 95). Digression is "simply" what there is between the beginning and the end of the book, since language is not any more than life *about* what it purports to say.

But why talk of digression, then, if it is so generalized? Sterne's metafiction has one more loop. The hyperbole of "digression which is everything" has an ironic value too: it is self-denouncing. Not all discourse is narrative; digression functions, in relation to the core narrative, both as a discreet, almost secret adjuvant ("my main business does not stand still") and as antinarrative, a delaying procedure against narrative that names and consummates death (writes its sum), against the main business, which is that of dying.

When Nabokov writes of Colette, the autobiographical(?) "forerunner" of Lolita, and her model, in *Speak Memory*: "I had a gold coin that I assumed would pay for our elopement. Where did I want to take her? Spain? America? The mountains above Pau? *Là-bas, là-bas dans la montagne*, as I had heard Carmen sing at the opera,"[49] he knows that fictionality is the mental gesture that attempts to hold together Colette (nine and a half years old) and here in the same world, and fails protractedly; in the same way that narrativity attempts to hold together Colette (nine and a half years old) and Colette (dead many years ago) in the same world, and unfortunately succeeds without delay. Metafiction is, among other things, an intratextual echo (imitation, response, parody, and redundancy) of intertextuality; it seeks to develop a pathos of textual interaction. Sometimes intertextuality strikes back in the least expected way, as when an MLA bibliographer, misreading my article on this topic, lists one of the subjects as "sources in Colette, Gabrielle-Sidonie,"[50] thus "lolitizing" Claudine in a daring anticipation of our nostalgic modernity. Metafiction does not hold Time and real reference at bay; it exposes their traps, so that we know better what we have to come up against, and where to fall. Allegory is not quite as honest about it.

Allegory

> Toujours la mer n'est pas en butte
> Aux ravages des aquilons;
> Toujours les torrents par leur chute
> Ne désolent pas les vallons . . .
> Espère donc avec courage . . .
>
> [Not always is the sea exposed
> To the blasts that play havoc;

> Not always do the torrents by their fall
> Devastate the valleys . . .
> Be brave and do not lose hope.][51]

Tzvetan Todorov hesitates between several definitions of allegory, including those of Quintilian ("the development of a continued metaphor") and Fontanier: "Allegory consists in a proposition with a double meaning: a literal and a spiritual meaning at the same time,"[52] and concludes that "allegory implies the existence of at least two meanings for the same word" and "this double meaning is indicated *explicitly* in the work; it is not dependent on the interpretation (arbitrary or not) of any reader whatsoever."[53] Without arguing about strange meanings that do not need a decoder, let us keep in mind the principle of duality and try to determine at what level of the semiotic process it is operative. Let us recall also the distinction drawn by Fontanier between allegory and allegorism: in the first, the literal meaning subsists, survives interpretation; in the second, which is a developed metaphor, the literal meaning should disappear, the figure must be reduced, in order that the correct meaning may be constructed. In any case, allegory, often confused with personification under the influence of the terminology of art history, promotes a "moral" sense by means of a "physical" representation. It has an orientation toward information and action; it is teleologically didactic and pragmatically coercive. Making the most of all these elements, it should be possible to reconstitute the allegorical procedure step by step on the given example.

> Not always is the sea exposed
> To the blasts that play havoc . . .

As we read these lines, there is no need to look for a double meaning (polysemy) to make sense of them, but, even when polysemy is activated by literary reading, logical and chronological priority is given to real reference; the certifying Discourses will all confirm that tempest is not a permanent, universal phenomenon and that there are always quiet seas after the heavy seas; the assertion in these lines is welcome as truth by meteorology and, probably, personal experience.

> Not always do the torrents by their fall
> Devastate the valleys . . .

In the wake of the first lines and under their training, we shall certainly refer this segment in the same manner, in order to get the same reward, but the second time over is disappointing; the structural undertones of tautology turn it into incipient monotony, when literal truth is so true that it borders on truism. We know that we could go on and on with this game, for more identical rewards, marginally depreciated each time:

Not always does raging fire
Destroy the green forests,
Not always does the black plague
Wipe out entire nations, etc.

If the text is supposed to convey information, there must be some other point to these self-evident assertions. We realize that the poem juxtaposes two areas of the physical Real of reference (nature): the open sea and narrow valleys (*vallons*) in a mountainous zone, which could hardly be "relevant," "of concern" simultaneously for a subject living in this physical world. Simultaneous relevance lies only in the structural homology of the propositions, when we take into our purview the semes shared by "sea" and "valleys," on the one hand, "blasts" and "torrents," "play havoc" and "devastate" (actual synonyms), on the other hand. For a subject equally acquainted with or distant from the sea and the valleys, the two propositions can be reduced to their common denominator or rather their common semantic locus by a process of *abstraction*: "Not always is a quiet X damaged by the irruption of the corresponding violent Y." This formulation presupposes (1) that things can change in time both ways, from state 1 to state 2, and vice versa, and (2) that each X has a corresponding Y that threatens it and fights it. But all this would be uninteresting if it were not directed toward the cognizance of another Real that will be, this time, "moral," that is, human and amendable by human behavior to some extent. The conclusion reads: "Not always is the course of our lives subjected to woes and sorrow," and the "moral" consequence is the stated injunctive clause: "Be brave and do not forsake hope!" This finality justifies the retrospective reading, the translation of the first two sentences given by Fontanier: "Their common purpose is to make more tangible [*plus sensible*] the idea that *setbacks and misfortunes do not occur every day; they are only temporary.*"[54]

We have acted so far as if there were no generically given rules of the game, as if we had to discover these rules in our context-free example, and we have described a structural marker of allegorical *comparatio*, so as to show its implicit presence and the necessity of taking it into account in view of a coherent and purposeful message. Double reference, however, is always at work, and we have not yet fully revealed its process. There are really three phases: in the first, I give the status of reality to the signifieds of the first statements; in the second, I deny it or reduce it by an effort of conceptualization that leads me to a truth in *logos* (imaginary reference); in the third, I return to Reality, but to a reality of a different order. The first real reference had value in a constative framework, whereas the second works in a normative framework. The trick in passing from the constative to the injunctive is to weaken resistance by an appeal to imaginary reference; in the process we have been conned into accepting as a general truth something that is just wishful thinking, since no evidence has been adduced that human life is ruled by the same laws as the physical world at large. Moreover, the advice given to the reader ("Be brave and do not lose hope") would make no sense if it were addressed to the sea and the valleys, which have no ears or means of defense.

Allegory mimes the structure of syllogism:

> All torrents destroy / like misfortune
> All torrents stop destroying after a while
> Hence misfortune also stops striking after a while,

but allegory is not a syllogism, since the relation between the two terms of the major premise is not definitional but analogic. In other words, we can also see that, if the devastation of flooding torrents is a kind of misfortune that has an end, this does not entail that all kinds of misfortune have an end.

Allegorical reading combines a maximum of *comparatio* with maximum real reference, even though it is likely to contain a fallacy. If we lexically transform our example as follows:

> Not always is Delta exposed
> To the destructive blasts of the Klingons;
> Not always do mega-ants
> Eat away the green moon,

we change nothing in the syntactic and rhetoric structures of the first four lines, but it will be at least risky to draw the conclusion "Be brave and do not lose hope." If imaginary reference is dominant in the beginning, we shall also find it in the conclusion. This is why science fiction and fantasy literature are never allegorical, properly speaking, unless their mode of reference is inverted by the previous reduction of their signifieds considered as metaphorical (as we tend to do when we read Ray Bradbury or Ursula Le Guinn).

Final Remarks

1. In order to simplify, we have approached the various genres of fictionality as if they were uniform throughout the texts considered and their successive readings. This illusion was made easier in several cases by the exploitation of very short or fragmented examples. In fact, it is the rule in most extensive texts that they (make us) move through two or more successive genres of fictionality, even in the course of the first reading. Todorov suggests something of the sort when he stresses (excessively, in my opinion) the instability of the fantasy genre, which tends to be resolved or to dissolve into the marvelous or into realism (by means of a "natural" explanation of the phenomena), and again when he says that Gogol's tale *The Nose* places itself right away in the marvelous before inducing allegorical interpretations that become in turn unsatisfactory.[55] But this shifting of genres of

fictionality is the common lot of narrative communication, with differences of degree, intensity, and frequency. It is rarer to observe a leap from metafiction to documentary than a gradual passage from realism to allegory, but all the shifts are possible and, probably, exemplified.

In the fairy tale *Blondine*, by the Comtesse de Ségur, that we shall examine again in chapter 6, the first sentence, "There was a king called Bénin, everybody loved him because he was good," contains no explicit or implicit marker of *comparatio*, so that we have to compare possible references under our own responsibility, and the result is virtually complete undecidability: why not refer to the Real? why not to the Imaginary? The genre is romantic (see the listings on p. 118). After a few sentences, we notice that all the characters, like King Bénin, have names that denote or connote their most salient physical and/or moral characteristics: Doucette, Blondine, Léger, Turbulent, Fourbette, Brunette, Gourmandinet. Such a motivation of the names is a rather trustworthy indication of allegory, in which physical reality and moral reality are joined through imaginary reference. One more page, and Blondine is seen riding a pretty little car drawn by . . . ostrichs; we arrive at the edge of a "magnificent and immense forest, which was called the Lilac Forest because it was full all year long of lilacs always in bloom."[56] Toponymy confirms onomastics in its motivation; linguistic designators in this presented world are certainly adequate to what they point at, but there is a first slip or drift from a motivation *of* names to a remotivation and revision of the world by names: the Lilac Forest is called the Lilac Forest all year round; "therefore," its lilacs are lilaclike and at their best, in bloom all year round!

"Nobody ever entered the forest: people [*on*] knew that it was enchanted and when one [*on*] entered there once, one [*on*] could never get out of it again" (ibid.). How could one know that one could not get out, if one had not entered? And if those who had entered (no one?) had never come out to tell the others that . . . it was impossible to get out? The search for the origin of information is defeated by an enunciative vicious circle, very much like that of the one-way forest. We are now in a world whose dominant reference is clearly imaginary—characterized by irreversible space and, probably, reversible time—and about which the comparison of references is forbidden or severely hindered by the inapplicability of the principle of noncontradiction; the genre is the marvelous.

Striking effects of surprise, fear or illumination, but also comic effects, will often result from abrupt or repeated changes of genre of fictionality; such is the case of the joke about three horses and a dog quoted in chapter 5 and all the best tales of Alphonse Allais.[57] Even in many great novels of this century such as *Ulysses, Remembrance of Things Past, Doktor Faustus, The Castle, Paradiso* or *The Recognitions*, as well as in the sports column of your favorite tabloid, the genres of fictionality are in competition. A class of narrative genres could be determined by the criterion of the mutual relations of the genres of fictionality and their *dispositio* in the act of narrative communication.

2. The genres of fictionality depend not on the nature of the events reported or of the objects described or defined but on their predisposition for reference by techniques of enunciation that develop constraints both on semantic concretization and on semiotic drift—this idea was expressed by Michel Charles under the name *mise en place rhétorique*[58] of the text generator of literary effects. We have seen the remarkable weight of shifting enunciation on the referential *fort da* at the beginning of *The Red and the Black*; we shall see that of an enunciating third-as-first person in *The Recognitions* (chapter 7). In the poem quoted earlier: "The warm night Aurora flows around you / Slow like honey flows around a dead bee," the second person leaves the choice open between an allegorical and a realist regime of reference, but it forbids in principle genres like the documentary and the marvelous. Todorov again remarked that the fantastic is associated with first-person narration—it would be better to say: with a first → third-person type of narration—such that the object of the fantastic encounter may appear as a third party to both the narrator and the implied reader.

3. As indicated earlier, the division of worlds of reference between imaginary and real is considered valid for "contemporary Western cultures" that have acquired, from the modern era on and particularly in the nineteenth century, a certain idea of scientific truth and experimental evidence that they maintain to this day. But other cultures and other periods, past or future, of our civilization, may well divide the worlds of reference differently. In a similar sense, Pavel writes, "[In] a more archaic frame of mind [than ours] the fundamental distinction is not between actual and fictional but between the insignificant and the memorable."[59] This should not lead us to think that "whereas belief in the myths of the community is compulsory, assent to fiction is free and clearly circumscribed in time and space" (ibid., p. 61) since (a) myth too is a game of make-believe whose key difference from "fiction" is that its rules and conventions have not been exposed, and (b) assent to fiction is largely determined unless we posit rule-free free agency for a generalized ideal subject whose "perceptions" of "the real," moreover, are not informed by fiction in the first place. But the paradigm "profane versus sacred" would be an excellent candidate for the ruling configuration of possible worlds of reference in theocratic and deeply religious societies. J. Huizinga, in *The Waning of the Middle Ages*, quotes some reflections of Michelangelo reported by Francesco de Holanda:

> Flemish painting pleases all the devout better than Italian. . . . This is not a result of the merits of this art; the only cause is the extreme sensibility of the devout spectators. The Flemish pictures please women . . . and also monks and nuns . . . who are not capable of understanding true harmony. In Flanders they paint, before all things, to render exactly and deceptively the outward appearance of things. The painters choose, by preference, subjects provoking transports of piety.[60]

We could say that Flemish painting was sacred because of its servility vis-à-vis the image of Creation (of God's creatures), whereas Italian painting was profane or humanist because it abstracted and constructed harmony in a way that was not God-given to the naive eye. The former referred in the first place to the work and world of God, in its evidence, the latter to the human world and work, the unearthing of secrets. The coexistence of these two vectors of reference is what makes fictionality and art in our sense of the word already possible in the early Renaissance, even though the possible worlds taken into account differ from ours.

But we can wonder whether a monoreferential society, one where myth and life are one, if such a society exists or has ever existed, could be aware of the rift of representation and, consequently, whether it could cover it with the sealant and glitter of fictionality or, for that matter, whether it would need narrative to weld together an unbroken time. The conclusions of love legends like that of Leander and Hero, with the theme of "love stronger than death," express the nostalgia of such a Golden Age when art and narrative were not necessary:

> Et après mort, qui amants désassemble
> Se sont encore tous deux trouvés ensemble.[61]

In our own age, we are perhaps on the brink of a new change of referential paradigm. The future may oppose abstract or fundamental reality to *technê*, or even analog and digital worlds. The coexistence of two or more paradigms in the same culture is a cause of complication and enrichment of narrative and its fictionality, as it certainly was in the baroque, or as it appears to be in the "emergent literatures" of Africa and Latin America.

Chapter 5
Who's Who and Who Does What in the Tale Told

Narrative meaning is concretized through the production and comprehension of narrative units of discourse (transactive and/or nontransactive narratemes) which involve noun phrases (NPs) as well as verb phrases (VPs). Moreover, the text of a linguistic narrative is also made of all sorts of discursemes that have subjects. It is now time to raise some of the many questions involved and propose some methodological directions in a field that has so often been obscured by ideological interests alien or opposed to a science of discourse.

After a brief survey of two conceptual pairs of opposites that remain relevant and useful although their analytic power has been much exaggerated, we shall study the main functions of narrative agents and consider the extent to which they may be constitutive of narrative types, reserving for the end of the chapter some suggestions about three arduous and fascinating problems (subjective coherence, person, and onomastics in narrative).

Doing Something and Being Somebody: Actants and Actors

The linguistic reinterpretation we have proposed for *dramatis perso-nae* . . . in the first instance seeks to establish a distinction between *actants*, having to do with narrative syntax, and *actors*, which are recognizable in the particular discourses in which they are manifested. . . . we know that the relation between *actor* and *actant*, far from being a simple relation of inclusion of a given occurrence into a class, is instead twofold. . . . We have learned that if an actant (A_1) can be manifested in discourse by several actors (a_1, a_2, a_3), the converse is equally possible, just one actor (a_1) being able to constitute a syncretism of several actants (A_1, A_2, A_3).[1]

To paraphrase Tesnière, from whom Greimas borrowed the term "actant," we could say that the actants are the abstract operators that "participate in the process, in any capacity whatsoever."[2] They are the subjects and objects of classes of actional predicates, defined in accordance with these classes of predicates ("functions" in the Proppian sense) and their functional positions relative to such classes. Thus the "function" called "addressing" would allow us to link, and to oppose to each other, an *addresser*, an *addressee*, and an object *addressed* by the former to the latter; or the "function" called "killing": a killer, a victim, and a life taken or a death inflicted.

The actants are *names of roles*; therefore these roles can be fulfilled in a text by NP's which may have complex denotative and connotative semantic contents ("lexematic figures") beside or "on top of" their intervention in a particular role. The reference of an NP, as we have seen in chapter 4, is not any more than its denotation strictly linked to the actantial roles it commands in a particular text. Some roles are simply more appropriate, expected, or "grammatical" than others. NPs considered in this perspective are *actors*.

In the framework of the class of predicates labeled "giving," let us pick up three givers, three objects, and three receivers:

Givers: A = Father; B = Heaven; C = Julie
Objects: X = wealth; Y = love; Z = genius
Receivers: J = son; K = poet; L = lover.

These elements instantly offer twenty-seven possible combinations, of which three seem to be the most "natural" or clichéd:

AXJ: The father gave wealth to the son.
BZK: Heaven gave genius to the poet.
CYL: Julie gave love to the lover.

Several more combinations remain readily acceptable:

AYJ: The father gave love to the son.
AZJ: The father gave genius to the son.
BYL: Heaven gave love to the lover.
CZL: Julie gave genius to the lover.
CZK: Julie gave genius to the poet.

Other combinations sound "strange," ranging from the unusual to the almost nonsensical:

CZK: Julie gave wealth to the poet.
AYL: The father gave love to the lover.

The "accuracy" of the various triads depends on their conformity with the semantic contents attributed to each NP by language and our special *doxa*. Fathers and sons are lexically defined in relation to each other, and fathers are supposed to be generous and general givers to their sons. Heaven is supposed to be a universal giver in the guise of Providence, but its giving capacity has some moral limits that may exclude BYL from the field of narrative possibilities in certain contexts. Fathers are definitely not supposed to condone illicit love affairs, or women to maintain poets; nevertheless, these possibilities cannot be discarded on simple lexical-logical grounds, nor do they require a metaphorical interpretation to make sense, like, say: "An apple gave Mary to Peter." Moreover we should note that many of the NPs involved could just as well occupy a different position in the aforementioned actantial classes: Julie could be the given object in a BCK combination ("Heaven gave Julie to the poet"), or the receiver in an LBC combination ("The lover gave Heaven to Julie").

What remains interesting in this dated approach is certainly less the forced reduction of any narrative to the concatenation of a number of elementary strings than, on the contrary, the double allegiance (predicative *and* nominal) of narrative that it has eventually accepted, with the corresponding tension or struggle between these two constraints. Narrative suspense and the hermeneutic code are in fact just as dependent on this double bind as on the time factor; time requires the institution of "currency," a substitute for immediate use value, but it has no power to decide *what* can be exchanged for another thing.

If the datum of a narrative is taken to be the propositional value of a predicate, the questions asked will be questions of identity bearing on the fleshing out of actantial roles by actors, and related modal questions of status, necessity, and so on. For example, the datum "reproduce" will give rise to such questions as: "Does anyone reproduce, when, how and why?" and, in the affirmative hypothesis: "Who reproduces what, with whom, for what purpose, and for whom?" But, if the datum is an NP or a set of NPs, potential subjects and objects of narrative predicates, the questions will now primarily bear on predicative filling: "What's going to happen?" "What will Joe do next?" and "What will be done to Joe?"

Although one group of questions may be more pressing than the other at a particular moment of the narrative construction of meaning, or even throughout the reading and totalizing process of a full-length narrative, the two kinds of questions always combine insofar as the identity of a subject amounts to the sum total of predications, especially actional, in which this subject has been, is or is likely to become involved: "Jack is the guy who killed his father, married his mother, blinded himself, and saved his city from the plague." Conversely, any actional predication is a synthesis of identities established in the milieu: "To conquer an empire is to do the same as Alexander, Caesar, Napoleon, or Citizen Kane, to name a few." Any formulation and application of causal principles, every affirmation of necessity or contingency, and every questioning of the same—all rely on the double bind of narrative.

In the examples mentioned earlier, the flexibility of the actors was due to their definitional openness, but defining them more precisely would be tantamount to positing some of the possible transactive and other predications as contextually preactualized: for instance, "The father begot the son," "The poet has genius," or "Love unites Julie and her lover." Narrative and nonnarrative utterances collaborate to constitute "identity," what the subject "is," as narrative utterances become stratified into layers of the subject's portrait. Varied attributes may be the motive force of a narrative: it is not easy for anybody to be, in one breath, a son, a poet, and a lover; these attributes may be the point of departure, if the narrative is about choice, or they can serve as successive goals when the overall design is to complete the circle of the possible phases or stages of a subject. But any genre of narrative maintains, within its own limits, a measure of competition between enigmas of the subject (actorial) and enigmas of event (actantial). Although the question asked about marriage in an adventure story tends to be: "Will X get married?" and, in romance, "Who will marry whom?" the answers given to these questions also mean the victory of one way of approaching our relation to action over another *and* the final impossibility of dissociating these approaches, freedom from determination, or intention from programming.

Doing or Having Something Done to You: Agents and Patients

This distinction was particularly elaborated by Claude Bremond in a context more mimetic and representational than logical and linguistic.[3] It should be an important factor for an ideological analysis of narrative, since the distribution of "active" and "passive" roles according to social class, sex, age, ethnic group, religion, and professional training can be significant of strife or security, acceptation or rejection, resignation or struggle: Marxist manifestos depict the preparation of the proletarian revolution as a transformation of a passive exploited class into a conscious and organized, active class that will take in its hands its own future along with the accelerated actualization of the necessary course of history. But, notwithstanding its obvious interest, the agent versus patient pair is fraught with problems of evaluation, evidenced by the difficult application of Bremond's definition: "We define as playing a role of patient any person whom the narrative [récit] presents as affected, in one way or another, by the course of the events recounted" (p. 139).

First of all, what are the size and complexity of the textual units to be taken into account: a phrastic or a transphrastic unit? a simple or a complex sentence?

a surface structure actualization or a deep structure S? a sequence or a multise-
quence text? It is in fact quite common that a subject, agent, or character who
behaves "actively" in a particular surface narrateme be actually a "patient" in the
actantial figure to which this narrateme belongs: this is the main rhetorical
(ironic) resource of fate in tragedy. When Oedipus meets Laïos at the crossroads,
he is *apparently* active in killing him, but he actually acts according to a plan he
did not devise and could not choose not to fulfill.

When we consider a struggle, the weaker of the two contenders may nevertheless defend himself, even by taking some rest, or make, at times, an offensive gesture. His physical, material defeat in the limited framework of the sequence may
be a deluding strategic move in a wider scheme, or a survival lesson taught to
the presumptuous hero, or even the other face of a moral victory over himself,
an act of conversion. The distinction between agent and patient could be operational only in a univocal narrative; using it carelessly entails the risk of a hasty
monosemic reduction. Ordinary language, as well as the Freudian analysis of
parapraxes, shows the extent of the problem and its metaphysical resonance;
when you "get caught by the cops," he "gets his fingers crushed under a sledge
hammer," and she "gets pregnant at fifteen," are you, is he, is she "active" or
"passive"?

Even though there is no conflict or hesitation at one level of analysis, doubt
becomes the rule when we shift from one level to another. If we view the narrateme "Peter killed Paul" synthetically, we are sure that Peter is the agent and Paul
the patient; but if we analyze the narrateme into its underlying nontransactive
components ("Peter became a murderer" and "Paul died"), the difference is not
so clear any more.

In "Childhood III," the poem by Rimbaud studied in chapter 2, the surface actualization of the text presents the subject "you" and/or "one" as exclusively passive: he is, finds himself in the woods, is stopped, made to blush, and eventually
chased; but a role of "agent," in Bremond's sense, is necessarily implied all the
way through: to be detained in the woods, you must have entered them, and, to
be "chased away," you must want or have wanted to stay (otherwise you would
be "helped out"). The opposite situation is frequently found in narratives of transgression: any transgression is based on a "patience" and a passion that are not
necessarily manifested on the surface of the text or can be disguised in the form
of mysterious, symbolic influences. This applies to the "unmotivated" (overdetermined) murder of an Arab by Meursault in *The Stranger*: we could validly say
that the combined pressures of exile, semipoverty, and the "white man's burden"
come to bear so heavily on this character that he is unable to perceive them as
such and turns to arbitrary violence to express symptomatically his suppressed
manhood and take revenge for his forlorn, inhuman condition.

In conclusion, no participation of a subject in an action or event can be considered active or passive per se, but the presentation and representation, intra- and

extratextual, of activity and passivity, are invaluable keys to the narrative autonomy of the text and the concepts of authorial and narratorial authority prevalent
at the time of its production.

Ways of Being Involved in Narrative

The four facets of NPs in narrative can be schematically represented as follows:

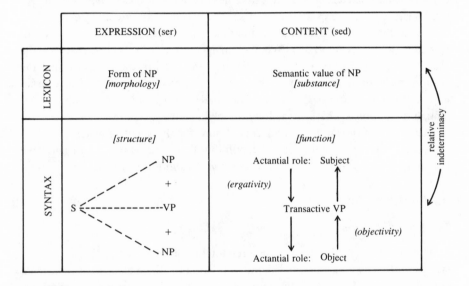

Remarks

Quadrants 3 and 4 illustrate an ordinary transactive utterance. If we considered
utterances involving more or fewer than two NPs, the diagram would have to be
modified accordingly. Two-way arrows in quadrant 4 symbolize the retroaction
of the verb on the subject, of the object on the verb and, through it, on the subject
(partial redefinition); this retroaction causes the relative indeterminacy in the hierarchy of values between quadrants 1 and 4: the initial a priori semantic value
of NPs is modified, as we have said, by their involvement in narrative and other
utterances; for instance, an empty personal pronoun receives some semantic content. But, at the same time, a given initial value of an NP modifies the meaning
of a predication. If somebody states, "He went mad," we can at least answer tauto-
logically the question "Who is *he?*" with: "just a guy who could go mad." But,
if the utterance reads, "The madman fell in love with the king's daughter," "falling
in love" is automatically qualified, connoted as not serious, crazy, or, at best,
hopeless. Finally we should remember that, under the regime of literariness, but

also in other regimes of communication, the plane of expression (morphology and structure) is caused to signify semiindependently through the processes of hypersemanticization (described in chapter 3): these additional significations may enhance narrative meaning or interfere with it.

In its broadest sense, *an agent is an NP that plays a necessary role in the semantic concretization of a narrative utterance*. This means that agents must be considered in their "qualifications" or "habilitations," in their relations with nonactional predicates, such as descriptemes or equatemes, as well as in their "active" positions regarding the narratemes in which they are involved. Agents are bearers of the text at the level of the utterances (sequences) in which they are involved explicitly or implicitly. Whether an agent "speaks" or not, it is always the shadow or the reflection of the enunciator at the level of the utterance (but the shadow must not be confused with the prey). Philippe Hamon wrote of the character that it is "the bearer of the conservation and transformation of meaning."[4] Although the notion of character will be somewhat narrowed down in our perspective, this definition can be fully accepted here for the agent in general.

Agents have three main means of fulfilling their role as bearers of narrative communication, which we shall call *cardinal agential functions*.

Agential functions

Dynamic Function.

The dynamic function is the structured totality of all the actional roles successively fulfilled by an agent, considered in relation to all the other narratemes that constitute the total narrative discourse of a narrative. The narrative function, insofar as it includes the agent's narrative programs as well as its involvement in actualized (fully textualized or necessarily concretized) narratemes, can also be compared with the sum total of moves carried out, or which could have been carried out by a particular piece in a chess match; it is therefore not distinct from the dynamic aspect of the agent's particular plot (see chapter 7). In its dynamic function, the agent is the subject or object of verbs of "doing"; it transforms situations or offers opportunities for situations to be transformed.

A young aristocrat marries a pretty shepherdess and fathers two children by her: he changes a situation in which the valences of two agents were, in principle, free, into one in which these valences are, in principle, fixed; then he creates a second new situation characterized by the presence of two new agents. The same man loses his wife and children in a plane crash: he does not have to be the pilot, the direct or indirect cause of this new transformation, to be dynamically involved in it. The new situation will be, so to speak, named after him as "his loss," "his sorrow" or "his lack of feeling"; he is just as much the bearer of narrative meaning as if he had deliberately poisoned his family with Tylenol (popular consciousness associates misfortune with guilt for obvious reasons of narrative logic).

An apple falls on Newton's head, helping him to discover the law of gravity: both Newton and the apple are dynamic agents in this sequence. Without Don Quixote's presence at the inn of Maritornes and his adventurous purposes and fantastic interpretations of the circumstances, no such thing would have happened as his being beaten up and prevented, together with Sancho, from enjoying any rest during the night. However distorted they may be by the Knight's spurious representations and confused perceptions, events take shape in his own and his squire's bodies:

> "If [enchanted persons] do not suffer themselves to be seen," quoth Sancho, "at least they suffer themselves to be felt: if not, let my carcass bear witness." "So might mine," cried Don Quixote.[5]

Yet we should realize that the dynamic function of each agent can occupy different positions and be of varying relevance regarding the overall dynamics of the tale told. It may be principal and subordinating, or accessory and subordinate, or function as a paratactic relay; it may appear as the driving momentum or in opposition to rival dynamic functions. The hero who tries to conquer and organize a kingdom in a period of chaos and general degradation is very likely to manifest a dynamic function that will be, in content and modality, the exact opposite of those of most other agents in the tale. On the other hand, a hero who comes "at the right time," the captain of a victorious army, whose feats are listed in the narrative will "naturally" embody the overall dynamics of the tale with minimal distortion. There exist, finally, erratic or episodic agents with a very restricted subplot, whose dynamic function is difficult to integrate and who question or jeopardize the unity of the tale, while others manage to create confusions about the functional quality of their interventions because of their performative use of language, or when action and perception are made hard to distinguish.

A very interesting instance of this borderline superposition of functions can be found in the character José Fago, of Galdós's *Zumalacarregui*. From the very beginning, the strange, almost devilish nature of the man, is manifested by the effect his very name has on the character he visits in his cell and confesses before his execution:

> The words *My name is José Fago* were like a shot that threw back the unfortunate prisoner against the pile of broken lumber, where he stayed put away, hands and legs spread out, his head rebounding against the wall.[6]

This blow of the name doubles in hyperbolic fashion the horror and irony of the situation, when José Fago, who abducted and ill-treated Saloma, Adrián Ulibarri's daughter, is called on to absolve the prisoner moments before his shooting by the Carlist general's troops. But later on, Fago, through whose almost exclusive mediation we are acquainted with the eponym rebel leader, undergoes so strong a process of projection/identification with Zumalacarregui, that he will even die of no known physical complaint, at the very same time as the general. During his wanderings with the Carlist army, the combination of a privileged point of view with Fago's uncontradicted belief that Zumalacarregui's strategy is a mere reflection of his own thoughts, results in a two-way assimilation of the dynamic, panoramic, and focal functions:

> The Sergeant-Chaplain was meditating: in the eyes of the general he had certainly recognized his own thoughts, by virtue of a miraculous transfusion, and he said to himself: "All that I think he also thinks; but he thinks it after me. . . . He is convinced that they are going to attack us on the front and both wings and he has taken measures to make their project fail. (p. 835)

Panoramic Function.

This function consists in offering things to see or, more generally, to know, as they are or might or should be. In this function and whether or not he is *also* a narrator, the agent is particularly the bearer of descriptions, judgments, interpretations, and other units of nonnarrative discourses. Whether or not he travels, a character always makes us travel thanks to "representations" (mental images) that are supposed to form in his mind, or simply due to his presence someplace. He contributes to the motivation of paranarrative or nonnarrative elements of the tale told and provides them with a common locus. The panoramic function is the seat of the modality of knowing, but, even though it is considerably developed in narrating characters—be it with direct, direct reported, or indirect speech—its practice does not require that the agent itself know or perceive the data presented by the text. It is sufficient that the occasion for information, true or false, be provided by the agent.

Narratives with important blind characters do not lack descriptions any more than others; on the contrary, the agents who keep company with the blind have to describe and comment all the time: "Here, there is this and there is that, a flight of stairs, one more step, a corridor, the door, an armchair on your right," and so on. In a story of *lazarillo* (*de ciegos caminantes*), the panoramic function is shared between the *lazarillo* and the blind man, without whom most descriptions would be unnecessary. The blind man provides the motivation and sometimes causes contradictory descriptive utterances to be produced: thus, in the *Lazarillo de Tormes*, the right information is given to the reader and the wrong information to the blind beggar, in order to kill him by making him throw himself headfirst against a stone pillar.

In a less sinister, more seductive register, we could think of Gide's *La Sym-*

phonie pastorale in which Gertrude's "first education" leads the minister-narrator to construct complex synaesthetic systems, before Gertrude juxtaposes her own "fantastic" description of the landscape to that of the minister, a description generated by "the eyes of the soul," the vision of love, and, due to the miracle of well-arranged words, more convincing than all the details a seeing person could accumulate:

> "I told you, Gertrude: those who have eyes are those who do not know how to look."
> "If you could but know," she then cried out in exalted merriment. "If you could but know how easily I can imagine all this. Look! Do you want me to describe the landscape for you? . . . Behind us, above and around us are the high firtrees."[7]

Beside this extreme type of panoramic intervention and the other pole at which the panoramic agent doubles as writer or storyteller ("Minneapolis is very cold; I was there last winter"), one very common presentational model, particularly in the classical novel, is that of a panoramic agent who does all or a good part of the seeing, while the narrator does all or most of the talking:

> Cordero observed everything and gave very prudent opinions on all the preparations. On the following days and nights he took his family on sightseeing tours of the retinues and illuminations and invited them to admire the great novelty: the allegorico-mythologico-bawdy triumphal float, ordered by the corregidor Barraócn, aboard which several beautiful Madrid women embodied the nymphs; among them, *Pepa la Naranjera*, on the highest step, represented the goddess Venus.[8]

The ironic, sophisticated tone of the passage dissociates rather crudely the panoramic agent, a mere tool, from the describing voice, which passes harsh value judgments.

The situation is different when the describing voice seems on the contrary simply to help the perceiving agent by lending him the words he lacks. Although it is known to be a repetitive device in Zola, this presentational mode could be found virtually identical in eighteenth-century and earlier narratives. Let us compare:

> Pierre did not grow tired, he could not stop looking from one end of the horizon to the other. He stopped to contemplate the noble lace, the proud grace of mounts Sabina and Alban, strewn with cities, whose belt bordered on the sky.[9]

> And, before he came in, he looked at Paris for a while; the huge sea of the city was displayed at his feet.
> After two terrible months of cold, snow, and ice, it was a Paris drowning in a shivering and drab thaw.[10]

Némorin casts his gaze on this vale and is captivated by the sight. In a space of one square mile, surrounded by mountains, he discovers a meadow.[11]

As the most commonplace analyses of Robbe-Grillet's *Jealousy* have shown, descriptive discourse apparently not borne by a presented character does not fail nevertheless to generate character image: Bruce Morrissette, for example, has called it "the husband."

The practice of the panoramic function gives rise, among others, to the problems of "covision" — "vision with" or "vision against" — which will be discussed in the following chapter, since they are closely related to enunciative strategies.

Focal Function.

Agents are seen, observed, described by others. Questions are asked about them and answers are given, sometimes, when some agents are deciphered and depicted by others who play the role of "inscribed readers," models and anti-models of reading and interpretation for any actual reader. It must be noted that (1) when an agent displays its focal function by becoming an object of attention, one or more other agents necessarily exert their panoramic function as a counterpart, even when there is an extradiegetic enunciative relay, as in the previously quoted examples. In the passage from *Los apostólicos* by Galdós, Pepa is focal and Cordero panoramic, despite the telling done by the voice of the extradiegetic narrator; (2) the focal function may have, either separately or jointly, two different, opposite and complementary aspects: *inquisitive* and *assertive*. A silent, mysterious, secretive, or invisible agent, or a deceptive or elusive agent, will provoke multiple questions, formulated as puzzles or problems. Other agents will ask, "What is it?" "Who is he?" "What is he really like?" and so on. An open, outward, transparent, "up-front" agent will be a topic for affirmative statements, admiring, disparaging, or bored: "She is a beautiful lady"; "They are damned rogues"; "He is so predictable!"

The more an agent is in view, in question, in the public eye, an object of interest or concern (the more focal it, he, or she is), the more panoramic other agents are bound to be: Gary Hart should have learned this rule of narratology. But their attitudes toward the focal agent may vary widely. Besides asking questions about him, they can ask *him* questions, present their conjectures to him so that he may confirm or disprove them: "Is it true that you spent the night with this girl?" The focal function is often developed in the framework of dialogic enunciation (e.g., interrogatories). Or questions can be asked also or exclusively of third parties, so that the focal agent is investigated by two or more detectives, attorneys, witnesses, and onlookers (as in a "cross-examination").

All these techniques are used and stretched to their remotest possibilities in Ivy Compton-Burnett's "novels":

"Do you mean [Lady Heriot] opens [letters]?" said Madeline.
"Tell me of another method," said Angus.
"How did she know it was one that concerned herself?"
"She did not know. She was finding out."
"So you mean she does open letters?"
"No, only those that excite her interest."
"Can you understand her doing it?"
"Yes, I think so. Most letters excite mine."[12]

As Angus is interrogated by Madeline about their mother, Lady Heriot, his own answers become a test and an object of scrutiny for Madeline, focality becomes shared by Angus and Lady Heriot; the focality of the *absent* character is direct and that of the character interrogated, indirect. Moreover, in such a dialogue, the interrogator himself or herself is often led by the interlocutor's answers to ask certain questions rather than others, or particular questions in a particular tone; the answers turn out to work like implicit questions to the asker about him- or herself, which results in the asker's assuming a focal position in his or her turn: "Tell me what you ask, I'll tell you what you are." The supreme irony of the passage quoted is that it deals precisely with the focal function, with being seen and being known:

"Is there something you would be afraid of?"
"One thing. Of being found out."
"Yes, of course," said Hermia. "We are all afraid of it. There are
things we are right to fear." (ibid.)

The focal function can also be revealed in many other ways, such as mirror images offered by the double or the portrait (*The Portrait of Dorian Gray*), deliberate or involuntary imitators, self-analysis and the presentation of documents or summoning of witnesses to testify about the agent, as well as by a systematic withdrawal of information combined with allusions and suggestions that build up curiosity.

The first case is, to some extent, that of Don Quixote and Sancho, as at the end of Part I, when Sancho delivers a premature funeral speech, in his master's own style and jargon:

"O flower of knighthood," cried he, "that with one single perilous knock
art come to an untimely end! Thou honour of thy family, and glory of
La Mancha; nay, and of all the world beside, which, now it has lost
thee, will be overrun by miscreants and outlaws, who will no longer
fear to be punished for their misdeeds."[13]

Indeed, by "recalling" the image of Don Quixote in this manner, Sancho also "recalls to himself" the knight who had passed out and seemed to be as good as dead.

The second case is notably that of paranoid and megalomaniac characters, boasters, and autobiographers in general. Anteo Crocioni, in Paolo Volponi's *Worldwide Machine*, almost begins his self-presentation with "false testimonies" copied from the "RECORD OF THE PROCEEDINGS OF THE SPECIAL COURT OF IN-QUIRY," as if to protest his very existence even when nobody is interested in him any longer. In the course of the narrative, he has to renounce glorification, grati-tude, and understanding on the part of his fellow human beings, but he transforms his quest into that of a "pure" sense of personal achievement that will still provide some visibility for him, however remote and intangible:

> Instead [of an actual proof] I am leaving a luminous beginning that travels through the sky like the tail of a comet. As soon as it passes over my immediate horizon at Fossobrone it will be visible from Mon-tegiove above Fano . . . and it will circle the earth like the stars that now are shining above my head and only a few hours ago were shining over America.[14]

The third case is obviously that of detective stories and psychoanalytic case histories in which enough traces, clues, and symptoms are manifested to call forth questions of identity and motivation ("Who done it? and why?"), but not enough clear information is provided to come up with easy answers. In metafiction and similar acrobatics, the device can be used to draw the reader's attention to the fabrication of the text and hence to the author himself: Roussel, in *Impressions d'Afrique*, Ricardou in all his fiction, or, to a lesser extent, Richard Brautigan and Raymond Federman, have thus deliberately stressed the artificiality of their tales, hoping that the clever maker of their textual worlds would become an object of inquiry. And it works, more or less. Brautigan avails himself of this technique, in *The Abortion*, to include his name as the author of one of the manuscripts brought to the queer library run by the character Frank, in the same way that Hitchcock appears, however incidentally, in all his films. Among twenty-three "books" brought in on an "average evening," we read the following description (an entry in the Library Contents Ledger):

> MOOSE by Richard Brautigan. The author was tall and blond and had a long yellow mustache that gave him an anachronistic appearance. He looked as if he would be more at home in another era.
> This was the third or fourth book he had brought to the Library. Ev-ery time he brought in a new book he looked a little older, a little more tired.
> "What's this one about? I asked.
> "Just another book," he said.[15]

Conversely, as we shall indicate later, the magician who gives *too much* to see — that is, more than seems useful in view of the circumstances — can also become an object of wonder and determine the fate of the narrator who takes charge of his existence in the text. More generally, with or without an intradiegetic narrator, encyclopedic, profuse, and garrulous narratives like *Tristram Shandy*, *Ulysses, The Recognitions, Le Bavard* or *Paradiso*, stress a strongly inquisitive focal function in favor of the teller, in the most perverse way, because they exhibit the risk of destroying the reader's interest in the process.

Functions and Typologies

John Frow notes at the beginning of his major paper "Spectacle Binding": "The concept of character is perhaps the most problematic and the most undertheorized of the basic categories of narrative theory."[16] He also very rightly remarks, concerning Grivel's approach and my own 1979 article on the topic, that "the insistence upon the textuality of character and the denial of any continuity between character and person rests upon an assumption that the two are quite different: the person or subject cannot itself be thought in textual terms" (p. 230). It is therefore a pleasure for me to contend that, in its new elaboration, my theory of the three agential functions in the tale told (not to be confused with Proppian "functions") represents an effort to break "the tied dichotomy of humanist plenitude and structuralist reduction" (p. 232) rather than a further complication of an already intricate jargon that would merely add categories to the existing terminology. Beside its evident analytic power, this theory should be able to simplify and rationalize some established approaches, rescue the question of the subject out of oblivion and reconcile rigorous linguistic inquiry with the broad anthropological scope that should be that of literary theory. Some invaluable tools of investigation discarded in the structuralist and early poststructuralist eras will be reactivated by the same token.

Characters and Forces.

In his brave, if naive, defense of the notion of character, Seymour Chatman revealingly posits the semantic feature "human" as so natural and basic that he is paradoxically led to consider subtracting secondary "people," "walk-ons," and the like from the ranks of characters to include them in the "setting."[17] But he also finds that the importance for the plot of some "existents," such as certain obsessive object devices in Hitchcock's films, is not sufficient to "qualify them for characterhood" (p. 140). Distinctions like the one between "flat" and "rounded" characters, made by E. M. Forster among others, are certainly linked with a demand for correct representation in a humanist perspective, but if we examine creative practice and critical tradition over a long period of time, while firmly maintaining the actant/actor dichotomy, we might find a way out of these difficulties.

"Character" was officially banned from formalist and structuralist approaches for obvious ideological reasons: it was associated with ethical motivations or psychological imitation. The former seemed to imply a "referential," utilitarian, didactic, socially subservient, heteronomous concept of literature that was seen as abiding by moral and political constraints when it sought to promote directly applicable values and norms of behavior. The latter also reduced the autonomy of literature by foregrounding "content," structures supposed to be those of things out in the world, in the psyches of people, for instance, rather than the unique signifying material of verbal art, words and their arrangement. Once rejected from the literary canon and the critical code by the formalist/structuralist counternorm and, to a large extent by mythocriticism and a number of other trends, the facts of ethical motivation and psychological imitation (modes of "building conscience" and "presenting consciousness") were most unscientifically ignored, as if an "unscientific" object were irrelevant per se to science and threatening to epistemology. In this perspective the distinction between force and character should be one of the very first to be delved into, since both archaic irrational fears and irrational rationalizations have a hold on it.

Among actors in narrative, common belief would have the character versus force dichotomy follow one or more of the dividing lines between human and non-human, person and thing, animate and inanimate, or complex and simple agents. All these distinctions are interesting because they involve elements of modal logic that must be activated in the process of constructing narrative meaning. An inanimate object cannot be said to cause an event in the same *sense* as an animate being; we rather associate it with "happenings": if you curse a rock for stumbling on it, you know nonetheless that *you* only are to blame and that cursing the rock can only help discharge your irate feelings without blaming yourself, the road engineer, or God—and having to face retaliation by those insulted.

Two major difficulties remain. First, the componential semantic analysis of an item like "human" or "anthropomorphic" is infinite in principle, or, if a limited number of sememes are chosen, this choice and the hierarchy of major and less important components cannot help reflecting a sociohistorically determined vision of human beings that is likely to lack interpretive validity on a large scale and to make diachronic and intercultural comparison between narratives virtually impossible: before Freud, "man" had a soul but no unconscious; before the Wright brothers "man" could not fly, and there are still communities today in which anyone who eats pork or practices *coitus a tergo* is considered to be an animal and not a person.

Second, a lexical definition cannot adequately bridge the gap between the qualification of the subject (attributes, presuppositions with regards to its ergative role) and syntactic practice; let us illustrate this point with an "after-dinner joke":

> The three famous race horses—Red Rum, Nijinsky and Arkle—were chatting in the stables one afternoon, when Red Rum turned to Arkle and said: "Do you know, Arkle, every time I've won a race I get a pain between the buttocks."
> "I don't believe it," said Arkle. "It's a funny thing but I was just

about to tell you that every time I pass the post first I get a sharp pain under my rear end."

"Would you believe it," butted in Nijinsky, "exactly the same happens to me when I win a race."

Just at that moment a greyhound came running past, but he pulled up by the stables and said: "I've just won another race at White City and I got a sharp pain in the bum."

All three horses looked up at each other in amazement, and Red Rum said: "Jesus Christ, a talking dog!"[18]

Besides many things about genre, style, context, and horizon of expectations, this tale teaches us that a supposedly essential human characteristic like speech is not important in itself for narrative qualification: it becomes significant, here as in most narratives, only in relation to reported speech and overtly delegated enunciation. Moreover, a context-bound convention, related to agential functions, is more efficient than any lexical predetermination. We are shocked, not to "hear" the horses talk, but to see that *they* are shocked that a dog can talk too. We humans wrongly assumed that, when horses talked, any "animal" could do the same, whereas the horses made a sharp distinction between themselves and animals, just like humans do when they are not fabulating. But we are all proved wrong; we humans, because we had generalized too quickly, had seen things in an irrelevantly broad context in which the horses' point of view was not dominant as it is in this particular text, in their own world; and the horses because they were too narrow-minded, unable to conceive of the class "animals" or at least to envisage that this class could include them. If we do not want to behave like these horses or their readers, we must devise a new way of distinguishing between characters and forces.

I shall propose, tentatively, the following criteria.

1. The three agential functions can be carried out by characters without any restriction, and functions can be distributed equally in any character. But forces are essentially endowed with the dynamic function (mainly in its "active" version); their focal function is more inquisitive than assertive; their panoramic function is nil, or however little of it they may have is manifested symptomatically through action.

2. Characters, not forces, are the exclusive bearers of certain modalities of predication, like duty and willing *in mente*, closely related to the two functions denied to forces or much reduced in them. In order to *wish* for a different state of the world (not just to tend to modify its present state), a subject needs to "know" what the world is like and therefore provide, directly or indirectly, a vision of this world by engaging in description or motivating it. In order to *have to* do something (deontic modality), a subject must display a complex set of characteristics and a degree of flexibility that will allow the observer to evaluate the greater

or lesser conformity of the actions planned or carried out with the initial portrait and the expectations it entailed.

Fate and fortune are blind; they can teach us nothing about the world or themselves except their own inexorability and the arbitrariness of design that defines them; their unknowable design is the empty double of their action, the shadow of happening when we cast on it the light of unanswerable questions of origin: "Why, how, and when did it all start?" The deification of woman ("Beauty," "Idol," *femme fatale*, etc.) does not compensate for her depreciating sexist vision but manifests it unequivocally by amputating her essentially human dimensions: gods can *do* more than people because they *are* less. On the other hand, the "mechanical" image of the slave or the "primitive" disseminated by racist literature also exalts certain of their powers (sexual, in particular) in a frightful, quasi-divine manner.

Ambition cannot *become* disinterestedness or apathy, it can only be replaced by one or the other. I imagine this is the reason why characters treated mainly as the seats of opposite, conflicting forces also tend to change names according to the dominant force that occupies them at one moment or other: Dr. Jekyll and Mr. Hyde, God and Satan, Jean-qui-pleure and Jean-qui-rit. Such changes presuppose the existence of a supersubject whose proof of identity may be the biological continuity of a single living body or yet the transhistoric testimony contained in a body of Scripture (uninterrupted tradition). When a single purpose combines with the near-perfect consistency of purposiveness ("intention"), as it occurs in allegory, epic, adventure stories, and so on, we can see that there is often a fine line between "flatter" characters and "rounder" forces, the lover and his Love (*Cuer d'Amours espris*), the adventurer and the spirit of adventure, the prophet and his truth, a mother and motherhood, and so forth.

The distinction between character and force, obscured by actantial analysis, should be revived as a tool of literary and cultural critique. The whole history of Christianity or Marxism could probably be rewritten along these lines, in terms of a competition between tales of forces and tales of characters. On the one hand, we have stories of sin and redemption, light and darkness, faith and disbelief, capital and labor, infrastructure and superstructure, progress and reaction; on the other hand, stories of father and son, friends and enemies, chiefs and slaves, inventors and censors. The first group of stories tends to be dominated by the repetitiveness of actantial roles: they are square, clear-cut, absolute, categorical. Stories in the second group tend to be more relativistic, revisionist, open to exchange and conversion, sometimes confusing: they rely on the mobility and malleability of actors. More often than not, these two types are found together in extended narratives; the models of combinations realized — agonistic or collaborative — might be one of the best ways to characterize period and individual strategies against nonchange, stillness and death, in favor of change as life (movement), or in favor of nonchange as life (continuity, survival, reproduction).

Major and Minor Roles.

As Philippe Hamon showed most conclusively, this is an immensely complex problem that has gained little from recent developments in narratology.[19] I shall try not to add to the prevailing confusion but, even if I did, I believe it would still be better than dropping the matter altogether, since hierarchies of power, privileges of initiative, and preferred representations of people in social communication are the main concerns of innumerable narratives, from the realm of ancient myth to Hollywood, from local politics to the Bible, and from Cabinet meetings to office small talk. Major and minor roles, those of characters particularly (when forces are subdued, concealed, or scattered and absorbed among characters) are often decisive mediations toward the production and traffic of value in literary communication. The "central," "key," or "dominant" position of a character—whatever these adjectives may cover—is an important factor in the choice and acceptance of the didactic message of a narrative, since key characters are among the main prisms through which modes of reference and, consequently, types of fictionality, criteria of verisimiltude, and so on, are selected by the reader.

Should we decide to elect Dulcinea del Toboso to the post of main character in *Don Quixote*, the whole thematics of the novel would be completely upset: the relegation of women to the dark unknowable background of perpetual virginity, with general sexual deprivation normalized by the Counter-Reformation, could appear as the most central issues of early seventeenth-century Spain rather than, say, the difficulty of that country in adapting to a market economy. But why should we decide to elect Dulcinea rather than Sancho or, for that matter, Don Quixote rather than the talking head? Hamlet rather than Rosenkrantz and Guildenstern? Even when the effects of a particular selection of major roles are rather conspicuous, the criteria and motivations, both textual and situational, are extremely varied historically. The emphasis placed on one criterion rather than another by different methodologies or schools of thought might itself become an interesting object of study, for the concepts of value that it reflects. For instance, my earlier definition of the hero as "the bearer of the largest number of words in the text,"[20] could be seen as revealing an obsession with quantitative productivity, possession, and presence on stage, rather than seduction and obliqueness, which ultimately have become more fashionable. On the other hand, John Frow's insistence on character as "effect of desire" reveals this anxiety of being that is the characteristic legacy of radical deconstruction, obliging us to perform acrobatics in order to found the very discourse that tries to get rid of all ontology:

> "Character" is an effect of the self-"recognition" of a subject which is
> not preconstituted but which assumes a specific identity in the identification of and, hence, identification with the identity of a character.[21]

In the present context I shall retain the definition of agents as bearers (seats and supports) of the conservation and transformation of meaning (by the reader-viewer through the text) and, simultaneously, as bearers of text at the level of utterances, but I shall insist on the qualitative aspect of the correlation and the functional specification of dominant roles. My first and chief example will be an inquiry into the hierarchy of roles in *The Magus*, by John Fowles (1965).

From the beginning we are confronted with two contradictory signs of preponderance: the title, which invites us to invest our curiosity in an eponymous, extraordinary leading character, and the autobiographical manner of the narration:

> I was born in 1927, the only child of middle-class parents, both English, and themselves born in the grotesquely elongated shadow, which they never rose sufficiently above history to leave, of that monstrous dwarf Queen Victoria. . . . I began to discover I was not the person I wanted to be.
>
> I had long before made the discovery I lacked the parents and ancestors I needed.[22]

John Fowles's own remarks about the influence of *Le Grand Meaulnes* and *Great Expectations* on his belated adolescent novel (I paraphrase the foreword to the revised edition, published in 1977) can only confirm that we are dealing with a classic case of family romance (on this topic, see also chapter 10). The enunciated "I" of the first-person narrator, alias Nicholas Urfe (orphan Orpheus?), is a middle-class antihero, a "modern Everyman" in search of the family, particularly the father (Santa Claus?) who would lend him by right of birth the qualities (freedom, audacity, spirit of invention, assurance, good taste, historical indeterminacy) he feels he is most cruelly lacking. This predisposition will naturally lead to the encounter with Conchis, when "the mysteries begin" (read: the coincidence of actuality and origin, history), a multiple, changing narrative of the past substituted for the eventlessness of the present. "Before anything else, I knew that I was expected": this is meant to be understood in a "deeper," more powerful symbolic sense than the simple "two-ness of the teatable" that is offered as a setting. Conchis is "a man whose age is impossible to tell" (p. 79); he combines an obscenely vital baldness with the immemorial "not quite human" penetration of his "simian eyes": a father allright, but the father as alien to the foundling or bastard "self"-exiled on the fascinating, grotesque and almost desertlike microcosm of Phraxos (also "fracture" of praxis), the father as beast, and the beast as rival. After the second visit to Bourani, Nicholas describes himself as "an Oedipus still searching for his destiny" (p. 157).

In his relation to Nicholas, Conchis exerts mainly the panoramic and focal functions in the beginning. He shows Nicholas around Bourani, a setting that combines an art gallery, an encyclopedia, and unchanging nature. He also shows him around his lifestory, firmly set in the midst of world events like a historical novel. He fuels many questions and rejects questioning by his narratee, telling more stories instead and thus stretching almost impossibly the usual separation between the two faces of focality that builds up suspense, requires the protracted exercise of language, and widens the margin of uncertainty that any attempt at truthtelling inexhaustibly creates about itself. The dynamic function of Conchis seems at first to be similarly split between two temporal fields: the narrated past in which his former self is the central actor of his own present tale, and the narrating present in which he seeks to act on Nicholas and Nicholas seeks to reap the benefits of his "election" while at the same time deceiving the old man by participating in the Godgame more superficially than he believes is requested of him. ("If this is the price, I'll seem to be his fool; but not be his fool" [p. 137].)

However, as Conchis's stories become illustrated by various sensorial devices, in a quasi-hallucinatory manner, the boundary between the panoramic and dynamic functions is repeatedly crossed with disconcerting ease and therefore almost erased for the narratee. This new turn of the screw, by actualizing the illusionistic reading of narrative that it pretends to denounce, outlines a plane of reality within fiction and casts all preexisting "reality" in the role of a representation—of another, more elusive reality? Of another, more masterly fiction? Conchis, not content with fulfilling all three agential functions with an obsessive completeness, also demonstrates something more than their complementarity: their effective overlapping; he appears to become rapidly, in a disturbingly transparent sense, the author of Nicholas, imprisoning him rather than involving him in his textual territory. As Nicholas would say later: "What Conchis had done, or was trying to do, was to turn Bourani into a gallery [of automata], and real human beings into *his* puppets" (p. 322), or June, in a clever allusion to Gide's *Counterfeiters*: "It's not just that he wants to be mysterious to us. He wants us to be mysterious to him," (p. 318).

The varying frequencies of pronominal couplings are revealing too. In the first part, when Nicholas Urfe still enjoys a monopolistic foregrounding, we have a combination of "I → me" ("I grew the habit of . . . ," "I considered myself as . . . "), "I → third person," and a few instances of "third person → me." The meeting with Conchis radically upsets the balance, the new characteristic pair now being "he → me," hardly counterbalanced by some "I → him." Then, as the masque develops on an all-embracing scale, we find more instances of "They → me" than of "I → them," complemented notably by a good number of "He → them" relations. Particularly in a spectacular context like that of the Godgame, the dominant role needs helpers, were it only to flaunt the whole scope of its power at the spectators, and in the process this role runs the risk of receding behind the "apparatus," the crowd with which it surrounds itself, the *machina* that bears witness to the not-so-subtle presence of the god.

Paradoxically enough, the supreme trickster builds himself out of sight, and we realize, with a shock, that he has always depended on witnesses for his very existence, that the framing narrator gives him birth and death, speech and silence at will. To this extent, the whole Magus business is a huge *mise en abyme* of what the fictional narrator Nicholas manages to do to us: attract our attention, seduce us, induce us to invest our "real" feelings, desires, and power of interpretation in a world that remains only partly verifiable. In Part 3, Nicholas begins—half reluctantly—to take over the responsibilities of an initiator in the presented world, for example, when, instead of warning the young American, Briggs, who will be his successor at Bourani, he simply wishes him good luck. But this belated complicity with the Magus in the presented world is yet another way of making us forget that he has been the true Magus to us from the beginning in the world of fictional communication—a Proustian twist. By the time the antihero, the mean little middle-class Englishman, lets us see through his trick, by the time (many years in the presented world, many pages and many hours of reading in the communicational world) we realize that he has begotten a father-hero to his own idealized image, we can no longer withdraw without, at least, admiring his cunning. He who states that the web is without a spider, and the mask faceless, implies that he is or has become himself the bearer of appearances, the spider, the face, the Magus. The reader, in turn, can only deny this quality by assuming the role himself or offering it as a reward to the author. In either case, if such a major role as that of magus is efficiently constructed by a narrative text, it can only be dismissed by silence, oblivion, and stupidity. The role is contagious. As soon as we say something like: "The truth about this narrative is . . . ," we are acting just like the dominantly panoramic major roles; reading the Rorschach text is always a contribution to its effectiveness as a projective test.

The theatricality of Conchis's world results logically in a wide distribution of the dynamic and focal functions across the entire "hierarchy" of minor roles and walk-ons. Although such roles are essentially instrumental, the question of their relative autonomy with regards to Conchis, and to the total narrative design in which Nicholas is involved as an experimental subject, is crucial for the latter, who can never quite believe that roles are roles and that the course of events is determined by a combination of roles rather than by some intrinsic human properties, psychological or otherwise. Among all the hard lessons taught to Nicholas, those concerning women, sex, and love could be considered in this light with much profit. Nicholas needs to classify people so that predictable pleasure can be experienced: in other words, he makes narrative dependent on description, characterization, habilitation; even unpredictability is such a category for him, where one should remain if one belongs there. If your partners are predictable or predictably unpredictable, you enjoy the security of knowing their parts better than they do themselves. But, once Nicholas is trapped in Conchis's world, addicted to it, he becomes the single character who does not know his lines; far from giving him an edge over the others, however "minor" or episodic they may be, his cherished freedom is his worst handicap, a mere lack of training. Conchis, a figure of destiny, seems to favor those around him who act according to plan; they reflect and multiply his power; they also partake of it, while Nicholas's only care – that of his own image – turns him into a puppet, a weakling. He will be a man when he accepts being part of a broader design, a cog on the universal wheel, not its axle. Through this relativization of the hierarchy of roles, *The Magus* offers a profound reading of the nature of the tragic plot.

But to relativize and to destroy are two different things. Parallel to the trend of continued elucidation of the relations between roles as an exemplification of their relations to their determinants, the hierarchy of roles, with its long dramatic tradition, has been attacked and eroded to the point of unrecognizability from several sectors of twentieth-century literature. Unanimist and social realist techniques, building on certain aspects of nineteenth-century melodrama and historical novels, have often scattered agential functions among many bearers in order to promote a collective subject, thus encouraging in fact an underground return of the author, the only possible sense giver behind the fragmentation of action, value, and point of view in the text. More radical or, at any rate, more conscious techniques tending toward the "eclipse of the author"[23] by means of a dehierarchization of roles are those metafictional and new-novelistic devices that foreground the properties of language and *écriture* in particular, among them the arbitrariness of the sign (with the corresponding liability to remotivation) and the resilient automatic effects of rhetorical organization. Interchangeability of names and features between human roles, or even between anthropomorphic and other actors, is typical of a great many contemporary "popular" genres: science fiction, fantasy, pornography, detective stories, and so on; it has been borrowed extensively by "high" experimental literature.[24] The use of anthropomorphic agents, with the values they carry, appears to be limited to the quest of a second-hand, parodic symbolism; every reader will recognize a figuration of the order of the novel in the following scene:

> Don't worry about the men. They are only men after all – a tractor
> could have done the job as well.
>   The composition would have suffered, Thomas said. Think of it: Up
> there, the nineteen, the Old Incorrigibles, hauling the cable. The line of
> the cable itself, taut, angled, running from there to here. Finally, the
> object hauled: the Father, in his majesty. His grandeur. A tractor would
> have been très insipide.[25]

Other narratives have contributed to mess up the division of labor between roles; they are those that make a metaphysical exhibition of language as a noncommunicative, sterile, mechanical, and, perhaps, cancerous deadly artifact. With that "walling in of psychological functions"[26] carried out by authors like Blanchot and his imitators, for example, recent literary narrative in Western cultures is often marked by the leveling out of characters rather than by the "death" of character, as it was so much boasted. *L'Arrêt de mort* is striking in this respect; whereas the first part seems to focus on the death throes of a single young woman, J., in the final stage of tuberculosis, the second part multiplies female agents but makes them virtually indistinguishable from one another, since their occurrences in the text appear to be subordinated to similar circumstances: compulsions or phobias related to closed space and limits, problems of recognition, being caught unawares where one should not be . . . A "thought" without truth or content, whose force is perhaps nothing more than the shell of its name, becomes (or had it always been?) the exclusive object of desire and consent on the part of the narrator himself; this "thought" is probably not different from his own being-in-words: "To have lost silence, the regret I feel for it is immeasurable. I cannot tell the misfortune of a man who once began to speak. A still misfortune, itself sentenced to dumbness."[27]

Agents and Unity of Narrative

If agents afford the substantive constants without which paradigmatic couplings and macronarratemes would be equally impossible, the question I shall address myself to at present has two parts: how do the agents achieve this unifying role in narrative, and what are its limits? My examples will be two books that are high reading risks from the point of view of narrative unity but that still manage to provide a feeling of totality clearly different from that of a lyrical text (the presented worlds are moving as a whole in one direction). *Las afueras* (The surroundings), by Luis Goytisolo, has had many editions since its publication in 1958, but like *La Chambre des enfants*, by Louis-René des Forêts, first published in 1960, it enjoys little international recognition.

These two works are not subtitled "novel," "fiction," or "short stories"; they bear hardly any decisive paratextual sign of being either collections of discrete anecdotes or of forming a single continuum each. The blurbs on the back covers make some choices in this respect, but they show a certain consciousness of the delicate positioning of these works in a generic void or in a fluctuating and uncharted in-between:

> The four tales that make up this collection [*recueil*] share the same inspiration and illustrate, through differences of plot and structure, the essential preoccupation of the author of *Le Bavard*. They are like steps of a long patient journey [*démarche*], sometimes oriented, wandering at other times, but always in search of some perhaps inaccessible aim. (*La Chambre*'s 1983 edition)

> *Las afueras* is the novel of a broken fragmented world, a narrative developed along seven chapters without initial connection, but which in-

tertwine page after page, overlap and complement one another until they form a single collective drama whose protagonists, as if pushed by some internal dynamics, seem bound to integrate the backdrop of some quiet and desolate surroundings. (1971 edition)

The two short summaries are well worth analyzing in terms of their revealing clumsiness.

1. They both say that the contents of the respective volumes are not random or even circumstantial *varia*; they insist on the intended coherence. Individual parts are building blocks cemented in the same structure; the disjunction of the pieces is only superficial and temporary; like a puzzle, its educative aim is to make us strive for completeness, even though closure may remain elusive.

2. In *La Chambre*, unity is caused by the author; as a sign, it does not refer outside the relationship between the author and his text. In *Las afueras*, the deep unity and its initial or permanent limits are mimetic, imitative, iconic.

3. In both cases, apparent disjunction and actual reunion of parts are functional; they serve a purpose of improved comprehension and are to be taken in a particular narrative succession, from greater initial disorder to greater final order.

If we want to appreciate the part played by narrative agents in the achievement of some textual unity (unity of significance), we must first of all consider other factors that play either for or against this unity.

In *La Chambre*, each of the four tales (*récits*) has its own title, the title of the book doubling as that of the second tale, pointing at a private space inhabited by characters, whose door, in the presented world, cannot be opened by the listener/narrator. The seven chapters of *Las afueras* are simply numbered. In *La Chambre*, superficial thematic unity is much more severely limited than in *Las afueras*, place and time have nothing to share but their vagueness, their referential indeterminacy (no names of streets, towns, or institutions); the conceptual nucleus of each story seems different: phenomenal strangeness in the first story, the solipsism of the dreamwork in the second, obsessive memory in the third, emotional possession in the fourth. The level of abstraction, a pseudoallusiveness, not the recurrence of concrete references to a shared encyclopedia, is a factor of unity. In *Las afueras*, in contrast, fairly precise geographic and historical reference is maintained throughout the seven parts: to Barcelona, the Catalan coast, and a narrow strip of inland country, and to approximately the last sixty years, with a double concentration on the *posguerra* and the weight of the Spanish civil war; the economic and cultural conditions of classes ranging from the poor peasantry to the high bourgeoisie, traditional family structures and their interplay with power, desire and violence in male sexuality, are also evoked in some detail.

In *La Chambre*, stylistic and rhetoric unity is so strong that it blurs any possible distinction between voices, even in reported speech: a factor of authorial or enunciative unity reinforced by a dominant abstract lexicon to be interpreted as a deliberate confession of artificiality, as a statement on the necessary separation of literary language from natural language. *Las afueras* shows a measure of "dialogism," although no character speaks Catalan in the text, a feature that emphasizes the figural, constructed nature of literary narrative. As far as the varieties of predication are concerned, *La Chambre* and *Las afueras* are opposite. Narrative discourse is generally scarce at the phrastic level in the former (even in "Les Grands Moments d'un chanteur," where there are more textualized narratemes, narrative intention seems to be more and more defeated by the proliferation of commentary and tabular discourses), while intradiegetic narrators are numerous and often at work in the latter (sequences are complete, detailed, presented as exhaustive accounts, which turns their frequent analeptic redevelopment into a "special effect").

The very complex interdependence between voice and character will be evoked in chapter 6, let it suffice now to note that, in *La Chambre*, the positions of enunciation, defined by the pronouns that explicitly rule verbs of saying, are initially diverse and finally confusing. In *Las afueras*, however, a Σ narrator is clearly present behind all third- and first-person utterances—these confined to reported speech. In conclusion, although stylistic, thematic, and enunciative features are too constant in each book to allow for a plurality of authors, genres, or visions of literary communication, there is still more to their internal continuity and total significance than all these features, considered separately or together, can explain.

I shall presuppose rather than demonstrate, for lack of space, that there is, in *La Chambre* as in most compartmentalized extended literary works, at least a degree of homology between the processes by which the unity of individual parts and the unity of the whole are generated. A description of leading NPs in the third story, "Une Mémoire démentielle," will be used as a shortcut.

The story begins with a third-person pronoun "he": "He had been too young to indulge in this [*cet*] elating and reckless exercise" (p. 93). Let us consider provisionally that the pronoun "he" lacks a textual antecedent. Any noun or, even more, any pronoun in this case, as it opens a blank space for speech, has practically no other semantic value than its syntactic valence (subject of an assertive predication) and, at best, some determination in gender and number. Like the *je* of "Longtemps je me suis couché de bonne heure" at the beginning of *La Recherche*, the cataphoric "he" will receive its semantic content retrospectively from the utterances in which it is anaphorically involved as subject, object, and so forth, either in the guise of pronoun or as a substantive, a proper name, or even in periphrastic form. Anaphora is a largely automated process of referentiation, but its other face, cataphora, is best served by an apparently careful respect of the horizon of expectations; here, for example, by the antithesis in the second sentence: "When he was older, he did it again exclusively to challenge nature," which combines thematic coherence with drawing a temporal axis. Progressively, the subject "he" establishes itself as polyvalent and extends its field of action toward the present, the "now" of the time of writing from which it was initially separated.

Its situation regarding the point in space "here" evolves in a similar but much slower fashion, as if the spatial parameters of meaning did depend indeed on the previous construction of a literary, textual space. The first deictic, *cet* (indifferently "this" or "that"), which can hardly refer to the title NP, works cataphorically like the subject "he" itself, but it implies a space of communication in which the spatiotemporal parameters of the virtual reader are involved. The emphatic *c'est . . . que*," often used after the second page, is also a figure of enunciation in the utterance, so that a progressive superposition can be achieved between the nunegocentric systems of the enunciator, the enunciated third person, and the virtual reader as text function. The numerous demonstrative pronouns and locutions (*ce qui, ce que, celui, ceux*, etc.) combine their necessarily anaphoric referentiation with a small number of demonstrative adjectives and their potentially deictic referentiation (e.g., *ce corps*, p. 96), so that this other mode is projected on the earlier one and becomes partly confused with it. Vincent Descombes would find here a textual manifestation of reductive referential fallacy: "all the signs being treated as words, all the words as names, all the names as symbols,"[28] but, precisely, paying attention to the functional division between parts of speech, as we are doing here, makes this textual process significant and fruitful.

The first *voici* ("Here is" and/or "such is") that bridges the "here" of enunciation and the "here" of the enunciated world appears also on page 96, and the first *ici* on page 98. On the following page we find successively, in reported speech, a first-person object in a subordinate clause, a first-person subject in a subordinate clause and then in a main clause. The point "here" more and more closely unites textual space with the space of the presented world. Eventually, the demonstratives will mediate the ultimate substitution of "I" for "he" in direct speech: "I am this man of letters. I am this maniac. But I was perhaps that [*cet*] child" (p. 131). We gain a feeling, as with Blanchot, that narrative can refer only to its enunciation, whether it is compulsive, reticent, or dictated by some law beyond the power of the narrator: "Eh bien soit: parlons, écrivons, n'hésitons pas, puisque nous ne saurions échapper au mal commun"[29] (So, let it be: let us speak, write, without hesitation, since we are unable to avoid the general disease [and/or "evil"]).

The goal of the all-embracing rhetoric of des Forêts, including his denial of rhetoric, would be to persuade the reader that, not just "this time" but "always," any "he" is an "I"; any main role is always, in the end, a speaker. There would be no other source of unity for the subject—or for narrative. Narrative unity would eventually depend, through the anaphora of the (speaking) subject, on the recurrence of the communication situation, neglecting the particular functions of characters and forces. But is this so? In fact, although speech is, logically and inevitably, a given—not a gift—from the very beginning, making the silence it breaks unthinkable and the question of origin at the same time ever more acute and ever more *dépassée*, the duality of the subject, generated or worsened, fostered and broadened by the fact of enunciation, turns speech into a disputed object whose appropriation would mean the victory of a singular, unified bearer of text: a victory over the reader as well as the disintegrating power of language (the obverse of the encompassing power of *voice*). It is an unending task: the enunciated "I" will never be able to coincide with the enunciator it presupposes; the effort toward directness and control is infinitely regressive, so that the apparent dynamics of the divided self is actually entirely geared to displaying its exponential division. The unity of the narrative space constructed is that of a hall of mirrors in which looking and being looked at are strictly interdependent. The panoramic and focal functions are exercised simultaneously, like an affirmation always associated with its questioning or its negation, like a sound whose existence could be proved to itself and to us only by its ironic echo, and which will find whatever completeness it can achieve in the second, ultimate silence. Similarly a desired and desperate inexhaustibility is concentrated in, not contradicted by, "tag line" endings in Beckett.[30] In each part of *La Chambre* there emerges a protagonist whose task it is to take over speech as if he did not have it already; but a progression, or rather a kind of outbidding, takes place from part to part as the imaginary fight becomes each time harder, the possession of speech more ambitious, more extensive, more destructive of the dynamic function and the autonomy of other characters. The much desired domination loses its objects as it resorbs them into effects of speech; it recedes as far back as the statement of its own intention with the hope of proving that unity is not at the same time self-destruction and self-exhibition. But unity is produced by the "unending" exhibition of its own destruction.

The single most striking textual gesture of *Las afueras* is the recurrence of proper names through variations of qualification and context in the different sections of the book. In the first part, we find the following designators: Victor, (Don) Augusto, (Doña) Magdalena, Claudina, Ciriac, Dina (alias Dineta or Bernardina), (Don) Ignacio, Roig, Domingo, Julio, Adrián, Tonio, Patalino. All but one are first names, diminutives, or nicknames; one is a typical Catalan patronym without a first name. All these designators then, like personal pronouns, share an ability to refer to different individuals in fairly open categories: halfway between ordinary nouns and fully specific proper names that exclude homonymy (like Peter the first of Serbia or Elizabeth Cleghorn Stevenson, Mrs. Gaskell), the names in *Las afueras* paradoxically depend on context, that is, on the acquisition of semantic content, to be recognized as specific designators, a specificity that will be threatened by any recontextualization, whether within a narrative sequence or, even more, through different sequences involving different forces, a different casting, different roles. "Victor" is present or mentioned in five of the seven parts of the book. In Part 2 he is the dead son of Don Augusto and Doña

Magdalena, and the father of the boy Bernardo; in Part 3, as in 1 and 2, he is married to an unnamed woman, but he is now the father of Alvarito (he was child-less in Part 1), as he will also be in Parts 4 and 7, and again the son of Augusto and Magdalena. Nevertheless, an old man by the name of Augusto appears alone in Part 5. In every case, the family is middle class, but it can rank very differently in this class. Ignacio or Nacho, a country physician in Part 1, reappears as a bank executive in 3 and as property manager in 4. On the other hand, Claudina, a peas-ant woman in Part 1, was married to Ciriac, in jail for theft like Claudina's hus-band, Ciriaco, in Part 6; in 6 *they* have a child called Bernardo, but in 1 they had a *daughter* called Bernardina, and Claudina of Part 5, daughter of a Mingo (Domingo), like Claudina of Part 1, is now an unmarried girl who should become the wife of the innovative young farmer Tonio.

Some characteristics of the system must be listed:

1. None of the names is present in all seven parts (systematic asystematicity);
2. the frequency of a name is not related to the importance of the role played in one sequence or another; thus Nap, the handicapped son of Mingo in Part 5, is a protagonist of this sequence but not even named anywhere else, while Adrián, always in the background, recurs three times;
3. Some names undergo morphological variations, others do not;
4. One name, with the corresponding variations, changes sex;
5. Most names bear several constant features of habilitation: Victor is always a bourgeois with something secret about him; Claudina is a young woman of peasant origin, whether or not she lives on the land . . . But, notwithstanding this strong link between names and roles in the presented world, the distribution of functions among major roles and others is the key to narrative unity even when it runs counter to the superficial unifying contribution of names.

The main roles are never converted into Σ narrators like "he" in "Une mémoire démentielle," but they always provide points of view and bear the panoramic function in competition with one or more subjects who enjoy a certain mobility between extra- and intradiegetic positions. At the beginning of Part 1, the text successively offers descriptions of the setting from where Victor is approaching on the road, of Victor "appearing"—seen by a third party—and acting in a way that can be recounted indifferently from his or from another point of view. In all of Part 2, it becomes clear that hiding and showing rather than doing things, are the privileged modes of existence of the three characters in the presented world; Augusto, Magdalena, and Bernardo are peeped-at Peeping Toms, a stock ironic or even comic situation turned dramatic in an existentialist manner by the ontological dependence of the characters on its structure. Like Meursault in *The Stranger*; they have no reality in their own eyes until they are reported, accused, denounced. Like Meursault again, Victor, in Part 1, is deprived of his ergativity at a crucial moment of the causal dynamic chain, when the bird, the golden oriole, is shot: there is a gun in somebody's hands, and then a life is taken. Similarly, in Part 2, the geraniums have been uprooted by "someone." Events that occur *in absentia*, as they do in the classic detective story, generate or justify the dominance of the panoramic/focal axis in the process of the quest for an "author" of the action incriminated, but, contrary to the detective story, the quest remains unsuccessful, or the solution known from the beginning is first omitted and later erased by the quest itself. As narrative develops, it further deprives the characters of the responsibility of their actions, which becomes shared by a combination of the narrational force (language actualizing itself in discourse) and various unnamed forces in the presented world, which the reader is led to reconstruct and formulate: a regressive social structure, the loss of identity of winners and losers alike after the civil war, and so on. Narrative utterances, like the events reported, are born incidentally at the intersection of two oblique glances; language, like action, sinks into an inescapable, tragic futility: "Someday perhaps . . . Anyway, why talk about it? See you tomorrow" (p. 180).

We can now conclude that, although the recurrent distribution of functions is indeed the main factor of narrative, ideological and aesthetic totalization, the lexical actualization of the agents is never neutral. In "La Chambre des enfants," for instance, the final restoration of the lost name is at the same time a reassurance for the pronominal subject and a distancing that will make projective communion forever impossible, or, in "Dans un miroir," the ghostly nature of our beings (*qua* representations) is strongly associated with naming: "Qui sait si elle aura encore la force de détourner son regard du fantôme compromettant que j'ai nommé Louise, et si moi-même et si nous tous tant que nous sommes, à voir ici le nôtre s'animer" (p. 191). Naming opens the abyss of infinite definition at the same time as it tries in vain to enclose each agent in its absolute, impossible singularity. The series—that is, partial repetitions, with semantic differences—of names in *Las afueras* have a double effect: when new signifiers appear, the reader should expect a different behavior, but he is disappointed; when the same signifiers recur, we expect them to work fully as well-defined lexemes, but we are deceived again. Semantic arbitrariness and unreliability are necessary ingredients of personification; they are indeed the conditions of possibility of authentically narrative transformations. They reinforce the subject by giving it command of a wider spectrum of predicates, although they also weaken it by threatening its unity and increasing its indeterminacy; they render its status somewhat similar to that, totally unpredictable, of [god] or [chance] in language. Conversely, the semantic reliability of names (i.e., rigid characters) tends to produce pseudonarratives of the kind described in chapter 2. And narratives that are characterized by a high recurrence of predicates ruled by changing NPs, that is marked by ergative transformations, imply the underlying laws of forces that will use any agents to reach their aims and manifest their empire:

Peter loved Mary,
then Peter and Paul loved Mary,
then Peter loved Jane,
then Mary loved Peter,
then . . .

Chapter 6
Voices: Knowing, Telling, and Showing It or Not

This chapter deals with the operations (of reading and inscribing) pertinent to the representation of enunciation in narrative. Genette writes in *Nouveau Discours du récit*:

> In the most sober narrative, someone talks to me, tells me a story, invites me to hear it as he tells it, and this invitation—trust or pressure—constitutes an unequivocal attitude of narration, hence the attitude of a narrator.

And also:

> Whether it is a narrative or not, when I open a book, it is because I want the author to *talk to me*. And since I am not deaf or dumb yet, I even answer him sometimes.[1]

The critic-as-reader expresses his desire of being "talked to," his need for a special addresser somewhere, which is a vital part of literary communication, not the fact of a human presence here, which remains always phantasmatic at this end of the act of communication. Therefore we shall call *voice* the product of the reader's quest for the origin of the text. "A voice": such is the vague, empty answer that we must give to the question of "who speaks," at least until we can describe more or less correctly the situation at the other (sending) end of the act of communication. By this time, the voice will usually become subdivided into different levels associated with the several structural mediators to whom a competence (certain qualities, skills, and limitations) is attributed as a function of their performances.

Just like in "real life"—of which literary communication is part and parcel— voices do not need to be embodied in a physical image in order to be credited with sense-making potential: they can be voices in the night, recorded or remembered; they can remain anonymous. But they must occur in a particular situation or "context," out of which no intention or compulsion to say something to somebody could be imagined or analyzed (hence no reaction could take place and a message would not be constructed). At the same time as we decide to consider a set of sounds and/or visual stimuli as a text, rather than as noises, stains, or erratic natural phenomena, we presuppose the existence of at least one voice "behind" the text, somehow actualized in it. The original questions, "Is somebody speaking?" and "Who is speaking?" are in fact syncretisms of many more questions, some of them relatively independent from each other, and some of them logically stratified: "Why?" "What for?" "In what circumstances?" "With what knowledge of the world and the addressee(s)?" "With what aims?" and so on.

The vertical, authoritarian view of communication, artistic in particular, which considers reception as ancillary to text production, and some apparent reactions to it that extend the act of reception backward to its total inscription in text production, have both contributed to an extraordinary inflation of the study of narration, with a correlative loss of specificity. Narration was the center of interest for two-thirds of *The Rhetoric of Fiction*, half of *Story and Discourse*, and nearly all of Stanzel's *Theory of Narrative*. Our concentration on the *tale told*, on the narrated as the object of narrative transaction, does not mean, however, that narration has become unimportant to us, but that it is only one theoretical moment of this transaction, and one we can only know through its traces (texts) and its outcome (meanings and values).

Although the entire field of study should eventually be reorganized, it seems useful to start with a clarification of the two traditional concepts: "narrator" and "point of view." The former at least can give access to some aspects of narrative communication, if it is redefined, not reified.

Narrators

The compulsory constitutive task of the narrator is to fulfill the *narrative function*, called *representative function* by Dolezel. This function is always combined with the *control function* [*fonction de contrôle ou de régie*], since the narrator controls the structure of the text in the sense that he is able to quote the discourse of the actors. . . . Beside these two obligatory functions, the narrator is free to practise the optional *interpretation function* or not.[2]

The narrator does not have a personality but a mission, perhaps nothing more than a function: to tell [*contar*]. He fulfills it well insofar as he does not stray from it. . . . The narrator, then, is an abstraction.[3]

These two quotations from recent theorists are characteristic of the more or less successful contemporary attempts to draw a distinction between narrator and author, and another between narrator and character, both in terms of functions. The author would be responsible for the whole text, using an intermediate specialized instance—the narrator—to tell (within the text), whereas characters are elements of content in the presented world whose role is to be and to act. However necessary it may have been to avoid collapsing all the levels and relays of presentation, projection, and identification into one huge divine chaos that reeks of false familiarity and abolishes the constitutive distance of artistic communication to the benefit of fusional misunderstanding, some limitations of this approach are immediately apparent: (1) the narrator is said to be an abstraction, but he *has* a function, or better a "mission" or task; our theorists speak of "him" as if he were a human being or perhaps a spirit, without a personality, but still capable of good and ill will, success and failure, authority and interpretation; (2) *the* narrator is viewed singly in principle, even though "he" may end up subdivided or multiplied; (3) "narrator" is not taken specifically as the conveyor of *narrative* discourse any more than "narratee" was a specific receiver for Prince or Rousset.[4]

Any meaningful utterance U presupposes an act of enunciation reconstructed by a receiver in the form: "X says U." We call X an *enunciator*. The enunciator is a narrator if U has a narrative effect or is part of a set of utterances, explicit or implicit, from which narrative meaning can be derived. The enunciator of the isolated remark "The sea is blue" is not a narrator; the enunciator of "Ulysses returns to Ithaca" is one, but so is the enunciator of the utterance "Ulysses is prisoner on an island," if this utterance belongs to a text that includes the utterance "Ulysses eventually regained his throne"; the former utterance, in the context of the latter, implies that, at some stage, "Ulysses was released."

A narrator is the subject of enunciation of one or more utterances that either contain a narrateme or are involved in the production of a narrateme by the reader.

Narrating is a particular actantial role at the level of enunciation; at this level, the same actor-enunciator can also play other roles such as those of describer, or giver of orders, as does Mentor when he says to Telemachus: "The sea is blue. *Ulysses is returning to Ithaca.* Let us find him and go with him." The frequent confusion between narrator and enunciator in general is due to three factors:

1. The differentiation of predicative types of discourses is often insufficient (for example, the injunction in the third sentence of the example contains a potential narrative of the future, yet to be actualized in the presented world).
2. One enunciative act can be embedded within another, since "Men-

tor says to Telemachus 'The sea is blue. Ulysses is returning to Ithaca,' " etc., also requires a general enunciator who will indirectly embrace both narrative and nonnarrative information.

3. To speak is always, at least in part, to act: an enunciator, whether in the presented world or outside, is easily perceived as a reporter of events, because he is the subject of the "action of speaking."

For all these reasons, without losing sight of a possible specialization of the actantial roles of enunciation, we do not have to rebut systematically the tradition of labeling as "narrators" the various instances of enunciation in the framework of narrative communication.

Subjects of enunciation as such are involved in a triple set of relations: with the utterances enunciated, with other subjects of enunciation, and with the addressees, intentional or not, of their acts of enunciation. It is these relations that we will encounter repeatedly in the next two sections.

Paratactic and Hypotactic Relations in Narration

There is no such thing as a nonnarrated story, although the receiver may lose consciousness of the act of enunciation, together with any awareness of his act of understanding-imagining, as happens in a dream. The situations in which such losses occur and the textual devices used to achieve the "illusion of pure mimesis" are worth studying, but they should never hide the fact of enunciation, which it is the task of the critic to identify and unmask, always smoldering under its pretended absence or the mockery of its own exhibition. Actually, there is no difference of *nature* between all the subjects of enunciation in a complex act of enunciation like that involved by the transmission of an extended narrative. For any utterance in a text or for a text as a whole, the subject of enunciation is always a construction of the receiver, *not* the grammatical subject of the utterance, set of utterances, or complete text concerned. This is true even of performative utterances such as: "I swear that x happens"; the subject of enunciation here is not "I," subject of the enunciated verb "swear," but "he who says 'I swear,' subject of the verb "say" in the receiver-formulated, extratextual utterance "He says that he swears."

On the other hand, the radical separation between subjects of enunciation and subjects of the enunciated means that, while the latter are essentially heterogeneous, the former, which can exclusively command verbs such as "communicate" (in the receiver-observer's speech), are essentially all alike. They differ in only two ways: scope and modality of communication. Can they say much or little? Do they suggest, state, or imply? Do they affirm or question? Do they state what they say in their own names, or report it? Do they share the enunciation of the text with others, or do they enjoy a monopoly? Is there a clear delimitation of the textual segments uttered by them? In narrative communication, then, things are much simpler in certain respects, and much more complicated in others, than they are presented by most theorists. The distressing proliferation of instances endowed with variegated attributes can be replaced by a spatial distribution of roles, easy to conceive and more productive as a descriptive and heuristic tool.

That the subject of enunciation is always exterior to the enunciated explains that hypotactic relations are usually present in the system of enunciation, and paratactic relations (juxtaposition, coordination) automatically imply them. Enunciation without subordination would require a complete set of independent utterances (without any reported speech or verb of communication), a pure report of action, and inventory of items, excluding thoughts, speech, and expressive behavior. Delegated or embedded narration, most noticeable when a second narrator (or subsequent narrators) enunciates large segments of text, either in diversion or in partial duplication of the overall narrative (digression, *récit à tiroirs, mise en abyme*), is nevertheless the absolutely dominant system of enunciation. One makeshift example will be examined in the first place.

Hypotaxis: Complex Embedding and Its Consequences

> "My grandmother used to tell me how she had fallen in love with a young officer who had declared his passion for her, although he was not rich enough to marry an heiress," said Max. "Was the officer your grandfather?" interrupted John. At this, the two men started to laugh.

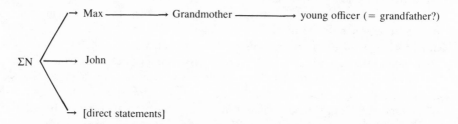

In the preceding text, an anonymous narrator reports speech from two agents, Max and John, and makes a statement about an action carried out by them (starting to laugh). Max reports, in indirect speech iterative summary, a narrative or fragment of narrative told by his grandmother, in which another agent (the "young officer") intervened again by speech in the form of a reported performative ("declared his passion" = telling + acting out). John contributes to the narration by asking a question that activates the hermeneutic and proairetic codes and, at the same time, suggests possible answers.

If this text is a narrative about upper-class marriages of olden times, Max and John are its intratextual but extradiegetic narrators, whereas the instances "grandmother" and "young officer" appear as intradiegetic narrators, embedded to the first and second degree, respectively. The asymmetry between "grandmother" and "young officer" should make us realize that the reported narrator does not coincide in time with the agent in the love story. The words "used to tell" also suggest that Max's grandmother "*re*-counted" rather than just told the story, which could imply yet another intermediate narrator: the grandmother's younger self. But, whether this is a narrative about love affairs, or a narrative about telling them, repeating and using them in conversation, there can be no doubt as to the necessary existence of an extratextual enunciator who names and quotes Max and John. In the first case, the overall narrator ΣN collaborated with Max and John practically at the same time as they were submitted to ΣN as delegated narrators; in the second case, the paratactic relation disappears, because Max and John become intradiegetic narrators. Conversely, the choice of seeing a subject rather as an actor or as a narrator, when it is possible, will change the "point" of a narrative, the theme that guides the construction of meaning and value; let us remember that this is one of the devices that can alter the genre of fictionality, shifting it from realism, for example, to metafiction, as happens in *Tristram Shandy*.

Complex hypotactic relations in narration, of which the preceding text is only a moderate example, show a strong tendency to blur the origin of enunciation. The segment "although he was not rich," reported by Max, is given as uttered by his grandmother, but it is not clear whether the young officer in the story confessed his poverty himself. The more embedded a narration is, the more difficult it becomes to report speech directly: John: "My wife said: 'My husband told Peter: "Peter, don't say: 'Jane will go!' " ' " Indirect speech makes enunciated contents more easily transferable from one enunciator to another, finally restoring homogeneity under the N's hegemony, in the guise of delegation and dispersion. In any case, multiple narrational framing tends to distract the receiver from the contents of the deepest frame, if any, and concentrate his attention on the art and artifice of narration, as in the joke:

> There were ten Boy Scouts around a camp fire; the first Boy Scout got
> up and said: "There were ten Boy Scouts around a camp fire, the first
> Boy Scout got up and said: 'There were ten Boy Scouts . . . ' "

This is what one could call structural punning in narration. It blocks reference to other universes of discourse very effectively, serving metafiction and humor, whereas realism will tend to avoid it and have recourse to paratactic relations between the narrators, as happens in the detective story, or to minimal delegation (quoted speech) under a single powerful narrator. Yet, the degree of narrational subordination must be considered.

Hypotaxis: Forewording and the manuscrit trouvé Technique.

Let us read the prologue of the *Epic of Gilgamesh* in the English edition by N. K. Sandars:

I will proclaim to the world the deeds of Gilgamesh. this was the man
to whom all things were known; this was the king who knew the countries of the world. He was wise, he saw mysteries and knew secret
things, he brought us a tale of the days before the flood. He went on a
long journey, was weary, worn out with labour, returning he rested, he
engraved on a stone the whole story. . . .
    In Uruk he built walls, a great rampart. . . . Look at it still to-
day. . . . Climb upon the wall of Uruk; walk along it, I say; regard
the foundation terrace.[5]

The earlier edition by Alexander Heidel[6] shows that, if tablet 1 actually contains an invitation to admire the wall as monumental testimony to the hero's gran-
deur, there is no overt narrational proclamation of the sort that Sandars made up
in the interest of the general public. It is worth noting that Sandars felt the necessity of contriving a first-person, although anonymous, narrator who fulfills a
number of functions. This "I" disappears completely after the single initial page
of the prologue; it asserts itself only to abdicate before the hero, whom it extolls,
thus signifying respect and veneration for him. At the same time, the hero who
replaces the narrator materially in the text confers retrospectively some of his
powers on this narrator; the engraved text of his deeds becomes one with the tale
told by the narrator, which the receiver will climb to visit like a monument of
stone. The later absence of the narrator, which can only be felt as something
amiss, after his initial presence was forcefully established, makes it seem that the
hero—albeit in the third person—tells his own story; it acquires the overwhelming
power, dramatic in essence, of facts witnessed by the receiver. The fragmentary
translation of fragmentary texts, in the Heidel edition, tempered by scientific
doubt and bearing so many marks of the reader-interpeter's work, left no room
for the remarkable illusionist strategy adopted by Sandars to transform the epic
into a "readerly" text.
    Revealingly, a very similar strategy is used, on a lower key, by many modern
storytellers, especially the naturalists and Costumbristas (nineteenth-century
authors of Spanish and Hispanic tales of manners), who could see the advantages
of narrational features borrowed from popular traditions (or their idea of them)
when they sought to recreate a feeling of quasi-conversational, oral immediacy.
In oral transmission, as with the African *griot*, the storyteller, to a certain extent,
speaks for the hero or heroine, aristocrat, or dynasty, and thus, through his diction, rhythm, chanting, and mimicry, a physical part (fetish or relic?) of the
characters is invoked. But, in its written literary transposition, the overt framing
storyteller who does not provide the physical presence of the voice and gestures,
supplies an apparently candid, primary text, which turns the framed narrative into
a solid object; at the same time, he frees himself of the responsibility of author-
ship with regards to this narrative: the framed narrative, even when it is unreliable (as in fantasy or horror stories), becomes autonomous, is placed in the same

situation vis-à-vis the reader as it is supposed to be vis-à-vis the framing narrator; it is like some raw, uninterpreted reality, mysterious because it is "real."

Maupassant offers a fine example of this technique in his short story "Allouma."[7] The initial narrator, a tourist in Algeria, gets lost one evening in the country, where he meets by "pure chance" with a friend of a friend, who is a colonist there:

> Fifteen minutes later, I was dining hungrily in front of my host, who was still smoking.
> I knew his story. After spending a lot of money [*après avoir mangé beaucoup d'argent*] on women, he had invested the remnants of his wealth in Algerian land and planted vineyards.
> "But, what about women?"
> " Ah! . . . Resources are somewhat limited."
> "Only 'somewhat?'
> "I am going to tell you a story in which [my manservant] plays a major role."
> When the man was gone, he began . . . (pp. 11–12)

Auballe's love story involving the southern nomadic Arab girl Allouma, as told by himself, goes on for some twenty-eight pages uninterrupted by the listener; only the moral conclusion, with a possible alternative denouement, is brought about by a short final dialogue in which Auballe has the last word:

> M. Auballe had got up. He walked about the room and looked at me, smiling:
> "Such is love in the desert!"
> I asked him: "And, if she came back?"
> He muttered: "The slut! . . . But I would be glad, though."
> "And you would forgive her the shepherd?"
> "Well, yes. With women, you know, you must always forgive . . . or ignore these things." (p. 40)

We could wonder, then, why there is a ΣN at all, or, if you prefer, why Auballe is not allowed to tell his story directly; or, on the contrary, why the frame here is so asymmetrical. Besides those evoked earlier, many more reasons could be suggested.

1. The first-person framing narrator can hardly be distinguished from the "implied author"; his realist attitude and the reality effect of the embedded narrative are enhanced by the complete "literal" recording of Auballe's tale. Although Auballe may not tell the truth, the telling of the story *is* an indisputable event in the ΣN's "life."

2. The plane of literary production appears to emanate naturally, effortlessly, from life itself, where the ΣN finds it; narration is a natural, purposeless surplus

of life, of the life of others, instead of a painful task (if it were assumed by the
ΣN-implied author) or the manifestation of a need (if it were assumed by the protagonist). Narration floats between the two narrators without being appropriated
by one or the other, as if it were life telling itself. But, at the same time, the subjects seem to be less involved in the events described. The effect is double: to permit dramatization, on the one hand, and to distance it, on the other.

3. Narration happens "by pure chance," and, between two newly acquainted
people, it is doubly casual: no space for excessive emotion, no room for a *personal exchange* that would compete with the secret intensity of the embedded
story; indirect narration increases the luminous mystery of passion by structurally
turning the whole story of Allouma into a litote.

4. The ΣN dedicates almost three of his five introductory pages to a highly
lyrical description of the Algerian landscape seen as a sensual living being with
which nightfall could perhaps achieve the fusional loss that desire had suggested
and prevented during the day. The embedded narrator offers a kind of salvation
to the traveler by transforming the landscape into a character, and description into
narrative, as if there were more blood running in narrative. But the narrative remains open; the same signifiers are repeated; inescapable passion is reaffirmed,
its depths doubled by recurrent exploration, this effect is that of *fixation*.

5. The ΣN, who transcribes or recites and "gives to the public" a tale he has
heard, doubles as inscribed reader; his role as such is often extremely ambiguous,
however. On the one hand, he forbids direct "contact" with the existents in the
framed story; he maintains some objective distance and should prevent crude
identification of the reader with the characters. On the other hand, due to the same
distance, he facilitates an apparently safe access to the presented world and offers
models and countermodels of reading that make us feel secure (someone has already visited this world). But the presence of a guide who says, "This is just a
story," may well be a trap for our drives, exactly like the dream within a dream,
which further lowers the barrier of censorship.

Metafiction too has made a secret deal with the return of the repressed. The
device of the *manuscrit trouvé* is exceptionally frequent in two cases: where there
is stringent legal or social censorship, and when the story or stories "found" play
dangerously—promisingly—with our unconscious: "Convinced that this book
would never be returned to its legitimate owner, I did not hesitate to get hold of
it."[8] The text behind the text builds a monument in the place of a narrator, but
fantasy has left no one accountable for the narrative:

> The original papers, together with the scarlet letter itself—a most curi-
> ous relic—are still in my possession, and shall be freely exhibited to
> whomsoever, induced by the great interest of the narrative, may desire
> a sight of them.[9]

Parataxis: Narrative Relays and Conflicts.

The question of narrational parataxis is closely related to that of dialogism: it will be partly theorized in the last section of this chapter, but we should note here that it does not occur only in dialogue proper, and dialogic enunciation offers no guarantee of a paratactic narrational structure. With narrational parataxis, in order to establish a typology, we have to consider the narrative matter retrospectively as if it was a given (a *fabula*, in the formalist sense), when the fabula or story is actually constructed into narrative matter by the very division of labor between "parallel" narrators placed at similar levels of subordination. It will be profitable nevertheless to outline three main models of relations between "parallel" narrators, it being understood that they are never fully actualized in real narratives, but mixed and combined in varying proportions.

1. Sequential relay. Two or more narrators tell successive events and give successive information belonging to the same plot in *"linear"* chronological order, that is, in the order in which events are supposed to have occurred and cognizance of the relevant information may have been taken in the presented world. Narration, then, is ritualized, as it is in a mass, for example; or, more rarely, its arrangement in time will be justified by successive fragmentary witnessing of the events concerned by the narrators in their previous roles of panoramic agents. An extraordinary example is that of scene 2 of *Savannah Bay*, by Marguerite Duras, although the technique was also used elsewhere in her work:

YOUNG WOMAN: . . . He had seen on the white of that stone the small shape outlined in black. (*A long pause*) And then he had had seen her throw herself into the sea, swimming away

MADELEINE: She made a hole in the sea with her body. And she disappeared in the water hole. The water closed back.

YOUNG WOMAN: Nothing can be seen any more on the surface of the sea. (*A pause*) Then he shouts. (*A pause*) Then he stands up on the white stone and he shouts. That he wants to see again this maiden in a black swimsuit. (*A pause*) Hearing him shout, she came back.[10]

2. Concurrent or conflictive versions. The same "data," the same core events or the content of the same period of time in the same place, are covered by two or more narrators who confirm the same story or, on the contrary, contradict each other; this is typical of the classical detective story. Take *Murder on the Nile* or any other: X will say to Hercule Poirot that, at the time of the crime, he was reading a book alone on the deck; Y will say to the same Poirot that, at the time of the crime, she was having an argument with X in the first-class lounge. Since X and Y cannot both be right and sincere, or the information they provide should be taken as indicative of their living by different parameters, this technique serves the authority of a supreme narrator who will reconcile all the versions, negate, correct, or validate some or all of them, or confirm once again all concurring clues; the suspense bears as much on the narrational architecture as on the "reliability" of successive informers.

3. *Narrational crossfire*. There is some relaying in time, as in (1), but it need not be precisely chronological: there may be a conflict or convergence of information as in (2), but this is not very important, since there is no central core of events to link the different partial narratives between them, or the core is a pretext that is progressively diluted almost out of sight by successive narrations with different centers of interest. Anyone will recognize the narrational structure of *As I Lay Dying* in this description; the death and burial of Addie Bundren is iconicized by the several rounds of narration creating her absence, of which further proof is given by her materially central intervention in the book, out of place, yes, but unable to reverse her own death by the metaphoric affirmation of Anse's death at her side. Narrational cross fire thus contributes less to narrative suspense than to the promotion of a lyrical mood, such that the object of the tale told, the object of the reader's quest, becomes ever more evanescent as its portraits are multiplied in a distorted space from which the hypothetical model is banned.

Let us note finally that, first, the paratactic dimension of narrational organization always implies a powerful organizer (ΣN, implied author or chief editor, as you prefer), an enunciator manifesting itself mainly by its control function, so much so that, when this dimension is dominant, the Σ narrator generally remains behind the scene, extradiegetic and even extratextual; its necessity is brought about as a projection of the reader's requirement of textual unity. Second, paratactically associated narrators tend to be dramatized; they are textualized as agents fulfilling their panoramic function; they force polyphony up to the surface of the text, but this is as much or more a question of multiple "points of view" as of discrete narrational acts. The effect (kaleidoscopic, discordant, or unanimously converging) on reader-produced narrative significance can be very similar in narratives where characters exert their panoramic function passively, just happening to be where they are, rather than by plentiful narrative speech acts.

First-and Other-Person Narrations

We have progressed a good deal in the study of voice without so far taking into consideration the question of the narrational grammatical person. It would be wrong to neglect it completely, but I am equally ready to insist that it has been widely overemphasized — and misunderstood.

The subject of enunciation is "he who speaks" according to the discourse of the receiver receiving who, as soon as he produces a discourse on communication, becomes an observer. The same is true of the enunciating agent in the communication situation, so that, strictly speaking, the act of enunciation, even when it is figuratively practiced ("metalinguistically described," according to Greimas) in the first person, is not knowable *in* this person: "I mean, *you* know," or, from another angle, "I know *he* means." Greimas and Courtès stress that one should not confuse the enunciative act (*le faire énonciatif*) with the uttered or reported enunciation (*l'énonciation énoncée*), which is only a simulacrum. Nevertheless, I disagree with their deduction that "the 'I,' 'here,' and 'now' that we find in the enunciated discourse in no way represent the subject, space, and time of enunciation"[11] because they are an "unscientific" projection. In fact, the problem with these anchoring elements is the leap on which they rely: they re-present an act of enunciation that is never present or presentable. Once we understand and accept the theoretical difference and separation between the space of communication in which the producer(s) and receiver(s) of a text evolve, and the narrower space of the text itself, we still have to account for what the items 'I,' 'here,' and 'now' in a text are intended to mean, stand for, and cannot but mean a priori. They mean that the subject of enunciation manifests propositionally his oneness with the subject of the utterance (a oneness that can be modalized in as many ways as any other proposition). Now any person used in an utterance presupposes a first person against and with which it makes sense, so that the enunciating 'I,' unknowable in its act, is however always represented in any text; and any receiver must determine his position in relation to it. This indisputable fact had to be settled to clarify that first- and other-person narration cannot mean narration made *by* a first person (always true) or another (always false), but refers only to the varied textual strategies used in the representation of enunciation through a paradigmatic system structurally identical to that of the communication situation constructed by the observer. In other words, the configuration of explicit and implicit persons (in a loose sense) is a textual factor of the concretization of "voice" by the reader, such that even its literal acceptance remains a figural game: a game of figuration of the ever-absent enunciating 'I.' This is why some of the best recent contributions on the topic, notably in the genres of autobiography, the epistolary text, and the lyrical, are rhetorical studies.[12]

But we should still reformulate one capital observation made in chapter 1. Narrative, I hope we know by now, is concerned with change, a narrateme being the paradoxical (magic) imposition of identity on subjects whose identity is negated by the predicate: "John has changed" can be rewritten as "John$_1$ ≠ John $_2$." This has three important consequences:

1. A textual narrative first person, as in "I went to bed," is not only representative of and different from the enunciative subject of these words, it is also split into two or even three instances, subjects of "not be in bed," "move," and "be in bed," respectively. The narrative subject is always plural; it undermines the unifying work of its re-presented enunciation. This is one of the reasons, perhaps, why autobiography is such a perilous exercise, particularly when it is subject oriented.

2. But, regarding this threat and the means to fight it, all persons in narrative are grossly equal; the fact that one of them, the first, bears preferentially the weight of voice figuration does not affect narrative meaning fundamentally. We can see it when Julius Caesar refers to Julius Caesar in the grammatical third person, or, for that matter, when a schizoid character in a novel does the same thing:

> "She must go for a long walk, for today she has had nothing to eat,"
> she said to Otto.
> "Yes, but you . . . I mean I heard that you . . . that something hap-
> pened to you last night . . . "
> "Last night," she repeated, looking away from him, "last night she did a
> very foolish thing, turning on the gas."[13]

Although, in this last case, the change from Esme's expression in the first person to the third person does constitute a narrative event, it is to be constructed, like many other narratemes, through the juxtaposition of fragments of tagged reported speech.

3. The very same threat that narrative poses to the unity of its enunciated subject (and thus, indirectly, to the enunciating subject) by the semantic content of predication, is limited, compensated for, or even canceled by the *form* of express narrative predication, the narrative verb, which welds again together the *schizé* it has registered: "Veni, vidi, vici."

Three types of the enunciated person that would deserve better treatment than they have generally received, because they strongly affect "voice" through the mediation of the addressee and the receiver, are the second person, the first-person plural, and the indeterminate person (one, *uno, on,* etc.). All of them have been exemplified and explored in contemporary French narrative (e.g., respectively, in *La Modification*, by Michel Butor, *Les Eoliennes*, by Pierre Silvain, and *L'Opoponax*, by Monique Wittig). Contrary to the first- and third-person types, these three "persons" have the *faculty* of including the implied reader in their referential field, a faculty that can be indulged in or negated, depending on the predicative content of the utterance, but whose exercise is always impending and places permanently on the actual reader the onus of defining himself in relation to the text and its enunciator. The three types, which work slightly differently because of the varying relation between otherness and addressing in them, share the key characteristic that they blackmail the reader into negotiating and measuring his existential involvement in the meanings and values that can be construed from the text. When Shlomith Rimmon-Kennan states that, in *La Modification*, "the narrator, addressing himself in the second person, seems to be verbalizing his actions while performing them,"[14] she completely misses the aesthetic and philosophical originality of this work, since it relies in great part on the resistance test to which it submits the reader: "You see telegraph poles rushing across the train window?" "No, *I* don't, do *I?* But, don't I?" And, if the weary reader happens to accept that, yes, he does this and that, the text jumps back at him with the other function of you: talking to and *of* oneself as to and of another person. "You" represents the enunciative "I" as one who is forever separated from the enunciated; identification and even identity are all the more ready to be shattered that they seem close and tempting. But these phenomena cannot be fully analyzed by themselves, without taking into account the population of the textual possible worlds and the ways they come into being for the reader (see chapter 4).

Points of View and Information

The notion of point of view, overgrown and overworn, has become an object of incredible confusion in narratology, probably because it is situated at the junction of the narrational and narrated planes in one of its acceptions, and at the intersection of meaning and value, in the other. My aim is not polemical here; I will give only a few examples to show the necessity of a fresh theoretical start in this matter.

Bernard Valette writes:

> The presence of the narrator among the characters, or his absence (omniscient author) answers the question "who speaks?" The notion of "restriction of field" (or authorial intrusion) *concerns the narrator, not the point of view*. Point of view depends in fact on the question "Who sees?" and relies exclusively on the opposition between internal and external vision. (my italics)[15]

and: "The most frequent point of view is internal focalization" (p. 35), purporting to use Genette's terminology. The awful jumble of categories in the passage quoted is not, however, a constant feature of the book, and the author's complete ignorance of recent international research on the subject does not suffice to explain the misunderstanding. I quote Genette, writing well before the publication of Valette's handbook on the modern novel: "By focalization, I mean indeed a 'restriction of field,' that is in fact a selection of narrative information."[16]

Wallace Martin, the latest writer to date on narrative theories, fares hardly better than Valette, without the excuse of ignorance. It is apparent that, for him, "point of view" is interchangeable with "manner of telling" and "narrative method," which means that the widely accepted paradigm "time/mode/voice" is rendered inoperative. On the other hand, Seymour Chatman made the very exaggerated claim that

> perception, conception, and interest points of view are quite independent of the manner in which they are expressed. When we speak of "expression," we pass from point of view, which is only a perspective or stance, to the province of narrative voice, the medium through which perception, conception and everything else is communicated.[17]

For Chatman, point of view is plural and voice singular. For Lotman, it is virtually the opposite:

> The concept of "point of view" is analogous to that of perspective in painting and film. The concept of "literary point of view" unfolds as the relationship of the system to its "subject" (or "sentient center"). . . . By "subject" we have in mind some consciousness which is capable of generating a structure of this kind, and hence, is reconstructible through the process of reading.[18]

The notion of "point of view" still hovers between a descriptive use related to the panoramic function of characters and/or of an author/narrator considered as intradiegetic even when he is not, and an ideologically critical use related to the referential bias or grid through which the representation of an otherwise existing world (mimesis) can make itself pass for the presentation of a fictive world, or vice versa.

To avoid all these uncertainties and some of the half-truths they can lead to, I propose to consider "point of view" as a relation between two components or parameters of voice (projected or reader-represented enunciation). One of these parameters we have called "narrators." A narrator is a grammatical position of a subject of enunciation with regards to an utterance or a set of utterances; it can be described in terms of *scope* (the amount, linguistic variety, etc., of utterances placed under its command) and of *position* in the system of narrators. The other parameter is the *informative performance* of a voice, itself related to a presupposed *informative competence* and to an inferred *cognitive competence*. Point of view, then, if we care to keep it at all, could be reduced to two factors: *distance* and *sanction*. These aspects will be developed through some examples analyzed later in this chapter, but let us summarize first the theoretical space concerned here in a simple diagram:

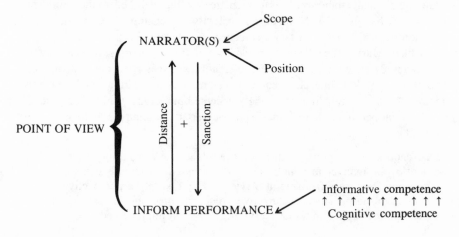

The informative performance of a voice can be very poor in spite of a high cognitive competence, if the informative competence is poor: the diplomatic secrets of imminent World War III are communicated in a code not accessible or only partly accessible to the implied reader of the overall narrative. This poor performance is carried out through a numerous bunch of paratactically and hypotactically organized narrators, composing the "rumor," the most subordinated being those who use the inaccessible code ("X says that Y says that N—the national leader—says ?"). A Σ narrator (with the widest scope) sanctions positively the whole chain of transmission. The text will run like this, in a James Bond story (do not take literally):

> We have just been in touch with our special agent 007 who says that, according to Sean Connery's faithful report, Captain Fleming has come across several handwritten copies of a document that reads: "Alliance between Bananas and Tornado against Misfire imminent."

It is the various discrepancies between competences and between distance and sanction that produce a comic effect by stretching excessively our logical gullibility with little reward. In another thematic and generic context, similar discrepancies and incompatibilities will generate the marvelous, as we have seen in chapter 4. But the "reality effect" of a text also depends to a large extent on the same system of voice, used in a different manner. *Ethan Frome*, by Edith Wharton (1911), occasionally compared with *The Europeans* and *Wuthering Heights*, will be our key example in the present section.

Ethan Frome is the story of a poor New Englander who runs a sawmill. Married to Zeena, a hard, selfish hypocondriac, Ethan falls in (reciprocated) love with the delicate, pretty, young, Mattie Silver, who has full board at their home in exchange for domestic help. Zeena wants to hire a paid servant instead. With no money and no hope of being reunited, Ethan and Mattie, after a last few hours of tenderness and despair, decide to commit suicide together by running their sleigh into a tree; but neither of them dies in the crash. Twenty-four years later, Ethan, lame and crooked, is "but the ruin of a man," and Mattie, a quadriplegic, still lives at his home, where Zeena takes care of her. This we learn from the framing narrative of the narrator's acquaintance with the protagonists and a few other characters in the framed story. The narrating subject is extradiegetic with regards to the core story, but intradiegetic as a witness of the epilogue contained in the two parts of the framing narrative. The framing narrative presents an overt first-person narrator, the framed narrative does not. Two diagrams will help visualize the narrational and narrated planes:

Order of the Narrated (story).

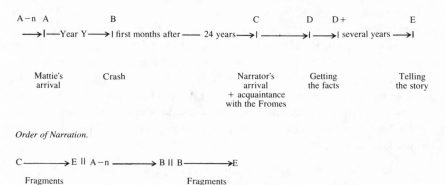

Order of Narration.

C ────────→ E ‖ A−n ────────→ B ‖ B ────────→E

Fragments   Fragments

The first segment of the framing narrative motivates the telling of the tale and the search for the information that led to its composition: Ethan Frome is a striking character; Starkfield is a harsh, strangely desolate, fascinating place. Since its people are isolated and secretive, it was necessary to gather information from several of them in order to know more, but a visit to Ethan Frome's home was vital to provide a "key." The overt narrator (enunciated enunciator) is quite explicit about the origin of information and his intervention in narrative composition: "I had the story bit by bit, from various people, and, as generally happens in such cases, each time it was a different story."[19] He is even so explicit about it and uses such a crude device to involve the implied reader in the presented world ("If you know Starkfield, Massachusetts . . . If you know the post-office you must have seen Ethan Frome") that this segment seems, like many nineteenth-century beginnings and prefaces, to solicit our interest for storytelling in general rather than for the particular story about to be unraveled: "I had the sense that the deeper meaning of the story [told by Harmon Gow, a Starkfield resident] was in the gaps," (p. 7). We do not know yet whether the significance will take the shape of such gaps in the central narrative (reduced narrative performance) or whether it will arise from the filling in of the initial gaps by the framing narrative.

In fact, in the central narrative, we are at first somewhat surprised to encounter a (re)presentation of Ethan's consciousness (sensations and thoughts) from inside, that is, facts not directly accessible to anybody except the presented person. There is nothing in the first or the second segment of framing narrative to corroborate an oral or written transmission of these precise and intimate experiences of Ethan to the Σ narrator or his informers. We read, for instance: "The effect produced on Frome was rather of a complete absence of atmosphere . . . 'It's like being in an exhausted receiver,' he thought" (p. 27); "Ethan was suffocated with the sense of well-being" (p. 82); "Ethan's heart was jerking to and fro between two extremities of feeling" (p. 108); and so forth. The inner states of Zeena, Mattie, and the minor characters remain largely undescribed, and the little of them we are entrusted with is presented through the mediation of Ethan's perceptions and reckonings at the time.

Except in some sparse reported speech, however, Ethan Frome never appears as the subject of enunciation of the narrative information concerning him and other characters; should we dispense with a more sophisticated narrational analysis, we could easily accept the central narrative in *Ethan Frome* as a perfect illustration of Chatman's rule: "The perspective and the expression need not be lodged in the same person."[20] Unfortunately, this does not hold true under closer scrutiny. Near the three passages quoted earlier, we also find the following utterances:

> *Young Ethan Frome* walked at a quick pace along the deserted street.
> (p. 26)
> [His interrupted studies] had *fed his fancy* and made him aware of
> *huge cloudy meanings* behind the daily face of things (p. 27)
> "Well, Matt, any visitors?" he threw off, stooping down *carelessly*.
> (p. 83)
> "Is that what the new doctor told you?" he asked, *instinctively* lowering his voice. (p. 109)

In all these utterances, it is clear that a good part of the information conveyed is not mediated by Ethan's consciousness. "Young Ethan" implies a temporal distance that would be at odds with the access given to his consciousness at the time of the events narrated, not later (no prolepses in the central narrative). And none of the other three examples can bear a first-person transformation without undergoing a severe semantic change: "I stooped down carelessly," for instance, would imply feigned, calculated carelessness. As Wharton herself was well aware, the linguistic matter of narration (lexicon, syntax, rhetoric) is as determinant in assigning the origin of information to a subject as any narrated "fact" in the presented worlds:

> If [the looker-on] is capable of seeing all around [the characters], no
> violence is done to probability in allowing him to exercise this faculty;
> it is natural enough that he should act as the sympathising intermediary
> between his rudimentary characters and the more complicated minds to
> whom he is trying to present them. . . . only the narrator of the tale
> has scope enough to see it all, to resolve it back into simplicity, and to
> put it in its rightful place among his larger categories. (pp. viii–ix)

In other words, although Ethan Frome is a highly panoramic character in the context of the central narrative, he is not a primary informer in this context and he is essentially focalized from the framing narrative. Perspective and expression do coincide. The narrator produces and proffers Ethan's mental life on an empathic "as if" mode: "as if I had lived his life" and "as if he could tell it in my words." In her introduction, Wharton is very proud of the narrational device that permitted the reconciliation of her "subject" with temporal (and cultural) distance in spite of her, self-confessedly, not having invented it. In fact, the framing narrative and its peculiar relation to the framed narrative are not only a token of commonsense logic, a tribute to verisimilitude, and an aesthetic bonus, compared with the "classical" unframed "omniscient narration"; they allow the narrator-as-character to penetrate physically, if belatedly, into the lives and setting of the Fromes (end of first segment and beginning of second segment), an exceptional favor, as Mrs. Hale remarks, there to experience the incommunicability of distress that the central narrative, contrary to Ethan Frome, attempts to overcome by expressing it. Wharton considers Balzac's "La Grande Bretèche"[21] and Browning's *The Ring and the Book* as her narrational predecessors and models. *The Scarlet Letter* and *Wuthering Heights*, because they are novels, could even more legitimately claim this privilege.

In the latter, too, we have Lockwood, a first-person narrator of the framing narrative whose apparent motivation for investigating the past is mature Heathcliff's singular aspect and temperament; but the framed, central narrative is also told to him by an overt first-person narrator, Nelly Dean, who supplies firsthand, unquestionable information. Belonging to all the successive presented worlds, as she does, she effectively kicks Lockwood out of *Wuthering Heights* as well as out of Wuthering Heights. Lockwood, the character, a stranger, is unable to make Catherine Linton, Jr. love him or even find any interest in him; he cannot prolong the story on his own account any more than he can repeat either Heathcliff's or Edgar Linton's role. Both perspective and expression come to coincide again in Nelly Dean. She combines cognitive and informative competence, leaving to Lockwood the sole grotesque task of transcribing his own failures: the failure to narrate equals the failure to participate in the presented world. The visible discrepancy between his apparent position of Σ narrator and his dispossession signifies his foolishness; he is manipulated from within the communication situation of the presented world by Nelly Dean and, from without, in the realm of conscious literary communication, by the implied author who thus appears to take sides with Nelly Dean. We could say that Lockwood manifests an instrumental aspect of writing rejected by the Brontës' romantic aesthetics, while it is highly valued by Edith Wharton.

Now we could wonder whether the congruence of "perspective" and "expression," or, in our terminology, the indissociable wholeness of "voice," from cognitive competence to narrational scope, still holds true in conventional "omniscient" narration (extradiegetic Σ narrator). Let us see what happens with *The Europeans*:

The first Sunday that followed Robert Acton's return from Newport witnessed a change in the brilliant weather . . . Felix Young, without overshoes, went also [to church], holding an umbrella for Gertrude. It is to be feared that, in the whole observance, this was the privilege he most thoroughly valued. The Baroness . . . on this particular Sunday morning of which I began with speaking . . . stood at the window of her little drawing room . . . ; the long arm of a rose tree . . . appeared to have a kind of human movement—a menacing warning intention. The room was very cold. . . . Then she determined to have some fire.[22]

A traditional narratologist would say that the narrator is ubiquitous ("Meanwhile, back at the ranch" style) and has access to all the consciousnesses involved, or that, in the passage concerned, the point of view or perspective is first collective and impersonal (from above) before it shifts to either Felix Young or someone close to him, and then to the Baroness. But it is perhaps time to remember Genette's options: "I use 'narrative *information*' in order to avoid 'representation,' which seems to me a mongrel compromise between *information* and *imitation*. . . . There is no place for imitation in narrative, imitation being always short of (narrative proper) or beyond (dialogue)."[23] Although I do not agree in general, insofar as an absolute stance against representation underlies a negation of reference, it is true that an extradiegetic Σ narrator, particularly when it is overt, as in the preceding example, must be equated with the implied author inventing and forming the story; *and* he plays with the possibility of his own insertion in the presented world on an *as if* mode, as a quasiexperience, showing the reader the way to one or various possibilities of projection/identification. The same subject serves alternately as signifier of narrator, performing witness and narratee, but remains the only source of information as well as the name of the only voice.

Enunciation and Information in a Fairy Tale

We have already seen that genres of fictionality, and especially internal shifts from one to another, are closely associated with positions of enunciation and the use of shifters that work as indexes of these positions. Now, while assuming that a particular genre of fictionality has come to be firmly established in one segment of text, we shall study in some detail the interrelation between voice and diegetic information through a close examination of chapter 4 of Ségur's *Blondine*.[24]

Two initial points must be made. First, the marvelous frame of reading does not involve complete logical anarchy or a necessary inversion of all the rules that are supposed to help us "make sense of our world" in common sense or scientific Discourses, for any of the parties concerned: implied author, narrator, character, narratee, and implied reader. Second, in a formulaic genre like the fairy tale, we should not overrate the distinction between the first, supposedly "linear" reading and subsequent readings; we can even neglect it to a large extent, since the implied reader of a formulaic genre is itself formulaic: it already knows, by definition, most of the structures of the tale and many of their potential actualizations.

In chapter 3, Blondine got lost in the enchanted Lilac Forest (from which "one cannot return"); let us work our way through chapter 4:

1. Blondine dormit toute la nuit

Due to the poverty of specific context, the voice is identified as that of the Σ narrator, as it spoke at the very beginning of the narrative ("Il y avait un roi . . . "), that is, a narrator whose interest in telling the story or whose sources of information need not be justified for the time being. But the determiners "toute la" are interesting. The night in question ("*la* nuit") is an anaphora of "cette nuit" in the final interior monologue of Blondine in chapter 3 " . . . si encore les loups ne me mangent pas cette nuit." The new statement thus appears as a kind of *answer* to Blondine's worries as expressed in her diegetic loneliness. "Toute" reinforces this trait, since it answers the hypothesis of a night cut short by a possible attack by wolves. The narrator's voice is in close contact with Blondine's thoughts before her falling asleep. It works both as a silent witness of her sleep and as a protective presence; the following negative statement contributes to this stance:

2. aucune bête féroce ne vint troubler son sommeil

But statements of nonevents are not only "dialogic." As commentaries, they generate distance between narration and narrated. They relate to codes and may constitute trial-and-error markers of genre: "Contrary to what you assumed (with Blondine), little girls who spend the night alone in the forest are not always eaten up by wolves."

3. le froid ne se fit pas sentir

The pronominal turn is equivalent to an *on*; it has an ambivalent totalizing quality, such that it may involve Blondine, the beasts and plants of the forest, *and* the narrator's "presence," all together, or only some of the potential feelers of cold.

4. elle se réveilla le lendemain assez tard

Blondine is not known to have a watch or be able to read the time by the sun, or even see the height of the sun: it is difficult to attribute the evaluative "*assez* tard" to her, even as an impression, because her belatedness seems of no concern to her in the following lines. "Assez tard" is rather an addition and a corrective to "toute la nuit" = she even slept in the morning, after the sun was up; this is "late" compared with the norm for young children. The connotations, therefore, are those of sensual satisfaction in laziness ("grasse matinée") and infringement of the norm, and the information appears carried by an external, well-informed, and norm-bearing Σ narrator.

> 5. *elle se frotta les yeux, très surprise de se voir entourée d'arbres, au lieu de se trouver dans sa chambre et dans son lit. Elle appela sa bonne*

This is a fairly complex passage, in which the value of information varies considerably, depending on the positions of enunciation, themselves dependent on syntactic analysis. Two distinct paraphrases of the first two clauses are clearly possible: (1) "elle se frotta les yeux *et, commençant à distinguer* . . . , fut très surprise," and (2) "elle se frotta les yeux, *étant très surprise de se voir.*" It is typical of apposition to render the apposited clause logically ambiguous; here we cannot decide whether it is (1) consecutive or (2) causal. Option 2 offers some more intimacy between the narrator and the character than option 1, which more or less turns the former into an eyewitness, if Blondine's surprise shows on her face. This is a form of "reserved commitment" of the narrator to the character's psyche and, consequently, to the information brought by it—by way of speech, for example, which makes of it a narrator in its own right.

The subsequence "se voir entourée → sa bonne" poses another problem, because it is illogical to call for your nurse when you realize that you are in the forest, not in your bedroom. The inconsistency can be interpreted in at least two different ways: Blondine is illogical because she is distraught, or Blondine is illogical because she knows or suspects that she is in a world where traditional logic does not fully apply; she already behaves as an inhabitant of this world. In other words, the information is overdetermined, implying a double stance of the voice. But, if we consider the next sequence:

> 6. *Elle appela sa bonne; un miaulement doux lui répondit*

we realize that Blondine's illogicality and the narrator's teleology (forward motivation) are one. Blondine's state of want and the narrator's need to present Beau-Minon as an answer, however displaced or metaphorical, to a persistently masked question, act jointly to allow the expression of a generic need, a need for gender as well as a need of genre.

> 7. *Etonnée et presque effrayée, elle regarda à terre . . .*

Inconsistent as it may be as a reaction to "un miaulement *doux*," Blondine's feeling is easy to understand in response to the substitution of meowing for speech and a male cat for a female nurse. Blondine, in the process, stands for the narrator, since she is dumbfounded in its stead and shocked by its own audacity:

> 8. *et vit à ses pieds un magnifique chat blanc qui la regardait avec douceur et qui miaulait.*

The embedding of "étonnée et presque effrayée" between "un miaulement doux" and its quasi repetition "avec douceur et qui miaulait" is evidence of a not-so-soft transition from the narrator's voice to Blondine's own voice in the next paragraph, mediated by the intervention of the cat's voice at the same time as it mediates it: the narrator reveals its role of go-between, and the metaphoric status of Beau-Minon is thus enhanced.

After so many signs of a confusing and confused, troubled enunciation, we can now go a bit faster and see its deep homology with indirect, tropic information, in the double form of on-the-spot substitutions and processual transformations.

From fragments 6 to 8, the variation from "un miaulement doux" to "la regardait avec douceur et qui miaulait" synaesthetically equates "voice" with "gaze," an equation that has simultaneously a regressive and a prospective effect: (a) the questions "Who speaks?" and "Who sees?" should not be dissociated; the narrator is automatically justified and further confused or at least symbiotically associated with the character; (b) the equivalence of "speech" with "gaze" prepares new sensory equivalences, notably between "sight" and "touch," and "food" and "sex," all prevalent in Ségur's work, but which need to be reaffirmed for a correct subconscious reading to be carried out.

Blondine's pleasure in caressing Beau-Minon is defined both by the Σ narrator and by herself in her reported direct speech, as visual, caused not by the softness and length of the cat's hair but by its beautiful snowy whiteness. The antithesis "snow versus warmth" brings evidence of a metaphorical sublimation, to be reduced by the competent reader, while maintaining the connotative bonus of purity or innocence. In the wake of her initial naïveté, Blondine does not hesitate to ask Beau-Minon to take her to *his* house (but she must eat something first). When she has eaten, she asks him to take her to *her father's house*; and when Beau-Minon declares that it is impossible, she opts for *just any house* ("une maison quelconque"): the provisionally final result is that he will accompany her to *his* (and his mother's) house. The destiny of nubile girls under patriarchal rule is thus clearly a vital element of the social code whose actualization in Blondine's life can be forecast with a degree of certainty. No need to insist on it, but it is fascinating that Blondine herself is in charge of the expression of the rule. The simple *mise en abyme* of the code and the story would be much less effective if they were borne by the Σ narrator or by any voice other than that of the eponymous character; later developments will seem to be predicted, wished for, and dictated by the character herself, not by the narrator. The subordination of the former to the latter is reversed, the task of the narrator will be merely *executive* from now on; the initial display of power (naming, constructing an asymmetrical and Manichaean world, etc.) dissolves into the apparent enunciative autonomy of the character-disciple who condones institutional perversion. The benefits of this reabsorption strategy (the pseudoreabsorption of the narrational level into the narrated) are such that, when Blondine becomes silent and the Σ narrator must take the cue, its voice becomes a forceful cohesive factor in the presented world. Let us conclude with a few notes on the second to last paragraph of the chapter.

9. *"Beau-Minon, pour toute réponse, s'élança dans les buissons, qui s'ouvrirent d'eux-mêmes pour laisser passer Beau-Minon et Blondine, et qui se refermaient quand ils étaient passés. Blondine marcha ainsi pendant une heure.*

Magic and the symbolic code go hand in hand. We should not be surprised (no more than Blondine) that green forest = Red Sea. Yet we may admire how incidentally we learn, how "unwittingly" the narrator lets us know that Beau-Minon is God. Even subtler is the way in which the wandering creatures come to form a still fragile couple: "Beau-Minon," "Beau-Minon and Blondine," "Blondine" are the successive subjects of the verbs "leap," "cross," and "walk," but the origin of knowledge is different in each case. "Pour toute réponse" implies Blondine's point of view, quite literally, but turns Beau-Minon's action into a *speech* act (she looks at Beau-Minon and reads his response to her question); "laisser passer Beau-Minon et Blondine" is supported by an impersonal narrational instance that can include Blondine, but excludes Beau-Minon unless or until he looks back; "pendant une heure," like "assez tard" at the beginning of the chapter, is a statement exclusively supported by the Σ narrator's ability to measure time. But now the narrator will become involved in the presented world in a much more ambiguous fashion than before; its involvement will be a far cry from that of a legislator or a judge, shouldn't we say, when

10. *On voyait de jolis oiseaux qui chantaient.*

The positive correlation between visual appearance and speech detects the copresence of Blondine and the narrator, a complicity between them. But, since Beau-Minon and Blondine are the only conscious creatures visible and reported to be in the forest, "on" must include Beau-Minon, humanizing him by the way: a cattish cat would be rather upset by the birds singing close to him, if he could not catch them! There remains a possibility that Blondine projects her own feelings onto Beau-Minon, but, in this case, she expresses her desire that he share these feelings, her trust that he can become a human partner. When the three of them (Beau-Minon, Blondine, and the discreet narrator) stroll through the woods, the narrator too is in some need of embodiment in the presented world; it is building a niche for an adequate new character combining a witness function with decision making. Bonne-Biche will be this new character.

11. *Blondine . . . était enchantée de tout ce qu'elle voyait*

The forest was earlier called "enchanted" because one could not leave it; it was a woeful forest, a prison. Now it is Blondine's turn to be "enchantée," in the opposite sense of feeling free, happy, and confident. The forest's enchantment was known to "one" (the narrator, adults, people who had prior or a priori knowledge of things, of the real world); Blondine's "enchantment," due to the conjunction of immediate sensory experience, discovery, and the belief that she is going to see her father again soon, is known to her in the first place, and to Beau-Minon, who

12. miaulait tristement quand Blondine faisait mine de s'arrèter.

Beau-Minon, endowed with consciousness, has become the mediating witness between Blondine's inner experience and its textual expression. Something even more important is given to him at once by the narrator: a secret that he cannot reveal, even if he wanted to, the sealed knowledge of his identity, which becomes an object of desire for Blondine and for us, together with the double knowledge that Blondine must not stop in the forest because she is not going to find her father there, and that she is going to find him in the end, transformed and regressed into that prince that Beau-Minon was once, a worthy husband for her. The greatest gift a narrator can make to a character, and the most productive investment for the narrator's own sake, is not speech but golden aphasia, withheld knowledge.

Dialogic Enunciation

The novelistic dialogue itself, as a compositional form, is indissolubly linked to the dialogue of languages that makes itself heard in the hybrids and the ideological background of the novel.[25]

Although I am ready to take sides with Bakhtin and denounce with him the devaluation of the communicative function of language by most schools of linguistics, which a new narratology must focus on if the discipline is not to fall entirely into disrepute, the context of the quoted passage unfortunately obliges us to see that the indissoluble link postulated between novelistic dialogism and the dialogic form of enunciation is essentially, if not exclusively, a mimetic relationship. Dialogic enunciation in the literary regime of textual production should thus represent and serve a sociolinguistic model of the formation of utterances given in "reality" by "communion of speech" on the one hand, and the encounter of diverse and contradictory dialects, registers, or discursive formations, on the other. Such a model of production that posits individual or collective speaking subjects as constituted before the sense they can make, a one-way model, both subjectivist and populist, runs a serious risk of conflicting with a more authentically "dialogic" concept of social communication and self-communication. According to this view, the forms of enunciation and utterance themselves are in constant competition for the production of value. None of them can stay in its appointed territory, so to speak, and each of them in turn contributes to manipulations of meaning for which it is not iconically cast. Due to displacement, condensation, contamination, rhetoric action, due to the complexity of social links and exchanges and associated strategies of communication, each form is always about to break up the enclosure of its functionality and run loose, away from its "legitimate" domain, to places where it will mean differently. The dialogic form of enunciation is no exception to this rule, unless we consider its legitimacy as exclusive and universally established, thereby rejecting any other structure of enunciation into a limbo, treating it as a screen, a fallacy, an illusion, a con trick.

If we accept these premises, the dialogic form, crystallized in drama, philosophical argumentation, the novel, and film (in its visual dimension too), with aims and functions that are not totally different from each other, should be seen as competing "dialogically" with monologic and choral forms of enunciation. We should also remain aware that it may be imitated in "life" as much as it can borrow from conversational techniques found in "life."

It is therefore very important to examine dialogic enunciation where it is most regulated, rigidly codified, and aesthetically functional *before* we can analyze and understand the most ordinary and apparently anarchic negotiations of meaning in everyday practice. As we know, the "dramatic mode" of presentation has often been contrasted with the "narrative mode," recitation, and exegematic address. At the same time the conditions of equivalence and processes of translation that allow the mutual substitution of scene for summary, or vice versa, are generally not understood (see also chapter 9 on the narrative transcription of drama). In the framework of a brief survey of functional possibilities offered by overtly, externally dialogic enunciation, we should ask at least the following questions:

- Which are the functions of language that dialogic enunciation can typically fulfill or whose role it may stress?
- Does dialogic enunciation necessarily involve and reflect Bakhtinian dialogism or can it not sometimes be a trick, an illusionistic device that conceals actual monologism (thematic and ideological monism) and helps it to reign? Is it not able to draw a smoke screen over the deepest conflicts?
- Can it not be also a means of erasing or blurring the distinction between narrative and other predicative genres of discourse, or even an artifact that launches and promotes polyreference and fictionality independently from any real plurality of "visions" or "points of view" within a textual world?

First of all, let us imagine examples of dialogic enunciation for each of the six traditional Jakobsonian functions of language. The functions themselves are not rediscussed here, and the examples are interpreted in a moderately pragmatic perspective:

1.X: Wow! That's wonderful!
   Y: I am very pleased for you.

2.X: If one is not born French, how can one become a French citizen?
   Y: By naturalization or by marriage to a French citizen.

3.X: Blue are her eyes and deep like the sea.
   Y: Blue are her eyes and blacker than the raven . . .

4.X: Nice day today, isn't it?
   Y: How are you, Mr. Smith?

5.X: I want milk.
   Y: You should not say "I want," but "May I have some milk, please?"

6.X: Will you be a good knight?
   Y: Yes, I shall be loyal and faithful to my Lord.

Without excluding some interplay of functions, examples 1–6 are meant to be clearly representative, respectively, of one function each: 1, emotive (expressive); 2, referential; 3, poetic; 4, phatic; 5, metalingual; and 6, conative.

It is obvious that the cooperative principle is at work in all these dialogues, but we should already note some remarkable differences as to the extent of its role in the definition of the prevalent function in each dialogue. In 1, both individual segments are emotive, and their junction in dialogue has a dual effect: on the one hand, it reinforces expressiveness, but, on the other, it introduces, implicitly at least, other elements, metalingual for example, by juxtaposing formally different utterances sharing the same subject matter. They "comment" on each other in a way that could not be achieved by simple monologic repetition—this phenomenon can be observed in comic dialogues like those of *Do You really Love Me?* by R. D. Laing.[26] In 2, if we take it that letters X and Y stand for names of actual individuals (whether "real" or "imaginary"), the dominant function is referential; both X and Y deal with things as they are in their shared worlds of reference, and Y adds a new element to those already possessed by X about this world, that is, to the presupposition set involved in his question: X believes that one can "become French," and Y confirms it and explains how. But, if we consider that X and Y stand for "Question" and "Answer" roles, the dominant function of the whole dialogue is immediately reinterpreted as conative: the Discourse of Law speaks itself in dialogue in order to better enforce a certain code of behavior in a subject defined in relation to it, dependent on it—this is the "confession of faith" model that we shall study in greater detail in chapter 10.

Conversely, 6, in which X and Y are at first understood as simple roles of enunciation and which is seen as conative, could be reinterpreted as a referential set of utterances, if X and Y were meant to represent two individuals, two friends, for example; but, even in 6 and under the first hypothesis, in spite of the authority implied by the interrogative segment, the answer collaborates with this authority by giving an obligatory semantic content and a motivation to the value judgment suggested by the verb phrase "be a good knight."

In 3, each of the two segments separately is poetic to some extent, but, after Y's intervention, we can retrospectively interpret the adjectives "deep" and even "blue" as more definitely metaphorical and undecidably ambiguous, since it now appears that "blue" is both a color and a noncolor, blue and black having ceased to be incompatible on the paradigmatic axis shared by the two speakers. In 4, neither of the two segments taken separately seems to fulfill a markedly phatic function; the phatic function results almost entirely from their juxtaposition, which shows, through referential heterogeneity, that X is not any more interested in the weather than Y is in X's health, while both X and Y are trying out utterances for the mere sound of words, at best using them as formulaic greetings and probably in order to begin a conversation on some topic totally unrelated to the two non-topics evoked initially. Thus X might reasonably proceed by saying, "By the way, Y, did you watch the World Cup on TV last night?"

In 5, taken separately, the first segment is almost purely conative and the second segment is also conative to a large extent, but their juxtaposition underscores a displacement of interest on the part of Y, who comments the form of expression of "I want milk" instead of the actual need or wish signified by X; retrospectively, even an utterance as apparently straightforward and monofunctional as "I want milk" appears as expressive and even metalingual itself, insofar as it implies a utilitarian attitude regarding language as well as an aggressive attitude vis-à-vis the addressee.

I shall now present three more examples of very simple dialogic texts in which specific functions not listed by Jakobson emerge with really surprising strength:

7. X: The inhabitants of this town are all wicked.
   Y: You should not generalize.
   X: I know what I am talking about, I know them only too well.
   Y: But you must make some exceptions—don't you live here yourself?

8. X: This girl is very pretty.
   Y: She has beautiful eyes.
   X: And beautiful hair too.
   Y: She has a perfect body . . .

9. X: Peter was lonely and unhappy,
   Y: Then he met Jane . . .
   X: They fell madly in love,
   Y: And Peter was very happy ever after.

In 7 we encounter the full force of a POLEMICAL relationship between utterances, which was already present in 5 (and in 1, if Y's response was understood ironically), but which had been neglected thus far because of the monologic perspective of Jakobson's frame of analysis, whereas Bakhtin stressed it throughout his work in a basically Marxist (dialogic-dialectical) perspective. With Bakhtin (and Mallarmé), we consider this phenomenon not only as an occasional structural characteristic of some particularly complex utterances, but as one of the fundamental functions of language in its own right that we shall call POLEMICAL function; it is different from the conative, the referential, the poetic, and all the other previously accepted and defined functions, even though it is copresent and mixes with them, as the six other functions do among them.

In 8 there is no opposition of any sort between the segments uttered by X and Y; in fact, these segments could be uttered by a single speaker without any thematic, ideological, or stylistic shift. The same speaker could very well say "in the same breath" that "this girl is pretty, with beautiful eyes and hair, and a perfect body." One speaker, or a collective speaker, a choir, or a chorus, could sing or proclaim her praises simultaneously. In the two cases, dialogic and choral enunciation, there is a sharing of utterances and multiplication of the subjects of enunciation; only the temporal disposition, alternate or simultaneous, differs. Comic situations with identical twins often play with these cognate processes: sometimes a twin will repeat what the other has just said, and sometimes they say the same thing in unison.

In 9 again, there is no opposition between X's and Y's segments, but their complementarity, although it does not involve any specialization of roles, acquires the new dimension of an apparently necessary instead of an arbitrary order; in 8, the succession of segments was an effect of the successivity of the linguistic medium, but in 9, linguistic succession pretends to imitate actional succession. Both 8 and 9 are examples of enunciatory relays (paratactic), one in the service of descriptive discourse, the other in the service of narrative discourse. The contribution of dialogic enunciation to the overall significance of the text is, at least at first sight, strictly cumulative: it enlarges the original field of veridiction by a kind of "wide angle" process in 8, instead of competing for value in the same closed field as in 7. We shall call the new function exemplified in 8 and 9 CONSENSUAL function.

The CONSENSUAL function is to some extent the opposite of the POLEMICAL function, because it seems to manifest the compatibility and harmony of the utterances possible within one language, but we shall realize in the forthcoming analyses that the relation between the POLEMICAL and CONSENSUAL functions is not a simple inversion of signs: POLEMICAL is not −CONSENSUAL, since they can coexist and even collaborate in the same text. This proves that they are authentic functions of language, not mere semantic contraries or modalizers.

We should now examine a collection of texts in which dialogue is a particularly salient feature of enunciation, more or less strictly ruled by systemic constraints, in order to differentiate and foreground the POLEMICAL and CONSENSUAL functions and evaluate how far they can be enslaved to the demands of narrative meaning or, on the contrary, tie it down to an instrumental role. The texts chosen here are of unequal length and vastly different in style, theme, and aesthetic investment: *Pedro Páramo* by Juan Rulfo (1955), *La Sylvie* by Jean Mairet (1627), and *Manservant and Maidservant* by Ivy Compton-Burnett (1947).

Guerilla ad vitam aeternam

El Tilcuate siguió viniendo:
—Ahora somos carrancistas.
—Está bien.
—Andamos con mi general Obregón.
—Está bien.
—Allá se ha hecho la paz. Andamos sueltos.
—Espera. No desarmes a tu gente. Esto no puede durar mucho.
—Se ha levantado en armas el padre Rentería. ¿Nos vamos con él o contra al?
—Eso ni se discute. Ponte al lado del gobierno.
—Pero si somos irregulares. Nos consideran rebeldes.
—Entonces vete a descansar.
—¿Con el vuelo que llevo?
—Haz lo que quieras entonces.
—Me iré a reforzar el padrecito. Me gusta cómo gritan. Además lleva uno ganada la salvación.
—Haz lo que quieras.[27]

In these fifteen lines, neatly set apart by blank spaces from the surrounding text, only the first speaker, Damasio, alias El Tilcuate, chief of an armed band in the pay of Pedro Páramo, is clearly identified. The deictic value of "viniendo," combined with the centrality of the Media Luna farm in the presented world, implies that this is where the dialogue could take place, and that Pedro Páramo might well be the interlocutor. Nevertheless doubt is fostered by the fact that Damasio used to call Pedro Páramo "patrón" (master) on earlier occasions, and the tone of general approval adopted here by the answering party does not seem to be quite true to Pedro Páramo's temper and authoritarian attitude. Although a binary division of roles is maintained from beginning to end, a measure of anonymity certainly deflects possible dissent between the voices.

Tightly bound to the question of identity of the speakers is the problem of the chronotope in this passage. If El Tilcuate is the first speaker, the subject of enunciation of all the odd utterances (1, 3, 5, etc.), such statements as his could not be made without utter contradiction and incoherence in the one session or even over a short period of time. El Tilcuate's returns (to the Media Luna) are not only several ("siguió viniendo"), they take place over many months or even many years. Dialogue (direct speech), which is supposed to be the enunciatory type that most closely parallels narrational time (≈ reading time) and story time, is used here to form a summary rather than a scene. Or, to put it more precisely, its constructive steps are the following: (1) various separate scenes are summarized in a couple of lines on average, and (2) these summarized scenes are stuck, spliced together into one block of dialogue by the visual presentation of the text, the assumed identity of the speakers, the similarity of situation and topic, and the lack of temporal clues, except the vague succession of three civil wars indicated by the names of Carranza, Obregón, and a priest, certainly involved in the Carlista-style rebellion that took place in the years 1926–29. If we had "El Tilcuate volvió cuatro veces," the effect would already be different: we would feel somehow invited to cut up the block into four successive separate dialogues corresponding to a Carrancista period, an Obregonista period, a period of peace, and a Rentería period. The frequentative aspect would still operate to some extent, but it would not so easily be put to an iterative effect as the whole passage. In order to present successive dialogues in one block, we know that the specificity of each occurrence, on the two planes of content and situation, must be reduced; but, at the same time, this kind of presentation still induces a feeling of contradiction and incoherence, "as if" the same guerrilla chief could fight simultaneously for two or more antagonistic political leaders, "as if" peace and war, lawfulness and rebellion were supposed to be the same thing. José González Boixo has noted that this sequence (number 67, of 70) is "independent from the rest . . . and serves to establish a chronological separation between the death of Susana and the end of Pedro Páramo, in an indeterminate time that encompasses, more or less, part of the revolutionary process."[28] Indeed, we should also see that it derives its unique character from the fact that historical synthesis is given as possible, albeit in an ironic manner, while the fragments of individual lives cannot be stuck back together: Pedro Páramo will die "crumbling down like a heap of stones" (p. 195). The spatial center is, in both cases, the "Media Luna," a site far from everything, but the eccentricity of human lives cannot be fully compensated by "meaningless" repetition like the short, monotonous cycles of history. It is as if death, in history, did not die.

All the significance of the passage lies in a small number of such "as ifs," suggesting rather than naming absurdity, fatality, purposelessness. The ultimate balance between accumulation and iteration, their ultimate equivalence, cannot but teach us the paradoxical lesson about narrative itself that "the more it changes, the more it remains the same." No other mode of enunciation than dialogue used for its own rhetoric potential could signify it so efficiently, because it allows a faster change and a faster exchange of roles, to the point of unrecognizability; it can mix voices into one murmur or one outcry labeled "the voice of things," for the sheer impossibility of assigning this discordance to any single narrator. Here we can see how rhetorical devices combine at the level of enunciation itself to generate ironic significance, the polemical potential of each segment of dialogue being first canceled, then transferred to an apparent opposition between fragments that cancels itself in turn, or *almost*, through repetition.

The assumed recurrence of the speakers is based on metonymy, but its reassertion in spite of contradictory statements (e.g., speaker 2 — Pedro Páramo, if you want — agrees to all the opposite choices made by his mercenary) coincides with a metaphoric interpretation: in order to give sense to apparent contradiction, we must find one shared seme throughout several contradictory utterances. This seme will be a constant pertaining to description or characterization, a nonnarrative or even an antinarrative element, in this case, the axiom that all value rests on violence and destruction, probably the one thing about which all the characters (most of them narrators as well), from Pedro Páramo to Damiana and the anonymous initial narrator ("a son of Pedro Páramo," "Juan Preciado"), would seem to agree from beginning to end: "No vayas a pedirle nada. Exígele lo nuestro" (p. 64); "Después de unos cuantos pasos cayó, suplicando por dentro; pero sin decir una sola palabra," (p. 195). This is how dialogue, in the framework of narrative, often serves to express the final impossibility of actual verbal communication and a general consensus about this impossibility.

The Answer of the Shepherdess

The "Dialogue de Sylvie" is as rarely analyzed in depth as it is famous. The intrinsic reasons of its seduction will become obvious in a while, I hope. But extrinsic, a priori reasons include a form and a position in the play that make it belong and not belong to drama and performance: it can be recited privately as well as staged for an audience; it is intimately necessary to the coherence of the play, but, at the same time, easy to separate from it because it still makes sense out of context (it provides its own private context, apparently different from the total context of the play). Critics noticed this ambiguity — without explaining it — at least as early as 1905. Jacques Schérer, in 1975, virtually reproduces in the notes to the Pléiade edition the same remarks made by Jules Marsan. We may wonder whether this ambivalent status does not reflect and invert that of Bakhtinian dialogism insofar as the latter can do away with the dialogic *form* of enunciation.

Act 1 of *La Sylvie* comprises five scenes: 1, between Florestan, prince of Candia, and a knight called Thyrsis, who brings to him from Sicily the wonderful portrait of the royal princess of that island — this is the only scene that takes place in Candia, not in Sicily; scene 2, Sylvie's monologue, is particularly important in that it prepares for the dialogue in scene 3 and offers permanent keys for the interpretation of Sylvie's character; the dialogue of scene 3 is itself framed by two monologues of Philène; scene 4, between Thélame, Sylvie's lover, and his sister, Princess Méliphile, exposes the prince's passion and psychological features, which will never be altered all along the play; scene 5, between Thélame and Sylvie, amorous, lighthearted but also intensely erotic, stands in sharp contrast with scene 3. The first act thus seems quite conventionally expositional, as it introduces all the main characters in the play with the exception of the older generation, that is, Sylvie's parents and King Agatocles, Thélame's father. This particularity nevertheless places the act under the sign of desire, the pleasure principle, and the future; it also promises a more prominent role for Philène than will be achieved in the rest of the play; at the same time, the centrality conferred on scene 3 on the plane of literal plot will turn out to be deceptive. The centrality of scene 3, as we shall see, is rather that of an essential interpretant. In any case, the voice of authority is not heard directly in the act; it seems at first to be merely echoed by Princess Méliphile when she reminds her brother of his duty and his family's expectations. The later *pronunciamiento* of authority might make us revise our view of act 1 and consider it as a deceptive shelter under ominous skies, unless we analyze correctly the scope of the relation between enunciation and utterance in the dialogue.

PHILENE: Beau sujet de mes feux et de mes infortunes,
Ce jour te soit plus doux et plus heureux qu'à moy.

SYLVIE: Injurieux Berger qui toujours m'importunes,
Je te rends ton souhait et ne veux rien de toy.

PHILENE: Comme avecque le temps toute chose se change,
De même ta rigueur un jour s'adoucira.

SYLVIE: Ce sera alors que d'une course estrange
Ce ruisseau révolté contre sa source ira.

PHILENE: Ce sera bien plutôt que ta conscience
T'accusera d'un crime en m'oyant soupirer.

SYLVIE: Tes discours ont besoin de trop de patience,
Adieu, le temps me presse, il me faut retirer.

PHILENE: Arrête, mon soleil, quoy! ma longue poursuite
Ne pourra m'obtenir le bien de te parler.

SYLVIE: C'est en vain que tu veux interrompre ma fuite,
Si je suis un Soleil, je dois toujours aller.(45)

....

PHILENE: Au moins que ce bouquet fait de tes mains divines
Au défaut d'un baiser récompense ma foy.

SYLVIE: Tu n'en peux espérer que les seules espines,
Car je garde les fleurs pour un autre que toy.

PHILENE: O Dieux! soyez témoins que je souffre un martyre
Qui fait fendre le tronc de ce chêne endurci.

SYLVIE: Il faut croire plutôt qu'il s'esclate de rire
Oyant les sots discours que tu me fais ici.

PHILENE: Tu t'en vas donc Sylvie, ô Sylvie, ô mon âme!
Est-ce là le loyer que mérite ma flame?
Reviens, belle, reviens . . .

In view of the length of the complete text (lines 141–222, in the 1630 edition), we shall study only a few typical exchanges and draw our conclusions from these and a summarized reading of the whole.

Three major differences with the preceding dialogue become immediately obvious: (1) the dialogue from *Sylvie* does not result in the first instance from the combining and collapsing of several temporal sequences into one; the theatrical situation of performance/interpretation obliges the observer to consider it basically as a "naturally framed" single scene; (2) although the lines go two by two, not one by one, the dialogue is more clearly stichomythic here, because the speakers are unequivocally identified; and (3) this dialogue is threatened from the very beginning with being abruptly interrupted by one of the interlocutors: it is jeopardized from inside.

Sylvie seems to reject verbal as well as physical intercourse:

Insolent shepherd who always bothers me
I return all wishes, and I want nothing from you.
(lines 143–44)

Nevertheless, the very ambivalence of "je te *rends tout* souhait," or "*ton* souhait" in many other editions, lays the foundations for the pursuit of a verbal war game; this sentence can be understood either as, "I formulate the same wish for you that you have made for me: 'Be happier than I am,' " or as: "I return to you your unwanted wish, you can keep it." Not that the first interpretation would be much nicer to Philène than the second one, since "Be happier than I am," taken over by Sylvie, implies in her mouth: "I am displeased because you annoy me," but this is a way of dismissing Philène within discourse, while the second interpretation rejects him from verbal communication altogether. Sylvie has trapped herself in this alternative, and Philène, who believes his interest is to maintain verbal communication, with the correlative physical presence as a first step toward sexual intimacy, will draw on all the phatic resources of his language, while Sylvie's discourse will oscillate between a destructive metalingual attitude in her comments on Philène's words, and the crude affirmation of her desire to leave and be left alone. Then it becomes Philène's turn to exploit the antiperformative characteristic of any such farewell, in order to keep communication going.

It is remarkable that the whole dialogue is built on an extended syllepsis, first offered by Philène and unwittingly but wittily accepted by Sylvie as an object of derision. Once she has done this, she finds it extremely difficult to dispose of it; the more she tries to break it into its component parts, the more this bond between words through the double entendre of one word turns out to be a bond between her and her interlocutor who thus share at least one object, one bone of contention (in French, *pomme de discorde* [an apple!]).

The syllepsis in question binds the two denotations of the word "temps" ("time" and "weather"). It is prepared as early as the second line of the dialogue by a more obscure variation on it proposed by Philène, the suggested double denotation of "jour" ("day" as period of time or occasion, and as light of day): "Ce jour te soit plus doux." It was even announced by a paronomastic, punning antanaclasis in Sylvie's earlier monologue:

> ....enfin l'*heure* est venue
> Que sans rendre ma flame ou suspecte ou cognuë
> Je puis entretenir ces rochers d'alentour . . .
> ....
> Ce bois qui de mon *heur* fut la cause premiere
> Sera tantost forcé des traicts de la lumiere.

Then it appears explicitly in lines 145–46:

> Comme avecque le *temps* toute chose se change,
> De même ta *rigueur* un jour s'adoucira.
>
> [Like everything changes in time,
> Your rigor one day will melt.]

Sylvie is not tricked: she tries to ridicule the allegory based on the analogy of signifiers, knowing that no syllogism can be based on an analogy, even of contents. She denounces the error as follows, expressing her conviction that time, contrary to cyclic weather, is irreversible:

> In this case choosing a strange course
> This stream will flow toward its spring.

The narrative program that Philène sees in the syllepsis is a wrong prediction. Philène's sophistry, because of the naive Cratylism with which he hopes to possess Sylvie as easily as he enters the forest, is considered by Sylvie to be linguistic regression. It is her opinion that the form of expression should be placed under the control of the referent, not the other way around. But this does not prevent her from condoning analogical, metaphorical, and allegorical thinking *in principle*: the pastoral (known to us as "romantic") analogy between Nature and people, later analyzed by Delille as a system of echoic response. In order to be ironic, she is taken in by the inherent vice of antiphrasis and accepts in fact the entire code according to which people can be talked about in terms of Nature and vice versa, and space and time are so indissociably bound that the lexicon of one can be exchanged for that of the other. Sylvie limits her critique to certain applications of the analogy. Philène is thus confirmed in his belief that the more time he spends discussing any topic with Sylvie (even her "unlove" of him), the closer he will get to her body. When Sylvie realizes all this and tries to use the word "temps" in a monosemic way to signify her departure, it is too late:

> Tes discours ont besoin de trop de patience,
> Adieu, le *temps* me presse, il me faut retirer.
> [Your speeches require too much patience,
> Farewell, time is pressing, I must retire.]

Philène answers: "Please stop, my Sun . . . ," and so on, and it is clear that shepherds, as a class, have good reasons to read astronomical time climatically or perhaps climactically.

This classical syllepsis, like the canonic example "brûlé de plus de feux que je n'en allumai," unites a "literal" and a "metaphorical" meaning. In the "Dialogue de Sylvie," its striking expansion, for the reasons indicated earlier, draws on all the processes afforded by metonymy, synonymy, paraphrase, and even onomastic semiosis, in order to extend its own field of application to an almost cosmic scale, at the same time as it develops a parallel metaphorical field that is so contrived as to reveal eventually the utter pointlessness and artificiality of the dialogic relationship between Sylvie and Philène. A quick comparison with the later dialogue of Sylvie and Thélame (act 1, scene 5) is stimulating:

PHILENE: Ha! si tu n'aimais rien, ce bois sauvage et sombre
                Ne te retiendrait pas dans son sein tout le jour.

SYLVIE: Il est vrai que je l'aime à cause que son ombre
             Conserve ma froideur contre les feux d'Amour. (lines 169–72)

SYLVIE: Il est vrai que voici le lieu le plus charmant
             Qui se puisse trouver.

THALAME: Loing de la complaisance
Je croy que sa douceur lui vient de ta présence,
Que tes yeux seulement le font gay comme il est,
Que c'est par ta beauté que la sienne me plaist.
(lines 448–52)

In the first exchange, Philène suspects that Sylvie stays all day in the wood because she is waiting for another lover, but, intially she lies to him, she resorts
to metaphoric "logic" to disguise the truth: she pretends that she cherishes her
"coldness," and the darkness of the wood helps her protect it. Her own name is
associated, she knows, with the forest, so she wants Philène to opt for the connotation of wilderness carried by the cliché. On the other hand, her exchange with
Thélame is hardly metaphorical at all: the wood is seen by the lovers as a very
practical place to enjoy physical intercourse. In fact, it has no intrinsic properties
like those contained in the metaphorical/allegorical code; all its qualities are lent
to it by the lovers' purpose, by their physical *transports*, not by any coded displacement of signs:

C'est luy [l'Amour] qui tient expres ces rameaux enlassez
Pour défendre au Soleil de nous voir embrassez.
(lines 495–6)

Nevertheless, such an instrumentalization of Nature does not simply mean a complete victory of culture; it will often cover and reveal a displacement of Nature
from the landscape to the human body where it will operate in the guise of passion
with the unsuspected force conferred on it by its repression/compression. This
will be the new power source, opposed to the king's cold blood ("espris dissipés,
pesans et refroidis") in the august chambers of his palace.

There is another very interesting difference between the two dialogues in
scenes 3 and 5: formal symmetry, the ritual exchange of identical forms in which
Philène has the initiative and the lead, goes with physical incompatibility, the rejection of Philène by Sylvie, while physical agreement between Thélame and Sylvie goes with a rather informal exchange, cues of various lengths and even some
lines shared by the speakers (cut at the hemistich, as in the example quoted).

It is only after Philène has requested a first and last kiss that Sylvie lets him
in on the truth (i.e., that she loves another man), but even then she does not depart
from the "eye for eye" rhyming technique:

You can only hope for the thorns
Since I keep the blooms for another than you,
(lines 215–6),

thus signifying that the strict rules of verbal exchange are definitely exclusive of any physical transaction. The polemical function of dialogue certainly implies an agreement on how to build a body of text, but constructive cooperation in this respect is incompatible with sexual communion, which does not let the text form along the lines of gender division. In a sense, the rhyme scheme of the "Dialogue de Sylvie" already announced this fusion, each of the speakers being equipped with the same A-feminine—B-masculine lot, but the mechanical character of the device betrayed its inadequacy for the spontaneous motion of real love that does not stick tongues out but secretly entwines them.

The technique of the "Dialogue de Sylvie," its polemical structure and its superficial consensual effect, are laid bare where the bodies of the speakers are not. Thélame knows better than to try to conquer Sylvie on the ground of language games, or at least, so he says:

SYLVIE: Pleust aux Dieux vissiez mon âme toute nuë
            Pour juger de sa flame.

THELAME: Elle m'est trop cognuë,
            J'aimerais beaucoup mieux te voir le corps tout nu.
            (lines 425–27)

In conclusion, if Sylvie's collaboration with Philène in the dialogue is relatively easy to interpret and oppose to her different complicity with Thélame, her extreme verbal cruelty still wants to be further explained: why does she not flee earlier from her unwanted suitor? Why is her repulsion so extreme that, without being physically threatened at any moment, she pronounces an actual *votum mortis* against Philène—unless it is a survival wish, so that he can be slowly consumed and put to death by the flames of his passion as if they were those of Hell. Philène could say to her, like Saint-Amant to his own Sylvie:

> . . . vos rigueurs sont si grandes,
> Que j'ay beau les flater des plus dignes offrandes;
> Je croy qu'elles voudraient que je fusse immortel,
> Afin tant seulement que mon ennuy fust tel.[30]

Sylvie does not hide from Philène that he deserves death for "the crime of having undertaken too much." She uses the same arguments that will be those of the king some time later when he considers her execution as the aptest means of preventing her—"a handsome witch," he says—from seizing the scepter and tarnishing the name of Sicily. Does she feel that she already belongs to the princely class of rulers because of Thélame's commitment to her, or does she consider herself as "queen" for her own qualities, her beauty and her wit? I would answer yes to both questions: the mastery of language is the criterion of an aristocracy that will soon be able to vie with aristocracies built on blood and money. Philène is a rich shepherd whom Sylvie humiliates and reduces to beg for something "priceless': a smile, a sweet word, a kiss. But she also exploits his wealth of words and clichéd metaphors. Later on she will marry him off, against his persistent will, to Dorise:

> Philène, now you must lose any hope
> That of possessing me your heart could hold.
> (lines 2231–32)

Sylvie rejects her vocation of object to constitute herself into a law-giving subject thanks to her *supériorité en repartie*, her superior ability to reply, first of all in the order of poetic eloquence that she finds already formed in the select milieu of the pastoral debate. The agonistic aspect of the dialogue shows that Sylvie is the most accomplished rhetorician in the play, and it is also that which announces under a disguise the nature of some future radical change in society and communication: the advent of the power of persuasive discourse, instead of the imperative, a change that, unfortunately, she cannot carry out to the end.

A Lie and Its Truth

With the (imperfect) exceptions of Miriam, the kitchen hand, and Horace, the master of the house, at the beginning of the novel, all the characters in *Manservant and Maidservant* seem to distrust words, in the sense that speech shows a strong tendency to *lie* (to say something else than what it is supposed to). But, at the same time, they easily overvalue words for their capacity to *belie* all the deep, dark, intended meanings that they are not supposed to carry, all the actual meanings distinct from their face values but which can be deduced by reducing figures. In the "Dialogue de Sylvie," desire was not shared by the speakers, or rather Philène's desire met with Sylvie's aversion. In *Manservant and Maidservant*, sexual desire is virtually absent, or it is so weak and silenced that it does not exist for its own sake; it is just somehow in the background (only one character, Magdalen, proves to be "really in love"). Status and material goods, made scarce by the hierarchical, highly stratified social structure, are the objects exclusively sought and fought for by all the personnel of the novel. Speech is primarily an instrument of power, sometimes offensive, sometimes defensive, but always basically polemical.

Speech is the best-shared capacity of people in the presented world; only the lowest characters on the social scale, like George and Miriam, are reduced at times to a "direct," nonfigural use of it, and, worst of all, to gestures; however, they soon learn the art of insinuation. But, if speech is well shared, it also entails that no individual can speak for very long at any one time and that each of the contestants must occupy the speech of the other with his own meanings and interests (reinterpret it) instead of developing his own line of thought in an autonomous vocabulary and syntax. The reorientation (recycling and reinterpretation) of other people's speech is mediated again by one or more interpretants that are supposed to be shared by the speakers and thus appear as necessary presuppositions of the utterances of the first speaker. Let us take a couple of examples in a passage belonging to the last third of the novel.[31] The poor cousin Mortimer had plotted to live with Charlotte, Horace's wife and the real owner of the family's wealth; their plan was discovered because Horace opened a letter that was not addressed to him. Mortimer had to leave the house, but, after a few days, he returns:

"You have not a high opinion of human nature, Mortimer."
"No, I have not. And it is not because I judge people by myself. That is a thing I never do." (p. 218)

Horace suggests that Mortimer has no right to judge other people, since he is also guilty. Mortimer takes the hint and begins to reverse the situation, something he will achieve over the next three pages by managing to make Horace himself feel guilty: if he, Mortimer, does not judge people by himself and still thinks badly of them, it must be that other people give him a poor idea of mankind, whereas if he, Mortimer, judged other people by himself, he would have a high opinion of them. The first "other" is, by necessity, the second person, Mortimer's interlocutor. But his justification of this insolence is indicative of an even more insolent — and irrefutable — stance: "to judge people by oneself" is implied to be a selfish, unChristian attitude that Horace should reprove as a matter of principle; if one's own criterion is insufficient, then one's own standard cannot be assumed to be better than that of others. In fact, Mortimer insinuates through the irony of this double meaning that Horace is a hypocrite who judges people by his own invalid criterion and in an unjustified comparison with his own (actually low) standard. The falsely slick appeal to Mortimer's complicity against himself has been taken literally and rejected: Horace does have a poor opinion of human nature, and he is right insofar as he judges other people by himself, because his judging other people by himself proves that he is not worth much:

"Mortimer, I must ask you one thing. Can you see Charlotte hour by hour and day by day, and remain master of yourself?"
"It is nice of you to welcome me back."
"You have not answered my question." (p. 219)

In the present conversation, Horace has just said that "Mortimer [had] not his permission to stay in [his] house," but Mortimer has scored a point by revealing to Horace that he knows how Horace discovered the plot against him. In the preceding exchange, Horace obviously poses a condition on which Mortimer may stay: he must keep quiet and not interfere with Charlotte again. Mortimer chooses to consider only the implication that Horace would be glad to welcome him back [if possible]. By bracketing the condition of possibility, he can be understood either as disregarding it or giving it an affirmative answer. Since Horace is never "nice," Mortimer's reply may also mean, ironically, that Horace's proposal is insincere or proffered unwittingly, his real presupposition being then that Mortimer will *not* be able to leave Charlotte alone. In this case, Horace was just seeking from Mortimer a confirmation of his assumptions, but Mortimer shifts the emphasis from doubt about these assumptions to the formally reduced scope of the interrogation. In fact, by translating Horace's question into a statement that he is welcome back, Mortimer all but considers the question as so negligible that an affirmative answer to it would appear as not serious. Horace is not in a situation such that he can afford to be excessively subtle anyway, so that his plain lack of subtlety in answering "You have not answered my question" is a case of necessary verbal defeat. In the next few replies, Mortimer will build on this advantage to inform Horace in a mockingly compassionate tone that he, Mortimer, is no longer interested in Horace's wife: "It is a difficult subject, my dear boy." In all these pages, Mortimer manages to reverse his inferior position almost completely by making *more sense* of Horace's utterances than Horace is conscious of their having, by exposing Horace's lack of talent as an interpreter, and finally by making him state bluntly all that shows him under the worst possible light. Eventually Horace will be robbed of everything but his precarious (usurped) economic power over the household, a power that is worthless to the overhearer.

In the first quotation, the relation between dialogic exchange and narrative meaning is very indirect, whereas in the second it is almost immediate; Mortimer transforms a seminarrative question into a purely narrative answer as he gives it a definite temporal frame. This is also a way of exerting or conquering power in the context of a narrative horizon of expectations—the reader's horizon. We can see that the peculiar situation of dialogue in literary (i.e., spectacular) narrative communication adds to it a dimension that is not an intrinsic parameter of "ordinary" or "everyday" dialogues.

In the passage studied, Horace and Mortimer agree on most facts and norms as far as the subject matter of their conversation is concerned, but they disagree on the identity of the addressee: Horace talks essentially to Mortimer, but Mortimer speaks "to the gallery"; he includes an overhearer, a potential reader in the communication situation, invokes him as a witness to his wit, and thus enlists him on his side. Horace is once again his own worst enemy and finds himself all alone: he reenters our narrative field of interest only through this dubious motive for compassion, that is, through the pursuit of characterization by the reader. Such situations are not unknown in "everyday life," but they certainly take literary (or theatrical) communication as their model: they impose on one interlocutor, or on both of them, an image of himself, of his speech—of themselves, of their speech—such that an important part of the meanings taken into account for narrative or argumentative progression in dialogue can be attributed only to the distanced, metalingual position of a third party, a "public" or audience who does not think the less for remaining mute.

The last words of Ivy Compton-Burnett's novel are: "Horace could only be silent." This final silence relates, rather enigmatically, to a remark of Bullivant, the butler, about "much of the world being woman" and it not being "a thing that one would speak against" (p. 299). This silence no longer means defeat for Horace, but it is in need of sustained interrogation and continued interpretation, at the end of three hundred pages of dialogue. Dialogue creates a space that gives more meaning to the unsaid. Its extreme abundance, as in the work of Dame Ivy, can even elicit narrative value from the sudden emptiness of the rare outbreaks of the Σ narrator's discourse; thus, the (falsely) imminent death of Horace, close to the end of the book, is manifested more by the absence of collective enunciation than by the very words in the text: "The house was hushed, vibrant with covert emotion, charged with fear and hope" (p. 276).

Chapter 7
Binding and Unfolding:
on Narrative Syntax

Like "discourse," "syntax" is, in our context, one of the words that demand an accurate redefinition for a limited purpose, lest they invade with a battalion of loaded linguistic concepts our modest attempt to theorize the system and process of narrative communication. It is worth repeating: narrative is neither a language nor a chain of events but a particular manner of imposing design on a presented world and of presenting worlds through the operations required by the constraints of this design.

Although syntax will still mean for us in this chapter "the study of principles and processes by which S's are constructed in a particular L,"[1] its goal will no longer be strictly "to construct a grammar that can be considered as a kind of device to produce the sentences of the language submitted to analysis" (ibid.). We shall rather take S's as narrative meanings and L as narrative communication. The preposition "in," therefore, in the first sentence quoted, no longer signifies a simple one-way spatial-axiomatic relation of inclusion such that all possible αS's are contained in the αL in question and αL should contain exclusively αS's, with an α grammar summarizing the essence of αL and defining the receivability of αS's in αL. In our perspective, S's are constructed into a particular L, a particular L is constructed from particular S's, and vice versa; and the relation between the two terms is subject to numerous tropes: metaphor, metonymy, synecdoche, simile, and so on. A binding generative model can be built at the level of minimal units of discourse, not at the level of the significance of a complex act of communication that is, by definition, cooperatively produced and situation dependent. A descriptive-interpretive model like the one toward which we are going to work

now is only able to predict certain probabilities. Here, the relevant S's can be juxtaposed (without a mental order of precedence), successive, or embedded within
one another, depending on the levels of analysis and the moments of synthesis
considered. Moreover, grammar and semantics are tightly interdependent. The
syntax of narrative should be understood as a compound of the grammaticaliza-
tion of semantic data and the semanticization of grammatical data, very much in
the same way as Jakobson would balance the grammar of poetry with the poetry
of grammar.

This syntax is the study of cognitive operations, more than — and before it can
become — that of the conditions of inscription of a text to come under narrative
analysis and criteria of valuation. Unlike early "grammars of narrative" and some
later semiotic systematizations,[2] it is concerned with the production of effects of
change rather than with the mimesis of actions, and it takes into account the "surface" structures of the communicated-communicative text as much as the
reduced-reductive "deep" structures it is supposed to embody. Even though it is
not directly within our reach, our object of study consists in the quasi-mimetic
actions of a "receiver" or would-be addressee who arranges to secure under the
sign of narrative significance a certain adequation of his decoding/recoding operations to what he judges to be the code and norms of the text, whether this rewarding adequation is produced by homology, analogy, or symmetry. Genealogical
projection (the "voice" or "voices") always plays a role in this process, but the
weight and nature of this role depend on the receiver's perception of the situation
of communication. The semiotic conventions by which narrative marks its particular order (in all the senses of the word) in, with, and against another order (linguistic, for example) are also important, but no more than the special rules of discrimination between narratemes and nonnarratemes of all sorts that apply to each
semiotic medium. Local, regional, and hegemonic markers that encourage or dis-
courage the fixation of meaning at the narrative level of discourse (the formation
and stabilization of representative narratemes by the receiver) should all be examined, as well as the markers of continuity and discontinuity between textual narratemes and nonnarratemes, and narrative and nonnarrative metaphrastic textual
units (paragraphs, sequences, chapters, etc.), all factors that contribute to determine narrative significance, the ascendancy of narrative meaning over a certain
span of text — itself partly demarcated and unified, initially or finally, as a function
of its relation to narrative meaning.

The Principles of Narrative Syntax

Narrative syntax has two main facets: (1) the articulation of narrative and nonnarrative discourses within the decoded/recoded narrative text and (2) the ordering

of narratemes recognized (comprehended and apprehended) at different moments of the dual process of implication/explication.

Discursive articulation and narratemic ordering are practically interdependent: it is impossible, for example, to articulate a description with a narrative sequence without determining the narrational and narrated orderings, the narrative *dispositio* that constitutes the aforesaid sequence; conversely, this *dispositio* may well be influenced by the paratactic and hypotactic *dispositio* of the description. But since discursive differentiation and (inter)discursive articulation are inseparable and the former is *logically* prior to narrative ordering, we shall deal with interdiscursive articulation first.

Interdiscursive Articulation

How do we detect nonnarrative discourses in a narrative, or how do they manage to remain unnoticed? In what sense can we talk of their subordination to narrative discourse? Is this subordination final? Does it reflect the structure of the generative model of discourses? We are dealing here with a field of interferences, a pluridimensional network of interventions that would demand that we take into account a large number of parameters if we tried to produce an exhaustive study of these problems. The duality of narratemes (transactive and nontransactive) can break up narrative meaning as well as it can prompt the search for narrative significance. Interdiscursive articulation is a matter of thresholds and secret alliances; it is an important part of narrational strategies and generic determination. In order to simplify, without neglecting the richest implications of the metasystem, we shall concentrate on the question of the relationship between descriptive discourse and narrative discourse.

Gérard Genette tells us that this question was of no great concern to theorists before the nineteenth century,[3] but they have caught up with it since. The peculiar problems of the French *nouveau roman* and "poetic narrative," the revival of rhetoric and argumentation, the questioning of narrative conventions by techniques of fragmentation, multiplication of delegated narrators and "points of view," the sociological and cultural trends in contemporary historiography, the new coalitions or polemics between semiological systems (words in painting, concrete poetry, etc.) with the correlative "spatialization" of discourse—all these are factors that can be evoked to understand our renewed curiosity about description. Jean Ricardou and Philippe Hamon[4] are two of the authors who have most persistently and successfully investigated this discursive level. I shall seek, like the latter, to "avoid the traps of a referential approach,"[5] which is not equivalent to eliminating the horizon of reference. I must also insist that discourses present before they represent; description is not any more than narrative a free-floating modality of figuration applicable to just about any kind of given objects to be denoted; it is just as impossible to "describe an action" as to "narrate a landscape." Discourses make their contents be; the differences between description and narration *have* a semiotic existence.[6]

In his early research, Hamon defines description provisionally as "an *expansion* of narrative (in the same sense in which syntax talks sometimes of expansion from the kernel of a minimal sentence)."[7] We have seen that descriptemes may be obtained from narratemes by analysis, but descriptions do not necessarily owe their existence to that of given units of narrative discourse. The expansion evoked by Hamon is also, curiously, "an interruption of the syntagmatic [axis] of narrative by a paradigm" (p. 468). In these two remarks, Hamon seems to rally to a basically linear notion of the text, like the narrator of *Tristram Shandy*. Description would form a loop, lengthen the trajectory by expanding a point, interrupt the straight line with a curve; compare:

1. Gilgamesh took up two kids
$$\longrightarrow$$

2. Gilgamesh took up a kid, white without a spot, and a brown one with it.

Any description would then be a sort of *in*cident, at once mutilation and excess, a lack of integrity, insofar as the continuity of the temporal flux is a necessary condition of the unity of the textual body, and surplus of content, insofar as substantives and verbs are sufficient repositories of narrative meaning. Description, adjectival in essence, would be attached to the interrupted, mutilated body by a bond of possession, legal ownership, not by an ontological, natural, or organic bond. This contradicts another view according to which description, if it is an autonomous or dissident form of discourse, lists items, works like an inventory. These two views show that description can be interpreted almost indifferently as engaged in a process of analysis or synthesis, deconstruction or construction in relation to its total signified, summarized in its title.

In the preceding example, we must certainly presuppose a kidless Gilgamesh, prior to the act of taking kids, as a necessary presupposition of this act, but we cannot logically assume the existence of colorless kids before they are labeled white and brown, respectively, by the text. Although the difference in deep structure between narrative and descriptive discourse is thus very obvious, the articulation of discursemes of the same level between them is essentially similar regardless of the level considered, and so is their surface syntax, with minimal variations. Identical paratactic and hypotactic processes can be found at the descriptive and narrative levels:

3.   The basket was full of pears, peaches, apples, apricots, and plums.

4. We ate all the pears, peaches, apples, apricots, and plums from the basket.
5. The man I had hurt by banging his head against the wall went mad.
6. The valley hidden by overlapping cliffs widened after a few miles.

The successivity of reading is often projected by the reader over the simultaneity of existents in the presented world. The metadiscourses of transversal communication narrativize and dramatize the production of meaning, easily mistaken for the primary semantic content of the text. Moreover, the analytic phase of narrative comprehension can permanently reduce narrative discourse to descriptive discourse if some other motivation, aesthetic or psychological, for instance, happens to block the obverse synthetic movement. From the paratactic sequence:

7. One kid was all white and another brown

we can derive a paranarrative interpretation: "There was a white kid, and *then there appeared* a brown one." And from this other paratactic sequence:

8. Gilgamesh took up one kid, and another kid,

we can construct the resulting "picture":

9. There were two kids in the hands of Gilgamesh.

Units that belong to hierarchically contiguous levels imitate or parody each other with the ultimate result of letting ideology speak injunctively without showing it (see chapter 10). The ideological novel, the *roman à thèse,* and much of historical Discourse rely on the multiplication of interdiscursive bridges to naturalize the Law by making it "paradoxically" indissociable from narrative discourse: "Things happen as they do because they are as they must be." We are led to hypostasize some kind of hypersynthetic operation that makes all types of predication virtually indistinguishable for the reader, when state and process are equally reduced to objects in the presented world or mediators of its total, quasi-textual significance.

> Together they went down into the forest and they came to the green mountain. There they stood still, they were struck dumb; they stood still and gazed at the forest. They saw the height of the cedar, they saw the way into the forest and the track where Humbaba was used to walk. The way was broad and the going was good. They gazed at the mountain of cedars, the dwelling place of the gods and the throne of Ishtar. The hugeness of the cedar rose in front of the mountain, its shade was beautiful, full of comfort; mountain and glade were green with brushwood.
> There Gilgamesh dug a well before the setting sun.[8]

This passage is particularly interesting because we can see how collocation, coordination, and subordination all collaborate in the articulation of narrative and descriptive discourses, so that their mutual finalities engage in a process of almost endless reverberation. The qualificative "green," at the end of the first sentence, separates the mountain, thus specified, from the unspecified forest, but, at the same time, it maintains the mountain in the forest by making explicit the seme "green" shared by both lexemes in this context, although it was not yet apparent in the sole noun "forest." The incoming narrative does not put an end to description so much as it reinterprets it as motivating for narration instead of ancillary to it; "there," at the beginning of the second sentence, seems at first to fulfill the supposedly classical, instrumental role of description with regards to setting, decor, and accessories, spatial and psychological parameters of action, but it ushers in a series of pseudoactional verbs ("they stood," "they saw") that can even accept inanimates for their subjects as in "the hugeness of the cedar rose." Description here is heavy with future narrative, but it devalues the special ergativity of human and animate subjects, turning them into spectators, leveling them with nature, in order not to preempt the outcome of the struggle that will question and activate the most fundamental paradigm of all in the symbolic order, the opposition between man and nonman. Where man is debunked as prime mover of action, he is reintroduced as judge, aesthetic or otherwise (the shade was "beautiful"), and user or consumer of nature (the shade was "full of comfort"). Interpretation, as we shall see in the third section, is the typical two-way bridge between description and narrative, because it is a discursive activity that can use several levels of predicates indifferently. It provides transitions as well as closing statements or interrogations; this move is very apparent in the anaphoric series "the mountain of cedars, the dwelling place of the gods and the throne of Ishtar." We should not think that narrative can be self-sufficient any more than description; in fact, narrative discourse is geared toward its own destruction: in the epic, it will be the acquisition of a permanent status by the hero, which will make him share the nature of things, eventually describable, definable, engraved on stone, petrified and repeatable. The meeting point of narrative and descriptive discourses is, at the same time, a meeting of the passionate character with the object and means of his passion, in this instance, of an ambitious demigod with the glorifying place, at the same time enemy and helper. Humbaba, guardian of the forest, is also the spirit of description that any narrative must challenge and defeat publicly to appropriate its virtues.

A complete study should be dedicated not only to the rhetorical effects of the various modes of interdiscursive articulation, but also to its rhetorical means, of which only some have been investigated (extended metaphor, allegory). Comparison, as was shown by Maarten van Buuren,[9] is an essential ingredient of classical and modern descriptions alike, even when they purport to get rid of their anthropocentric orientation, but its contribution to the articulation of discursive levels *between them* should be emphasized. Typically it allows the reintroduction of narrative in the midst of description, and vice versa, juxtaposing them without operating a bold predicative translation. At the same time, the border between animate subjects and inanimate objects becomes porous; mythic or clichéd narratives solidified in our universes of belief are evidenced, and marginal narrative programs can be tried, either for future development or as traces of abandoned options, or even as clues and indexes cleverly woven into the aesthetic carpet. There is a little of all this in a sentence from a Greek romance quoted by R. Debray-Genette: "For the pale rosy amethysts of Ethiopia resemble a rosebud opening up, as they begin to blush under a sunray."[10]

Inasmuch as description (or definition, for that matter) is not a mere list of parts, measurements, and properties, it has a strong tendency, like the riddle, to rely on similes and quantitative comparisons to determine its object within a class, and it puts to work the reader's encyclopedia to move from the better known to the unknown or the not-so-well known:

> Valencia is like a seagull flying inland, riverless like a drunkard who has stopped intoxicating himself, smaller than Barcelona and yet virtually endless, with equal parts of heavenly climate and hellish provincialism. The young man whom we have seen landing there on a warm Spring morning of 1967, was not in a mood to condescend to its paradoxical charms.

But whether it is mainly an enumerative chain or also an explicitly comparative development, description will often work as a *relay* between two flights of narrative discourse that have a different thematic scope and/or a different fictional regime; it is ready to act, for example, as a mediator between realist verisimilitude and fantastic or marvelous make-believe. It is efficient in the area of familiarization *and* defamiliarization; it helps us to play more freely with narrative logic. This broad function should be added to all those already listed by Hamon with regards to the narrative text, namely:

a) a demarcating function (to emphasize the articulations of narrative)
b) a delaying function (to interpose an amount of text before an expected denouement)
c) a decorative function (to integrate the text in an aesthetic and rhetoric system)
d) an organizing function (to contribute to the logical chain, to the readability and foreseeability of narrative)
e) a focusing function (to contribute to the anthropocentric character of the narrative by bringing a certain amount of direct or indirect information on one character or another—often on the *hero*.[11]

We should note that all these functions are at least partly reversible and some of them act in opposite directions. When there is *relaying*, as we have seen, *demar-*

cation becomes smoother or even inapparent; where *organizing* and increased *foreseeability* prevail, *delaying* becomes inoperative, as in melodrama when description reveals that the orphan and the lost father are in fact reunited and they will soon know it, or in the *novela rosa* when description designates the chosen couple as it already did in the Greek novel. On the other hand, the *decorative* and *organizing* functions can reinforce each other: the integration of the text in an aesthetic system through "descriptive systems" and stylistic features in description (such as maidens with long golden hair, dark towers with thick walls, and metaphoric enumerations of jewels to describe a beautiful face) entails a particular generic frame and the accompanying structural expectations. Conversely, the structural features of descriptions in a detective story are likely to attract the reader's attention on a romantic *style* of description as an oddity loaded with second thoughts or even perhaps as a cryptic metaliterary statement. The *demarcating* and *delaying* functions are effective by interposing heterogeneous textual masses in the supposedly linear first reading or in those parts of successive readings that replay the first. They are therefore more closely related to the ordering of narrative discourse itself than to the articulation of distinct discourses within the text; they are more involved with the temporal dimensions than the thematic series and isotopies, which are at first perceived as spatial forms; finally, they can be fulfilled just as well by other nonnarrative discourses (definitional, injunctive), by intranarrative ruptures (e.g., narrative digressions), or even by enunciative shifts (in *As I Lay Dying* or *The Hunting Gun*).

Narrative Dispositio

Here we shall deal principally with the so-called temporal dimensions of narrative, with its special successiveness as superimposed on and playing with that of the linguistic medium and other kinetic media, or contrasting with the relative indetermination of temporal parameters in the plastic media (painting, photography, etc.). This is the set of questions that early narratologies tried to investigate under a variegated constellation of terms including: plot, action, story, sequence, scene, summary, order, duration, frequency, chronology, exposition, suspense, catastrophe, and denouement or catharsis. Insofar as we take up and adapt part of this terminology, which is inescapable, each of the concepts will be treated as denoting an operation in a praxis, a move in a quest for significance, not textual objects. These operations, however resilient their textual markers may be, should not be hypostatized and foreclosed into a finite, final product that could be retrieved, identical to itself, by another operator or by the same operator on a different occasion; they seek and trigger off encounters, either memorable or almost unnoticed, between the trajectories of the various projections and retrojections that constitute, with as many side steps, narrative communication.

The basics of a nonneutral terminology will help to clarify a methodology for the study of narrative *dispositio*, the impact of its features on the narrative meaning of a text, and guidelines for a possible typology.

Plot.

A plot is a set of narrative *situations* or, more exactly, pro-narrative, narratogenous situations characterized by tensions, conflicts, imbalance or unstable balance (whether actual or potential) between agents. In other words, a narrative situation contains one or more narrative programs, depending on the codes that rule the world in question, and particularly the valences of the agents as a special aspect of code. Where there is a conflict of codes, the codes themselves can be considered as agents (forces).

In a text of a certain complexity, a plot normally consists of two or more *subplots*, that is, microsystems that center the situations on the individual agents or groups of agents; the various subplots can be more or less closely linked between them, their overlap can vary.

In Racine's play *Andromaque*, the initial plot can be summarized as follows: "Orestes loves Hermione who loves Pyrrhus who loves Andomache who loves Hector's memory." The subset of situations involving Pyrrhus (e.g., Pyrrhus and Hermione, Pyrrhus and Andromache) is Pyrrhus's subplot. In the *Princesse de Clèves*, where the situational bonds between the characters do not form a straight, coherent, and continuous chain, the differences between the various subplots can be seen even more readily; let us consider one (rather superficial) version of the plot: "M. de Clèves loves Mme. de Clèves who loves Nemours who loves Mme. de Clèves who has respect and friendship for M. de Clèves who is jealous of Nemours who flirts with the Dauphine who is attracted to Nemours," and so on.

The richness of the subplot radiating around one character is one of the criteria that contribute to turn this character into a protagonist, as we have seen in chapter 5, or, conversely, its poverty can turn a character into an auxiliary, although a tramp who meets all the characters on the road, or a lift boy who meets them in the elevator, is not necessarily central in the same sense as Mme. de Clèves in the novel by Mme. de La Fayette. But the situations also involve *forces*; subplots are formed around honor, desire, greed, and so forth. When such subplots are thematically dominant, we are dealing with the allegorical genre or regime of fictionality.

Subplots, structurally similar to thematic isotopies in this respect, can be more or less autonomous in the course of a narrative, in the sense of the relative continuity of the network, the number, quality, and frequency of the points of intersection, and the distance between them measurable by the number of intermediate steps; for example:

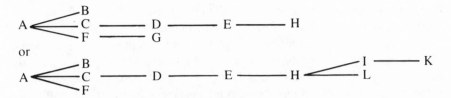

In the French classical tragedy, the rule of the three unities ensures a tight interdependence between subplots; in *The Recognitions*, initially independent subplots tend to converge through a rare combination of circumstances (see the second section of this chapter); in some "slice of life" and unanimist narratives, several subplots may never meet at all.

Structure, Story, and Related Notions.

The narrative *structure* of a message, in its broadest sense, is the systematic schematization of the way in which the plot, considered at each point of unfolding of the text, is transformed into another plot: it can be compared to the notation of all the actual moves in a chess game. (My "narrative structure" is not essentially different from the abstract core of "plot" as defined by Peter Brooks: "We might think of plot as the logic or perhaps the syntax of a certain kind of discourse, one that develops its propositions only through temporal sequence and progression.")[12] The various narrative structures (in their actual or possible, idiosyncratic or typical diversity) consist of more or less complex combinations of plot transformations, with their articulation (mode of transition) and syntagmatic order.

Transformations should not be understood here in their strict generative sense. Moreover, even if they are manifested on the surface by a suppression, an omission, or a disjunction, *all narrative transformations are cumulative*: they all add up toward the total narrative significance produced as that of the text by the act of communication based on this text. Thus the transformation thematized or concretized as "loss" of an object should be added to the acquisition and retention of the same; we could say that narrative structures are a kind of double-entry bookkeeping. Any transformation in a series involves, at least virtually, the complete series with all its instrumental and modal options, as well as the corresponding "contrary" and "contradictory" series according to the semiotic square. "Acquiring," for instance, should not only be situated on an oriented axis between "not-having" and "having," but it must also be confronted to "not-acquiring," "losing," and "not-losing."

Il visconte dimezzato (The cloven viscount), the first tale from Italo Calvino's trilogy *Our Ancestors*, will offer a simple illustration of these ideas. At point x of our reading, we have been informed of a plot consisting of the viscount's incompleteness, physical, moral, and mental, his exactions against all the people of the county, and his being "in love" with the shepherdess Pamela who does not want to become his prey and be held prisoner in one of the towers of the castle. At point y, we have been informed of a plot consisting of the same key elements, plus the contrary action of the viscount's other half, as perfectly good and saintly as the other is bad and devilish, equally in love with Pamela and ready to marry her; the good, left, half's subplot now at least balances the bad, right, half's subplot, since the former maintains, directly and indirectly, relations with the narrator-as-character and most of the other characters, which are important or potentially decisive for their respective fates. At point z, the plot consists of a single (two-in-one) well-balanced viscount facing all the ordinary tasks and problems of a powerful man's life. These plots are cumulative in that they do not erase the preceding plots as they come into reading focus (and become the thematic focus of the text). Earlier on, at point $x - 1$, half of the viscount's body had seemed destroyed, crushed by a cannonball, but, even before it returns, as alive as the other half, the absent part, significantly, makes more sense for the remaining one than the two together managed to do for each of them or for the whole person before. The same accumulation works at the end too:

> "My Uncle Medardo became a whole man again, neither good nor bad, but a mixture of goodness and badness, that is apparently not dissimilar to what he had been before the halving. But having had the experience of both halves each on its own, he was bound to be wise. He had a happy life, many children and a just rule. Our lives too changed for the better."[13]

No transformation can be purely negative or canceled out by another one; there is no such thing in narrative as a *mere* "restoration of order," or a "circular structure" on the plane of the narrated. This is of the essence of narrative economy (see chapter 8).

As far as the articulations between the different transformations are concerned, they are best described in rhetorical terms; for example, the duel between the two halves of Medardo, as a result of which they would both die without the intervention of a third party, but which is at the same time a necessary precondition of their reunification, shows clearly the argumentative structure of the parable. In a love romance, a walk of the two lovers hand in hand between a period of separation and their final reunion, works obviously like a foreshortening of married life and an anticipation of a honeymoon trip; it is, therefore, a metaphor that can be reinterpreted later, depending on the final outcome, as hyperbole, litote, or irony. These articulations between transformations contribute as much as the transformations themselves to situate the narrative text in a particular aesthetic perspective and in a specific socioideological "context"; they are subtle loci of the "poetics of the norm."[14]

Modalizations (other than aspectual) of narrative transformations of the predicative type can generally be analyzed as the result of the conjunction of certain actional predicates with a tabular (infranarrative) predicate. For example:

1. *Nonmodalized Series.*

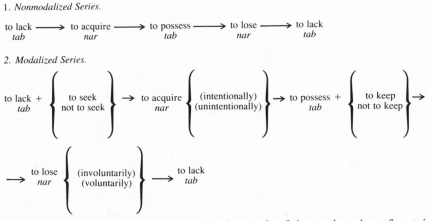

2. *Modalized Series.*

The modality of duty can be seen as the result of the conjunction of certain actional predicates with an injunctive predicate. Aspectual modalizations will be studied later in this section under the heading "Aspect, Time, and Logical Spatial Forms."

A *story* is the totality of the narratemes in a narrative, reordered within the limits of narrated time set by the text, according to the chronological criteria accepted by the reader in the situation (criteria that originate in the pragmatic and symbolic temporal codes of the cultural community to which the reader belongs).

In a classic detective novel, we meet a corpse first, then a detective, then traces, clues, witnesses, tracks, and finally a murderer; its chronological reordering will give the story of a crime followed by its detection and (sometimes) punishment. The story is a fact of social Discourses (legal, historical, etc.); it must not be mistaken for the logical and other presuppositions that condition the production of narrative meaning, since it is due to a reduction and a rearrangement necessarily carried out *after* the recognition of narrative structure. Although a gross temporal frame may be given from the beginning (*A Day in the Life of Ivan Denisovich, Une Année dans le Sahel, The Life of an American Writer, 1943–1954*), each narrateme designs and redesigns the temporal texture of the whole tale told, which provides the grid needed to construct a story. Even if a narrative structure could be perfectly "linear," that is, if the syntagmatic order of transformations could coincide perfectly with the chronological order of the micronarratemes, the story would remain a superimposed structure whose aim is to return to conformity and necessity, in the guise of a motivating Gestalt, the irreversible arbitrariness of what happened to be told.

It is worth noting that my distinction between story and structure does not coincide exactly with Tomashevsky's dissociation of *fabula* and *sujet* as explained, for example, by Meir Sternberg:

> The *fabula* of the work is the chronological, or chronological-causal sequence into which the reader, progressively and retrospectively, reassembles [the] motifs; it may thus be viewed as the second degree "raw material" . . . that the artist compositionally "deforms" and recontextualizes. . . . The *sujet*, in contrast, is the actual disposition and articulation of these narrative motifs in the particular finished product, as their order and interrelation, shaping and coloring, was finally decided on by the author.[15]

Beside the often criticized confusions this terminology is prone to generate, our narrative structure is to be seen as primarily produced by the reader who works it out from the text, like the story, but freer from social pressures at large and, conversely, more dependent on textual markers. The idea of a symmetry between the inscription of the text by the sender and the production of meaning by the receiver is the illusion that changes the "story" into hypothetical "raw material," but it is indeed contrary to the radical asymmetry of narrative communication. Motifs, like the Proppian functions, are centered on a subject; they do not take into account the general remodeling of relations and potential involved in each transformation of plot. Finally, a story is by definition a commonsense justification of narrative structures, the reduction of events to a factuality that disposes of cognition and the text in favor of the security of social and legal time; it may serve mechanical memory, but it is a regressive instrument of oblivion regarding the event of communication itself.

Even in conditions of realist or scientific mimesis, the linguistic material introduces a high degree of arbitrariness in the "order of events," since it prevents in any case an iconic rendering of simultaneity. For example, should we say, "As the lift goes up, the counterweight goes down," or, "As the counterweight goes down, the lift goes up"? Or, very often, phrastic syntax does not reflect the "order of things"; typically, in Latin: "Aliquem Augustus convenit." Whatever the semiotic vehicle involved, we have to do away altogether with the idea of a natural or faithful presentational order of events; it is impossible to start from the beginning and finish at the end. In the film *The Quiet Man*, studied in Chapter 9, the narrator says he will begin with the beginning, but he is immediately forced to stop his protagonist in the middle of the road to make him tell who he is and where he is coming from. The speaker or inscriber who presents events exerts or transmits the ordering powers of language, Discourses, and genres.

It is clear that plot and narrative structure, on the one hand, and story and narrative discourse, on the other hand, are tightly bound. The close association of these two systems in some epics and in the so-called classical novel should not blind us to their dissociation in other narrative forms. Those who doubt the preponderance of narrative discourse in Robbe-Grillet's *Jealousy* and say, "Nothing happens in this novel," are not completely wrong. The efforts of more or less humanist critics like Bruce Morrissette[16] to "reconstruct" a story, a chronology acceptable by everyday standards, are all in vain when there is no single temporal frame that would offer a "commonsense" alternative to the order of enunciation of the narratemes; the blurring of narrower temporal frames also casts doubt on the transformational status of individual predicates. The same is true of multiply embedded narratives branching out on partial overlappings, like Potocki's *Manuscrit trouvé à Saragosse*. But, in spite of its aborted narrative discourse and absent story, *Jealousy* does offer a successive set of narrative situations organized in subplots that amount to different, transformable plots at separate moments of the reading experience: we are dealing with a rhetorical narrative structure rather than a causal or chronological *dispositio*; *Jealousy* is a *hierarchical* narrative of a particular kind in which there are several conflicting macronarratemes (see chapter 2). William Burroughs's "narratives," as well as the more recent work of Juan Goytisolo, or Raymond Federman's hyperfictions, arrive at the same result using different means.

Even with a simple quantitative narrative, it is not always possible to formulate the corresponding story. Very often there are a number of narratemes floating in the chronological or chronocausal frame suggested by the text. The paleographers who pieced together the fragments of the *Epic of Gilgamesh* were facing precisely this problem; Sandars gave it the most conventional solution, capping the whole thing with an archetypal sequence, more revealing about the functions of narrative in general than about the ancient civilizations of the Middle East: "He left—he traveled—he returned—he wrote—he died." We are so ready to do the same to any narrative that many contemporary forms rely on our training to integrate any event in the "normal course of things," to adapt the news to the *doxa* and make us repeat what we believe we know already about ourselves and our world.

These are excerpts from a newspaper obituary for Marshall McLuhan:

The world's pioneer communications theorist, Professor Marshall McLuhan, whose phrase "the medium is the message" became the byword of a generation, died at his home in Canada yesterday.
His death at 69 followed failure to recover from a stroke in 1979.
. . . Professor McLuhan was Director of the Centre for Culture and Technology at the University of Toronto's St Michael's College for the past 17 years. . . . A prolific and diverse writer, he produced 14 books. His first, *The Mechanical Bride: Folklore of Industrial Man*, was published in 1951.[17]

The only other chronological data are a doctorate at Oxford in 1942 and international fame won in the 1960s. It is then very difficult to guess the place of *Understanding Media* in the chronological frame of reference (namely Western historical time, 1911 to January 1, 1981 = McLuhan's life, or even 1951, first book, to 1979, stroke) or in relation to his other published works and his many honorary degrees. This and other uncertainties, and the resulting shapelessness of the story, are not innocent; the life of McLuhan, a "pope," a star of the intellect, is reduced to that of a vast category of men who "left, traveled, returned, wrote, and died," and furthermore to a single unsituated phrase that encompasses his whole existence: "The medium is the message," which the newspaper correspondent, unwittingly, proves right.

Other typical obituaries finish with a statement to the effect that: "Mr. Smith is survived by his wife, Helen, and two children, Rod, 15, and Kim, 12," without giving any information about the date of Mr. and Mrs. Smith's marriage or, obviously, the state and fate of their accumulated capital. The story is vague, but nobody cares because the narrative structure of the obituary focuses on the narrateme "Mr Smith died" and the transformations inferred from it (e.g., the change of status of the protagonist's actions, which cease to belong to a becoming and are turned into signs and evidence of their own causes).

Now, if we consider the "story" of the typical mad criminal (the "Yorkshire Ripper") as narrated by the daily press, it is reduced to a mechanical succession of narratemes of the type "X rapes and kills Y," all identical but for one variation: the name of the victim. The "gratuitous" horror of the repeated murders corresponds to the almost complete absence of narrative situations (no conflict exposed, deficiency of characterization, etc.). Narrative structure reaches its degree zero in pure repetition. The only variation—the name of the young female victim—does not indicate a transformation, nor does it even confirm a narrative situation; it is a self-referring sign that signals nothing but repetition itself and, through it, the passage of time. In short, there are *structural* narratives that offer a basic trajectory from narrative situations to narrative structures, and *storical* narratives whose trajectory runs from narrative discourse to story, in the sense that the former, which fail to induce the production of a coherent story, make us revert to structures and dwell longer on them, whereas, with the latter, we rush through weak structures to reach the story and stay there. This distinction does not duplicate that between *hierarchical* and *quantitative* narratives, since the criteria and levels of analysis are different, although there may be a measure of coincidence in practice.

Aspect, Time, and Logical and Spatial Forms.

Temporal notions are so indissociably linked with narrative communication, whether as its source and motivation, as its material, means, and constraints of production, or as its effect, that dissertations about time and narrative or time and the novel will generally do very little to clarify the consequences of this fundamental fact and the modalities of its manifestations. Time is a single object only inasmuch as it is nothing but a fetish, a god, or another object of belief. In relation to narrative, it is vital to distinguish between *presented time*, a thematic item, and *presentational-experiential time*, intertwined with the reception situation, and again, for each of these two times, between continuity and rupture, on the one hand, and condensation and expansion, on the other hand. For instance, even though Ricardou's pioneering article "Temps de la narration et temps de la fiction" relied on the first distinction, the mechanical calculus of tempo he attempted to derive from it proves erroneous on key examples. Quoting the famous passage at the end of Flaubert's *Sentimental Education*:

> He traveled.
> He came to know the melancholy of the steamboats, the cold of
> dawn under the tents, the tedium of landscapes and ruins, the bitterness
> of interrupted friendships.
> He returned,[18]

Ricardou spoke of a "tremendous acceleration of narrative" that he opposed to "the slowing down, even reaching standstill," imposed by reading a description. In order to determine the tempo of a narrative text, he was content with labeling as *récit* all the utterances denoting actions or events, and *descriptions* the other utterances. We know that descriptions can be the material of narrative meaning, and sometimes its sole material, and also that apparent narratemes, without the right temporal frame or vector, or under the frequentative aspect, may not narrate at all. The passage quoted from Flaubert is a third case, the intermediate *iterative*, which has recently become the object of some very elaborate studies.[19]

The iterative is characterized by the fact that a single occurrence of predication denotes several occurrences of the corresponding phenomenon in the presented world. This plurality may be explicit ("He came to know the melancholy of the steamboats") or implicit ("He traveled"). The number of occurrences can be large or small, more or less determinate, and they can take place over a longer or shorter period of time (narrative iteration) or in a larger or smaller space (descriptive iteration). In the passage quoted, the number of occurrences of individual trips (how many different steamboats?), the temporal limits of the total period of traveling, and the duration of each trip are all rather indeterminate; we can only infer a long or fairly long time in view of the distances evoked and the nature of the psychological reactions. All connection with the preceding chronology is provisionally broken, this is *the* event iconically figured by the abrupt leap from a singulative into an iterative narrative. Although the passage is a *summary* (few words for many events), we could say that, far from being accelerated, "time" is conjured away until a new date is mentioned. I do not see why the reader should speed up his cognitive process; the low density of information is emphasized by the unusual blanks in print, which are supposed to be filled out by clichés *ad libitum* on the model of the two lines between "he traveled" and "he returned." The dynamics of the production of meaning and value with the iterative is fascinating because it is really dialectic: narratemes are first apprehended through analysis and synthesis; their frequentative character virtually confers on them a descriptive or even definitional value, but the explication of these predicates involves again the activation of their narrative programs that, not being guided by the text, is heavily dependent on the cultural codes. Such "temporal ellipses" or summaries are often in fact the occasion of considerable expense to the reader who stops working out the "action" in order to develop and/or assimilate the inscription of social Discourses and, generally, the genealogy of the text. In our example, Flaubert's supreme irony consists in making us perceive how clichéd Frédéric's behavior is (traveling to forget) at our own expense, by making us do exactly the same thing with his text.

Contrary to the implications of the classical opposition between *scene* and *summary*, which is supposed to entail the isochronicity of the former (time of narration = narrated time), a dialogic scene can be as iterative as a summary in the voice of a Σ narrator. We have already come across a good example with the dialogue from *Pedro Páramo* studied in chapter 6. This dialogue compresses into one synthetic scene several encounters far distant in time in the presented world, but there is no need that a dialogue be arranged in such an original fashion for it to fulfill an iterative function in the construction of narrative significance: long-term characterization constants combined with high chronological indeterminacy give an iterative quality to a vast number of dialogues in *Pedro Páramo*. The "self-contained" framing and the anonymity of speakers produce the same effect in most of the dialogic scenettes of R. D. Laing's *Do You Really Love Me?* We must remember that literary, even theatrical dialogue, is always reported speech, quotation; its singulative or iterative character depends on a combination of narrational features and selected semantic content. The sharp contrast between a monologic frame and a dialogue on the one hand, the specific questions and answers made on a first encounter, make us read a dialogue as singulative, if the characters involved are sufficiently autonomous; the exemplary strength of a dialogic moral fable or parable often relies on this kind of compromise with a realist device. For example, from Hermann Hesse's *Siddhartha*:

> Siddhartha went to see Kamaswami, the merchant. . . .
> "I have been told," the merchant began, "that you are a Brahmin, a learned man, but that you seek service with a merchant. Are you then in need, Brahmin, that you seek service?"
> "No," replied Siddhartha. "I am not in need and I have never been in need. I have come from the Samanas with whom I lived for a long time."

"If you come from the Samanas, how is it that you are not in need?"[20]

I would like therefore to propose a more workable notion of *scene*. This notion, used by prestructuralist Anglo-Saxon criticism as well as by Baquero Goyanes,[21] Gérard Genette (as an element of analysis of narrative rhythm),[22] Seymour Chatman (grossly for the same purpose),[23] and Jean Rousset (as a criterion of a "fixed form that belongs by right to the genre of the novel"),[24] in fact owes its existence to the Aristotelian division of genres and is associated with the "dramatization of narrative" by which "the author wishes to achieve the illusion (for the reader) that the tale tells itself."[25]

I shall say that *the scene is a textual unit (or group of units) whose unity is determined by the conjunction of a certain population of characters in a particular presented space.* I use it then in its strict dramatic sense, except for the mode of enunciation that may, but need not, involve direct reported speech. Diegetic time is an effect of textual presence; it is either a projection of the existential time of reading or comprehension of textual assertions about time, or even and more commonly a combination of these two factors, but what it cannot be is simultaneously a criterion (a cause) and the signification (consequence) of the scene. The scene is different from the "picture" (*tableau* or *eidyllion*) in that it requires agents that work as such, fulfill more or less their three functions, and thus generate narrative as well as nonnarrative discourse. The scene can receive a title that will be also a name of *sequence* — or of a fragment of sequence — as defined by Barthes ("a logical succession of nuclei [= elementary narratemes] bound together by a relation of solidarity"),[26] for example, "a gift," "a meeting," "a departure." The scene is thus the first privileged unit in which to observe interdiscursive articulation, but it is also important and useful in many other respects.

The scene appeals to our most naive experience of transactions with the outside world and with ourselves (in dreams and in daydreaming), and it is a model for the formation of unconscious images. Therefore it tends to naturalize narrative. Its coincidence or noncoincidence with the external divisions of a tale (paragraphs or chapters in written enunciation, continua between pauses, telling sessions in oral enunciation) will have a marked aesthetic effect, as they play with distanciation, realism, and tradition, *muthos* and *epos*. Metafiction is a great enemy of the scene, as it dismantles it or disrupts it to superimpose the adventure of telling over the tale of adventure, or even it uses it, like fantasy literature, for purposes contrary to its supposed singulative vocation, by repeating it or making it easily repeatable, not unique. But popular genres and milieus of communication give it a similar treatment to confirm their own preponderance over the narrative subject matter (the presented possible worlds) and, at the same time, generate suspense; the serial and the extended comic are great scene cutters: "Is Nick going to kill Ted? . . . Meanwhile, back at the ranch . . . " The scene is an essential ingredient of narrative (whether it is actualized or not), not because it liberates it from the supervising presence of the teller, but on the contrary because it has to do with the subject, with all the subjects involved in narrative communication (subject of enunciation, subject of enunciated enunciation, subjects of narrative and other predicates, subject of reception, subject of enunciated reception). Its constituent form is a "there and then," mirror image, metonym or metaphor of the "here and now" whose quest or assumption determines the subject. "Here and now" is the semantic complex whose manifold negations constitute the logical forms of all narrational and narrated moves, for example, "not here but now" (mental, imaginary narrational displacement), "not now but here," earlier (mental, mnemonic narrational displacement), later (mental, speculative narrational displacement), "neither here nor now" (narrational or narrated displacement). A scene can be viewed as the concretization of a narrative situation and, reciprocally, a situation as a conjunction of characters and forces in a mental locus, that is, a mental scene.

Something must now be said of the notion of *narrative program* (not in the sense of the Paris school of semiotics).

The narrative program of an utterance or a group of utterances in general is the complete set of narratemes and ordered chains of narratemes that can be derived from it.

Let us consider the statement "X is bald"; its negation can be situated either before or after the time T of the state of affairs considered, as can the negation of the negation:

1. X was not bald—X is bald—X will not be bald.
2. X was bald—X is bald—X will not be bald.
3. X was bald—X is bald—X will be bald.
4. X was not bald—X is bald—X will be bald.

Depending on whether we consider only the relation between the present and one not present state of affairs, or the relation between the present and the two not present states of affairs (past and future), there are either two or four primary narrative programs, as follows:

1. X has become temporarily bald.
2. X will finally cease to be bald.
3. X will never cease to be bald.
4. X has become definitively bald.

Each of these programs can be enriched by taking into account cause and/or consequence, duration of process, and so on, and can be actualized-concretized in many forms by contextual adjunctions. For example, the primary program "X is bald ↔ X will not be bald" can give rise to explanations such as: "X is getting a hair implant," "X is buying a wig," or "X's hair is growing (again)," or to consequential developments such as: "X will look better," "X will look younger," or "X will no longer catch head colds," but *not* to other narrative statements such as: "X's feet will get sore." Narrative programs are dependent on the lexical content of the utterance considered, not on the truth-value of this utterance. The primary narrative program of "X is bald" is the same whether X is "the present king of France," "Louis XIV," or "Mr. Smith." The contents of secondary narrative programs are affected by these lexical fillings out of X, notably because some of them are substantivized predications (e.g., "a king rules France now") that have their own narrative programs, but the *relevance* of possible narrative chains to the utterance from which they are inferred has nothing to do with the truth-value of the utterance.

I must stress that all well-formed utterances have narrative programs, whatever the transformational level of discourse to which they belong, except the ontemes and equatemes, which *cannot* be negated because they cannot be displaced in time. But narrative programs can vary immensely on scales of openness versus closure, necessity versus arbitrariness, and probability versus improbability, as a function of the nature and content of the utterance or group of utterances that gives rise to them. For example, "The scarf is red" has a much more open secondary program than "Peter killed Paul" or "Open the door!" Utterances with very open programs, such as "The scarf is red" or "It was nine a.m." typically contribute to the symbolic articulation of a narrative text (see the third section) because they fit with almost any narrative development while being relevant to only one or a limited number of symbolic codes; the need for textual unity and determinacy makes these codes seem operative on narrative logic precisely because the utterances concerned themselves are not.

I shall not prolong the protracted debate on the spatial form of narrative[27], but some sense must be made of the notion in relation to narrative syntax. First of all, any confusion must be avoided between denoted space and presentational or narrational space; the latter is manifested by the number and length of words and blanks on a visual support, the size of the support itself, and the corresponding time of contact in reading, or by the time and intensity of contact in oral communication. Linguistic narrative space is doubly oriented, but memory makes it reversible—in the same way that Euclidean space must be; and memory is vital to the production of narrative meaning, significance, and value. The reality and homogeneity of narrational space must be assumed in order to understand repetition, simultaneity, forking out time, ambiguity, and options; its reversibility is implied by the perception of symmetries and so-called circular structures. But what deserves detailed study is the complex relation between presentational and presented space on the one hand, and between presentational space and semantic space on the other hand, plus the relations between the two systems. Generic determinations, rhetoric and aesthetic effects, and the production of value in the cultural context (milieu) of communication are largely related to these three sets of spatial relations, as they are also to the corresponding sets of temporal relations.

It is most interesting in particular to observe whether there takes place a projection of the plane of narration on the plane of the narrated, and vice versa, along this axis, and which means of projection are used: is the crossing of a desert iconically figured? And, if so, will it be by an unending repetitive narration, as in Pierre Loti, by a few words interspersed with blanks as in *Sentimental Education*, or by a liberation of the space of the screen as in the film *Lawrence of Arabia?* The metaphorical redundancy of presented space, semantic space (varying distance between opposites or quasi synonyms, closely related or virtually unrelated terms), and presentational space may in turn abolish "distance" through an effect of harmony and at-oneness, or hyperbolically underscore it, depending on the dominant codes of figuration in the situation of communication.

The Role of Nondeclarative and Negative Utterances.

These difficult questions, in particular that of interrogative utterances, would require long developments in the framework of a theory of argumentation[28] and its intersections with narrative theory. At present, I shall make only a few remarks.

1. As far as the transformational level of discursemes is concerned, an interrogative utterance is in no way different from an assertion: "Was Paul killed?" and "Who done it?" are narrative. "Is the rose red?" is not.

2. However, an interrogative utterance is fundamentally different from an assertion in that it cannot be syntactically self-sufficient, or rather it exhibits a lack of self-sufficiency that other utterances conceal under their assertive form. A question asked in a text, if it is unanswered, attracts either another question of the reader: "Who is asking?" for example, or a supportive clause of enunciated enunciation in order to cancel as far as possible the imbalance introduced by the interrogative "Was Paul killed?" → "X asks (himself) whether Paul was killed." And, if the question is actually answered, the interrogative utterance is immediately integrated into a dual enunciative system: "[X asks (himself)] 'Was Paul killed?' "—" 'Yes, he was' [answers Y] or [X answers himself]."

3. The interrogative renders utterances unstable and makes it easier for them to join in with others in discursively nonhomogeneous chains; for example:

"Did Peter kill Paul?"   → "[No] He was at the other end of the country."
　　　　　or   → "[Yes] He was in love with Paul's wife."

Especially in dialogue, an interrogative utterance will often bridge the gap between a narrative and a nonnarrative utterance. Moreover, a deeper application of the notion of implicature allows us to go even further. Let us examine again the example proposed by Wilson and Sperber:[29] to the statement "I am going to the bank" someone responds "It's twenty past *five*." There is certainly, in the second segment of the exchange, an implicature that "the bank closes at five, you are too late," but also, due to the cooperative principle, an implicature of the question "Can I still go to the bank?" in the assertive utterance "I am going . . . " The response is also an answer: it makes the original assertion slide toward the interrogative. Is it not precisely because the two assertions are not of the same discursive level? (One is narrative; the other is descriptive.) If, to the same statement, the response had been "*I* am going to the post office" or "I'll go *tomorrow*," nothing of the sort would have happened.

4. Interrogation, explicit or implied, is a prime mover of the codes that Barthes called proairetic and hermeneutic (actional and interpretive).[30] "Is Peter really guilty?" and "What happened then?" are multifunctional relays and punctuations. They contribute to formulate the enigma or work as decoys and temporarily prevent the correct formulation of the enigma, which always has the same result of attracting our attention. Such utterances mark a cut between two narrative sequences or between a narrative sequence and a nonnarrative syntagm. They change "focalization" (the ways of information) and shift agential functions. They serve as transitions between different voices, and as identification bridges: the reader is always the one who is supposed to ask questions, except when there is a sphinx. Unless he considers the enunciator of the question a usurper and an unfair rival—which is already a bond—the reader is obliged to project-identify himself with this enunciative role, a good way of transgressing (apparently) his passive, submissive position and getting "into" the text.

5. Negative statements always clearly imply the possibility of the statement they negate; therefore, they work largely as responses-answers to questions they imply and whose scope they delimit. For instance, depending on the emphasis, "X has not become bald" will work as an answer to the question "Is X bald?" or to the question "Has X become bald?" The negativity of the negation casts doubt back on its own certainty as well as on the propositional validity of the statement.

6. Finally, although all the examples given here are on the phrastic scale, for the sake of commodity, we should think of the status and sign of an utterance as a feature that can mark the propositional value of extended textual units (entire narrative chains, pages and chapters of text), if seen in a holistic perspective.

Textual Memory: The Syntax of *The Recognitions*

Repetition and recollection are the same movement, only in opposite directions; for what is recollected has been, is repeated

*backwards, whereas repetition properly so called is recollected
forwards.*

—Kierkegaard, *Repetition*

The Recognitions may be seen as a desperate and failed attempt to transcend this opposition-in-the-mirror or, less naively perhaps, to reveal its falsity, since the mirror of opposition is not less constitutive of repetition than the tracing paper of re-presentation. The mockery of Echo is irony: at the same time the negation of identity contained in its manifestation (my voice must come from thither to be heard) and the negation of difference. Is there nothing new then but time itself? Are all encounters bound to be *re*encounters (*rencontres*), calling cries, reminders, and narrative—the discourse of change—a recourse against impermanence?

Copying and counterfeiting, the universal lack of authenticity are, at first sight, the recurring themes of *The Recognitions*, the point in question and the very principle of construction of the novel. Wyatt, the son of Reverend Gwyon, is a painter who, unable to complete his dead mother's likeness from a photograph, gives up the production of "original work" and produces fake Old Masters profitably introduced on the New York and international market by two accomplices, Recktall Brown and a Hungarian double agent named Basil Valentine. Mr. Sinisterra, who caused the death of Wyatt's mother on board a ship, the *Purdue Victory* (where he was hiding, posing as the ship's surgeon), is a counterfeiter whose life's goal is to be praised by the *Counterfeit Monthly* for the quality of his work, when his notes are seized by the police. Esme, Wyatt's model, "writes slowly, with no effort apparent but as from memory, in confident trust as poetry is written";[31] her pieces, however, happen to be by Rilke. Otto, the young lover of both Esme and Esther (Wyatt's wife), writes a play called *The Vanity of Time*, with a main character, Gordon, lifted entirely from the "real life" Wyatt, who happens to speak in quotations; later Otto will wander about New York with his arm in a sling, pretending that he was hurt in a revolution in Central America. Mr. Feddle is always going to have a book of poetry published; he is present at all the literary cocktail parties in the Village, signing books from the shelves by famous authors, until he is unmasked carrying a fake book of his: "Then pages flashed, the laughter broke.—*The Idiot?* That's the title of your book? *The Idiot* . . . the laughter came on,—by Feodor Feddle . . . ?" (p. 1000).

But, at the same time, imitation and faking seem to be the secret of reality itself, the nature of its nature, and the process of its own achievement, as well as the means and conditions of poetic justice. Recktall Brown dies as he falls on the stairs clad in a suit of armor; Mr. Sinisterra finds his death at the hands of a professional killer, as he bears the Romanian passport of a certain Mr. Yak: he had planned to sell a fake mummy to an Egyptologist who happened to be, in disguise, the killer sent to Spain to execute Mr. Yak. While Wyatt is looking for the remains of his Protestant mother, Camilla, killed by Sinisterra, and Sinisterra for a potential mummy, they find instead the body of a young girl who is to be canonized because she worked miracles after being raped and murdered: during the Spanish civil war, the bodies had been exchanged and Camilla's will become the relics of a Catholic patron saint, while the girl's will become an Egyptian mummy. All this takes place at San Zwingli, a swindle, a contradiction in terms and a referential impossibility in Spain, since Zwingli was a radical reformer; but we also remember that Gwyon, Camilla's husband and Wyatt's father, had turned progressively from Protestantism to the solar worship of the Golden Bull, while his idiotic servant was printing her own version of the Bible. Otto, on his return to Central America, actually has his arm broken in a local revolution:

> The demonstration was noisy, but he looked on it with a tired eye, refusing to be taken in by such foolishness. Until a policeman rode toward him, swinging a saber; and the policeman's neck was covered with blood.
> That suddenly, it was real. (p. 778).

Earlier in New York, Otto had a date with his unknown father, Mr. Pevsner; having mistaken the counterfeiter Sinisterra for his father, Otto had received from Sinisterra the five thousand dollars in fake notes that forced him to flee from the United States. With a small part of this sum, he had bought a dressing gown for Mr. Pevsner, who is arrested and consequently lobotomized—he had been unable to make it to his first date with his son because the police had mistaken him for a drug addict (he injected himself with insulin for diabetes).

We discover in fact a second principle of organization and production of meaning: the creative mistake. Where and when fiction fails, it generates reality; reality cannot anticipate its own course, it can only manifest itself through the structures of fiction, for it is, in and of itself, structureless. Imitation is its source, even when it fails. An imitation is successful—it is believed to be the real thing—only when it is defaced by an imitation of imitation, the typical clumsiness of modern alterations and restorations: if nobody, wanting to produce a fake, faked so poorly, then the painting (the book, the love, the revolution, etc.) must be original. Eventually, all evidence that there ever was something else than what there is (i.e., fakes) will be destroyed. *The Recognitions*, an immensely parodic book, relies on the construction of a textual memory that supersedes and destroys the encyclopedic intertextual memory by which it is nourished; for this purpose, it gives itself the necessary time and space that make it world-substitutive.

Applying its own Borgesian axiom that a transparent fake is an original—the untouched presence of itself as event—*The Recognitions* points insolently to its imitation of *Ulysses*, to the extent that the "central quester" is given the name Stephen. Visible imitation, enjoyable in itself, as classical aesthetics had already dictated, cancels resemblance, the duality of objects, before and after or side by side; it should leave us with the pure event of passage, without origin or destination. The three fathers (Gwyon, Sinisterra, and Pevsner) and the various father figures (Brown, Valentine, Hemingway) are poorly treated in the novel; nothing happened before except what is happening now: the impossibility of being born of oneself. We understand now why there is one exception to the rule of the transparent fake: paper money. Currency, the instrument of exchange, cannot be successfully imitated because, contrary to the work of art, it is defined from without; it is traced back to its source of emission, not down to its effects. Lacking any intrinsic value, determined and controlled by the law that it embodies, the least authentic and original of all things, currency poses nevertheless as the unfalsifiable, unforgeable standard of authenticity. So does, one might think, the realist work of art, in contradistinction to the modernist work.

The power assigned to textual memory is a means of offsetting all other forms of memory. Yet, even though verisimilitude is ridiculed by the most contrived coincidences, cognition is a coincidence, it is always recognition: the illusionistic effects of repetition come back with a vengeance. All the characters, whether they know reality is apocryphal and existence secondhand, or whether, like the musician Stanley, they still believe in one original God and one original accomplishment, are equally disposed of. They cannot forget that they are made of the stuff of memory, and it drives them to madness and death, Bosch and the Ship of Fools.

To the madness of memory, there is nothing to be confronted but another loss, even more severe perhaps, and it is the inconsistency of the present; the scene, particularly the "party," is its *topos*:

—Oh, said the tall woman recovering,—I support my husband. *He*
writes. He's an editor, you know. He's editing Esther's book.
—Who's Esther?
—Why, my dear, she's our hostess. There, talking with the tall fellow
in the green necktie. (p. 606)

People, when they are together, cannot recognize and therefore cannot *know* each other: the little girl who comes several times from some apartment downstairs to collect sleeping pills, remains always in the present; ever new to those she approaches, she is forgotten without being identified. Is she or her mother going to commit suicide? No one cares, no one will be informed, no one will ever ask this question; the little girl does not begin—or cease—to exist, since she does not "make memory" for any subject. If it is not weaker than absence, which is uncertain, coexistence is anyway the weakest and dimmest form of existence: "My mummy sent me up to get some sleeping pills, but I can't find the lady who . . .
—Now, don't you bother the nice lady, said Agnes, rummaging in the bottom of her large purse" (p. 638).

However, if time is useless with regard to the myriad events that destroy it at each moment, the reader's memory too can encompass only the most enduring successive repetition into the simultaneity of one scene. Textual memory is the condition of possibility of repetition, but it also levels out occurrences to the final reduction of narrative significance. The closure of narrative, its finitude, collapses the encounter of an incomprehensible past with an obtuse present into a falling façade: the text of all texts passing by.

William Gaddis knows and shows that repetition and rehearsal, not change, are the foundations of narrative, and that its function is to hide and pass off as change the repetition of death. Textual memory is the artificer of the forgetfulness built into custom; narrative syntax is its preferred trick: we shall all be one block between our beginning and our end, and our work "will still be spoken of, when it is noted, with high regard, though seldom played" (p. 1021). When Michel Zéraffa wrote: "Ruled by a historical-chronological principle, the novel excludes, refuses repetitiveness, but it must accept it because of its mythic antecedents and references,"[32] he showed an acute awareness of some fine historical nuances in the last couple of centuries, but he was perhaps not fully conscious that he was detecting, like William Gaddis, the deepest strategy of *all* narrative: a token offering of discourse to the law of time, yet another offering with the secret, ever-disappointed hope that time will reject it and return it to the realm of being, unknown in discourse, or will shield from memory the future that it alone can generate as a variation on the model of the past.

Open and Covert Discursive Articulations in Dante's *Vita Nuova*

Dante's *Vita nuova*, so obviously composed of prose and verse, narrative sequences, lyrical poetry, and exegetic commentary, could easily pass for the ancestor of many contemporary metageneric or even metafictional attempts, or for a model of scholarly edition, of those that provide all the relevant genetic data, literary context and some account of the initial reception of the text. As in a French *explication de texte*, each poem is sliced up into thematic and logical sequences, so that little room is left to the young or uninitiated reader to exercise interpretive freedom. In this kind of book, discursive articulation should be easily describable, perhaps exemplary, but, at the same time, one can wonder whether its very obviousness is not, at least to a certain extent, a disguise or a snare. Is there not a secret or hidden articulation, more meaningful to the discerning reader who would dispel the screen of transparency, and nevertheless active at a subconscious level on those who will not recognize and name it? The *Vita nuova* has often been considered as a cryptic text, especially in order to justify its theological translation as if it were another version of the *Song of Songs*; but what interests me is that this cryptic character, suggested by semantic contents and structures in many places, is the instrument of a dialectical relation between processes of articulation that modify and enrich the provisionally final significance of the narrative.

Open Articulation

There are slight variations of discursive disposition among all the chapters that contain self-quoted verse; sometimes, as in chapter 21, the motivation for writing a sonnet is supposed to be the all-too-simple desire to say something more about the same topic as before:

> Poscia che trattai d'Amore ne la soprascritta rima, vennemi volontade di volere dire anche in loda di questa gentilissima parole . . . [33]

Such "weak" transitions certainly have a role to play, in addition to affirming the coercive "self-generative" power of writing on the writer himself: variation on a theme is in the nature of things for Dante. But chapter 24, like so many others, begins with an "appresso," followed by a demonstrative:

> Appresso questa vana imaginazione, avvenne uno die che, sedendo io pensoso in alcuna parte . . . (p. 58)

The first syntagm, which refers to the vain (not so vain) imagination described and accounted for in the preceding chapter, is polyvalent: (1) it announces and situates an as yet untold event in the chronology of the presented world, it is a tool for story building; (2) it contains a summary and evaluative commentary of the last-told event, thus qualifying it as a text; (3) it borders or even overlaps on the plane of narrational statements and binds into a single narrative structure the narrational, narrated, and story planes. The syntagm is then logically exploited and develops forward into three elements relevant to the narrative situation of the new chapter: (1) "avvenne uno die che" (temporal ordering and frame of duration, on the plane of the story); (2) "sedendo io in alcuna parte" (presentation of the subject of the action, spatial situation, on the plane of the narrated); (3) "pensoso" (mood of text production, on the narrational plane). The high degree of mechanism and the analytic quality of composition are striking; before questioning what they can stand for, we must examine the rest of the sentence and the beginning of the next one:

> . . . ed io mi sentio cominciare un tremuoto nel cuore, cosí come se io fosse stato presente a questa donna. Allora dico che mi giunse una imaginazione d'Amore . . . (pp. 58–59)

We have two narratemes, one of quasi-physical process and one of quasi-mental process, mediated by an explanatory hypothetical comparison that is rooted in the metaphorical potential of "tremuoto nel cuore." While proposing a *virtually real* cause of the "imaginazione d'Amore," the comparison is still predominantly placed under the sign of imaginary reference by the unreal aspect of the verb. The appropriate place of "dico" is precisely at the intersection of real reference and imaginary reference, since saying or, better, writing will always transform an imaginary percept into one or more actual textual objects that will circulate in the presented world and influence the course of events in it; this is the obverse and natural compensation for the opposite phenomenon of derealization by figuration. Such textual objects, contained in the narrative prose introduction of each chapter, are very composite; they subordinate narrative discourse to other types of discourse, and it is the paradoxical task of the narrative introduction itself to bring and accumulate nonnarrative discursive components and guide and prepare the future subordination of narrative to similar nonnarrative components in the poems and their analyses.

Four verbs occupy the narrative prose part of chapter 24 in an obsessive fashion: "dire," "parere," "vedere," and "venire." They are reinforced by some of their semantic cognates such as "nome," "parlare," "parole," "chiamare," for "dire." In only thirty-five lines, "dire" itself occurs eight times, "parere," seven times, "vedere," three times; and "venire," six times; the cognates for "vedere" are numerous: "guardando," "mirabile," "considerare," "parate" (in Latin). Without undertaking a detailed analysis of narrative discourse in the passage, I shall simply note some characteristic transformations based on the five initial lines quoted:

- "Parere" was only implied there in words like "imaginazione" and the "come si" logical-rhetorical structure;
- "Dire" occurred only at the very end, in a present tense that made it contemporary with the time of enunciation and gave it a performative function;
- The "I" subject in the presented world was static ("sedendo"), with only his mind and his heart in movement;
- This subject did not see anything in the presented world about him; the decor was not indicated to us, so that the character's panoramic function was monopolized by an inward turn, for the inner scene of "cuore" that became the necessary locus of words and action.

In the bulk of the prose before the sonnet, the key combination is nevertheless proposed in a compressed form from the beginning: "dico . . . che mi parve vederlo [Amore] venire" (p. 59), an utterance in which we find all the possibilities of ordering in one block:

- the hypotactic order corresponding to linear reading and enunciative priorities: "I say that it seemed that I saw that it came" → I say, then I modalize, then there is perception, then there is a perceived object;

- the inverse paratactic order on the other hand, which accounts narratively for the successive events leading to the production of the text: "it came, then I saw, then it seemed (I modalized), then I say."

Note that in both cases the pivotal place is occupied by perception (seeing) and interpretation-cum-modalization (seeming), which are the obligatory relays between a nonverbal action (coming) and a verbal action (saying).

Logical duality, chronological duality, and ordering duality will be developed and reflected in the next thirty-four lines, but transformed into dual narrative components of the narrated scene: (1) duality, doubling, and, one could almost say, dubbing of the female character (Giovanna and Beatrice); (2) doubling of the coming of that character (Giovanna first, then Beatrice); (3) doubling of the naming of the first (Primavera/Giovanna); (4) doubling of the reasons for this naming (the pun on "prima verrá," plus the New Testament story of John the forerunner); which in turn confers (5) sexual and religious ambiguity on Beatrice, who is no longer akin to the Virgin Mary only but becomes at the same time a Christ-like figure; and, finally, (6) doubling, many times over, of the first-person character with regard to whom Amore plays the roles of forerunner and annunciating angel, who has a triple temporal status, as perceiver of the vision, writer of the quoted poem, and commentator-narrator at the time of writing the *Vita nuova*, and who makes of his best friend an alter ego both at the origin of the poem (coaddresser) and at the receiving end (coaddressee). Duality is, as we know, the analytic deep structure of all narrative, but the stress placed on it at this point, however compensated by the presence of a supranarrative (injunctive) component—"Pensa di benedicare," "parate viam Domini"—leaves us in need of a more synthetic realization of the materials, which the sonnet should be positionally designed to fulfill.

In fact, this is, rather curiously, what it seems to do in the first place:

> Io mi senti' svegliar dentro a lo core
> un spirito amoroso che dormia:
> e poi vidi venir da lungi Amore. (p. 60)

The lack of the hypothetical, "unrealizing" modalization contained in "parere" (seeming) contributes to this clear dynamics of narrative, as if it were not filtered through an a posteriori reflective stance, although we must take into account the fact that the very form of the sonnet may largely play the part of the lexically absent modalizer, since it constitutes in itself an index of figurality. But the sonnet turns out to defeat our narrative expectations by reintroducing the self-justifying injunctive "Or pensa pur di farmi onore" and culminating in a repetitive, nonnarrative note: definitional naming, at this border between definitional and ontological discourses that we could call the axiomatic level proper. With "e sì come la mente mi ridice" and "Quell'è Primavera / e quell'ha nome Amor, sì mi somiglia," even the "seeming" modality reappears in a transformed guise; the logical connectivity of "resemblance" with "appearance" has become an interpretant for the whole passage, revealing clearly one fundamental conversion pattern (in Riffaterre's sense) which has been used to produce a lyrical poem from a narrative matrix. All that is left to do is to read and reread the sonnet; then the final directives where surface descriptive discourse becomes progressively exclusive appear as a normal outcome.

Like most other concluding commentaries, this one is in two parts. The first retraces the narrative origin of the thematic material with, again, a close collocation of "sentire," "apparire," "parere," "vedere," and "dire," now all subordinated to the description of location in the poem. The second limits itself to deictic location (intrareferential description) in the sonnet taken as an object.

To sum up the features of open articulation in a rather typical chapter of the *Vita nuova*, we could say that (1) narrative discourse, which comes first, seems to be the prime mover of text composition and its initial material; (2) in the framework of an exemplified narrative of the production of lyrical poetry, surface narrative discourse is bound to be defeated by the end result of the action and event of writing, and recede behind nonnarrative discourses (NP-oriented, dominantly injunctive and descriptive levels that bracket out the narrative levels); (3) in the process, there takes place an implicitation of narrative, not its destruction; as we read, the explicit narrative of text production is progressively replaced by the narrative program of the reading directives given to us.

It would be relatively easy to show that the structure of open articulation in each chapter mirrors *en abyme*, with the necessary modifications, that of the *Vita nuova* as a whole. This text is presented as a fragment found in the book of the Σ narrator's memory, remodeled and selected to make a legible sample: "io trovo scritte le parole le quali è mio intendimento d'assemplare in questo libello, e se non tutte, almeno la loro sentenzia" (p. 7)

All this could be good news for those committed to self-referential theories of the literary text, but I am afraid that I am obliged to dampen their enthusiasm: even a cursory survey of covert articulation will lead to rather different conclusions.

Covert Articulation

We shall start with two clues evoked by the study of chapter 24 of the *Vita nuova*: (1) the "I" character is duplicated threefold three times, and (2) "apparire" and "parere" are closely associated in the conclusive commentary of the sonnet. Even though these features are not very prominent in the passage and could pass for fortuitous details buried in its profuseness should we consider this textual unit separately, they must be seen nevertheless as a kind of figure in the carpet when they occur repetitively *together* at all the decisive points of Dante's narrated life in relation to Beatrice. Indeed, we have learned to recognize these turning points thanks to the presence of these clues. The initial placing of the two signs, both in terms of the text (in chapter 2) and at the beginning of the "new life" for the Σ narrator and protagonist, assigns them "by definition" the value of markers of decisive events in the narrated world. I quote Menakhem Perry:

> The first stage of the text continuum . . . creates a perceptual set. The reader is predisposed to perceive certain elements and it induces a disposition to continue making connections similar to the ones he has made at the beginning of the text. . . . Certain items in the subsequent stages of the text appear particularly relevant and essential, and are placed in a prominent position [by the reader], while others are given much less weight . . . and are relegated to the background."[34]

This analysis could be complemented by Edward W. Said's more philosophically minded meditation:

> The choice of a beginning is important to any enterprise, even if, as is so often the case, a beginning is accepted as a beginning after we are long past beginning and after our apprenticeship is over.[35]

So when we read the famous inner beginning of the *Vita nuova* (pp. 7-8):

> Nove fiate già appresso lo mio nascimento era tornato lo cielo de la luce quasi a un medesimo punto, quanto a la sua propia girazione, quando a li miei occhi apparve prima la gloriosa donna de la mia mente, la quale fu chiamata da molti Beatrice li quali non sapeano che si chiamare,

we are predisposed to treat further narratemes associated with "nine" and "appear" as signifying major events. Examples of this are the circumstances of chapter 3 (the "second coming" of Beatrice, nine years later), chapter 22 (the hallucination during Dante's illness) and chapter 29 (Beatrice's demise). When we know that, in this last case, Dante must have recourse to the Syriac calendar in order to link Beatrice's death with number nine, we could even question the intrinsic weight of the character, if it needs such a signal to increase the importance of her death. But what is really the discursive valence of number nine?

Any dictionary of symbols will say that nine is the number of successful pregnancy and parturition, of the sky-heaven and perfection (trinity multiplied by itself). Nine, then, contains both a static, perfect, hypostatized component, and a narrative program of fecundity and birth. The two are related insofar as birth is the achievement, the perfective outcome of pregnancy, but in the case of the Virgin Mary, we find heavenly perfection at both ends, a complete, perfect, spherical narrative cycle. Beatrice (Beata Beatrice) is akin to the Virgin Mary, but to whom or to what does she give birth? Announced by a forerunner, she is also akin to

Jesus Christ, but, if she comes from heaven and will return to it, if her place was not on this earth, why did she come, whom will she save by the sacrifice of her incarnation and subsequent death? Furthermore, although it may double (or duplicate) her perfection, does not her duality, and the corresponding ambivalence of gender, jeopardize her perfection?

"Nine" is definitely a very complex signifier; it grows even more entangled if we take into account the inevitable pun on "nove"/"nuova" or "nova" that assails us from the title, the heading of the legible part of the "libro della mia memoria": *Incipit vita nova*, and the first line of the inner beginning in chapter 2: "Nove fiate già." Through the hypersemanticization of the signifier, "nine" becomes associated with "new" in the double sense of novelty, a narratively charged first occurrence (e.g., "new age" = youth), and with renewal and repetition (e.g., "occurring anew" = rebirth). And through formal features in the vernacular, the same signifier insists on the aesthetic revolution of the "stil nuovo" within the tradition that has established the alliance of amorous communication with the artistic text. With all these factors in hand, we could build a vast number of combinatory scenarios, of which I shall mention just three examples.

1. Beatrice, an incarnation of the Virgin Mary, is met by Dante when she is nine. Their chaste relationship, nine years later, will give birth to the book of the new life (in this version, Dante, the author, is God and visits the Virgin). Once the book is completed, Beatrice, who has done her (passive) lot on this earth, returns to the realm of God, where she belongs, united with Dante-God, the character, in his heavenly book.

2. Beatrice, an incarnation of Christ, comes, after nine years, to the rescue of the human Dante who does not yet know the good news of the new law; she saves him from his ignorance of God, thus giving him, after nine years, a new birth. Dante, after Beatrice has returned to the realm of his/her Father, will spread the news: in this version, he is an evangelist, and the *Vita nuova* is the gospel, whereas in the first version, the book was the body of Christ, Dante's and Beatrice's baby.

3. Beatrice, whatever heavenly being she represents, is an exile on this earth—a fact unknown to Dante and to her until they have both reached an age that doubles that of their first perfect encounter. In this version, Dante must save her by putting her to death, which he will do in two ways: by becoming Christ and Christ's executioner (by committing anew Christ's redeeming suicide, for which the Father will abandon him on the cross), and also by reversing Beatrice-*qua*-Christ's destiny: thanks to Dante's writing, the Word made Flesh will be made Verb again and start a new life, the life of the Book of the New Life in which Beatrice and Dante have become forever indissociable.

All three scenarios are equally and simultaneously acceptable as interpretive guidelines. They have two characteristics in common: first, they are narrative summaries of love rewarded in the tragic mode—like Tristan and Isolde—in which love's victory is achieved at the expense of the union of the lovers in the (real) world, and second, the book is instrumental for the spiritual union of the lovers; it is the subterfuge and its writing the stratagem by which this union is achieved, as it provides an artificial place for the common sense of the couple.

Consequently, the "apparire/parere" paradigm regains all its sense. Beatrice's appearance, when she makes it, is only "seeming"; it maintains in Dante, the addressee, certain illusions that he must fight by giving them the fixed bodily appearance (aspect) of the word, so that they can be exorcised, separated from their essential, unutterable origin. Beatrice will be liberated, together with Dante, from her terrestrial spoils, when she leaves them in the book, new and naive in comparison of their eternal perfection. Unfortunately there is always an irony in the simulacrum. The solid mask keeps on reappearing as the original or the model of the elusive face; everything must be done again and again:

> Sì che, se piacere sarà di colui a cui tutte le cose vivono, che la mia
> vita duri per alquanti anni, io spero di dicer di lei quello che mai non
> fue detto d'alcuna. (p. 94)

Hence the *Comedy*.

From this new perspective, the descriptive and injunctive levels of discourse are no longer dominant in the *Vita nuova*, but completely subordinate to narrative discourse, which alone has the power, however ephemeral, of exorcising the dreadful illusion of nonverbal incarnation, as illustrated in chapter 3, in which the reclining hero gives the poet's heart to eat to the naked lady sleeping in his arms. Does it mean then that the open articulation should be neglected? I believe on the contrary that it is just as important as the covert articulation, that both of them are equally necessary to the aesthetic and didactic success of the work. The double, antagonistic, articulation is itself an icon of the double status of "I" in autobiography: I was the one to whom it happened, but I, telling the tale, am no longer the one to whom it happened. Narrative is the only means of trying to fill the gap between these two doubly antinomic statements, but *this* narrative is not for the inscribed narrator to tell; it is for the reader in his mind and his flesh, in his heart endlessly devoured by the naked lady—thanks to the book ("farei parlando innamorar la gente"). We ourselves may end crushed between the branches of the symbolic ambiguity: "nine makes news."

Chapter 8
Narrative Economy: A Dissident Approach to Logic and Necessity

At this stage of our inquiry, should we see narrative as a living species, we know probably a bit better how it is built, its anatomy and its locomotion, as well as some aspects of its physiology, but we have formulated only some very general hypotheses about its goals and motivations, its processes of reproduction, and its relations with the environment—"passive" adaptation and "active" modification. In other words, we have left value, demand, work, investment, profit, and interest on our horizon. This does not mean that such notions and, consequently, the metabolism and ecology of the narrative species are secondary, auxiliary phenomena that we could expeditiously dispatch in a couple of footnotes. On the contrary, these forces, these energies, are so intimately bound to narrative communication—literary or not—and artistic communication—narrative or not—that it is difficult to isolate them. My intention in this chapter is then to conceptualize these energies, to bring them to the surface of my metadiscourse, so that they cannot be easily forgotten in the future.

General Economy and Textual Economy

In the recent past, we have known two principal kinds of sociologies that have included "narratives" in their fields of investigation—besides producing narratives from or about a social state of affairs: they are a sociology of literary institutions and a sociology of literary texts. The former was interested in the facts of literary life, whatever it means, in the behavior of its actors, and the fate of its objects (texts-as-objects): Who writes what? Who reads what? Who publishes what? What are the functions of a book and a magazine? Do they differ socially and how? How are texts chosen to be printed and sold? At what price are they offered to the public? What is the socioeconomic status and the cultural capital of the reading or listening public of such and such texts? And so on. Textual sociology dealt mainly with "contents" and, to a certain extent, with the forms of contents. A good example is unfortunately to be found in *Sociología de una novela rosa* by Andrés Amorós. The book is divided into six chapters with the following titles: "The Heroes," "The World," "Things," "All-powerful Love," "The Novel," and "Hidden Motivations." The last three, which could make us think of semiotic, structural, aesthetic, or psychoanalytic approaches, are deceptive: a narrative, for this author, is nothing but a collection of referential existents arranged in a certain order, as if the reader were ready to sit and indeed could jump on an enunciated couch.

These two sociologies, despite some progress carried out in the school of "sociocriticism" led by Edmond Cros,[1] showed and still show a strong tendency to develop in mutual ignorance of each other, not because they are incompatible but rather because they rest assured that the findings of one will confirm those of the other, so persuaded are they that there is a deep, natural, and automatic homology between the institutions and the texts produced or transferred by and around them. In fact, both sociologies seem to aim deliberately wide of communication; one is concerned with its "context," its instrumental preconditions, the other with its means or its pretext. Whether value for them is external or internal, it is not in transit but safely in one place.

Lucien Goldmann wrote that

> the literary work is characterized by four features of equal importance: its strictly *unitary* character, its *richness*, the character of real or virtual *universe* of the total set of elements that make it up, and its *nonconceptual* character. . . . Its signifying structure is constituted by its *unity* and its character of *universe*, the aesthetic nature of the expression of this structure depending also on its *richness* and its *nonconceptual* character.[2]

The literary work passes for a reflection of the social causality that it manifests, but it concentrates value in itself apparently well beyond the hoarding needs of "society" (what society?). The four terms that characterize it intrinsically are evaluative and three of them highly meliorative; the fourth is clearly the lack, deficiency, or untold—in other words, the gap through which ideology emerges and can be detected by the specialist. I consider with Philippe Hamon[3] that silence is an ideal, all-too-easy object to be filled and explicated by the critic who does not care to be contradicted by a text, and that Pierre Macherey[4] should have meditated on the anecdote of the "Purloined Letter" before equating the truth of a work with its secret and its aesthetic character with its theoretical incompetence and axiomatic aphasia. The character of universe of the literary work of art is an obvious effect of the attitude of the receiver-observer who channels his intellectual quest through the special, central attention he dedicates to this semiotic object; under this light, any text of sufficient extension and complexity can acquire a character of universe. As far as the unity and richness of the "literary work" are concerned, we already know that they do not *belong* to texts as much as they are (some of the) effects sought by the manipulations characteristic of the various regimes of reception in their quest for value. There is probably a lot to learn about a "work" (a text) seen as a repository, but little that will justify the name of "work" we give it. It is logically inconsistent to look for and, worse, to find, or worse still, to presuppose the value of a text, if we persist in positing that the realm of aesthetics is a closed playground; and if its supposed autonomy, which determines its value, is only an illusion, how can the illusion be exposed without ruining the value? Hence the fierce resistance of some academic (and popular) sectors to the "demystification" of the work of art by sociological and similar studies.

Where there is value there is heteronomy. Autonomy itself is heteronomous as a value because there is no value without exchange. Reciprocally, the communication of signs is always a form of exchange, and it is therefore productive of value along with other effects and affects. But value has little value if it is useless, if it does not serve a purpose—which need not be the purpose that has given rise to it. Our most fundamental question then is, what is the use of value? *General economy* is the science of this question. *Textual economy*[5] is not an image, a reflection, a metaphor, or an example of general economy; it is a special, limited area of it that concerns itself with the question, what is the use of value when there is text? At a further degree of specialization is *narrative economy*: what is the use of value when there is a narrative text—a text that gives rise to narrative communication? It is possible that this question can not be answered without further specifications; it is also possible that all the answers take the form of more questioning. But this initial degree of generality at least will avoid taking for granted and as final the social division of labor on which values are constructed. Indeed, although it has been denounced as illusory and allegorical, the radical vertical separation between infrastructures and superstructures continues to be practiced by many Marxists, thus saving and maintaining a transcendence of aesthetic objects that confirms the social division of labor well beyond actual practice in modern Western societies.

This division is a means of domination, exploitation, and alienation all the more powerful when it manages to conceal its own limits, that is, the measure in which the value of intellectual-cultural goods makes them exchangeable for material goods, as well as the extent to which the production of the latter is also a "symbolic" production. In summary, the social division of labor is all the more perverse when it is believed to be radical, thus concealing the collaboration of all individuals in society with the same system of values and its reproduction. A word like "political" in the works of Leenhardt[6] and Jameson[7] contributes in fact to bury under an ideal differentiation the self-reproducing collusion that prevails in our Western societies, a collusion that the ideas of general economy, textual economy, and ideological labor could expose. When Jameson writes (p. 45), in total confidence and in a tone of moral reprobation, that

> One cannot without intellectual dishonesty assimilate the "production" of texts . . . to the production of goods by factory workers: writing and thinking are not alienated labour in that sense, and it is surely fatuous for intellectuals to seek to glamorize their tasks—which can for the most part be subsumed under the rubric of the elaboration, reproduction or critique of ideology—by assimilating them to genuine manual labor,

we are really perplexed by a conception of labor typical of the early nineteenth century and such that cybernetics would render any struggle for liberation obsolete.

The exploitation of man by man is also the exploitation of man by himself, which cannot take place without a constant ideological expense and production on the part of the exploiters and their aids, but also on the part of the exploited. Even if the "production" of texts and meaning were a metaphorical notion, which it is not, it would be nonetheless real and the production of metaphor is still production. Conversely, this attack should draw our attention to the rhetoric of production of material goods; when we acquire or sell goods with a high labor content, their worth is also that of a narrative solidified in an object, and when the labor content is low, the story of invention, technological progress, and liberation from material tasks is repeated in each object as well. In handwoven textiles and in fast food or printed circuits like those that help me put these words together, the same dreams of domination are inscribed through different narrative paths.

Narrative economy *stricto sensu* has to do with the "narrative text" on either side of it, where upstream and downstream operations of communication meet and define their shared ground.

Materials, Transformation, and Production of Narrative

To produce a narrative text in language, you need words, syntactic structures, a transformational competence, and referential valences, and you have to arrange all this in a certain order, with certain regularities in spacing and occurrences of items. The materials of narrative are linguistic, cultural, and compositional. Since we have already given an ample idea of their nature and their uses in the preceding chapters, we shall now work on a small number of specific examples in some detail.

Conventionally, a written narrative, and even very often an oral narrative, a joke for example, bears a *title* that permits us to catalogue it and retrieve it in libraries, order it and shelve it in bookstores, but above all to circulate it in all sorts of transversal acts of communication: you talk about it, you allude to it, you exchange it as a token of sociality or in an assault of erudition, you point at it in memory for your own pleasure, you use it as an analogon of the text, you question it as an oracle. The title symbolizes the unity of the text even when it is deceptive; it further closes, objectifies, and reifies narrative like a narrateme reduces the difference of change to its synthetic essence. Among the many types of titles that belong to our cultural repertoire, some are particularly frequent:

1. the proper name: name of person, with a vast choice of components (first name, patronym and matronym, academic, religious, or noble title, nickname); name of place; name of animal or even sometimes of a single object (*Ulysses, Emma, Napoléon, Eugénie grandet, Les Thibault, The Hunchback of Notre-Dame, King Lear, Oedipus Rex, Rome, Dubliners*);

2. substantives in general in association or not with adjectives and other determiners (*Les Choses, The Hunting Gun, The Serpent and the Rope, Pride and Prejudice*);

3. word for narrative or names of narrative genres, specified or not by adjectives or in combination with elements of the first or second type (*Histoire, Die unendliche Geschichte, La storia, History of the Conquest of Mexico, Les Confessions, The Autobiography of Alice B. Toklas, Cuentos completos*);

4. a simple clause, a simple or complex sentence or fragment of sentence containing or not a narrative predicate (*The Postman Rings Twice, El Coronel no tiene quién le escriba, Je l'entends encore*).

Each of these titles is culturally loaded with value(s) and endowed with particular semantic and syntactic valences in relation to the text it designates. A name of person implies that the tale is a total or partial life story and, more generally, that the archetypal model of all narratives is the biographical model with its particular successiveness and obligatory steps; the name of person is expected to be present in the text in the position of subject of narrative, occurrential, and equative predicates, failing which the set title + narrative will break up critically or parodically with the norm: "tale :: life" taken as raw material of all sorts of transformations. But the relation tale ↔ title is always one of mutual interpretation because the *effect of material* is as important in this case as the actual role of material at the effective moment of production of the narrative text (I mean the act of enunciation of the total text transmitted). The text of narrative appears as an expansion of the title seen as a generative signifier and a generative signified and, vice versa, the text appears as the material of its own condensation in the title, with all the rhetorical effects it can bear: redundancy and literality (*Napoléon* is the story of Napoleon), discrepancies (*Ulysses* is not the story of Ulysses, *The Autobiography of Alice B. Toklas* is that of Gertrude Stein, *Die unendliche Geschichte* actually comes to an end—hence a hyperbolic effect), metaphor (*La macchina mundiale*), litote, and so on.

When the title is treated as material, the text will be an instrument of added value as it disambiguates the title (*The Scarlet Letter*), reveals the secret designated (*The Mystery of the Yellow Room*), or, on the contrary, deflects conventional expectations toward a more imaginative realization (*The Life and Opinions of Tristram Shandy*, *The Education of Henry Adams*, *Las mocedades de Ulises* by Alvaro Cunqueiro). It is not only genetic criticism but any analytic reception (and the reception of narrative is always especially analytic in one of its phases) that construes as materials the deep structures, presuppositions, and other elements not necessarily integrated without previous transformation at any moment of composition, so that a differential between input and output can serve to measure the success of textual transformation. One of the functions of a title-as-material is to help recover also as materials textual components such as vocabulary, symbolic code, and archetypal narrative structures by virtue of the interactions that take place at this level in the course of reading and transversal communication.

Seen no longer as an effect of text but as part of an act of enunciation, the choice of materials, conscious or unconscious, voluntary or involuntary, is a decisive step in the production of narrative, as important indeed as the transformation of these materials by the performances of linguistic syntax, narrative syntax, and aesthetic composition. This choice depends on the encyclopedia of the producer of narrative, on the portion of it that can be mobilized and activated due to social, historical, and personal constraints in a particular universe of communication (the "legal" face of the milieu). In a comparative perspective, we can see that every society has at least two blind spots on the plane of available materials: the *unutterable* according to the law of language and according to the law of public, distanced, and delayed communication (public speech, the written word, the printed word), and the field of *ignorance* (the forgotten, the uninvented, the unimaginable, the unconceivable, or the other faces of memory, experience, and beliefs). The practice of translation, the reading of works by bilingual writers on the background of the language not selected by them, the almost universal silence of narrative about certain physiological functions, the almost universal invocation of God or fate even in the most materialist literature, are as many manifestations of these choices that do not mean in any way the exercise of free will or its lack, but simply that communication is primarily a filter.

To choose is to determine materials, to value things and signs *qua* materials.

The choice of materials by the actual producer of a narrative is already a labor of transformation in relation to the total narrative and discursive program of a language, but the relative possibility and probability of these choices, the capacity of elements of language and culture to be recognized as potential narrative materials, are already the beginning of the collective production of a vast general narrative: a society and a culture start to tell their own stories through the materials they make available to their narrators. The implementation of any material proclaims a competence; implementing, specifying a material, one also dictates its necessity, which, coupled with the competence claimed, implies preliminary value. Scarcity is established as justification and basis of value added. Fantasy, the surrealist novel, experimental narrative, and baroque plays present superficial evidence of an axiom verified by any narrative: materials are always rare, even when they are exceptionally banal.

Materials are not only forerunners of value, they contain pro-narrative energies and they are at the same time obstacles to narrative desire. To tell a tale you need a will to tell, which does not have to be yours or, for that matter, that of some ultrahistory craving to tell itself. Fredric Jameson, as we have seen in chapter 1, considers any producer of narrative to be the administrative producer of a more or less disguised history of class struggle: any narrative would be a kind of battlefield and a polemic dialogue of "ideologemes."[8] It amounts to a promotion of history, in its orthodox Marxist version, to the role of absolute model of which any particular narrative, whatever its Discursive allegiance, would present a "simple" transformation without ever being able to correct or modify the model in return. History is seen as narrative so that it can be passed on as material and repository of narrative rules from one Discourse to another (from its own Discourse to fictional, poetic, epistemological and other Discourses); but, at the same time, it *must not be* a narrative: otherwise, all the other narratives, as parts of the same genre or partaking of the same kind, would retroact on it and modify it. It is certainly not any truer, except in a very vague sense, that any story is an embodiment of history, than to say that the life of Everyman is a version of that of Oedipus, King of Thebes, or of Christ, King of the Jews. Nevertheless there remains a useful suggestion and perhaps some theoretical value: any narrative can cover and conceal another narrative; every narrative and, with it, the producer of its text, works for interests that are not the producer's own; any narrative inscribes but cannot fully narrate the story of its own production. We are dealing here with the violence done by enunciation to narrative-as-intention rather than with narrative's own violence with regards to the reader. This does not mean that the act of production *is* a narrative but that, in narrative, there is at least a measure of homology between the structure of the act of production and the form of narration inscribed in the text. The supposed circularity of *Remembrance of Things Past*, passing for an exemplary formalization of this relation, is alienated, if it remains unconscious, and perhaps mystifying, if the "awareness" of the relation turns the producer into a product of his work who could thus free himself from all other determinations.

The relationship of the teller with his materials, including the fundamental law of narrative discourse that seeks to *present* change *as if* it were past, is at once the simulacrum of a struggle *and* an erotic struggle for the simulacrum of pleasure. As in an amorous engagement, one of the most attractive moments is when pleasure is achieved by giving rein to the tactics of the other: projection of the plane of enunciation on the plane of the enunciated, and vice versa. One admirable example can be seen in a short story by Alejo Carpentier: "Viaje a la semilla,"[9] even in the difficulties involved in the double standard and in the final failure of the attempt.

In the first scene, an old colonial palace is being pulled down by professional house demolishers; in the last scene, when they return the next day to continue their work, they find that there is nothing left: following the model of unbuilding, Carpentier's story has wound back to the origins of the house and the family, ever newer, ever younger until there is nothing (yet) on the site: "Everything was transforming, regressing to its initial state. Dust returned to dust, leaving a wasteland instead of the house," (p. 92). But are materials consumed as they are used? In a sense, if their value arises from an alliance with time that transforms them into mnemonic objects, into the experience of loss. In this sense also, nobody can pay any attention to a straightforward narrative "because the sun travels from East to West and the hours that grow on the righthand side of clocks must be elongated with laziness, since they are those which lead most certainly to death" (p. 93).

Transformation, Displacement, and Profits of Meaning

In order to produce narrative, one needs all sorts of materials, and using them is a kind of spending, one that requires work on the part of the spender. Whether the narrative text mimics the production of material goods in society at large or conforms to it, or is even at odds with it, out of phase in one way or another, behindhand or prophetic, this text being produced is a scene of investment, labor, transformations, planning, and so on, best described in terms of its *internal economy*.

Every narrative, however open or fragmented, has at least one textual beginning and one textual end (on the narrational plane); most narratives also have beginnings and endings on the plane of the narrated and on the plane of story. Raymond Roussel made us more aware that one of the main problems of a producer of narrative is to provide a link or to trace a road between a beginning and an ending that cannot be identical but should have an air of family resemblance. The road of words and mental images will be paved with signifying intentions by the reader, if it is not by the producer of the text. Although narrative successiveness is, in a certain deep sense, alien to logical rules, since narrative violates the principle of noncontradiction in the first place, "common logic" is an ingredient of all narratives in that they are bound to play with a causal, etiological, and a final, teleological, orientation, which would provide an apparent rationale. As Carpentier's short story bears witness, the combinations of these two principles are severely limited in narrative production.

At another level, we can observe that narratives that employ characters have to get rid of them and their problems somehow in order to conclude, reach silence, shut up shop on some ground other than their own failure, boredom, or the mere eroding action of time. With the same economic aim, the solutions chosen will be very revealing of constraints belonging to the conditions of production, manifested in the generic, rhetorical, moral, and aesthetic fields. An autobiographical narrator cannot "kill" his character by reporting his own death, so that this death that resists the past-oriented mode of telling will frequently become the obsessional theme of all the other modes of telling (speculative, argumentative, etc.) in autobiography:

> When you read this, I won't be here any longer. I don't know what death is, but I am certain that my joys, pains and anxieties will not live on after I'm dead. So many thoughts about you . . . will soon disappear from this world. My body, my soul, everything will disappear.
> Nevertheless, many hours or many days after I'm gone and have turned into nothing, you will read this letter. And living after me, it will tell you the many thoughts I had while I was alive."[10]

Conversely, the heterobiographical narrator fulfills a norm of the genre (a norm of displacement) by recounting his character's death. But there are other manners of getting characters out of the narrative way to silence, like proroguing, adjourning them ad infinitum, eternalizing and monumentalizing them by various devices. Narrative discourse can progressively denarrativize itself by repetition ad lib of the same narratemes or by a change of spatial and temporal parameters that shifts the aspect of the verbs from the singulative to the frequentative: this is the typical happy ending of the love romance. Characters can cease to be the subjects of narrative discourse and become subjects of infranarrative discourses: they are taken out of the temporal flux. And finally, their elimination can be narrational rather than diegetic or discursive, when the Σ narrator loses sight of them, "forgets" them (stops talking about them), or delegates the reporting of their fate to an unreliable secondary narrator. In *The Recognitions*, Stephen—alias Wyatt—is last perceived receding out of sight and earshot, "withdrawing uphill slowly, empty-handed";[11] Don Bildow is abandoned naked in the toilet of a train between Rome and Paris; Esme is reported dead by Stanley, whom we have no reason to believe, since he is jealous and has already made up her pregnancy in another conversation. Distraction can also be brought about by a metaliterary shift, a thematic excursus, an unended digression, or a combination of all these, as in *Tristram Shandy*: "L–d! said my mother, what is all this story about?–a COCK and a BULL said Yorick–And one of the best of its kind, I ever heard."[12]

Although each of these choices takes place within the vast system of ideological production, it does not follow that they "reflect" ideology. Terry Eagleton is right when he insists: "Yet the structure [of the text] is not to be seen as a microcosm or a cryptogram of ideology; ideology is not 'the truth' of the text any more than the dramatic text is 'the truth' of the dramatic performance."[13] The dialectics of text and ideology, which begins at the time of production, continues with the reader's production of value, both cognitive and aesthetic, for as long as the text is received and commented.

Text production is the labor, spending of time and energy, of energy in time, which transforms varied, mixed materials–among them, existing texts–into text. Reading or listening is the labor, spending of time and energy, of energy in time, which transforms varied, mixed materials–among them the text received–into meaning. The labor of meaning production represents and justifies itself as *value*, but it also *disguises* itself as value projected on the text, its production, its producer, and the society that has given rise to the conditions of production and framed the existence of the producer. This is the source of one of the characteristic problems of a Marxist aesthetics. Just as the mental representation of a voice is, by turns, the necessary precondition and the necessary consequence of the reader's commitment to the delayed act of communication, "novelistic interest" or, more generally, aesthetic and cognitive valorization are the necessary corollaries of any reading that does not take place under threat or violence (or that is not aware of such threat and violence). Since any reception of signs is labor and expense, it seeks a profit at least commensurable with this expense. The differences between the production of profits of meaning by various types of empirical readers on the basis of different types of texts under the literary regime of communication, are basically quantitative, not qualitative; qualitative differences occur with the uses of the meanings produced, that is, with the critical dimension of transversal communication. Two very broad questions remain.

First, what are the textual sources of quantitative differences in the reader's production of meaning and value, and how do they operate?

The relative "richness" of a text is obviously not an answer, but it is true that the stimulating, productive text should be anything but average on the distinct planes of its various material and compositional features.

"Difficulty"[14] is due, for example, to the sheer volume of materials introduced in the text, to their heterogeneity, their cultural distance from the reader's encyclopedia, and the irregularity of their *dispositio*. We could list archaic, technical, dialectal, plurilingual vocabulary; archaic or regional syntax; the multiplicity of registers in these two linguistic categories; a demanding cultural allusiveness (allusions that are at the same time strongly marked but difficult to decipher because they are idiosyncratic, very fragmentary, or distant, referring to other places, classes, professions, and historical periods); a floating rhetoric in which the dominant type of figure changes frequently or remains undecidable; a high but eclectic role of generative signifiers (puns, anagrams, palindromes, crosswords). Baroque, esoteric, modernist, and contemporary metafictional narratives tend to offer all or most of these difficulties together; so does, in principle, the "dialogic" text in the Bakhtinian sense of the word. The length of a narrative can add to other difficulties (*Ulysses, The Recognitions, Paradiso*), but it can also be an obstacle of its own and compensate for the relative lack of the others (*Clélie*, the *Histoire de ma vie* by Casanova, modern sagas and serials, including *Dallas* and *Dynasty*), or it even sometimes contributes to solve the other difficulties by completing a coherent "universe of discourse" and providing enough context to allow the reader to formulate the particular code of the text. In any case, overcoming difficulties boosts the ego of the reader: "I have *read Finnegan's Wake!*" The reader is grateful to the text and its producer for it: he valorizes. Symmetrically, the very easy text that reads "like a novel" is a bargain, a time saver, a practical toy to avoid boredom on the plane: the reader valorizes.

Compositional *complexity* due to narrative syntax (fragmentation, informational delays, length of sequences, rhythm of discursive and narrational shifts) and plot (complex situations, multiple characters, intertwining subplots), even when each element is readily accessible to the reader, and its obverse, compositional *simplicity*, are valorized very much in the same ways as *difficulty* and *easiness*, but they appeal to other skills usually labeled "Narrative competence," such as the sense of games, strategic ability, the mastery of physical space and the environment.

Openness is due notably to narrative "gaps" created by the incomplete actualization of various codes (proairetic, hermeneutic, symbolic, etc.) leading to the perception of incomplete sequences, incomplete self-interpretation, incomplete motivation. The place of the gaps in the text and in reading is very important. The gaps that increase openness are those that are created early in the text and never filled, thus maintaining suspense beyond the limits of a first reading; those that are introduced retrospectively (analipses) or propsectively as decoys (prolipses), those which result from metalepses (authorial intrusions, projection of the plane of the narrated on the plane of narration); and obviously, those that appear at the material end of the "unfinished" narrative with the death of the narrator, his renouncement, or his failure to die (autobiography). Other factors of openness are the plurality of regimes of reading, the indeterminacy of the genres of fictionality, the plurality and competition between various types of preinterpreted materials (materials firmly rooted in characteristic established Discourses such as the sciences and technologies, philosophy, and history). Openness gives the reader a feeling of freedom and mental litheness; it invites him to daydreaming, verbal magic, and phantasmic constructions. The receiver believes that he produces text, that he completes the text the author was unable to bring to fruition; his universe becomes broader, wanders off limits: he valorizes in exchange for this gift. *Closure*, in contrast, protects the reader against transgressions, the vertigo of abyssal temptations, restores his security, allows fusional participation to an orderly universe—everything in its place, including the wanderer: he valorizes.

The second question is, what relation is there between aesthetic valorization, cognitive valorization, and pleasure?

This question is certainly the most difficult, because any possible answer would require an agreement not only on general economy but on psychological economy and on the particular economy that subtends the evolution of philosophical systems. Consequently, I cannot propose anything but some historically situated personal biases that have guided me in my theoretical construction.

1. Meaning is promised pleasure, deferred pleasure, the lure of a pleasure enhanced by its postponement; the production of meaning is deferral of pleasure, an investment for pleasure, a savings account that will produce pleasure at maturity, and also the pleasure of anticipated pleasure.

2. Meaning is a therapy or an anesthetic against displeasure, affective deficiencies, past wounds of the ego. Meaning, after a while, fills a lack, compensates for the disappointments of one's hopes by offering completeness on a different plane, another stratum of being (theoretical power, organization of representation and hence of self-image).

3. The beautiful and the meaningful, gracefulness and the intelligible, have exactly the same abstract structure, the same paradigmatic relation to lack and castration, the same function of switchplate between reality principle and pleasure principle, but they occupy different positions in space-time: meaning maintains a constant distance between need and satisfaction, while it points at the direction to follow; beauty shoots a close-up picture of pleasure, presents the desired object (hyperbolizes or sometimes supersedes it) in all the colors of real life; beauty shows us or makes us believe that the satisfaction of desire lies in being acquainted with its pleasurable object and that the intensity of satisfaction amounts to desire multiplied by acquaintance.

These considerations could perhaps help us to understand as a series of aspectual distinctions one of the oldest divisions between kinds of text: the triadic separation between essay, narrative, and lyrical poetry, which cannot be based on the same enunciative Aristotelian criterion as the triad drama-epic-lyrical, although many overlappings and confusions have enriched the literary scene for ages. The essay takes it for granted that it is not the function of text to provide pleasure, direct or vicarious; it offers knowledge instead. The lyrical takes it for granted that it is not the function of the (artistic) text to provide knowledge, but that it should exalt at the same time desire and the analogic form of its satisfaction. Both the essay and the lyrical tend to work in the present and for the present. For this purpose, they have to make their respective choices between knowledge and pleasure. Insofar as they take time into account, the essay and the lyrical treat it as space, as a place to collect moments of the same nature. But, with narrative, with the superimposed successiveness of the narrated, we have a protracted debate and a potential dialectics between pleasure and knowledge. Value, for narrative, can never be predetermined; it is not supposed to be a given. This is probably why the essay and the lyrical, as soon as they are "conscious" of the return of the doubt repressed at their very foundation, are seized by the temptation of narrative and must wage their warfare with it on its own ground, the former in the guise of argumentative structure and illustration by exempla,[15] the latter in the guise of the dialogical structure of request and response, and tropic developments (extended metaphor, allegorism, etc.). Narrative economy could lead us to a general theory of textual transactions in which the median, ambiguous position of narrative would offer a central vantage point. But, on the other hand, narrative communication itself, as we shall see, is not impervious to the media that channel it, to the Discourses within which or on the borders of which it takes place, or to the special social purposes it is always made to serve.

Chapter 9
Narrative within Genres and Media

Between the formation/cognition of narrative discourse and the construction of narrative significance, there is still one important mediation to consider: that of genre as technê and sociohistorical constraint. In fact, if we had not taken genre into account, implicitly at least, every time we studied individual examples of acts of narrative communication and their texts, we would have made an intolerable qualitative leap from the level of generality at which our method of analysis was situated to particular concrete situations. The purpose of this chapter is to put genre to work as efficiently as possible within the process of theorization itself.

The Reality of Genre

Claudio Guillén wrote as early as 1965:

> The concept of genre occupies a central position in the study of literary history, very probably because it has succeeded so well and for so long in bridging the gap between critical theory and the practice of literary criticism . . . , the theory of genre is coextensive with the theory of poetics. . . .
>
> Modern criticism has repeatedly demonstrated that the vocabulary of genre theory, paradoxically enough, adapts itself most sensitively to the apprehension of individual works.[1]

In his 1985 *summa*, he would again dedicate a long chapter to genre in comparative literature. But Gérard Genette, in his presentation of a "reader" on genre theory in 1986, seems to forget how neglected and repressed the notion of genre was in the 1960s and 1970s:

> The question of genres was for centuries—from Aristotle to Hegel—the central object of poetics and has only temporarily and partly vanished from the field of literary studies in a century of relative fading out of poetics itself before historicist and positivist approach for which nothing should be considered beyond individuals, individual works, and empirical circumstances.[2]

The date of publication of this collection as well as that of a French translation of Käte Hamburger's book,[3] the doubts and precautions of Hernadi,[4] Jost,[5] Barat,[6] Marino,[7] and Todorov,[8] all in the 1970s, make me think that the ahistoricity or the ahistorical oversimplifications of a large sector of structuralist poetics are as much to blame for the decline of research on genre as Lanson's reaction against Brunetière's biological evolutionist views: "The identification of literary genre, which survives by imitation, with a living species that perpetuates itself by generation, is purely verbal."[9]

The notion of genre is obviously nothing but a dim, changing constellation in the metalanguage of literature, if we consider literature to be a self-selected corpus of texts imposed on vertical communication by their own transcendent quality; genre would then suffer the same loss of status as any other means of desacralizing "the text." Conversely, if we take transversal communication into account, genre will appear as an essential element of communication *through* texts, since it does not belong to any text in particular or even to a finite group of texts. What Lanson and modern textologists seem to share is a belief in the fixedness of the text and in the strict determination of the nature and contents of communication by it, contradicted by the quest for accuracy in interpretation, on the one hand, and the search for new interpretations and valuations, on the other.

The notion of genre, in contrast, presents texts as determined by models at the moment of production, reproducible by imitation, and subject to all sorts of external influences on their reception, since they are themselves unstable compounds of many ingredients—each of them key to a different potential genre. The notion of genre is essential because it manifests the anxiety of the law, which destabilizes the text with the intention of doing the exact opposite. But genre should not be reduced to an aspect of transtextuality: if we take its normative character seriously, genre is so real indeed that it does not need any concrete textual realization to lead the life of an object of value in the communication system. Just as there is no need for any man actually to attempt to marry his great-granddaughter for this prohibition to be present and active in the law, it is not necessary that anyone attempt to publish a text in which each word would be a name of character for this prohibition to be present in the law of narrative communication. Any prescription is also a negative norm, any classification relies on a principle of exclusion; the negativity of genre, then, is probably the main factor of its independent traffic in the communication system.

But what has genre to do with narrative in particular? We have already used the notion twice, in very different contexts: once as a type of discourse determined by certain characteristics of predication resulting from generative rules in a transformational system, and second, as a type of relation between the signification of a text and certain rules applying in other possible worlds (universes of Discourse and universes of belief). How can genre be used again in a different perspective, and what is the link between the two previous uses and the new ones in this chapter? If genre is basically a means of discrimination between texts as bases and indexes of acts of communication, then the main questions concern (1) types, systematicity, and variations of generic criteria; and (2) the actual functions of genre in communication (vertical and transversal, synchronic and diachronic).

Criteria

We can tentatively divide the criteria for genre into six groups:

1. Dominant discourse. This was the criterion used to define narrative (chapter 2), but we should never forget that narrativity remains always *potential* in the surface structures of linguistic and other texts; narrative significance is the result of an actualization that is highly situation dependent. With repetition and ritualization, for instance, a text like the sacrifice of the eucharist can lose its narrative significance for most people and become invested with many other values. Other texts of our culture, from *The Odyssey* to *Remembrance of Things Past*, have undergone a more or less advanced process of social denarrativization, while others, which were descriptions or lyrical poems, have become travelogues or a mere support for the story of their own writing.

2. Systems of subjects (subjects of the enunciated, enunciative systems, and relations between the two; see chapters 5 and 6). These systems in relation to narrative are particularly sensitive to the socially prevalent concepts of the subject and its ad hoc embodiments (the self, the individual, the human being, etc.). First-person enunciation was perceived as lyrical not so long ago, still following the precepts of Aristotelian poetics; but recently it has come to be more commonly perceived as autobiographical (hence creating narrative expectations) wherever it occurs. Narrative, as we have seen, has no intrinsic reason not to be enunciated in the second person, which was largely the case of the epistolary form and drama: these two forms are in decline, so that the second person is no longer "natural" for narration. Or is a much deeper change in human relations at the root of all these phenomena? We can only touch on this matter when we present some of the constraints of dramatic form on narrative later in this chapter.

3. Referential systems. We have studied these in chapter 4, but only in the framework of fictionalization and fictionality, an operation and a result that many Discourses do their best to deflect. Narrative is the dominant genre of discourse of cosmology, psychoanalysis, and history, among other areas of knowledge and belief with claims to scientific truth; philosophy, theology, economics, and politics also express themselves in great part through narrative discourse, and these Discourses display nowadays an uneasy consciousness of their necessary collusion with narrative. Our questioning in this respect should be double: are there peculiarities of narrative, constitutive of extensive and durable genres, which are dictated by the needs and constraints of social Discourses such as history and politics; and to what extent are these Discourses determined in their own significance, ideology, and underlying worldviews, by their privileged—if awkward—relationship to narrative?

4. Channels. I include in this set of criteria the different semiotic vehicles (visual, graphic, static or animated, oral-aural) through which communication can take place. A further distinction should be made according to the degree of immediacy, which can vary considerably within the same semiotic vehicle. Orality, for instance, is certainly not an indivisible block; narrative sense is not constructed in the same way by a traditional storyteller and his public, or by someone who telephones the police because he has just found his house burgled. But painting, writing, music, drama, and film, each and all respond to their special spatiotemporal parameters to inscribe delay, expectation, confirmation, or invalidation of narrative programs.

Narratologies that lacked a communicational core have generally been divided between those of linguistic inspiration that looked more closely at textual structures, and those of semiotic or sociological inspiration that were concerned mainly with "narrative grammars" or "structures of content." For Genette, "the sole specificity of narrative [*le narratif*]" still "resides in its mode," which is "*stricto sensu*" verbal representation.[10] He justifies this restriction by the nonexistence of narrative contents: "There are [only] concatenations of actions or events amenable to any mode of representation . . . and which are labeled 'narrative' simply because they are found in narrative representation" (ibid.). In radical disagreement with this position, I plead for a general narratology that is not a theory or a repertoire of "contents" but a study of the relations between the different semiotic systems of communication and their respective narrative *outputs* (meaning, significance, and value), if any. The combination of these two considerations is clearly the source of genres that are generally perceived as operative in our culture: narrative versus "documentary" film; narrative (e.g., historical) painting versus landscape or portrait; narrative ("action") versus psychological drama; and so on. Genre is therefore a vital tool in the elaboration of a (truly) general narratology, one that can draw on linguistic narratology precisely insofar as the latter is conscious of its limits and its difference.

5. Modes of activation of the signifiers. A discussion of this topic was proposed in chapter 3, but some aspects must now be developed with the help of generic concepts. It has been noted that kinds of literature were basically segregated by tradition on the basis of three main sets of criteria: discursive (in my terminology), for example, narrative, description, essay, maxim; enunciative (lyrical, epic and dramatic); and "formal," for example, verse versus prose, long versus short forms, complex versus simple forms. There are obviously other sets of criteria, notably when we address ourselves to a vast number of semiotic media instead of just "language"; but many explicit or implicit genres throughout the spectrum of the media share either identical or structurally similar "formal" features that can be analyzed no longer as "forms," with implications of emptiness and/or aestheticism, but as constraints and/or productive assets in relation to a narrative output.

"Regular forms" or "fixed forms" like those of verse or musical structures, the relative length of a text (compared with a cultural average, as a function of ways of life, etc.), the degree of obligatory intertextuality (intertextual demands involved in the primary semantic concretization of the text), all these and other differential modes of activation of the signifiers should be studied in a comparative, historical, and intersemiotic perspective, that is, in particular through an approach of genre, generic change, and text transforms (translations, adaptations, and transpositions). This way we could know better how narrative outputs are produced, and the varied results of the challenges that narrative and certain forms have never ceased to send each other, creating some long-term dynamics (between narrative and series) and some rare conjunctions (the narrative madrigal, the video clip). Channel and activation of signifiers are not (only) related mechanically; they interact by tradition and due to the historical weight of their association.

Although lyrical poetry is no longer sung, accompanied with music, or even read aloud in general, its use of signifiers shows that it is still composed and received *as if* it were oral. Short narrative forms (the short story, the newspaper story – particularly in France) still presuppose a long-vanished orality, or they impose its resurrection with puns and sound effects or rhythms necessary to make sense of the message; so does written advertising, and this is caused not only by the resilience of ancient modes of communication but rather by competition with new oral media (radio, TV, etc.) on their own ground. The actual complexity of narrative can profit by competition and by the many compensations that each channel is likely to seek for its narrowness, but the hypersemanticization of the signifier thus obtained can also upset the construction of a narrative message (as in the "literary" or "poetic" film, in artistic comic strips, etc.).

6. *Markers and shifters of aestheticization.* These are related to all the preceding sets of criteria, but two particularities with regards to narrative genres must be stressed.

First, narrative aesthetics is bound to *thematics* and, with it, to *pretold stories*;

a simple epithet, an allusive distribution of figures across the space of the screen may attract and crystallize entire narrative programs that will coexist either in redundancy or in discrepancy with the explicit narrative structures of the text.

Second, narrative aesthetics, more than the lyrical, for example, is necessarily confronted with *triviality*, either as a material or as an opponent, since narrative discourse is involved in almost any act of everyday communication: it is a metonym of information and propaganda, which aim at making news or delivering it, even when it is two thousand years old and disproved.

Functions

On the vertical axis, as a set of norms of production, genre does not diminish the authority of the sender, even if it seems to restrain his supposed freedom. If an author respects a genre, imitating established works or imitating nature in the rules of the art (which is the same thing), he justifies his authority through conformity to the canon and the initiative of obedience to orders from above (it is the "proud to serve" attitude). If he does not respect a genre, he shows his independence, his creative, innovative spirit; he is the founding father of a new genre or its forerunner; he at least contributes to the dynamics of the genre. If you place yourself above the law, you still confirm the law in its principle. All texts are cases; their reception acquires jurisprudential value in the realm of discursive trials, they actualize the institution once again; hence the political justifications of the temptation of silence, and artful theories of the death of art. Each genre is the bearer of a narrative and contains the seed of its own destruction. Whatever an author does to a genre, he helps it accomplish its fate, and he receives in return some of the glory he has imparted to genre.

In reception, genre is recognized or chosen as a function of peritextual signs (titles and subtitles, names of collections, summaries), textual markers (combining various criteria, as explained before), extratextual pressures (classification by the university, schools and academies, handbooks and encyclopedias, gazettes and religious or state censorship), and subjective, psychological factors that are not necessarily individual. Genre limits the wanderings of the reader; it draws a portrait of the Model Reader and determines constitutive principles of behavior. Genre chooses and judges the empirical reader, selects and elects him as much as it is chosen by him. Genre determines the scale of competence on which the performance of the reader will be measured: it is a vehicle of authority and an instrument of self-control, introjection of social norms of reading. Genre gives freedom, a space to play under, around, and with the rules of the game; it channels and therefore multiplies the energies invested in reception. Genre is also the thrifty device that associates authority with freedom: the generic Model Reader reads instead of the empirical reader, substituting the evidence of ready-made sense for the awareness of sense-in-the-making; but, at the same time, it liberates the empirical reader from the tiresome exploration of irrelevant meanings and allows him to pursue the production of pleasure-loaded meanings.

Genres should not be considered, however, as essentially practical devices that can be superseded in the course of literary or artistic evolution. Genres first of all *are*, they are a precondition of existence of texts because they are the names given to the frames in which an act of communication can take place, that is, the locus in which semiotic structures are deemed compatible with and relevant to the situation. Genres are the intermediaries between milieu and situation, without which texts cannot bridge the gap between language and occasion. Because genre is a territorial principle that equally and symmetrically extols external difference, at its periphery, and internal resemblance, within its boundaries, it mimics the situation of the thinking subject and even more the vision that subjects, individual or collective, can form of themselves, of the range of their possibilities; it is as impregnable as the position of identity occupied ipso facto by the speaker of any language whatsoever. There is no stronger norm than that which forces us to speak its identity as well as ours as soon as we communicate, but, like languages and semiotic systems, genres are several: actual communication is the consequence of their plurality. The historic change of genres, sometimes presented as the "life of forms," and the synchronic competition of genres within the same texts or the same areas of communication, or around the same focus (narrative compulsion, for example), manifest the constant tension between the stricture of law and the threat of entropy that characterizes human societies.

If we see the distinctive features of a genre no longer as a grid through which textual features can be listed and a text described and located, but as a historically determined relation between texts and communication situations, these features can be called conventions, which become pertinent to wider and wider cultural codes, such as propriety, structures of kinship, modes of production, and forms of festivity. Cultural codes can be cognitive codes, codes of action or, more often, a combination of the two types, that is, symbolic or mythic codes, in a relation of injunctive/interpretive transforms to underlying narratives. The name of "conventions" should not mislead us into accepting a loose "contractual" notion of generic communication, like the overemphasized *pacte de lecture* fashionable among a number of French literary theorists.[11] Conventions should be understood rather as the space fashioned by multiple constraints that meet to define some human manifestation as an act of social participation. There are conventions of production and conventions of reception, but free will or conscious negotiation has no necessary role to play in their formation. On the contrary, the rationale of any shared practice is that its sharing (i.e., its conformity) takes the place of meaning. The hierarchy of conventions, from quasi-universal archetypes through stereotypes repeated in at least one total culture, historically defined (say, eighteenth-century England), to finer types characteristic of a subculture, leaves little margin for subversion; but conventions cannot produce their sedative, healing, affirmative effects, if they are not recognized as antagonistic to an immense shapeless reserve of possible aberrations. A *formulaic genre*, for instance, is a fortress island in the ocean of the atypical. Conventions of the lower orders manifest *and* transform those of the higher orders, so that the formulaic genre will never manage, however, to erase completely the difference of performance and resorb it into pure competence. Like narrative in general, it cannot heal the wound of change, which repetition will forever reopen to reenact its cure.

"Formal" Typologies and the Frontiers of Narrative

We shall examine briefly three cases in which narrative significance is put on trial by particular formal features or devices, or in which narrative discourse fights for its own through forms that do not welcome it as serenely as does flexible conversational or novelistic prose.

Short Forms

The shortest (jokes) are supposed to be the best. Not all jokes are narratives, but many of them are and many more involve a narrative program in an allusive form.

Let us compare these two examples quoted by Freud:

1. Two Jews outside the bath-house:
    One of them sighed: "Another year gone by already!"
2. A wife is like an umbrella. Sooner or later one takes a cab.[12]

Example 1 is at first sight a narrative consisting of two narratemes, the presentation of two events in a self-sufficient "there and then" frame: two Jews met . . . , and one of them sighed. But the *point* is not narrative; the anecdote is meant to express, by a falsely single, exemplary instance, the proverbial uncleanliness of the Jews. If the story read: "What do two Jews say when they meet at the bath-house? 'Another year gone by already!' " it would be much less funny, because the iterative question would give the show away. Narrative must briefly seem to be the point, in order to be immediately short-circuited by the *doxa*: "This is not strange, Jews go so seldom to the bath-house that they would say that!" In the absence of cotext, the receiver provides a context found in the *doxa*, and this context all but destroys narrative significance; not to seem stupid, the receiver must renounce a narrative reading in favor of an axiomatic reading. His temporary error about the nature of the dominant discourse in the message is reinvested as a further emphasis with an ironic turn: "How would one guess that this is not a narrative? Who would believe that Jews are so dirty that this is the sort of thing they would *normally* say at the bath-house?" As in the literary regime, the "story" of text comprehension is integrated into the significance of the text itself.

Example 2, at first sight, is not narrative. It is composed of two surface structure segments, one clearly equative and the other injunctive, insofar as it is the expression of a law, of the order of things mediated by the consenting or prophesying enunciator. In fact, as Freud remarks, the technique of this example is very complicated. "A wife is like an umbrella" implies rain and a subject trying to shelter himself while going somewhere; "wife" is a relational lexeme definable as "a woman married to a man." When we ask who wants protection from the rain, it can only be this other subject: "a husband, or married man." For the sake of unification, we transfer this semantic content onto the subject of the second sentence: "one." A cab offers more protection than an umbrella, so that "sooner or later" can only mean: "if it rains hard" (p. 119). Two situations are in opposition: (1) it rains: an umbrella or a wife is adequate protection; (2) it rains hard: a cab or a [what?] is needed. The only resemblance between a wife and an umbrella is that they are "personal belongings"; then the blank represented by [what?] in (2) must be filled in the class of women, adding a resemblance to cabs that will also be borrowed from the same paradigm as before, that is, private versus public. A cab is a public vehicle, hence the unnamed in the second sentence is a public woman, a whore, and rain stands in both sentences for sexual need. Explication of the joke: "When a married man needs sex, his wife is good enough on ordinary occasions, but when he needs special treatment (has a stronger need than usual or wants to go further), only a prostitute will do"; or even, "Sooner or later any married man will go to a brothel." The structure of this joke is really *allegorical*, in a very condensed form; it mediates between an Ur-narrative of experience ("the umbrella was invented for shelter from the rain") and a model for narratives of the past and the future, easy to concretize or exemplify: "X, who was a married man, went one day to the whorehouse"; "Y, who is a married man, will go to a prostitute one day." That married men are attracted to prostitutes is justified in the process as a law of nature (see chapter 4), but minimally contextualized narrative plays a vital role in the formation of the implied injuncteme: "If you are a married man and need sex badly, just go to the brothel like all married men do"; narrative significance is not canceled, it is potentialized by the lack of context. In example 1, in contrast, all additional narrative programs were regressive; they could only take the form of instantiations of "Jews are dirty," of which the text quoted was already an exemplification.

Casanova refused to tell the story of his escape from the prison of Venice in less time than he had set once and for all, as if there were a proportion to be respected between narrated matter and narration. Looking at a list of titles published by a famous Spanish periodical collection of short stories in the 1920s (*La novela de hoy*), one could well believe that there is such a relation: *El momento difícil* (no. 1), *Coincidencia extraña* (no. 17), *Un idilio de quince días* (no. 27), *Mis memorias de una noche* (no. 28), *La hora del pecado* (no. 42), *Una hora mala la tiene cualquiera* (no. 44), *Cuatro días en el infierno* (no. 47), to name a few. But narrative does not cut out chunks of "real" time, if there exists such a thing; it plays with two basic sequences: "I was born → I am alive → I'll die," and, "I cannot die → I write → I can die," under many forms and disguises that rhetorically encompass the totality of human knowledge and interrogations as placed under the sign of change.

Shorter narrative forms like the popular tale, the case, the anecdote, the parable, the short story, the fable, the biographical notice, the one-act play, the short movie, and the snapshot have a number of options to represent the basic sequences, when longer forms do not need to opt (most of my examples are taken from Santiago Sylvester's collection *La prima carnal* [1986]):[13]

1. They can *reduce exposition* in various ways, exposition being taken here approximately in Meir Sternberg's sense:

> It is the function of exposition to introduce the reader into an unfamiliar world, the fictive world of the story, by providing him with the general and specific antecedents indispensable to the understanding of what happens in it.[14]

Exposition will thus be confined to the beginning of the tale instead of being distributed in several points of it, or, more rarely, confined to the end, when the "antecedents" of understanding are confused with the enigma in a single question: "What really happened?" The first lines of "Tu amigo que te quiere" (Your friend who wishes you well) illustrate the concentration of exposition at the beginning:

> Two fundamental things made me feel close to Robusto Bitácora: childhood, since we had both been children once, and the fact that he wanted to be a writer and I did not.
> Robusto Bitácora, logically, was his pen name, and I can testify that he had chosen it with care.[15]

2. Exposition (essentially made of nonnarrative discourses) can occupy most or all of the tale, with markers that ask the reader to put to work its narrative program or programs. This is the technique of Robbe-Grillet's *Snapshots*, as well as of "The Philosophy of Furniture,": a text classified as an "essay" in some editions of Edgar Allan Poe's works:

> Even *now*, there is present to our mind's eye a small and not ostentatious chamber with whose decorations no fault can be found. The proprietor lies asleep on a sofa—the weather is cool—the time is near midnight: we will make a sketch of the room during his slumber.[16]

Among Sylvester's stories, "Un rezo por Amy" (A prayer for Amy), centered on an almost eventless scene, offers a modest variation of this process.

3. A complete sequence of the type "departure → adventure → return," or

"union → separation → reunion" is evoked by one of its extreme terms instead of being fully textualized; it is the reader-receiver's task to complete this sequence, using his knowledge of narrative discourse as contained in the intertext, in language, in his narrative vision of his own life. In "El protagonista," by Sylvester, an old man who has taken to writing fiction, a novel situated in Lisbon, spends an indifferent Sunday with his family, has a dream in which he is fired from his work ("You should write it, it would be a good story if you could find an ending for it," says one of his friends)[17] and leaves his home secretly for an unknown destination: "[When he arrived at the station], he was still half an hour early for his train." (p. 110).

4. The complete sequence can be concentrated in its central narrateme, which is also a figural duplication of the formation of narrative discourse itself. Embedded short stories, like that of Ethelred in Poe's "The Fall of the House of Usher,"[18] and telegrams from press agencies ("Last night in Honduras, a group of high-ranking officers seized power in a bloodless coup") often follow this model.

5. A complete sequence or two can be textualized in summary form; both exposition and the number of characters are reduced as, generally, in drama, but the entire narrative structure of longer forms is nevertheless present, like a miniature model. A scenario or a film script bears this relation to the expanded film text. Short stories such as "La prima carnal" by Sylvester[19] or "Los fugitivos" by Carpentier,[20] which appear as long stories cut short, give the contemporary reader a feeling that they would make "good movie scripts."

Narrative condensation can work very differently from what it does in the joke, when it offers just enough guidelines to fill in detail and incident (as the seventeenth- and eighteenth-century portraits of characters did in the order of description); it allows a more personal, perhaps more conscious, investment or projection on the part of the receiver who no longer has to accept blindly the tenets of the *doxa* in order to achieve narrative significance.

Verse

I have repeatedly contended that verse (*versus*, returning) is the born enemy of prose (*prorsus*, going forward) and, by the same token, of narrative.[21] These statements, made in a polemical context, are likely to seem counterfactual when one considers the huge corpus of straight epic in verse, as well as the mock epic and innumerable other narrative poems, including even sonnets, madrigals, and limericks:

> There was an old man called Nasty Nick
> Who arrived in this world
> With a corkscrew prick
> All his life was one long hunt
> For a perfect girl with a corkscrew cunt.

It would be interesting to show how this standard bawdy motif is put to different uses with the distinct, if not lesser, constraints of prose, for example, in *Les Bijoux indiscrets* by Diderot. In prose, the motif can be used ironically to denounce fatalism, the doctrine of predestination, and the myth of the sister-soul as a grotesque imposture, since the physical conformation of men and women shows that coitus can take place between virtually any partners: there are no *formal* limits to sexual freedom, but only perhaps degrees of enjoyment, depending on the conjunctions of changing tastes. As Fourier would put it:

> In order to deceive us on the evident incompatibility of marriage with the passions, philosophy preaches fatalism. . . . Not at all; it will suffice to invent a new mode of domestic society, adapted to the wishes of the passions.[22]

While, in a limerick, the name of the protagonist or his geographic origin (say: "There was an old man from London") is dictated by the choice of rhymes with a limited lexicon, the actual order of words turns this lexicon into a derivation of the name; the formal structure of the limerick, its form of expression, resembles somehow the *form of content* in a syllogism, so that narrative development, however arbitrary, is naturalized. Even with a "corkscrew prick," Nick could dedicate himself to many other activities than the "long hunt" (uncorking bottles in a wine bar, raising pigs, or drawing labyrinths), if he were not a being of verse. The *verse fallacy* in narrative could easily be compared with the "fallacy of four terms" in logic, except that its absurdity is not perceived before a thorough analysis is carried out, and it misses the refreshing comic effect of "All zebras wear stripes, and all prisoners wear stripes; therefore some zebras are prisoners"![23]

Yet not all verse acts on narrative in the same direction, determines it with the same force, not all narrative submits to verse as thoroughly as the limerick about Nick. The tension between verse and narrative (if narrative is the discourse of change), their antagonism, can lead to different outcomes; sometimes, exceptionally, as in the best operatic duets, both parties, both voices win, to the greatest advantage of the total significance of the text, of the sum of messages that can be constructed from all the individual acts of communication through the text. Let us look at a few samples:

> Heaven's winged herald, Jove-born Mercury,
> The self-same day that he asleep had laid
> Enchanted Argus, spied a country maid,
> Whose careless hair, instead of pearl t'adorn it,
> Glister'd with dew, as one that seem'd to scorn it.[24]

> Une acclamation douce, tendre et hautaine,
> Chant des coeurs, cri d'amour où l'extase se joint,

Remplira la cité; mais, ô mon capitaine!
    Vous ne l'entendrez point.
De sombres grenadiers, vétérans qu'on admire,
Muets, de vos chevaux viendront baiser les pas;
Ce spectacle sera touchant et beau; mais, sire
    Vous ne le verrez pas.
Car, ô géant! couché dans une ombre profonde,
Pendant qu'autour de vous, comme autour d'un ami,
S'éveilleront Paris, et la France, et le monde,
    Vous serez endormi.[25]

Il marche vers d'Ailly, dans sa fureur guerrière,
Parmi des tourbillons de flamme, de poussière,
A travers les blessés, les morts et les mourants;
De leurs coursiers fougueux tous deux pressent les flancs,
Tous deux sur l'herbe unie, et de sang colorée,
S'élancent loin des rangs d'une course assurée.[26]

    In the first fragment, in which Mercury falls in (physical) love with a shepherdess whose request of a "draught of flowing Nectar" will cause, with a short-lived revolution among the Gods, the future woes of Leander and Hero, the rhyme "laid-maid" is narratively operational and even generative; it formally relates sexual desire to the vision of a wench in the state of nature, emphasizing iconically that Mercury was feeling and acting as expected. Thanks to this rhyme, Mercury is "right" or "correct." But, at the same time, syntactically, "asleep had laid" rules "enchanted Argus" and has a completely different meaning, involving deception of authority in a high place. The next pair of rhymes, "adorn it — scorn it," stand in paradigmatic opposition as if it were ornament that the maid scorned, while a syntactic reading shows that the maiden's hair scorns the (cold or dampness of the) dew; but this scorn in its turn is not hatred but indifference, or even tolerance and complicity. In fact, she is adorned with dew instead of pearls: the phonetic equivalence is restored to the status of semantic and symbolic equivalence. The natural maid appears offered to the eyes of Mercury and the rhyme hides from him the ambiguity of nature and her attitude. Although the second rhyme fashions occurrential, descriptive discourse, it makes the most of its protonarrative potential.

    In the second fragment, we note one mixed series of adjectives, one polysyndetic series of nouns, two plus one appositions, two comparisons, and two interpellations as bearers of rhymes: these lines of Hugo seem full of chevilles and contain little information that is strictly and immediately useful to narrative meaning. In summary, the passage, built on a single antithesis, contains only two narratemes: "People will acclaim you (but) you will be dead." The same two narratemes are repeated three times, expanded with variations; the expansions of the first one are hyperbolic and those of the second are litotes. The thrice-repeated litote combines discretion – death is not named – with a full definition of the hypogram (to be dead is to be asleep, deaf, and blind); this combination has a periphrastic value and it will be further expanded. Although Napoleon can and should be named, his death is unnamable, for it is unbearable, but it must be repeatedly suggested, for it is unbelievable. The three litotes are doubly enhanced by the concision of the three hexasyllables and their position at the end of each stanza; these stylistic, compositional features, made possible by verse, give them additional expressive value: they are concise and final like death. Nevertheless, two of them are introduced by an antithetical vocative – the poet addresses the hero as if he were alive, and there is an important change in the third stanza in which the evocation of death appears as early as the first line; if we attach life and death signs to each segment of this last stanza, the sequence reads: life (own) – death (own) – life (own) – life (other) – death (own), and the general model structure of the passage appears clearly as the embedding of Napoleon's death in the midst of his nation's life: a mimetic structure.

Indeed, at a deeper level of interpretation, we realize that, while the nation perpetually mourns this death, bears death in its heart, Napoleon survives in its memory, bears in him some of the nation's life. The narrative exchange, again, is rendered possible by versification. A closer study would show that patching rhymes are not less functional: the apparent contrast between phonetic junction and semantic disjunction, for example, in "joint/point" and "pas/pas," indicates by its ambiguity that the primary narratemes are insufficient to give a full account of the narrative significance of the poem, that is, a secondary transformation such that the burial of the Emperor in the chapel of the Invalides will indeed be his ever-renewed "retour."

In the final fragment, although it is not always true in *La Henriade*, versification seems to be largely indifferent to narrative development, and vice versa. O. R. Taylor, editor of the 1970 critical edition, judges very harshly Voltaire's talent as an epic poet and revealingly contradicts himself. He finds "the narration fast, clear and easy, the verse equally tight and flowing,"[27] but style and versification are "conventional," dry, and repetitive; the lines are rendered "at once jerky and monotonous" (p. 229) by the abuse of antithesis. In short, *La Henriade* is not "poetic" or "romantic"; "it is rather versified history than an epic poem" (p. 228). Translated into a more proper critical language, the editor is really saying two things: (1) that "good poetry," imaginative verse, is not compatible with "straight" narrative, although it can accommodate "arranged" narrative (that is, influenced and modified or modalized by the lyrical – like Marlowe and Hugo), and (2) that Voltaire does not write "true" or "good" poetry, because he speaks fluent verse: facility is the mother of indifference (or vice versa?). I think this last, implicit, statement is very important. A distinction should probably be drawn between the periods and individual writers for whom fixed forms are not problematic, are received like a natural language or rather a well-mastered, quasi-mechanical technique, for example, Voltaire and many of his contemporaries, heirs to the established French classical tradition of the alexandrine, and, on the other hand, writers and periods for whom fixed forms are still to be defined or can be redefined, transformed, a process that raises the awareness of all the effects and modes of exploitation in the Renaissance and the early seventeenth century in France, in the romantic and "symbolist" periods in Europe. The relations between verse and narrative, in their tension and complexity, would vary in keeping with this factor. Let several of Edgar Allan Poe's poems, particularly "The Raven" and "Ulalume," bear witness.

The obsessive, throbbing repetitions of "Ulalume,"[28] already partly programmed in the title, could easily bring about an all but complete destruction of narrative meaning as it does in traditional litany or in Charles Péguy's *Eve*. It has been observed that the form of the ballad is, by itself, particularly favorable to patching, with only the chorus and a few other lines able to free themselves from the excessive constraints of the rhyme pattern;[29] the ballad would be caught in the opposition between its two original characteristics: that it was both a dance and a narrative, recurrent movement and the expression of change. Moreover, the role of a chorus is basically antinarrative. But, in "Ulalume," slight variation, a sort of skidding or slip, is all the more striking on the background of haunting recurrence. It takes the shape of an imperfect echoic duplication that figures the division of the enunciated subject of enunciation ("Of cypress, I roamed with my Soul- / Of cypress, with Psyche my Soul") at the same time as it prefigures the reencounter with the death of the beloved in the form of her tomb ("She replied — 'Ulalume-Ulalume — / 'Tis the vault of thy lost Ulalume' " . . . "And I cried—'It was surely October / On *this* very night of last year' "). The two enjambments of the sixth stanza had prepared the final fall into the terror of repeated death, death as repetition, that single unnarratable but inescapable event. "Ulalume" therefore illustrates yet another type of relation between narrative and verse: the restriction of thematic field, when the iconic value of verse form is strong and coherent. This is one of the most fascinating formations of compromise that can occur.

Drama

> And how . . . the duke of Albany ascended the throne of Britain after the death of Lear, is needless here to narrate; Lear and his Three Daughters being dead, whose adventures alone concern our story.[30]

I shall not resume the debate on the relevance of mimesis (vs. diegesis) to narrative, or the respective merits of telling and showing.[31] It has been made clear that the object of narratology is the study of all the acts of communication that carry narrative meaning and significance.[32] The preceding quotation would give more fuel to the excellent arguments of Michel Mathieu-Colas, agreeing with Ricoeur that "it must be possible to speak of dramatic narrative," as long as there is—in his terminology—"a minimum amount of actional content [*contenu événementiel*]" or a "represented content developing in time."[33] I would add that, if not all plays are narrative, neither are all texts of so-called narrative prose, and narrative discourse cannot stand alone in a novel or a newspaper story, on pain of unintelligibility and destruction of the narrative effect, any more than it can in drama. But drama will teach us something more about narrative if and only if we can determine some of its special ways of conveying narrative meaning, the place and status of narrative discourse in dramatic communication, in relation to other "surplus" discourses that take part in this type of communication. I shall proceed by remarks.

1. The last lines of the "King Lear" tale from Shakespeare, as rendered by Charles and Mary Lamb, show a temptation to emancipate it, on historical principles, from the relative unity of time and above all, "action," imposed by the stage: since Albany was not a central character in the story of the tribulations of Lear and his daughters, his ascension to the throne would be equivalent to introducing a different character *in extremis*. The "diegetic" tale owes its referential power, its capacity of presentation, to the structuring memory of the teller, which can display any segment(s) from an unlimited temporal continuum, while presence in drama is staged *as if given*: it can only expand from the presence of actors on stage; it can rely to a small extent on the mnemonic skill of agents or their foresight, but only at a second remove, in the background, through represented words. A tale told in words on stage is offered by hearsay. Drama increases the differentials of narrational distance and effects of presence between narrative contents. Theater in the theater could be seen in great part as a device to reduce again the differential.

2. Descriptive discourse shrinks in the verbal part of the dramatic text, except in conjunction with narrative told by actors. Let us compare two renderings from act 4, scene 4, of *King Lear*:

> [Cordelia is speaking of her father to the physicians] "Alack, 'tis he, he was met even now / As mad as the vex'd sea; singing aloud; / Crowned with rank fumitter and furrow weeds, / With harlocks, hemlock, nettles, cuckoo-flowers, / Darnel and all the idle weeds that grow / In our sustaining corn. . . . / He that helps him take all my outward worth." (Shakespeare, pp. 257–60)

> Lear having by some chance escaped from the guardians that the good earl of Kent had put over him to take care of him in his lunacy, was found by some of Cordelia's train, wandering about the fields near Dover, in a pitiable condition, stark mad, and singing aloud to himself with a crown upon his head which he had made of straw, and nettles,

and other wild weeds that he had picked up in the corn-fields. . . . By the aid of these skilful physicians, to whom Cordelia promised all her gold and jewels for the recovery of the old king, Lear was soon in a condition to see his daughter." (Lamb, p. 137)

The list of weeds that complete the mad king's attire is much shorter in the Lamb tale, but Cordelia seems to promise riches more pictorially to the physician(s). Leaving aside the simplification and modernization carried out by the tellers, it is easy to see that the first description on stage needs to be more "vivid" and rhetorical because it refers to an absent object and has to compete with the visual presence of the speaker, the physicians, the soldiers, and the setting (a tent), while a gesture of Cordelia pointing at her "outward worth," or even the simple visual presence of the gold and jewels she is wearing, is explicit enough on stage. The Lamb version creates a verbal balance between Lear's weeds and Cordelia's jewels, while the balance was established intersemiotically on stage. Another consequence is that narratemes in drama are not normally synthesized from verbal descriptions but from the interpretation of visual and other signs, *and* from other levels of verbally realized discourse through a rather more complicated process of analysis and synthesis. The injunctive and the various modalities of the conative function, emitted by the same speaker for different purposes in succession and perhaps in contradiction, will thus be interpreted as change (becoming) of this speaker, progress or regression of his designs. This phenomenon is also common in "diegetic" narrative, but it is less obvious for the reasons that follow.

3. As common critical vocabulary betrays, narrative drama is a matter of "action," efficient or impeded—it does not matter—rather than of happenings and becomings. The agents act on each other, or their problem is to succeed in doing so, even in tragedy where the force of destiny rules them all. Characters in the theater can hardly gain any existence from the speeches of others; not being granted the right to reply or not being able to find a reply can dismiss them from the scene forever. They are, on average, two parts speech and one part actor's body or hollow corporeal form demanding to be embodied, or one part of the former and two parts of the latter, but in any case, very little else. Sometimes they are allowed to leave a bodily imprint on others or receive it from them on stage (wounds, kisses, embraces, inflicted death, abduction, rape, rescue); more often, as on the French classical stage or the opera, bodies are rather the inescapable supports of voices and their extensions, metonyms of physiognomies, individual proscenia to manifest the corresponding souls, able to shed tears, burst out laughing, shiver, shudder, tremble with rage, and little more.

Drama is not mime and mime is not a Punch and Judy show, but even in a puppet show, in silent mime or, a fortiori in spoken drama, the dominant form of action is verbal, speech is dominantly actional, the illocutionary force of every utterance matters, the cooperative principle is constantly manipulated, and the dominant trend of narrative discourse is interactive on the narrational plane and transactive on the plane of the narrated. The beautiful, redundant horror of tragedy might well be the disqualification of characters by Fate with regard to their interactive-transactive function, a disqualification that runs counter to the most fundamental principles of dramatic narrative. Similarly, staged presence, the illusion of presence (bodies-for-speech and embodied speeches) would explain the universal reprobation for the *deus ex machina* in drama: each and every character must freely contribute an appointed share to the total god in formation, whereas in "diegetic" narrative, every character is undoubtedly an emanation of the narrating god, in one or more persons. Charles and Mary Lamb are visibly torn between opposite requirements involving a different philosophy of action. At times they dare to play the role of the all-powerful teller, at the limits or at the risk of metalepsis: "So we will leave this old king in the protection of his dutiful and loving child. . . . Let us return to say a word or two about those cruel daughters" (p. 138). But they often feel obliged to report the behavior of the characters in the presented world as *speech actions*, acts of discourse. The tale contains an average of ten words or groups of words denoting verbal communication per page; and, very significantly, many of the verbs like "say," "declare," "tell," and "pray" command several subordinate clauses, for example, "saying that . . . and that"; "told him that . . . , that . . . and . . . ; and she prayed him that . . . and . . . "; "called her a . . . , and said that she spoke an untruth"; 'And he bid . . . "; "And he spoke . . . , and said"; "And he cursed . . . ; praying that . . . or . . . that"—all on a single short page.

Drama does not "show" action any more than "diegetic" narrative, even when it does not integrate it in its text, but it conflates into action presented enunciation and the intended, actual, and possible effects of the enunciated content. We might venture to say that the competition of nonverbal, preverbal, or paraverbal expression in dramatic narrative forces narrative (which is always representation) to invest speech in a manner borrowed from nonverbal, preverbal, or paraverbal behavior.

Narrative in a Discourse of Truth:
The Case of Nineteenth-Century Historiography

My knowledge of the Discourse of history is far from being sufficient to sustain the credit of the wide scope that the title of this section would seem to claim. This title is meant as a mere frame of reflection and questioning. The bulk of our research so far has been conducted on the basis of textual examples that are currently found as tokens of literary or artistic communication in our societies. But narrative is present in almost all socially defined Discourses and dominant in many of them: what happens to it, how is it informed and shaped by the particular requirements of Discourses that are not centered or rooted in the production of aesthetic value, such as conversational autobiography, economic prevision, or metaphysics? And how do these Discourses use narrative for their own special purposes? What original constraints do they apply or impose on it to achieve their social functions and produce their own kinds of value? Before we evoke revolutionary propaganda (in chapter 10), some hypotheses about historical Discourse would come in handy. Without any pretension to generalization and well aware that Xenophon, Livy, Froissart, Gibbon, and the Ecole des Annales have little in common, I have chosen as my test case the work of a mid-nineteenth-century historian, praised for his conscientious research and the charm of his writing, published at a time when history was aspiring to convert its moral ideal of accuracy into a criterion of interest and a scientific ideal. I am using the 1889 revised edition of *History of the Conquest of Peru* by William H. Prescott, originally published in 1847.

The title page, like those of many other history books before this century, would deserve a thorough study by itself. The complete title runs: *with a Preliminary View of the Civilization of the Incas*. The stress is thus placed on the object conquered rather than on the merit of the conquest (compare the effect of a substitute title like: *with Complete Biographies of all the Main Conquerors*, or, *with Its Consequences for the Spanish Empire*). A "view," not a history, of the Inca civilization is proposed, with several possible implications: civilization is not a narrative subject matter, and only a synchronic picture, portrait, or description can be given; a history of the Inca civilization is not possible for lack of dated documents and because the Incas themselves had a concept of historical time radically different from ours; this civilization should be presented synchronically at the time of the conquest because the history of the conquest is that of its destruction (the view is "preliminary" for the same reason). That the title is overdetermined is evident from the two epigraphs that preinterpet the conquest as robbery: "Congestae cumulantur opes, orbisque rapinas accipit," from Claudian's political poem *In Rufinum*,[34] and "So color de religión / Van a buscar plata y oro / Del encubierto tesoro," from Lope de Vega's *Nuevo Mundo*.[35]

The historian will definitely not refrain from passing judgment on the Spaniards in the course of the book; for example, "From first to last, the policy of the Spanish conquerors towards their unhappy victim [Atahualpa] is stamped with barbarity and fraud."[36] At the same time, he will go as far as to exonerate Atahualpa of the accusation of immoderate cruelty (genocide) leveled against him by Garcilaso for the supposed massacre of his half-brother and rival Huascar's extended family. One of the organizing principles of the narrative is undoubtedly a demonstration of the wicked motives of the conquest on the part of Pizarro and Almagro, the prime mover being the "hard gripe of avarice." The moral demonstration goes hand in hand with a critical examination of certain documents: letters, early relations, and histories of the conquest. The criteria of the critique are of two sorts: the plausibility of the behavior of historical actors (monarchs, warriors, priests, etc.) as a function of their temperament and a reasonably sound perception of their personal and political interests, on the one hand, and the possible sources of distortions on the part of the witnesses, chroniclers, and historians, on the other hand. For example:

> Why was the massacre . . . extended to all, however remotely or in whatever way connected with the race? Why were aged women and young maidens . . . subjected to such refined and superfluous tortures, when it is obvious that beings so impotent could have done nothing to provoke the jealousy of the tyrant? (p. 166)

And:

> Garcilaso wrote late in life, after the story had been often told by Castilian writers. (p. 141)

Ethics, the search for truth, and common sense form a holy trinity that touches all the moments of historical communication, a chain actually longer than that of fiction, because historiography, as seen by Prescott, is fundamentally a kind of critical synthetic rewriting of preexisting texts for a purpose or, better, for a converging plurality of purposes.

The writing of history as rewriting is indeed striking in the case of Prescott who was almost blind and did not travel to the site of the events recounted or even to that of the sources:

> I sent to Spain to collect materials for an account of the Conquest of Mexico . . . the papers of Muñoz. This eminent scholar, the historiographer of the Indies, employed nearly fifty years of his life amassing materials for a history . . . a magnificent collection of manuscripts, many of which he patiently transcribed with his own hand. But he did not live to reap the fruits of his persevering industry. . . . his manuscripts were destined to serve the uses of another.
>
> The historian has rather had occasion to complain of the *embarras de richesses*; for in the multiplicity of contradictory testimony it is not always easy to detect the truth, as the multiplicity of cross-lights is apt to dazzle and bewilder the eye of the spectator. (pp. v, vii)

On reading these considerations, one would almost think the documents themselves are not narrative, but this is not so. In fact, the historian, a reader-writer, or a "spectator"-writer, to adapt Prescott's word, is more or less in the same situation as the spectator at the theater, and as a judge in a court of law. In the presence of a polyphonic or even cacophonic enunciation, of multiple speeches, many of them narrative and some not, but which in any case are never free of nonnarrative functions (command, request, entreaty, blame, defense, deception, self-delusion) and cannot occupy together the same referential space (principle of noncontradiction), the historian must choose logically compatible elements and arrange them in coherent sequences. Integrating a "fact" (a descriptive or narrative predicative content) into the narrative chain that forms the backbone of total narrative significance (therefore also axiomatic and moral) is at the same time the test and sanction of truth. If the fact "fits," it is good for narrative, and therefore it should be true; if it becomes a necessary link in the narrative, it will be passed on as true to the reader. There are, however, inherent risks and possible setbacks in this method, as Prescott is aware: if the truth is more difficult to detect in front of a "multiplicity of cross-lights," this also means that a single testimony, although it may be false, will tend to seem truer than several diverging versions of the facts or elaborations of the same themes.

In short, narrative unity is the necessary means to impart the notion of truth, but it can be misleading because there is always some truth in the tales told by previous narrators, with their own narrative unity. It is interesting to observe Prescott's empirical, prudent way out of this dilemma: a combination of design and diversity in the form of a hierarchy or, better, an orchestration.

Let us recall the three criteria of "what history should be," according to Saintsbury:

> In the first place, the author should have thoroughly studied and intelligently comprehended all the accessible and important documents on the subject. In the second, he should have so digested and ordered his information that not merely a congeries of details, but a regular structure of history, informed and governed throughout by a philosophical idea, should be the result. In the third, this result should, from the literary as well as the historical side, be an organic whole composed in orderly fashion and manifesting a distinct and meritorious style.[37]

The opinion of a literary historian on the norms of historical writing as a genre could probably be dismissed as spurious or, at best, symptomatic, if it were not corroborated by the theory and practice of many nineteenth-century professional historians. Prescott writes in his preface:

> The subject . . . , notwithstanding the opportunities it presents for the display of character, strange romantic incident, and picturesque scenery, does not afford so obvious advantages to the historian as the Conquest of Mexico. . . . The natural development of the story, there, is precisely what would be prescribed by the severest rules of art. The conquest of the country is the great end always in the view of the reader. . . . In the march of the events, all moves steadily forward toward this consummation. It is a magnificent epic, in which the unity of interest is complete.
> In the "Conquest of Peru," the action, so far as it is founded on the

subversion of the Incas, terminates long before the close of the narrative. (pp. vii–viii)

The "philosophical idea" that informs the "regular structure of history" is obviously also an aesthetic idea, or rather ideal, very close to that classicism of the romantics which finds its characteristic expression in *Hernani*. Art, like history, is imitative, "mimetic"; the one and the other find better topics — since the topics are also models — in some natural materials, ready to be transformed, than in others. The conquest of Mexico is a ready-made signifier to mean the forward movement, the purposiveness of both human history and historical narrative, even though the purposes are different, the former *telos* being the pursuit of power and the latter the pursuit of truth. But the conquest of Peru is bad, contradictory material for narrative: the Spanish protagonists do not strive for a greater unity of the empire; their ranks are torn by the rivalries of unruly adventurers; and they are divided within themselves by false consciousness, not being even thoroughly hypocritical. Pizarro, the swineherd, is to blame not only because he is a cheat and a murderer but also because he is not of the stuff that historical conquerors are made of when they bring unity of action.

One should not believe that this attitude is limited in time to the nineteenth century: the idea of putting history in *perspective* in order to write it is not exclusively motivated by the accessibility of documents or by the fear of distortions due to the psychological involvement of the contemporaries in the events; one of the main reasons of this requirement is the homogeneity of the resulting narrative. William L. Shirer thinks he can write his history of the Third Reich by the time it has taken the shape of a "rise and fall," and its narrative structure itself will never be repeated in the real world — the atom bomb, he believes, has made it impossible. The closure of the series crystallizes the narrative structure without threats of further variations. Moreover, historians who deal with confusing, messy materials also feel the need to find a narrative rationale for the mess, which gives it moral significance. Emile Témime begins his history of the Spanish civil war with a statement of Lloyd George's to the effect that it is an ideological war: the fate of democracy in the country is meaningful as a rehearsal for World War II. But let us return to Prescott.

Once "preserved," "the unity of interest which is scarcely less essential to historic than to dramatic composition" (p. viii), seriousness, the construction and preservation of truth, is afforded by the combined insertion of realemes (fragments of documents, previous histories, letters, etc., in view of the lack of monuments or rather of the archaeological ignorance of the time) and traces of composition that justify and increase narrative unity through its intertwining with an underlying argumentative structure. We find four categories of hierarchically organized evidence argumentatively arranged to support unity and its truth, while detracting from it by their individual contents:

1. "Notices" on major past historians, historic actors and witnesses, such as Sarmiento, Polo de Ondegardo, Garcilaso de la Vega, Pedro Pizarro, Montesinos, and Oviedo, delayed and placed after certain chapters;

2. Copies and translations of "original documents" placed at the end of the book;

3. Footnotes, mainly quotations from "documents" and early historians, commented on or not; their particular functions can vary widely, from the status of supportive statements by which the precedence of authority is reversed between source and modern historical writing, to ironic indignation echoing the text. First case: "A passage . . . is worth quoting, as confirming on the best authority some of the interesting particulars mentioned in the text" (p. 246 n. 1). Second case: "The secretary Sancho seems to think that the Peruvians must have regarded these funeral honours as an ample compensation to Atahualpa for any wrongs he may have sustained, since they at once raised him to a level with the Spaniards" (p. 232 n. 1);

4. Quotations or explicit summaries, with or without debate on their worth and authenticity, in the body of the text itself, for instance, this typical case of twice-reported speech: "He sought out Pizarro at once, and found him, says the chronicler, 'with a great felt hat, by way of mourning, slouched over the eyes,' and in his dress and demeanour exhibiting all the show of sorrow. 'You have acted rashly,' said De Soto to him bluntly; 'Atahualpa has been greatly slandered. There was no enemy at Huamachuco; no rising among the natives' " (p. 231).

We can wonder whether the main difference between historic narrative within history, Discourse of truth, and romanticized history or the historical novel, does not lie essentially in the different degree of textual integration of the sources: in the first case, a semiexternal, liminary, or marginal apparatus, juxtaposes diverging narrative programs to the core narrative course chosen by the Σ narrator; the truth and unity of the narrative are shown to be fragile constructions in need of reinforcing and reenforcement by the mediation of other discourses that more or less succeed in establishing it. In the second case, narrative unity is proposed fully realized by the Σ narrator, and it is presented as autonomous, naturally dominant, with the help of undoubtedly subservient descriptions. Lukács's preference for Walter Scott's technique of composition versus the "decadent" late nineteenth-century or even Heinrich Mann in the historical novel, is perhaps not solely the result of his political bias and the Marxist vision of history: "the multiplicity of . . . interactions between individuals and the unity of social existence which underlies this richness" and the fact that the "leading figure only appears at significant moments"[38] are equivalent on the plane of the form of content to the polylogical structure of enunciation furnished by the apparatus on the plane of the form of expression in the slightly later "scientific" historical writing of a Prescott.

Narrative through Non-linguistic Media

I have insisted several times that narrative communication does not take place exclusively through the linguistic medium: all media can, in principle, serve as vectors of narrative, whatever their primary sensory basis (aural: oral linguistic expression, music; visual: the plastic arts, film; tactile: fight, erotic contact; or even gustatory and olfactory) or the combination of senses touched by reading, multimedia spectacles, etc.), and whether their mode of existence is primarily simultaneous (photography) or successive (language, music), primarily static (painting) or kinetic (film, ballet). On the other hand, if we can talk of narrative communication through all these media, it means that some part at least of the narrative message can be transported into the linguistic medium, put into the natural language that is also that of our metadiscourse. But this should not lead the theorist to any of the following hasty assimilations and resulting fallacies; it is wrong that (1) although not all narrative communication is carried out through a verbal medium, it aims at a verbal translation; (2) therefore the medium is unimportant for the study of narrative communication; (3) therefore linguistics is the only adequate science for this study.

Although our operational theorization cannot proceed pictorially or musically, it does acknowledge that operations of pictorial and musical narrative cognition are *not the same* as linguistic operations and are not necessarily mere preliminaries; they share certain structures and processes of dissociation, association, comparison, transfer, and so forth, that permit transposition up to a point, but require a particularly careful comparative approach. In this section, due to the difficulties of textual illustration inherent in music, sound, and many other media in the framework of a book, and in order to avoid blunders caused by my incompetence in musicology and phonology, I shall propose succinct approaches of narrative through two basically visual media: the plastic arts and film.

Narrative Programs of Visual Texts versus Visual Programs of Verbal Texts

There is no order of precedence, either logical or historical, between plastic and verbal texts, but there are permanent differences on the planes of the mode of existence of texts and of their semiotization, which we cannot disregard.[39]

Bi- or tridimensional plastic objects occupy space in the first place. Not that they are necessarily "intemporal" or that they can remain so for long(!), but we are always in a situation of space sharing or competing for space with them: a space that they limit and define, which is defined and limited as soon as we begin to exist in space, which is, by turns, the condition and the effect of plastic perception. This compulsory sharing constitutes the fundamental otherness of the plastic text, its nature of object, the origin and abutment of relations that can vary from fascination to repulsion, from rejection to identification, but which could become indifferent only at the cost of our being-here. The second feature of plastic existence is the distance of the plastic object, never cancelable either for its producer or its receiver, even when the object is the body of the self, as it is for Narcissus. Before it motivates aestheticization or supports critical distancing, this distance is essentially the absolute third party. All plastic relations develop in its presence.

Verbal objects exist fundamentally in time, that is, in the unfinished; neither here nor there, with no place of their own, neither in myself nor out of myself: they are essentially frameless, until I take my own mortality into consideration and throw it at them. In *this* sense, "Death, on the human horizon, is not a given but something to do."[40] There is no distance between ear and throat, I can hear only what I utter, utter what I hear, even when hearer and speaker, myself or another, are two. The absence of a third party is the basic mode of existence of the verbal text, the opposite of the essential mode of the plastic text—before the intervention of figuration and narrativity in either of them.

Any plastic figuration introduces a temporal order in space: a model and its imitation cannot just exist side by side; the model is (in) the past of the imitation, the imitation is (in) the future of the model, but also in the past of its vision and of other imitations. An imitation as such is the negative model of a real-to-come. Without figuration a book would not be an object competing for space with other books and with ourselves. Figuration imposes spatiality on the verbal text and temporality on the plastic text. Narrativity is a special aspect of figuration, the figuration of movement or change, hence of "time." Figuration in general *implies* time, *enunciative* time through reference; narrativity *signifies*, thematizes time, *enunciated* time. The two facets can be dissociated in plastic as well as in verbal communication. Figuration, as such, temporally orders a framed space and an out-of-frame space, or several. Narrativity orders temporally within a single frame. Let us look at the two drawings on the next page.

In one, Marcel is a gardener; in the other, Marcel is a writer. If we consider the two scenes together, which amounts to replacing the blank space and the lines of the frames that separate them with a single dotted line or nothing, we can see that, since Marcel is unable to be seated and standing at the same time, or to hold a spade and a quill, one of the scenes must be temporally referred *before* the other, and vice versa. Possible verbal translations include: "Marcel, the gardener, becomes a writer"; "Marcel, the writer, becomes a gardener"; or, if Marcel is both a gardener and a writer, "Now Marcel tends his garden, and now he sits writing at his desk." As we have said earlier, narrativity breaks up the simultaneity of

plastic perception, but this is the simplest case of plastic narrativity, which involves the duplication of an item with variations within the same plastic space or the same frame. Examples can be multiplied, but they remain comparatively rare: the comic and the photo-novel are the main genres that use this device in our age. It should be stressed that, contrary to the generative rule of verbal narrative (at least in European languages), the "subject" *must* be repeated in this case; instead of a polyvalent fusion, we have an anaphora in the surface structure, as we generally do in a verbal narrative sequence.

But, if we take each of the scenes separately, we realize that they are not completely void of narrativity. Actually, their narrativity takes three different forms:

1. Narrative programs similar to those of verbal descriptemes, of which I shall give a few examples for the left-hand picture as suggested by these "relevant" or compatible questions:

- What was Marcel doing before? What will he do after?
- How long will he work in the garden?
- Is he planting or uprooting?
- Will he eat what he is growing?
- Is he paid for his work? And so on.

2. Narrative figuration as the figuration of movement: "Marcel is pushing the blade down into the ground by bearing down on it with his right leg." The narrativity is the same as that of a photographic snapshot, a photogram from a film, or the progressive aspect of a verb in verbal narrative. Figuration has taken a single sample state from a process, in contrast to Marcel Duchamp with his *Nude Descending a Staircase*, which adds up several states cut out from the process, makes them forcibly coexist in one frame: there, when parts of the body overlap,

we have a case intermediate between duplication of the subject and fusion into a narrateme, as explained earlier. This is also an intermediate mode between static and kinetic figuration, which can be closer to the one or the other, depending on two factors: the more or less detailed decomposition of process/movement, and the faster or slower displacement (scanning) of the eyes of the beholder. Cutting out and presenting one single state can give it an exemplary character, either as a privileged moment or as the representative type of a continuous process seen as a homogeneous sequence, perhaps repeatable or repetitive. The single "shot" tends to imply no variety because it bears none: Marcel's gesture stands for many more "identical" gestures, by him and others, throughout the world; if it is the human condition to till the earth, then narrativity is lost, very much as it happened with "A Day in the Life of Nancy."[41] Notwithstanding these generalizations, themes do play a role: in Goya's *Third of May 1808*, that which is going to happen is not repeatable with the same referential actors; but it is a limited role: the horrors of war are indefinitely repeatable and repeated in history and this is what makes them appalling.

3. Enunciative narrativity: "Who posed, and when, for the figure of Marcel?" "Will Marcel recognize himself?" And so on. To the extent that any work is the trace of its own production, (re)presents somehow its own creation and the anticipation of its reception, viewing a plastic text involves additional narrative programs that refer to its enunciation. Indeed, they are the only possible ones in "abstract," nonfigurative art, where all movement inscribed is that of the artist, not the model. The dynamic, gestural painting of Pollock, Appel, Hartung, and so on, makes it particularly obvious. But these enunciative narrative programs themselves can be more or less precise, open or constraining, as a function of the technique used, conventional marks of completeness, the foregrounding or not of a dialectics between material and transformation, idea and execution. "Vibrating" color means active light, light in movement, but it also means superposed layers of paint, accumulated work.

The possible superposition, the structural redundancy of narrative programs at the levels of enunciation, enunciated, and reference, or their discrepancy—critical, ironic, awkward, shocking, it does not matter—are indexes of the hypericonicity of the plastic text that, combined with a greater directness of sensory effects and the relative lack of a priori orientation of the medium, contributes to render plastic narrativity at once rich and problematic. We shall examine one famous example that will support this statement: *The Apparition*, a watercolor by Gustave Moreau (1876).

The five "characters" (plus the head) occupy vertically a little less than the lower two-thirds of the painting. The grandiose architecture in the background dominates the gaze of the spectator, concentrating on the figures, as it dominates the characters in the presented world. The light comes from above. The back-

The Apparition, by Gustave Moreau. Reproduced by permission of the Musée Nationaux, Paris.

ground wall without window or roof imposes verticality as the given mode of being of space. Nevertheless, the lateral distribution of figures shows that this law is respected only by figures on the right-hand side of the painting. The immense sword of Mannei is a guide for his posture. The head of Iokanaan is vertical too: profile, hair, and beard, prolonged by the fall of blood, more visibly because of its inscription in the concentric circles intersected by the vertical lines. On the left-hand side, in contrast, not one member of the group—all comprised under the high left-low right (HL-LR) diagonal—holds his or her body straight. Herod is stooping, bending slightly forward; Herodias, her hands clasped in her lap, is sitting back, with her head up and inclined to one side, like someone who is listening attentively, at the theater; the attitude of the musician is entirely dictated by her instrument at the center of the picture, and the necessities of composition. Salome is in the foreground, but set just a few inches back, far enough to mark stagelike distance; she is the only one in movement, and losing balance, with the upper body blown backward, while her legs are still dancing.

There are, at least, two scenes, as there are two spaces (stages) on which Salome is moving. The train of her dress and her plaited hair restore visual balance but draw her farther down and backward in the presented world. Her *left* hand, open in the strict line of the arm, points to the head whose glory does not blind anybody else. The right arm is folded without excessive contraction, letting the tips of the delicately folded fingers touch lightly the collar bone, or rather the collar band studded with jewels: Is Salome naively puzzled, coquettishly perplexed? Is she suddenly shivering (but her hand has found no stole to draw around her shoulders)? Is there a beginning of distress that has not fully reached consciousness? The gesture of the left arm, in contrast, is much more ambiguous: it points to the head and amplifies its presence ("A head! A head!), but it also repels the sight to protect the eyes and, with them, physical integrity in general; it expresses blame and amazement: "You! Why are *you* doing this to me?!" But the only witnesses she can call are an absent God ("My! What have I done?"), Iokanaan's conscience or compassion, if he can feel any, and her own weakness ("I am only a woman"). Despite the overhanging position of the head and the fixed, irate gaze that do not make dialogue easy, it is obvious that whatever is the matter is a problem between these two: Salome and the head. All the other characters are passive, safely in the shadow of the background, painted on a backdrop; Mannei has not even reacted to the absence of the head from the tray—he is tired, they are all tired. Salome and the head are not tired; they have other business to attend to; they feel something about their bodies, their lost bodies or body, one for two. They have a body to worry about.

The autonomy of Salome's lower body (under the LL-HR diagonal) is striking; it is like the hips and legs of a ballerina on a mirrored music box, which go on whirling and leaping long after the music has stopped and the old collector has died (in a thriller): a body that is independent from any other rules than those of its grace, its abstract, automatic perfection, such that movement seems to become another form of stillness; the upper body is physiognomy, entirely dedicated to expression, so much so indeed that it becomes profuse, illegible.

Although there is an anecdote, in fact a pretold story "under" Moreau's painting (in the cultural milieu of its calculated reception), we cannot help realizing how important the geometry of composition is for the narrative construction of meaning as well as for its symbolic construction. Moreau's composition, in this case as in several others, breaks away from the triangular perspectivist device of tradition. Verticality here is so decisive that horizontal lines are used almost exclusively to inscribe the head (the solid glory is comprised between the median horizontal and the upper golden rule horizontal) and maintain Salome entirely in the lower half of the picture.[42] But verticals and diagonals are thoroughly exploited, both as respected laws and as opportunities for test infringements. The autonomy of Salome's lower body is thus explained by its inscription—with the musician and the head—in the decisive triangle LL-HR-LM (low median) formed by two "good" diagonals, HR-LL for the entire picture, and HR-LM for its right half. This triangle is oriented downward as a beam, and also because of Iokanaan's falling blood. Because of this compositional feature, we are allowed to read: "Salome dances for Iokanaan"; "Salome dances for the head"; "the head wants Salome"; "Iokanaan wants Salome," and left to order these utterances narratively. Of Salome's upper body, only the left forearm enters this triangle, only the hand is in the right half of the picture, and the index only to the right of the HL-LR diagonal, penetrating into the territory of desire: the finger points at the cut throat in a line parallel to that which joins the eye of the head to that of Salome. On the right of the HL-LR diagonal, we are exclusively in masculine territory, with the head and Mannei, but the sword points downward to the empty tray, out of this field, and the finger of Salome points upward at the sign of the missing body of Iokanaan, into this field. Salome's body is strictly composed on either side of the HL-LM diagonal that crosses her sex and is followed in parallel by her falling phallic pubic ornament, while the symmetric HR-LM diagonal separates the head from the executioner (vertical body and sword). This story is about castration, but it is not simple.

In the nineteenth-century iconography of Salome, whether the head of John is on a tray, lying on the ground, or hanging in the air, in levitation, it is the sign of the absence of the body, which is neither fully compensated for nor explained by Salome's exhibition. The body of the dancer is an arbitrary sign trained to receive all the semantic investments of desire. This spared body, this savings-body where needs and losses fructify at a distance, does not belong to the dancer, she cannot even reclaim it. The right arm verifies for us this absence; the left hand points accusingly to the image of castration that a man has incited her to produce, as if a woman prostituted to the father could still lose something.

Now, if visual signifiers are narrative generators, we should also investigate the role of visual programs in the narrative reading of verbal texts, but since this would lead us to very long developments and the field remains virtually unexplored, we shall be content to adduce a few elements to justify this pursuit. We shall do it through an examination of a very short elegiac poem by Wordsworth:

> She dwelt among the untrodden ways
> Beside the springs of Dove
> A Maid whom there were none to praise
> And very few to love
>
> A violet by a mossy stone
> Half hidden from the eye!
> —Fair as a star, when only one
> Is shining in the sky.
>
> She lived unknown, and few could know
> When Lucy ceased to be;
> But she is in her grave, and, oh
> The difference to me![43]

First of all, what is meant by "visual program" of a nonvisual text? The answer is stimuli and directives leading to the formation of mental visual images by the receiver. In music, in verse to a lesser extent, and still less in "plain" prose, this phenomenon is largely synaesthetic, which does not imply that it is either completely arbitrary or completely regulated. It is well known that a high pitch generally suggests light and sharp forms, and vice versa; "program music" (i.e., "narrative" music) is based in part on such semiuniversal, semiconventional associations, but synaesthesias are also the preferential domain of individual experience, and few people will ever agree in whole with Rimbaud's colored vision of the vowels. In verbal texts, visual directives are partly synaesthetic, or derived from repetition, rhythm, and symmetries, as in music, but they can also be much more precise and direct through semantic commands. If you tell me "There is a red scarf on the white chair" and I form a mental image of a green beret on a blue stool, I have not correctly "decoded" or concretized your text. The visual programs of verbal texts can be as complex as the narrative programs of plastic texts (you just have to read my description of Moreau's watercolor without looking at the picture, to realize that), but they can be even heavier and more constraining, because three syntaxes at least compete for their organization: the syntax of the natural language concerned, narrative or descriptive syntax, and visual syntax with its many facets (of color, value, shape, size, volume, etc.).

In Wordsworth's elegy, I shall take into account only the most obvious elements and neglect completely the more obscure or arbitrary synaesthetic factors:

- Dwelt → dwelling (house)
- Untrodden ways → lines without footprints
- Springs → transparence, green
- Dove → subdued color, rounded forms, light (flying)
- Very few to love → a few human figures in the distance
- Maid → youth, femininity, pleasant softness of forms, fresh colors?
- Violet → violet color, neither cold nor warm, and green, softness of form; small, scarcely visible
- Mossy stone → dark green, rounded form, large in comparison with a violet
- Fair star → shining, small, pleasant to the eye, single in dark space
- Lucy → light
- Grave →dark, heavy, angular?
- Me → one human figure (at the side of the grave)

The poem is visually composed of two main scenes, juxtaposes two principal frames, one after the other in the order of reading. The first scene (idyll) is relatively rich in its directly descriptive part and considerably enriched by the effects of metonymy and metaphor: the maid can be seen at the side of her rustic house, near the springs, with one or more doves close by and a few people in the distance, standing still (the ways are untrodden); somewhere in the foreground, but not evident to the eye, the detail of a half-hidden violet. In the last scene, a grave with a name engraved on it, in empty flat space, and a man close to it.

The two compositions have in common that they are centered on a "dwelling" or abode with a human figure at the side, but the second is almost empty; their difference reads as impoverishment, dispossession. Not only shapes (soft and rounded) but light and color are missing. And now we realize that there is a third, transitional frame in the comparison of lines 7 and 8; the star alone in the sky implies night and a beholder. Although the violet provided the brightest, if discreet, touch of color in the first scene, the maid was not the source of light. When she starts to shine, she receives her name, Lucy, but a light can be consumed or blown; the name kills the maid. In fact, in the last scene, she has become invisible in the grave; light does not shine through the name, or ever so feebly. The light of being is hidden by something (hidden) as it will be later, in Mallarmé's poem "Prose pour des Esseintes," "par le trop grand glaïeul" of desire and suffering. In Wordsworth's elegy, it is then clear that a visual narration, showing the transformation of the hardly visible into the invisible, duplicates the central narrateme "she died." The beholder of the poem is left with the same sense of loss as the poetic subject, beholder of the presented landscapes, and with the same recourse of memory. Nevertheless, an elegy is not just a narrative, and the visual program has a lesser role in the construction of the lyrical mediation. Moreover, many examples could be found of verbal texts whose visual programs are completely at odds with their verbal narrative structures: the relations can be dialectical or merely contradictorry or even ironic. Unsuspected new fields are opened by the visual dimension to the complication and explication of narrative significance and to the rhetoric processes of its information. Film is the medium in which these phenomena have been best studied.

Narrative and the Kinetic Medium

The most fundamental characteristic of film as a medium is supposed to be the iconic figuration of movement. The moving picture does not simply stand for movement in the presented world; it is perceived as movement taking place in our world of "unmediated" experience, even if we do not hide under our seats when the train arrives at the station of La Ciotat. We have seen that the temporal successiveness of the verbal medium is not related to narrative discourse any more than the simultaneity of the plastic medium, but the moving picture is originally a mechanical means of reproduction of a visual perception in time; in this respect, its process of signification is essentially mimetic. Does this fact imply that the kinetic medium automatically entails narrative meaning or, on the contrary, that no additional device being superposed on the kinetic medium, narrative discourse is a distorting filter applied by the medium to everything it touches—so that distinctively narrative meaning could not be constructed through its mediation? If we are not satisfied with negative answers suggested by intuition, or if we feel tempted to accept positive answers because they offer a semblance of logic, we had better examine the problem and its ramifications, with the help of some concrete film analysis, concentrating on the picture track. I have chosen for this purpose a 1952 "classic," *The Quiet Man*, by John Ford, and selected one scene for detailed inquiry.

General Data and Context

• *Main characters*: Sean Thornton (John Wayne), "the Yank"—an Irishman and former heavyweight boxer who returns from the United States to his native village to stay; Mary Kate Danaher (Maureen O'Hara), a redhead with a bad temper who lives on her brother's farm; Squire Will Danaher (Victor McLaglen), a rich and rough landowner, brother of Mary Kate.
• *Setting*: Innisfree, a village of southern Ireland, five miles from Castletown, in the 1920s.
• *Summary*: Sean Thornton arrives by train at Castletown; an old man, Michaeleen Flynn, (Barry Fitzgerald) drives him to Innisfree. Sean wants to buy back his parents' small cottage and property, "White Morning," which now belongs to a rich widow whom Will Danaher wishes to marry. Sean sees Mary Kate for the first time with a flock of sheep, for the second time at church; they are immedi-

ately attracted to each other. The widow sells "White Morning" to Sean in spite of Danaher's attempt to outbid him. Sean finds Mary Kate in the house the first time he goes there to spend the night: she has cleaned it for him and built a fire. He kisses her. He sends Flynn, the matchmaker, to ask for Mary's hand. She accepts, but her brother refuses to give his consent. At a race, Sean's friends conspire to make Danaher believe that the widow will marry him if his sister no longer lives at home. He gives his sister away with a dowry of £350 and her own furniture. On the day of the marriage, he realizes that he has been cheated and knocks Sean almost unconscious. He will give the furniture but not the dowry. Mary Kate wants Sean to claim her dowry; she is angry with him because he is too quiet and passes for a coward for not respecting the tradition, and she refuses to sleep with him. The Protestant parson, Mr. Playfair, tacitly advises Sean to fight with Danaher, although Sean has abandoned his boxing career after killing an opponent in the ring. The Catholic priest, Father Lonergan (the verbal narrator), advises Mary Kate to fulfill her conjugal duty; she complies, but she is gone from the house the following morning. She is unable to leave Castletown because the train to Dublin is four and a half hours late. Sean finds Mary Kate at the train station and drags her back the whole way, walking and stumbling. All the people on the road follow them, expecting a "homeric" fight between Sean and Danaher (the challenge scene is analyzed in the next section). The fight is long and hard—a wonderful spectacle and the occasion for much betting. Sean wins. He and Danaher are now good friends; they have dinner together at "White Morning." The next day, all the villagers act together to make Reverend Playfair, threatened with being removed, stay in the village. They also applaud Danaher's formal engagement to the widow. Presented time: about six months? Duration of the film: 122 minutes, including credits.

The Challenge Scene: A Description.

This scene, situated fifteen minutes from the end of the film, belongs to a larger sequence between a change in black and a dissolve, which includes Sean's trip to Castletown to pick up Mary Kate and bring her back, and the whole fight. I have analyzed twenty-eight shots, all edited in *clean cuts*, with a total duration of three minutes and sixteen seconds, although, in its strict unity, the scene should include only frames 2–25: Danaher is not yet visible in frame 1, and Mary Kate leaves the screen in frame 25, until the men return from the fight.

Shot 1. The camera follows numerous people ascending a wooded hill toward the right of the screen (Sean dragging Mary Kate at the head of the procession), then stops to let them pass.

Shot 2. Danaher and workers, with heavy threshing machines, form a line at the top of the hill, as in a parody of Western war scenes with the Indians.

1

2

3

4

5

6

7

8

9

10

11

12

13

14A

14B

15

16

17

18

19A

19B

20

21

22

23

24

25

26

27

28

Shot 3. Closer view. A farmhand, on Danaher's left, speaks to him: "*I think you . . . your in-laws are coming to visit you, Squire Danaher* "

Shot 4. Reverse shot. Workers and a haystack; a crowd approaches from the far right hand on a background of trees. Sean and Mary Kate move to the center left.

Shot 5. Reverse shot. Danaher moves from right to left, holding a pitchfork.

Shot 6. Reverse shot. Sean and Mary Kate walk up forward toward left and then to center.

Shot 7. Danaher's rear view on right. Sean and Mary Kate are seen going forward, but still more remote than in 6.

Shot 8. Closer shot of Sean and Mary Kate (low angle): Sean occupies foreground on right; Mary Kate slightly behind on left. Sean to Danaher: "*Danaher, you owe me three hundred and fifty pounds. Let's have 'em.*"

Shot 9. Reverse shot. Mary Kate and Sean on left. Danaher at center right, with a machine and a worker in the right background. Danaher looks to his right where noises of marching men can be heard.

Shot 10. Two men (followed by others) enter on right, one of them an IRA man.

Shot 11. Upper body shot of Danaher looking to the right: "*So the IRA is in this too, huh!*"

Shot 12. Same shot as 10. The IRA man, showing something invisible in the background with his right hand: "*If it was, Red Will Danaher, not a scorched stone of your fine house would be standing!*" The other man (Flynn): "*A beautiful sentiment!*" Both men have especially heavy Irish accents.

Shot 13. Same shot as 11. Danaher looks back to left, sort of smiling: "*I'll pay it . . . never!*"

Shot 14. Same shot as 8. Sean: "*That breaks all bargains.*" Mary Kate looks up at him indignant. Sean throws Mary Kate forward to the right in a sweeping movement across the screen. Exit falling on right.

Shot 15. Same shot as 9. Sean on left, rear view. Mary kate falls and rolls to Danaher's feet at center. Sean: "*You can take your sister back. It's your custom, not mine. No fortune, no marriage. We call it quits.*" Mary Kate begins to get to her feet.

Shot 16. Closer shot of Danaher and Mary Kate rising (the black smoke-stack of the machine just behind and between them. Sean out of the field). Shot similar to 11 and 13, but with Mary Kate looking to left: *"You do this to me, your own wife . . . "*

Shot 17. Same shot as 15 and 9, with Mary Kate rising; she says: *" . . . after . . . after . . . "* Voice of Sean, with his back to the viewer: *"It's done."*

Shot 18. Reverse shot. Two foregrounded characters (railway workers) and another behind them, bent forward and looking to right (high angle shot), laughing. Camera pans slightly to right, showing more onlookers laughing. The laughter follows into frame 19.

Shot 19. Same shot as 9, but Mary Kate on right before the machine, and farmhand between Sean and Danaher, looking at the latter who takes money out of his wallet. Danaher to Sean: *"Here is your dirty money, take it. Count it, you sponge!"* as he throws the money (a wad of notes) at Sean's feet. Sean bends to pick it up. Camera moves slightly to right to follow Sean who walks toward Mary Kate. Danaher, as he passes before Sean: *"If I ever see that face of yours again, I'll push that through it"* (shaking his fist). Mary Kate runs toward the boiler to open its door.

Shot 20. Close-up of machine. Sean's rear view moving to right. Mary Kate enters the field, opens door of boiler. After a couple of seconds, Sean throws the money into the fire. Mary Kate closes the door, faces Sean to the right. Slight camera move to right. Sean grabs Mary Kate by left arm, places her to his left (right of field), facing the spectators. He looks at Danaher. Mary Kate, in profile, looks at Sean.

Shot 21. More distant shot, similar to 9, 15, and 19, but with machine at center. Danaher on left. Sean and Mary Kate walk toward spectators. Danaher tries to strike Sean as he passes by. Sean avoids blow as someone shouts: *"Charge him!"* Sean strikes Danaher in the stomach. Danaher falls on left.

Shot 22. Closer shot of Mary Kate and Sean (on left of field, i.e., to her right). Mary Kate turns to Sean: *"I'll be going on home now, I'll have the supper ready for you."* She turns around smiling, passes in front of Sean and leaves field by left. Sean remains alone in field, looking puzzled.

Shot 23. Reverse shot similar to 6, but with Sean's rear view on far right foreground. Mary Kate, seen from behind, goes down toward the crowd and enters it.

Shot 24. Reverse shot, as at end of 22. Sean looks on.

Shot 25. Reverse shot, as at end of 23. Mary Kate now in the distance. The onlookers are bent forward in expectation; one railway man starts forward hesitantly.

Shot 26. Reverse shot. Danaher getting to his feet, spitting in his hand, on center left. He strikes Sean (who turns his back, hardly visible on the far right).

Shot 27. Sean falling. Camera moves right and to lower angle to follow Sean rolling down the slope, and stops with him. He gets back to his feet, looking around. Crowd shouting: "*That way!* . . . "

Shot 28. Danaher on left (rear view). Head of Sean rising from ground on right, before a row of spectators. Sean, on his feet, puts his cap back, goes toward Danaher, strikes him after saying: "*You asked for it.*"

Note that the picture track of this film is supported by an "expressive" musical sound track which is not even always interrupted by dialogue (e.g., shot 3), but the scene itself takes place in absence of music (you can *hear* the silence) from shot 8 to shot 23. The scene is thus demarcated more narrowly, or twice framed, with a core development and "margins" (introduction and conclusion)

Some remarks on editing.

The average duration of frames in this sequence, seven seconds, with variations from about three to about fifteen seconds, is representative of the technique of visual enunciation in *The Quiet Man* in general, and different from that of many "modern" films. Movement in film picture, within a single shot, can be "diegetic" (something moves in the field), enunciative (the camera moves or changes focus), or a combination of the two. Camera movements are very limited in the film considered. There are only five, always to the right and of little amplitude, in the challenge scene: in shots 1, 18, 19, 20, 27; they work as adjustments of vision or continuity devices (where there could be two shots but excessive cutting would generate a counterproductive effect of fragmentation). The camera move in 18 is essentially an expansion, completed by the sound track, which prolongs the laughter of the onlookers into 19. The one in 20 is an adjustment that prepares a change of direction on the part of the characters, it is a hinge: the challenge between Mary Kate and Sean has been carried out or rather, consumed, and they can now proudly face the public (public opinion). The arc described in 27, like the slight move in 19, is an enunciative manifestation of interest: the camera follows the protagonist when he does something important or when something important is happening to him. But, when Mary Kate is thrown away by Sean, the discontinuity between reverse shots 14 and 15, compensated by a link in visual distribution (Mary Kate is on the right of the field in 15 as at the end of 14), is heavily overdetermined: (1) the depth of field is increased, so that Mary Kate seems to be thrown farther and with greater strength and violence; (2) she is now back with her brother and separated from Sean, as if the story could go full circle back to the initial situation ("We call it quits"); (3) the visual leap (reverse shot) signifies that the "ball" is now in Danaher's court, it is up to him to play; (4) alternate editing, reverse shots in particular, is extremely frequent in the whole film: a few words must be said about their organizing power and special value in the context.

At the beginning of the film, when Sean is on his way to Innisfree in an open cart driven by Flynn, the conversation between the two men joins them in the same frames, which is rather exceptional, but, as soon as Sean sees the familar landscape again, his panoramic function is marked by reverse shots; although the landscape cannot *see* Sean, it can speak to him in his dead mother's voice. This would seem to confirm a statement by Christian Metz, if we could take it in a very restricted sense:

> In film as in other media, description is a modality of discourse, not a substantial characteristic of the object of this discourse; the same object can be *described* or *narrated* [est *descriptible* ou *racontable*] according to the own logic of what is said of it.[44]

Sean's presence in the landscape would be narrated, not described, by the reverse shots, but in fact, this is not the "object" of the sequence. The object, always constructed through the position of enunciation, is narrative: it is Sean's sudden vision, discovery, and emotion in remembering, that is, events that happen at a particular moment and organize diegetic time around this moment. Moreover, there are two more generative moments in Sean's life; one of them is situated before the narrational beginning of the film, and the other very soon after the alluded moment of nostalgia in front of "White Morning." The first moment, which will be revealed only much later (contrary to the narrator's affirmation that he "begins at the beginning") is distant in space, not in time: it is the heavyweight championship in which Sean recently killed his opponent and subsequently decided to quit the ring; this flashback is also presented in alternate reverse shots, although the other man is dead. The other moment is the first appearance of Mary Kate as a shepherdess in the wood, edited in the same fashion: Sean, who is going to smoke a cigarette under the trees while Michaeleen and Father Peter Lonergan are talking (or observing him?), interrupts his gesture of throwing the match on the ground, he is transfixed by the sight of the maiden; she is equally stricken by the apparition of the good-looking, athletic wolf that she catches lurking among the trees.

Returning to his native island, Sean fulfills a romantic program of encounter(s) — "only an American could think of painting the door of his cottage emerald green," says someone. But this return itself is caused by an encounter of another sort, and Sean Thornton bears the same name as his grandfather, who was a convict in Australia (the ballad of Jack Dolan, the "wild colonial boy," is sung several times). Life is an encounter, you have to face it — not even the quiet man can dodge it in the end. This model, one of the two (with that of the quest) that rule the western, applies almost everywhere in the film. The alternate reverse shot has a symbolic and moral function as well as a narrative function. It is a dialogic structure, which places the Σ narrator *invisibly* in the middle, while an interactive, doubly transactive, narrative meaning is constructed by the receiver.

The other narratemes, transactive or not, that are enunciated by direct recording-reproduction within a fixed frame, such as Danaher striking Sean, Sean walking back home, and horses racing in the distance, are comparatively less important. They play the role of expositional elements leading to or explaining narrative situations, rather than that of transformations at the higher (more integrated, overarching) levels of narrative signification.

Provisional Conclusions

Although very brief clean-cut frames are reputed to be perceived as a continuum, especially when they are linked by factors other than thematic, which is generally verified in the classical film, with an unbroken sound track over several frames and correspondences of angle, orientation, and location of shapes on the screen from one frame to the next, it must be clear that their continuity should not be confused with the perceptual fusion that gives the impression of unbroken movement at a speed of twenty-four pictures per second. Movement of this type is perceived as a whole as in "real life" and does not bear narrative value by itself. Movement, or the figuration of movement, even when it is linear and one-directional, acquires narrative meaning when it is *broken*, dissociated, or decomposed. It must have a beginning and an ending, it must separate and unite discrete states between which transformations can be observed. Diegetic movements themselves as continua can play the role of signified states in their mutual, successive differences: "He ran faster before, he runs slower now: he has grown tired." Diegetic movement, in this frequent case, is the signifier of an equateme or a descripteme and, when it is decomposed, each of its parts has the same function. At the movies as everywhere else, the synthetic action of the "rational" receiver understands (conceptualizes and classifies) event and action *after* the same receiver has been confronted with the paradox of Zeno or analytic paradox, pertinent to verbal thought and human intelligence.

Danaher's fist would indeed never land on Sean Thornton's face if I did not consider the time it takes to travel through the air as divisible. The mental decomposition of movement (whether diegetic or enunciative) contrasts with its perceptual continuity whose function it is to signify the linear irreversible time vector, an internal paradigm that has been fully exploited by classical and modern filmmakers, but apparently not much theorized by the specialists. The typical punctuations of classical film (dissolves, changes in black or in white, shutters, and so on) were starters of analysis, not just markers of diegetic ruptures or narrational ellipses. For example, the change in black, about seven minutes before our scene, between Mary Kate and Sean's tender pose by the fireside, and Sean, in his dressing gown, coming out of the bedroom in the morning, should not be read simply as a narrational ellipsis manifesting and censoring the representation of a night of love; there are other changes in black in the film where a visual summary would have been "morally" possible, for instance, between Sean's installation at "White Morning" and a view of the cottage restored and repainted. It is not possible either to justify a change in black by screening time savings, when a five-mile walk can be positively figured in three or four frames of only a few seconds each. Interruptions of visualization such as these changes contain a major directive: you must break up the kinetic continuum; otherwise, nothing will change, nothing will happen (houses will not be built, maidens will not be deflowered, etc.). A lesson for many would-be reformist makers of history.

In contradistinction, modern films, even when they use other dividing devices, some of them very violent like the "chapters" and their titles in several works by Jean-Luc Godard, tend to lose narrativity with the length of the sequence frame and identical or virtually identical repetitions that overcharge and imbalance the input of narrative construction of meaning. The movie camera and the writing pen are very different instruments indeed, but, at the semiotic level at which narrative meaning arises, the analysis of the peculiarities related to one medium becomes illuminating for the comprehension of the other. Moreover, there is nothing in film that requires less training, less analytic power and judgment, than in the written verbal text. The force of the visual analogon, in the rather exceptional case of a contemporary realist film shot in your hometown, is a force of absenting that shakes your trust in your own memory; when the referent is unknown, "imaginary," not prememorized, the moving picture can only give it its own "colors of life." *You* put change and history into it: propaganda is the art of making us work to share somebody else's belief.

Chapter 10
What Tales Tell Us to Do and Think, and How
(Narrative and Didactic Constructions of Meaning)

I have hitherto described textual structures and the artistic communication system, among others, essentially as sets of material data and networks that constitute the preconditions for the formation of "primary" messages, that is, for the mental elaboration of relatively autonomous possible worlds. Such worlds could be considered mutually interchangeable in the eyes of an ideal, abstract "subject," since they were approached on the basis of their production rules, not from the viewpoint of their desirability. Similarly, a nation's industrial equipment and infrastructure can be described as able to produce heavy machinery and high tech means of transportation, without taking into account whether the aims of national growth are oriented toward liberation or imperialism, self-defense or international peace, and so on. So, we are now going to investigate *differences* between possible worlds on the plane of their respective values for their users, without forgetting that the patronage of these worlds must always be seen as the peculiar position of customers who also take part in the act of production.

The Didactic Construction of Meaning

In the modern Western world, we know that some worlds are held to exist independently from representation, especially verbal or artistic. They belong to the order of existential experience or to the realm of extraverbal being: they are the "real" worlds. Other worlds depend on having an image for their existence: they are "imaginary." Both types of worlds can be desirable or not for any determined, single or collective, subject whose identity in turn will be largely defined by a more or less coherent or contradictory set of desirable objects. Children and lovers are the same in this respect: their early conversations are always full of lists ("I like this, I don't like that").

It may seem paradoxical that the "real" is desirable, since its representation is deemed, by definition, unable to modify it. But the desirability of the "imaginary" is just as difficult to conceive, since its existence is in principle wholly given by its mental and sensitive image, its (re)presentation. The introduction of value into a system of possible worlds consists precisely in blurring and opening the borders between imaginary and real (or, in other cultures, between profane and sacred, intra- and extraethnic, etc.), which were initially posited as the preconditions of knowledge, action, and their multiple combinations (informed/uninformed action, experiential/secondhand knowledge, and so on). We can thus actually desire nothing else than the more or less selective abolition, deletion, or lowering of the barriers between categories of possible worlds, so that a metonymic movement is set forth and syntax successfully grafted onto the given paradigm. The act of communication that effects and/or mimics the destruction of borders—we call it fiction—provides both immediate satisfaction in the form of a release from the constraints of logical categories and binary oppositions, such as reality principle versus pleasure principle, in which time and mortality are inscribed with history and our own life story, and a model for future anticipated satisfactions in the form of a repetition of the return to supposedly primitive confusion: unity and at-oneness.

Persuasive or didactic communication consists in drafting obligatory paths between the two or more categories of possible worlds valid in the communication context (milieu) considered. Consequently, it presents certain items of these worlds as displaced or ill-placed; for example, according to a certain teaching, some supposedly real items are in fact imaginary (they will be labeled "vain illusions," "hallucinations of the senses"), whereas some reputedly imaginary items are "in fact" real, or even more real than the rest of the real (God's love for mankind will be called a "superior reality"). The mutual permeability of "real" and "imaginary" worlds is proved twice in the process, even when it cries out to be suppressed, according to some ideologies: it is attested once by the early displacement of items (disorder) and a second time by putting back in their respective places, "where they belong," unduly displaced or wrongly placed items. This is what any tale eventually tells, at the same time as it inevitably lays the foundations for an infinite number of other tales (many of them identical, that is, repeated).

Permeability between worlds, past and present or present and future, on the one hand, and formed according to different rules of admission, on the other hand, is the necessary basis of all narrative as well as the key to its repetitive-reproductive fate. But it must also be limited in order to make sense, that is, direction, which the pure assertion of infinite possibles would prevent from forming.

On the plane of narrative meaning, as we have seen, sense is made by temporal irreversibility, whereas the fusion of moments and durations in events manifests the permeability of temporal categories; we remember that cause and motive are the means of articulating these two opposite requirements. Similarly, on the plane of didactic meaning, the Discourse of law selects both the items that can be moved from one possible world to another, and the directions in which they can be moved. Successful passage from one world to another means necessity, moral and cognitive truth. Any didactic communication shifts items around from world to world as does any narrative communication, and time is always loaded with value. Consequently, all didactic communication should be narrative to some extent, and all narrative communication is inevitably didactic. The selection of mobile elements by the Discourse of law, whether tentative or final, can be derived from the study of transformations undergone by possible worlds considered as subsets of a changing textual world.

For example, in the following diagram, if textual world 2 (TW$_2$) is a final transform of TW$_1$ in a text T, we are dealing with the didactic construction of meaning of a typical, traditional Christian *Weltanschauung*. (Upper circles in the diagram are imaginary worlds, lower circles are real worlds.)

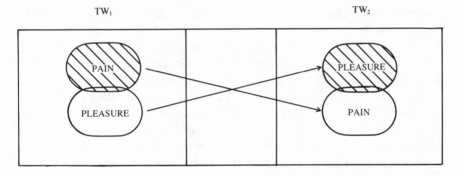

For an utterance to be construed as having didactic sense, two requirements must be met: its assertion must come under the scope of the modality of "necessity" (it must be unequivocally motivated); and the assertion made necessary in a particular context and situation must be transferable to at least one other context or situation without losing its necessity.

The construction of didactic meaning therefore presents two aspects: the construction of necessity in a limited contextual-situational field, and the construction of transportability (by broadening the contextual-situational field, by introducing new, changing, or otherwise replaced items into the field without loss of necessity). Hence the privilege of narrative communication as support of the didactic construction of meaning. But if all communication is didactic (referential and conative) to some extent, although it is not bound to be *clearly and overtly narrative*, we should examine the extent of the overlap and the processes and techniques of entwining between the two separate types of construction of meaning. Elementary philological investigation may be of some help before we examine didactic modes and means in more detail.

The Greek verb *didaskein* is roughly translated as "to teach," but rather than a simple concept, it is a fairly complex and unstable aggregate; the position of *genus didascalicum* in Melanchthon's treatise on preaching, for example, shows this clearly.[1] As for *docere*, it is variously translated by Latin dictionaries as "instruct," "inform," "show," "tell." The syntax of these and corresponding verbs in several modern European languages indicates that their semantic content relies on different visions of communication in its process and function. You inform someone, you teach something or someone, you show something to someone or someone something. In the semantics of "instruct," "educate," or "inform," *docere* and *ducere* become almost equivalent, since the object is the same: man, the addressee; in "show" and one of the constructions of "teach" and "tell," the addressee is not led, it is "things" that are led to him so that he learns to behave with them. On the other hand, "show" does not need the mediation of signs; it implies direct contact between signal and referent with no intervention of the addressee's intelligence, while "tell" points to the sign, underscores the presentational process. In the first case, if there was authority, it was understood as that of "things themselves," evidence; in the second case, it can only be the authority of the addresser or that inherent in speech, in discursive codes. It is interesting, then, that the verb shared by description and didactics is "show." Curiously, telling would be the only manner of *didaskein* compatible with the poetic function as defined by Jakobson. The verb "teach" denotes a not necessarily fruitful attempt, action, or endeavor, and "learn" implies success—failed or uncertain attempts coming under the heading of "study." In French, when *enseigner* (to teach) has a person for its direct object, it cannot be followed by an indirect object or another verb; it transforms the didactic relation into a purely personal one that does not require any kind of explicit content.

It results from all these turns of phrases that:

1. In spite of their association and frequent structural similarities, the didactic and narrative constructions of meaning operate at different levels, with discursive and sequential levels that are not necessarily identical, and in the framework of spatiotemporal parameters that can be at variance;

2. The didactic relationship can stress the economy of communication

(transmission of information and techniques) or positions of power
(a hierarchy of persons);
3. Consequently, the force of this relationship can consist essentially
    of transactions, or else of coercion;
4. The didactic relationship may aim primarily at producing a type of
    behavior, at inducing a praxis on the part of the addressee, or at
    modifying his consciousness and his conscience through new
    representations and interpretations, that is, cognitive contents.

Such diversity should not be discouraging for the study of didacticism, it only
reflects the universal enmeshing of symbolic and material values with communication. It also should not tempt us to limit our inquiry to an appreciation of actions
potentially incited by the didactically construed text. The right response to an
action-oriented text is not action—or inaction, for that matter. In most cases, the
line of action concretely advocated is impossible to take, irrelevant, or inadequate
to the receiver's situation: we cannot kill the emperor or propagate a dead faith,
even when endeavors of this kind are the avowed purpose of the text, interpreted
by us as the author's motivations at the moment of production. Nevertheless, explicitly conative texts of the past or those belonging to distant cultures are still
legible and literarily efficient in ways that beg to be determined: behavioral constraints on the reader are always in the first place rules of reading in order to produce value; impossible or rejected patterns of action response to texts remain active metaphors or metonyms of other actions that are mainly ways of
understanding (the text, the world, and oneself). The diversity of didacticism is
in fact not so much that of its aims and effects, since it does nothing but activate
the conative function of language, as that of its resources and processes.

Whether they are seen from the angle of text production or from that of reception
makes little difference to a survey of the main types of didactic strategies:

The sender may apply:	persuasion	exemplarity	authority
The receiver may enter into:	logical play	imitation	submission
The corresponding modes are:	deliberative	demonstrative	authoritarian

In any case, there is no didacticism without collaboration. I propose to study
the ways in which the terms of this collaboration are settled, how it is made profitable by and for the collaborators and to what extent a refusal to collaborate on
the part of either party—but especially at the receiving end—runs the risk of stall-
ing the production of meaning at levels other than the didactic, and may thus im-
poverish or even cancel the act of communication altogether.

1. The *deliberative* mode is based on reasoning, of which different kinds can
be distinguished, depending on the degree of certainty, probability or refutability

of the premises, and the degree of logical mechanicity of the sequences of propositions. We should note that:

- Persuasion is useful to didacticism in its two steps: logical (or otherwise) foundation of the necessity of a proposition, and foundation of its transportability through the generality or generalization of its truth-value; it is concerned both with evidence and relevance;
- Allegory is one of the most convenient techniques of the deliberative mode in narrative, since its argumentative structure made of successive transformations on a single oriented axis closely resembles narrative syntax;
- This mode can nevertheless use other techniques, such as true syllogisms, which have framing structures hardly compatible with certain narrative structures (those of so-called linear narratives, for example). Persuasion can conflict with narrativity as the main motor of message production; in order not to disrupt narrative functioning excessively, it will often have to locate itself within tabular zones of discourse and alternate with narrative zones proper.

2. *Authoritarian* didacticism is the type found in the Ten Commandments, constitutions, codes of law, military instructions, confessions of faith, and so on. In contrast to the deliberative and demonstrative didactic modes that find support in the referential, poetic, and metalingual functions of language, the authoritarian mode lays the conative function bare. Even when it does not make use of injunctemes in surface structures, it should allow us to derive injunctemes rapidly and efficiently from these other structures.

Neo-Latin languages, Spanish in particular, make the verb in the imperative mood agree in number and person, not with the subject of enunciation, but with the addressee; English shows a similar feature with the turn of phrase "Let + pronoun + infinitive." The subject of enunciation remains in hiding and, more important, the semantic content of the injunction is immediately given in charge to the addressee, as if the injunctive utterance were a preemptive presentation, as already accomplished, of the stance or action to be carried out. Many structures can perform this trick, providing they efficiently prepare (predict and induce) for the role change of the addressee who becomes an addresser through his acceptance of a place of subject in the sentence, always in principle more comfortable to occupy than that of passive object: strangely enough, we obey because we are not masochists.

Besides the imperative mood, the future tense, and the many-faced expression of the modality of duty, another favorite form of authoritarian didacticism uses dialogic enunciation (see the third section). Nevertheless, the articulation between surface structure or quasi-superficial injunctemes and often barely related narratemes may remain problematic in the framework of the tale and require an increased presentational complexity, with such devices as embedded segments, secondary narrators, epigraphs, quotations, allusions, and the vast play of an intertextual network. To tell, now, is no longer to do (oneself), but someone else to do and no one at all, or a very particular, estranged self, tell.

3. *Exemplarity* (the *demonstrative* mode) was particularly well analyzed by Jolles in his study of simple forms like the legends of the *Acta Sanctorum*.[2] According to this theorist, there must exist a mental predisposition to imitation in the actors of the communication situation. The community or institution (e.g., the Church) that rules and shapes individual lives then recognizes in them the "representation in action," qualitatively and quantitatively unique, of a moral concept (e.g., virtue) warranted by human witnesses and the divine evidence of miracle, which is at the same time the supreme manifestation of the concept. The simple form is born by arranging "verbal gestures"—strikingly similar to modern-day speech acts—"every time a mental process leads the diversity and multiplicity of being and events to crystallize into a certain figure." But the simple form must be actualized in a particular narrative that provides evidence of its necessity and extends its scope ("we can say that the legend contains virtually that which exists in life actually").

Imitation and exemplarity, which is its *virtus*, its propelling force, and its counterpart at any moment considered, appear together in a hall of mirrors, in a scene of infinite duplication. The life of the reader imitates the saint's *Life*, in the same way as the *Life* (actualized simple form) imitates the legend (virtual simple form), and the saint's life (material for the aforementioned actualization) imitated other *Lives* (beyond all of them, the Scriptures seen as our Lord God's *Life*), and so on. In demonstrative didacticism, repetition and narrativity are closely associated: together they must invent compromise forms that offset their ultimate incompatibility. At the receiver's end of this didactic mode, two types of response must also be reconciled: the production of meaning and the production of signals or, if one prefers, the cognitive and pragmatic responses. The legend is originally that which must be read before it is enacted: one might say that it is with these same two potentially conflictive responses to the (re)presentation of one's own history that psychoanalysis constantly comes to grips with.

Demonstrative didacticism is similar to the deliberative strategy insofar as both ask the addressee to try on or try out something; but this something is not the same. In the first instance, it is a mental concatenation with a broad axiomatic value, whose application, if it proves viable, will confirm the rule by and through a concrete case. In the second instance, the *narrative* of a life or one or more episodes of it, becomes the origin, the founding case of a possible general rule once it has been successfully reproduced, that is, embodied in one or more new lives that can be told in almost the same terms, as variations on the exemplary one. In deliberative didacticism the addressee is placed in the scope or under the umbrella of the rule; in exemplary didacticism, he himself becomes a necessary part of the construction of the rule, a *piece of evidence*: imitation itself is a proof of the validity of the *imitandum*.

Soft Didacticism; or, the Deliberation of Desire

I insist that all verbal communication is at least potentially didactic and that narrative has a particular vocation to didacticism, because it maintains an active relationship to time: the figuration of event implies the intersection of experience and project in occurrence. However, it would be all too easy to make this point on the sole basis of *romans à thèse*, folk tales, and other self-confessedly "authoritarian fictions" (in the sense defined by Susan R. Suleiman). This is why I shall examine some much less suspicious literature in this respect. Two short stories from the collection *Mondo*, by J. M. Le Clézio, have been chosen for this purpose. "Lullaby" and "Celui qui n'avait jamais vu la mer," different in this from other stories in the same volume (e.g., "Peuple du ciel" or "Les bergers"), have in common that they are narratively open at both ends. They neither present a biography or a neatly concluded adventure that would be automatically interpreted as compressing a life story, nor do they visibly fill narrative gaps shown early in the text: they rather build more gaps as they go, and broaden the early ones.

"Lullaby" is the story of a teenager, living with her mother in a French Mediterranean town, who decides quite undramatically, one day in October, not to go to school again. She walks along the seashore where she finds an abandoned villa, swims in a small bay, and meets a few people. There is a young boy who damaged his eyesight by looking at an eclipse; there is also a threatening man from whom Lullaby escapes as from a potential rapist, but he does not even touch her. After a number of days, she eventually returns to school where she is readmitted after a difficult confrontation with the headmistress, convinced that the girl has a boyfriend, and she is kindly welcomed by Mr. Filippi, the physics teacher.

Lullaby, then, is a young person who stands to some extent in opposition to the law (time tables, social order represented by an education geared for a career, work, productivity), but she used to be a "good element" at school and will be scolded, but not punished or rewarded, when she returns there: she is trusted to behave normally again. Her motives for playing truant are not stated any more clearly than those she may have to resume her course of study:

> Lullaby regarda tout cela [le soleil, des pigeons sur le trottoir, la mer, un bateau] et elle se sentit soulagée d'avoir décidé de ne plus aller à l'école. (p. 81)
>
> En marchant, Lullaby regardait la mer et le ciel bleus, la voile blanche, et les rochers du cap, et elle était bien contente d'avoir décidé de ne

plus aller à l'école. Tout était si beau que c'était comme si l'école n'avait
jamais existé. (p. 85)
Ça ne pouvait pas durer toujours, Lullaby le savait bien. D'abord il y
avait tous ces gens, à l'école et dans la rue. Ils racontaient des choses,
ils parlaient trop. (p. 110)

Lullaby's fascination with the sea would be her real reason to drop out, and public
opinion or her image in the eyes of indifferent people (the "qu'en-dira-ton?") that
which pushes her to settle down again in the routine. In a letter she does not send
to her father, she explains that she misbehaves (a little) because she could no
longer stand "feeling imprisoned." And to Mr. Filippi she can only say that she
has questions to ask him about light and the sea—but she has forgotten the questions. Even this attitude, interpreted as a sort of aimlessness by the headmistress
(who loses her temper when Lullaby denies that she has a boyfriend), is not sanc-
tioned by others or interpreted as a form of emptiness by the character herself;
she never seems to be bored or anguished by or indifferent à la Meursault to all
that surrounds her. The only precept implicitly affirmed by Lullaby is a romantic
"Burn what you love," not "what you have loved," and it is affirmed in a gentle,
lighthearted manner that greatly reduces the provocative power of the paradox.

A girl of exquisite sensitivity, nicknamed Ariel by her father, with a sentimental penchant for "ΧΑΡΙΣΜΑ," the "most beautiful word in the world," Lullaby
is remarkably cold-blooded about the events that have shaken her family—her
parents' presumed separation, her mother's (presumably mental) illness—and it
is perhaps what makes her exquisite, although the homage paid her on the streets
by motorists blowing their horns also evokes other, more tangible qualities. But,
if we grow wiser as a result of the story, we definitely do not do it by following
Lullaby as an example or a counterexample: her cautious serenity is not directly
imitable in actual social circumstances, mediated as it is, for most readers, by age
and/or sexual difference that transforms Lullaby into an object of desire rather
than of "identification." I think we should turn for an explanation to a much more
immediate, much less conscious level of communication than that of character
habilitation and explicit mimesis.

First of all, it is essential to pay attention to the text's surface syntax, in which
the paratactic mode (mainly juxtaposition) is far dominant over hypotactic expression. Two examples:

Il faisait bien chaud. La jeune fille chercha un endroit où elle pourrait
se baigner. Elle trouva un peu plus loin une minuscule crique où il y
avait un embarcadère en ruine. Lullaby descendit jusqu'au bord de l'eau
et elle enleva ses habits. (p. 90)
Elle avait envie de faire du feu. Elle chercha dans les rochers un endroit où le vent ne soufflerait pas trop fort. Un peu plus loin, elle
trouva la petite crique avec l'embarcadère en ruine, et c'est là qu'elle

s'installa. . . . [Les feuilles de papier] s'allumaient d'un seul coup
parce qu'elles étaient très sèches et minces et elles se consumaient
vite. . . . Lullaby pensait que son père aurait bien aimé être là pour
voir brûler ses lettres, parce qu'il n'écrivait pas des mots pour que ça
reste. (p. 102)

In these two passages, logical implication combines with covision to create a
mood of naturalness and harmony or at-oneness of narrator with character and
of the character's mind with her body, an alliance of her whole being with "Nature," both as natural and as humanized. The qualitative rather than quantitative
adverb "bien" means that the *pleasant* weather is known to us through the girl's
sensations, and her search for a place to swim follows immediately from this subjective state of things; it does not need any reasoning. (Compare with: "Since it
was very hot, the girl looked for . . . ," where the formal law of logic and an
external voice would compete with the "spontaneous" order of the presented
world for the construction of narrative meaning.) The unreal moods, "elle pourrait se baigner" in the first quotation, and "où le vent ne soufflerait" in the second,
are clear indexes of "subjectivity," implied by simultaneity in enunciation. With
the simple succession of "elle chercha → elle trouva," they contribute to place
all the sequence under the sign of effortlessness or, in other words, the obvious
necessity of events in the presented world.

The two occurrences of expressed causality ("parce que") in the second quotation should be analyzed in this light; although each of them is almost meaningless
individually, their parallelism makes a lot of sense and a very strong case for a
particular function of verbal communication. We all know that dry paper is easy
to kindle, but nobody is ready to believe that a father should be happy to see his
daughter burn his letters, especially when they are as emotional and literary as
Paul Ferlande's correspondence with Lullaby seems to be. The close association
of the two "parce que" contaminates a somewhat paradoxical reflection with the
obviousness of a natural, physical phenomenon, and vice versa. Physical causality, in terms of apparent destruction, not only justifies Lullaby's behavior, it
duplicates the affirmation of the value of all things ephemeral and becomes
retrospectively a metaphor of the exciting transitiveness of literary communication itself. Such an effect is made possible by the general parsimony of hypotactic
structures, particularly of causal and consecutive clauses. Their scarcity gives
prominence to an occasional and deviant usage of the same: we are led to accept,
not reject, a world in which evident necessity is the provider of "instants parfaits."
These exceptional moments reinterpret causality instead of dissolving it under the
disintegrating grip of anarchy or entropy.

At the diegetic level, Lullaby's firm and final rejection of the headmistress's
interpretation of her fugue coincides with this teaching: our autonomy begins just
beyond the understanding of those who abide by standard narrative codes; it coin-

cides with the bizarre, almost silent complicity of others, such as Mr. Filippi or Paul Ferlande, "the remote one," who are more interested in the formulas of significance than in the "reality" of social mechanisms. Lullaby does not put us to sleep, she helps us to maintain a precarious, secretly armed peace with "that-which-is." "Material extasis," then, is not conclusive, since it is as impermanent as narrative communication, but its very impermanence has permanent value; a temporary shelter for dissent, it is an unassailable fortress, because it vanishes in the hands of those who try to reduce it to a strategic invention.

"Celui qui n'avait jamais vu la mer" can now be read in a very similar fashion, although it goes even further than "Lullaby" in the dissociation of the character's action from the moral pattern.

The narrator in this short story acts as the single voice of a collective entity involved in the diegesis: he is the self-appointed spokesman of a group of students in a boarding school. In contrast to the narrator in "Lullaby," who floats or hovers about the protagonist's presence and consciousness, he is granted the security of the eyewitness in the beginning, but we realize very soon that this is the most difficult position for him, since he is given virtually nothing to "see": the single certain event in the story is a disappearance; the object of description he has to grapple with is the permanent absence of the protagonist. The title, which contains a narrative situation, does not come to be completed with the expected denouement: "The boy who had never seen the sea [at time T_1] has now seen it [at time T_2]." In fact, the only counterpart to the lack expressed in the title is another lack: "The boy left." The absence of the boy for his companions replaces the absence of the sea for the boy. The symmetry of these two factors is stressed by the fact that the sea desired by the boy was an impossibility; it was not touristic, accessible to all holiday makers, but ideal and absolute, the referent of the story of Sindbad, back in time and behind or beyond verbal representation, and the departure of the boy is "true, that is, without return" (p. 169). Nevertheless, this very symmetry, which prorogues the initial problem by transporting it to another plane, to another subject ("those who will never see the boy again"), calls for a more satisfactory solution in intellectual, if not affective, terms.

The first lines of the text show the way, thanks to a seemingly inadvertent ambiguity, at the moment of establishing the object of want for the protagonist: it will be "identity," coincidence with another textual subject:

> Il s'appelait Daniel, mais il aurait aimé s'appeler Sindbad, parce qu'il avait lu *ses* aventures dans un gros livre relié en rouge qu'il portait toujours avec lui, en classe et dans le dortoir. (p. 167)

Causality, deficient if the adventures read in the fat book are only Sindbad's, becomes fully efficient if they are also, or mainly, Daniel's own adventures. Like so many knights, his initial state is then characterized by the loss of a name that will have to be regained; and it will be the narrator's task to fill somehow the gap between Sindbad's sea and Daniel's desire, until the former can give his name to the latter:

> Ils s'étaient tellement agités en tous sens pour retrouver la trace de *Daniel Sindbad*, les professeurs, les surveillants, les policiers, et voilà qu'un jour, à partir d'une certaine date, ils ont fait comme si Daniel n'avait jamais existé. (p. 187)

"Celui qui n'avait jamais vu la mer" has something of a story à la Dupin in which Daniel's disappearance is the enigma. The adults, policemen, and others try to find traces and causes that would conform with the inventory of social aberrations, until they resorb the unexplainable, the unacceptable into statistical undifferentiation ("thousands of people disappear every year"); the narrator(s), Daniel's companions, develop the inner logic of signs until "they" receive complete satisfaction in the form of a story of imagination rewarded. By assuming this suppletive role in Daniel's absence, the narrator(s) transform this absence into a presence Daniel never enjoyed when he was physically there, a cosmic presence associated with all the variations of weather, no longer dependent on age, health, and human circumstances—no need to call it "myth," though. But the narrator(s) also acquire by the same token the qualities of ignorance and evocative illusion that were those of Daniel in the beginning:

> "Tu crois qu'il est là-bas?"
> Personne ne savait au juste ce que c'était là-bas, mais c'était comme si on voyait cet endroit, la mer immense, le ciel, les nuages, les récifs sauvages et les vagues, les grands oiseaux blancs qui planent dans le vent. (p. 188)

Banal naming, as exemplified by the typical adventure book, had prompted Daniel's disappearance in search of a referent, the narrator believed; now, by partaking *in mente* of his supposed quest, the narrator has empowered naming with a permanent capacity of actualization that words had always lacked, even for Daniel. The narrator knows, and we know with him/them, that there is no other sea than that which one never reaches but for whose sake one can depart from one's place of imagination. Daniel's companions, who perpetuate his memory, save him with their own means, as he has saved them from their shared dream of individual experience and palpable possession of the thing itself. The short story does not teach resignation, it teaches an exaltation altogether different from what we expected: the exaltation of the collective reader *qua* storyteller in response to the hero *qua* argonaut, robber of the "real" adventure. Even twelve-year-old schoolboys understand that the sea is God to Daniel when (in the narrator's imagination) he urges it to cover and dominate the whole world. We should also realize the deeper, more obscure lesson of Le Clézio's short story: God cannot be but somebody else's sea of desire.

It is clear that the two stories, although they are neither authoritarian nor exemplary, displaying no overt ideology or pattern of behavior, are nonetheless didactic: theirs is a rhetoric of persuasion or deliberative rhetoric, which guides our reasoning through precise channels drawn out at all the levels of the construction of narrative meaning, but with special emphasis on microstructures, phrases, sentences, and sequences, less invested by other didactic modes.

Some of these characteristics, along with a much more blatant effort to involve the reader sentimentally, would also be found in Saint-Exupéry's *Little Prince*, which makes extensive use of dialogic enunciation, but I think the actually profound difference between the respective didactic strategies will appear more clearly after we have described a model of the authoritarian genre.

Authority and the Play of Exchange

Differences in overt ideological and programmatic content between each of the two "Communist credos" by Engels, and with *The Communist Manifesto*, have been noted by the editor Dirk J. Struik[3] in terms of the growing influence of Marx and Engels in the Communist League and the progressive clarification of concrete revolutionary goals versus vague ideals of justice and brotherhood; but little seems to have been said by commentators regarding the "form" of these texts and its bearing on the efficiency of propaganda.

The "Draft of the Communist Confession of Faith" written by Engels in June 1847 (but discovered only in 1968) has twenty-two questions and answers over six pages, while the much expanded "Principles of Communism" consists of twenty-five questions and answers over some twenty pages; this gives the latter a "discursive" air that the former was lacking. Moreover, the pragmatic relation between questions and answers changes markedly both within each text and from one to the other. I must quote somewhat at length in order to analyze these relations and make them perceptible:

I. Draft
Question 1: *Are you a communist?*
Answer: Yes.
Question 2: *What is the aim of the communists?*
— To organize society in such a way that each of its members can develop . . .
Question 3: *How do you plan to achieve this goal?*
— By abolishing private property, replacing it by the community of goods.
Question 4: *On what do you base your community of goods?*
— . . . Secondly, on the fact that in the consciousness or feeling of every human being there exist certain tenets as indisputable principles,

tenets which, being the result of the whole historic development, are not in need of proof.

Question 5: *Name some of these tenets.*[4]

In the "Draft," the answering voice is supposed to say yes to question 1, that is, to acquiesce in advance to a program of behavior contained in the word "communist," a word that will be explained and displayed only through answers given to further questions. More generally, role B (of the second speaker) consists in providing answers expected and already known (owned and believed) by the asking voice (role A); it consists in *repeating* utterances that "happen" to coincide exactly with the answers discovered by the reader for the first time. A wants not information but confirmation; it only pretends to interrogate when it actually demands to recite; it does not ask (with direct object), ask for, or ask about, it asks to. B, consequently, only pretends to motivate its decisions; it provides information not to the asking voice but to the reader—if the dialogue is a show, a *mise en scène*—or then the reader's role is supposed to coincide with that of the asking voice; but, at the same time, it is clear that the reader will eventually have to share not the "curiosity" of the asker but the assurance of the answers.

In this form of the profession of faith, the initial questions have no origin, or else they have a circular origin, or even a hidden origin that will be progressively identified with historical necessity, a sacred narrative. Hence questions 8 and 9 ("Proletarians, then, have not always existed?" and "How did the proletariat originate?"), which give rise to a first, fairly long narrative development. Although some of the questions (7: "What is the proletariat?" 10, 11, and 12) seem to be definitional or occurrential (descriptive); they are all placed within a narrative framework set as early as question 2 ("What is the aim . . . ?"). The present itself is a narrative situation, a temporary state of affairs bound to change and which we must help change: we can certainly do so, because things have not always been the way they are now; the present is the result of past changes that can teach us how to change it in turn.

Thus questions 14 to 22 are again future oriented, after a transitional question, 13: "*You therefore do not believe that the community of goods was possible at all times?*" in which past and present are differentiated by the amount of future, so to speak, that they contain. From the point of view of narrative and argumentative sequence, the whole "Draft," which moves from conclusions to prior motives and then on to decisions and predictions, from the present to the future to the present to the past and back to the present and the future, appears to be rather awkward, notwithstanding the tenuous line of continuity provided by purport. It was deeply modified by Engels, to become the "Principles" of October 1847:

II. Principles
Question 1: *What is communism?*

Answer: Communism is the doctrine of the prerequisites of the emancipation of the proletariat.
Question 2: *What is the proletariat?*
Answer: The proletariat is . . . The proletariat, or class of proletarians, is, in a word, the working class of the 19th century.
Question 3: *Proletarians, then, have not always existed?*
Question 4: *How did the proletariat originate?*
Question 11: *What were the first results of the industrial revolution and the division of society into bourgeois and proletarian?*
Answer: Thirdly, the proletariat has grown everywhere in step with the bourgeoisie.
Question 18: *What will be the course of the revolution?*[5]

We note an almost complete reversal of roles in question-and-answer 1. The asking voice could now well be that of someone who wants to know (more) about communism and who is not yet, by way of consequence, a member of the Communist League; the response is no longer one of mere repetition and acquiescence, but a treasure chest of information revealed step by step. The first two questions are definitional; they address themselves to concepts (communism, the proletariat) whose content is historically determined and leads naturally to a narrative of the past, even though we know as early as the first answer that a future is held in store. At the end of answer 2, a clever transition with narrative is prepared within definitional discourse, so that consecutive questions and answers will all have to fulfill the task of providing a straight path, both temporal and logical, between a desired future and the means and methods offered by a well-known past through a hated and little-known present. It is interesting to observe how the shift from a wider to a narrower range of discursive units seems to go with a less authoritarian approach to didactics in which the deliberative mode plays a major part and "communism" is presented as an object of inquiry and desire rather than as the consensual basis for a pseudodialogue in which there was no transfer of information between the speakers, the confusion of wills (and persons) begging the very question of the possibility of conversion and thus defeating the purpose of the text.

Engels, in fact, was not quite satisfied with the first credo and wrote to Marx on November 23:

> Think a little about the confession of faith. I believe that the best thing is to do away with the catechism form and give the thing the title: Communist *Manifesto*. We have to bring in a certain amount of history, and the present form does not lend itself to this very well. I take with me from Paris what I have written: it is a simple narrative.[6]

Although this was not a really accurate description of the "Principles," the trend was clear and narrative was to form the backbone of Marx's *Manifesto*:

The history of all hitherto existing society is the history of class struggles.[7]

The first sentence of the *Manifesto* substantivates all the dynamic predicates that the subsequent text will simply unravel to perform its magic trick, its revelation of the corresponding hypostasis or reification of human work, production, and suffering by all previous social forms into a transhistoric "nature of things." An impersonal narrator offers his version of the past to off-textual debate, with the emergence and rise to power of previously oppressed classes (the bourgeoisie) serving as an imitable and correctible model for the emancipation of the proletariat:

From the serfs of the Middle Ages sprang the chartered burghers of the earliest towns. From these burghers the first elements of the bourgeoisie developed. (p. 90)

In a frame of mind that I do not plan to discuss here, Saint-Exupéry, in his *Little Prince*, settled for a compromise formation rather distinct from Marx's wholesale narrativism in the *Manifesto*. Jurate Kaminskas, drawing on articles by Greimas and Paulo Fabbri, stresses that "to impart knowledge is also to part (or break up) enunciation."[8] Dialogue occupies a prominent place as a dominant embedded structure of enunciation within a framing first-person narrative: "When I was six, I once saw a magnificent picture . . . " → "And now, obviously, six years have elapsed already . . . I have never told this story yet . . . " Dialogue occurs between the narrator and the Little Prince and between the Little Prince and various creatures he meets in the course of his systematic exploration of planets and asteroids, but dialogue is also inscribed, from the beginning of the narrator's direct telling, as an unsatisfactory or deceptive model of human communication: it should be, we hope, reenacted in a different manner after undergoing some deep transformation.

The narrator, we remember, starts with a recollection of his earliest drawings and the reactions to them elicited from the grown-ups:

I showed my masterwork to the grown-ups and I asked them whether my drawing frightened them.
They answered me: "Why should we be afraid of a hat?"
My drawing did not represent a hat. It represented a boa in the process of digesting an elephant. (pp. 411–12)

One of the "representations," the hat, is clearly descriptive, the other is evidently narrative: grown-ups repress their fear of "what comes after," their knowledge that there is death. Dialogic initiative is then, for the narrator, synonymous with a failed plea for intuitive recognition: "So, I lived alone, without anyone I could truly talk with, until a mechanical failure I had in the Sahara six years ago" (p.

412). Meeting the Little Prince will modify so deeply the narrator's attitude that the last lines of the text are an urgent request to the reader, asking him to meditate on the site of the Little Prince's disappearance and *write* to the narrator if the boy reveals his identity by *not* answering the traveler's questions. Writing, not answering, asking questions instead, giving physical signs of emotion, are all ways of maintaining a more real, nonmechanical communication. Carrying mail, reading celestial and terrestrial signs, and delivering messages were central concerns in Saint-Exupéry's life and profession.

It is certainly true that actantial roles held by the Little Prince undergo numerous changes that make him a "pivotal" character, but we should also see that he is instrumental in constructing a power that the narrator originally lacked: the power to relate and make oneself understood. Delay or différance, in the form of interpretive and *narrative* suspense, is essential in this perspective. The Little Prince is a gift from God, fallen from the sky, for the lonely narrator fallen from the sky, but the latter waits six years (of Creation?) before he can share his treasured memory with the public. Six years elapse between the blessed encounter (a second birth) and the final revelation, leading us back to that age of six when the first drawings were drawn and misunderstood by adults, but, this time, with a clear hope that verbal explicitness will make for the obscurity of symbolic meaning. The narrator needed all these years to digest the Little Prince alive, like the boa needed six months to digest the elephant; he reverses roles or boasts to make them reversible, like the fox saying to the Little Prince: "Tame me."

Parallelism and repetition—which are also, by the way, typical structures of prayer and lyrical poetry—are not just endemic in the didactic dialogue, as in the last conversation with the fox:

> "Farewell," said the fox. "I'll tell you my secret. It is very simple: one can only see well with one's heart. The essential is invisible to the eyes."
> "The essential is invisible to the eyes," repeated the Little Prince, in order to remember. (p. 474)

(They had both read Gide's *La Symphonie pastorale* and the Gospels.) Symmetry in succession suffuses narrative structures too. The character most respected by the Little Prince in the course of his interplanetary wanderings is the streetlamp lighter who faithfully repeats the same gestures dictated by the "rules" in spite of the ever-faster rotation of his planet. Even the asides of the Little Prince about unpleasant characters like the businessman are sweeping generalizations that reproduce the narrator's early opinions and will be repeated again by him: "Grownups are really queer people." The earth, the seventh planet visited, is almost as deserted as the other six: it is apparently inhabited by a single human being—the narrator. Dialogue, thus, is the model for a cyclical, ever-recurrent binary relationship that can only evolve from lack of meaning to loss of presence. For Saint-

Exupéry, narrative seems to be an inevitable datum, and the narrative framework fulfills a dual function: (1) it gives value to an object, the Little Prince, the ideal-identical other through whom the narrator valorizes himself and builds up his authority at the expense of our patience motivated by desire, and (2) it is deteriorated or even destroyed in the process as discourse of *change*, thus promoting an antihistoric, archetypal-story-like notion of history.

We now realize how closely the structural figuration of the modes of transmission of knowledge and belief come to iconicize and reflect the very concepts of history on which they are based and which they seek to put forward, either overtly or insidiously. Whether this vision of history is dialectic as in Marx and Engels, cyclical and self-canceling as in Saint-Exupéry, or that of a single, continuous teleologically oriented actualization of the Scriptures as in Fénelon, it becomes clear that didacticism, even in its authoritarian mode, must somehow be reconciled with narrative, with which it has deep-seated affinities. Some of them may be accounted for by the "violence of narrative" as has been studied by Ross Chambers,[9] but I wonder whether the sacrificial mask is anything more than the tip of the iceberg of the law of value, the symbolic return of time, the motor of value without which the instant would be worthless, and whether Time itself is any more than the godly name we give to our social being. Authority always originates in history—those teachings of the past whose knowledge and interpretation give us a superior right to predict and inflect the future; the basic, indestructible authority of an author resides in his being the (immediate) past of his work, as his voice and intentions are projected by the receiver in order to justify the labor of construction of meaning and make meaning and value possible. The authority thus confirmed is also transferred to the receiver as soon as he repeats the story in order to compensate for the loss of status incurred by submitting to the authority of the storyteller he has had to acknowledge in exchange for the various satisfactions the tale has brought to him.

The story-receiver eats his cake and then has it. All this was already perfectly understood by Fénelon and developed in chapter 6 of *De l'éducation des filles*, under the illuminating title "De l'usage des histoires pour les enfants":

> It must . . . be noted that, if the child has some ability of speech, he will naturally bring himself to tell to the persons he loves the stories that will have been most gratifying to him.
>
> You must try to make them prefer holy stories, not by saying that they are more beautiful, which they are not sure to believe, but by making them feel it without saying it. Let them notice how important, singular and wonderful they are. . . . You would have to be profoundly ignorant of the essentials of religion not to see that it is all historical: it is in a network of wonderful facts [*un tissu de faits merveilleux*] that we find its foundation, its perpetuity and everything that must make us practice it and believe in it. (p. 575)

In spite of a specialist's remark that the return of demonstrative rhetoric, under the influence of classical models, was largely responsible, with its "uncommonly positive . . . appreciation of God, man and the world," for "the emergence of the peculiarly Renaissance theme of the 'dignity of man,' "[10] we can still doubt whether narrative structure is a sufficient warranty of the autonomy of the reader, or whether it is not always ambiguous or even treacherous in this respect, because of its very "natural" subservience to the *principle* of history, where fathers are located, sought, and eventually found, when we enter it by retelling the stories they have bequeathed to us. The same trap of value is also operative, in a seemingly narrower context, with family romance.

Family Romance and Other Exemplary Narratives

My point of departure for the study of exemplary narratives will not be a traditional *exemplum* or the *roman à thèse*,[11] but a type of narrative that *apparently* originates in individual fantasy, not in a truth-telling institution or law-making social body, and which should be therefore deviant or even oppositional with regards to the *exemplum* as it is usually defined. I hope its confrontation with more orthodox types will cast fresh light on a generic notion that has often been overlooked or treated according to a fairly mechanical approach, as if exemplary narratives were bound to be simple, unequivocal, and based on the introjection of a crime-and-punishment model to produce their effects.

Family Romance According to Freud

Without trying to summarize or analyze in detail the well-known paper "Family Romances" (*Der Familienroman der Neurotiker*) published in 1909, I shall present a rapid survey of some elements of a theory of narrative, history and myth, which underlie it explicitly or implicitly.

In this paper, we find once again the constantly reaffirmed belief that human beings, facing time, should respond to it in a particular manner, neither by staying put, petrified, nor by a hasty and disorderly flight forward, but rather by well-tempered mobility, a rythmic march, a journey divided in regular legs. This applies to individual psychic development and to social evolution in general. Freud is a reformist. The deep parallel between ontogeny and phylogeny is never questioned, and it runs its red thread through all of his work. This permanent tenet has at least two fundamental consequences. In the first place, psychoanalytic theory itself adheres to a principle of reality viewed as the constraints of a moderate separation from that-which-is: an integratable, assimilable, recoupable breaking away. Second, if any vital event is caught between the two mirrors of past and future, there will be two kinds of repetition: one good and one bad.

The good repetition is *metonymic*: it involves, with the same verb content, an ergative transformation (a substitution of subjects) and a changed identity of the object. Generations follow each other and I become, instead of my father, the subject of *coitus*; thus I interpret the laws that society has given itself (me) and I (sort of) become my own legislator. Bad repetition, in contrast, is *literal*: I am, like my father, the subject of desire for my mother; I usurp the place of society to become its legislator; only the reference of the subject changes, not its semantic content; such a subject who does not progress but takes over an old name with an old personality, regresses. Moreover, the right repetition occurs on the plane of action, not representation, since the correct function of representation is precisely to deviate and distort, to be figural and amenable to intepretation, so that the real, in turn, may be difference, otherness, a desirable something else, not barely the given, that-which-is.

The generic type of the article "Family Romances" is mainly that of the essay, insofar as the critical, analytic, and argumentative strand frees it in part from the *post hoc propter hoc* fallacy and deconstructs the underlying narrative or narratives, but, being a metanarrative essay, it lets itself be carried away at times by a "logic of narrative" that builds up to a kind of synthetic ideal or arch-story. I shall recount it in my own language.

There exists a normal development or maturation of individuals, doubly related to social progress, since social progress relies on improved repetition of the parental model, and this maturation itself reflects the progress of mankind (our forebears reproduced and improved the parental model in their own time). The narrative outline results from the quest of a satisfactory compromise between two forces that pull in opposite directions and neither of which should completely offset the other, since they are both necessary: one is the *desire of identification* (to become [the same as] one's parents), which works for the sheer unaltered reproduction of the model; the other force is the *desire of difference*, which works for the production of a new subject and a new object for the model, without which the mere action of time would prevent the reproductive survival of the model. Opposition between these two forces generates in the subject a state of strain and turbulence in which a narrative phantasmic activity takes place to provide possible worlds serving an Ideal of the Self that would come into being without excessive sacrifice.

Depending on individuals and their histories, these possible worlds can play different roles in relation to the realm of action (which belongs to the possible world held as Real). At least three different cases can be described.

1. If the phantasmic tale becomes a magic substitute for the Discourse of the Real within empirical reality itself, we are dealing with neurosis or psychosis; the unconscious perverts the role of the conscious or usurps it and functions in its stead; this is the case of Norbert Hanold, of *Gradiva* fame.

2. If the phantasmic tale constitutes, *mutatis mutandis*, a model for a Real yet to come, or the key to a past Real, or both, it fulfills a utopian or cognitively novel function: this is what happens with creative personalities and also "all comparatively highly gifted people."[12]

3. If the phantasmic tale is just an automatic safety valve to provide relief from failure and disappointment in the Real, it actually valorizes reality in two ways: in that reality, contrastively, is at least here, solid and palpable, and in that reality already contains all the elements hyperbolized by the framing of the tale. As Freud says,

> The [phantasmic] parents are equipped with attributes that are derived entirely from recollections of the actual and humble ones; so that the child is not getting rid of his father but exalting him. (p. 240)

This would be the attitude of the conformist.

Four remarks need still be made in the perspective of an application of the Freudian model to public (vs. private) heterodidactic family romances.

First, the typical Freudian subject is here, as usual in psychoanalytic theory but not necessarily in literature, a boy, "hero and author," "far more inclined to feel hostile impulses towards his father."

Second, this boy *has* his father and mother and is brought up by them (he also tends to have brothers and sisters who figure as rivals in competition for the parents' affection); the phantasmic tale will then suppress, change, transform, substitute, or supplant "actual," known, living parents; it is an Oedipal crime.

Third, the Freudian subject's imagination is class determined: it is in essence a bourgeois fantasy in a society with limited opportunities for mobility and in which men monopolize sexual power (the right to experience orgasm) and economic power.

Fourth, phantasmic imagination, in spite of the occasional reassuring mention of "real recollections," draws heavily on bookish resources ("usually as a result of something they have read," or "in a way which reminds one of historical intrigues," writes Freud) to produce more genre-tied, literarylike narratives; consequently, it does not accept without modification the genres more closely derived from myth (the fairy tale, fantasy), it transforms them to meet some modern minimal requirements of "realism": "There is also the question of whether the phantasies are worked out with greater or lesser effort to obtain verisimilitude" (p. 239). In other words, the relative difficulty of inserting realemes—some of them structural, like "the sexual determinants of procreation"—is taken into account, so that real reference may become dominant at some key moments of the narrative and didactic constructions of meaning: Jensen insists on the equivalence of Norbert Hanold's cure with a modernization of the genre of the novella, which is particularly interesting in the context of the dubious aesthetic status of historical narratives at the turn of the century.

Orphanhood as a Didactic Device

In his brilliant study of *Great Expectations*, Peter Brooks points out that "as in so many nineteenth-century novels, the hero is an orphan, thus undetermined by any visible inheritance, apparently unauthored."[13] I shall discuss later in this section the interpretation offered. Nevertheless, I have shown elsewhere that this phenomenon is certainly not confined to the nineteenth century and its legacy.[14] In fact, regarding a major, largely transhistoric genre, the *novela rosa* or happy-ending love story (classified as "romance" by booksellers and publishers of the English-speaking world), it is possible to state the rule that the predestined protagonists (those who will be eventually united) must not have together more than two parents alive. Moreover, the death, disappearance, or removal of the parents from the scene by any other form of long-lasting absence (exile, confinement, etc.) must have taken place before the core (re)presented duration of plot, or happen at the latest at the beginning of this time span; and each of the protagonists should have in principle not more than one parent alive.

In *Daphnis and Chloe* already, the eponymic heroes were exposed infants, deprived of their biological parents (although all four of them are actually alive and will be reunited with their children in the end, just before their marriage). Whether there are foster parents, whether these are good or bad, whether biological or adoptive parents are eventually found, parents must be *missing*. This holds true through history from the Greek romance to Daphné du Maurier and beyond. Although the constraint is not as heavy, the rule remains extensively applied in other heterosexual love plots like the tragic romance (in which the lovers are separated but love lives on forever) and antiromance (in which the union of lovers degrades progressively). The picaresque hero is also an orphan or a foundling, as are, for all practical purposes, all the Robinsons of this world and many travelers.

The love story, the picaresque, and the Robinson story are vastly different models of narrative, only occasionally indebted to fairy tales and classical myth (which is often genealogical); all they have in common is to be unequivocally didactic. An approach of the functions of orphanhood in the light of the theory of the family romance should then help us to understand better how values and directives for action are transmitted by narrative communication. Orphanhood has two complementary faces: on the one hand, it is a *determination*, symmetrically inverse of the constraints to which the child brought up by his own legitimate parents is submitted; on the other hand, it accounts for initial narrative *indeterminacy* (or its pretense) by lifting the constraints of parental authority and protection.

Orphans are victims or even martyrs; they appeal to the warmhearted reader in more than one way. If they were abandoned by their true parents or others who had a duty to them, they are threatened by hunger, exhaustion, loneliness; they suffer and thus show clearly the satisfactions that a "normal" family should and would provide them. Orphans are often the victims of their legal custodians and relatives; easy prey for greedy and lascivious adults who covet their wealth and/or their bodies, they illustrate the difference between the unlimited generosity of the normal family, based on genetics and the reproductive instinct helped by religion, and the mere institution of family emptied of its instinctual motivation. If a surviving parent has remarried, the ill-treated child will make an implicit or explicit plea for sexual fidelity, even beyond death; but if he or she is loved and well cared for by foster parents, this new situation will again reinforce the "natural" family model by showing that it can be imitated, copied, or reproduced with a certain measure of success, but also by letting us feel some regret for the real thing, which would have been even better.

We should not conclude too rapidly, though, that the usual role of victim of the orphan signifies exclusively what Freud called the "overvaluation" of the parents by the child, of the family by the narrator, the author, and the consenting reader. Freud also writes that "the motive of revenge and retaliation, which was at the background at the earlier stage, is also to be found at the later one" and "[the] many-sidedness and . . . great range of applicability [of the family romance] enable it to meet every sort of requirement [dictated by] any other particular interests at work."[15] The suffering of children also bears an accusation against their *actual* parents, dead or alive, and bad parental figures are bound to be to some extent the work of displacement: they are safe substitutes that allow us to blame the real, supposedly good (but never good enough) parents through them. As determination of the child's fate, orphanhood proposes a structure whose correct interpretation will have to be conquered, notwithstanding any precautions that the text may take: this conquest is a builder of value, it is a vital part of didactic strategy.

Now, the tactics can vary from narrative to narrative. The figuration of communication plays a decisive part in shaping the reader's processes of valuation. If the orphan in the story is dominantly a narratee, if he *learns about* his story (like Oedipus) as much or more than he is responsible for it, the text structurally prepares our identification with him; it is our story too that—as present or, at any rate, future orphans, even if our parents are still alive—we must learn and plot in the form of general laws (of the world, of nature, and time: history and destiny) and moral codes that respond to them. The narrative with an orphan narratee is in fact an intermediate case between determination and indeterminacy as far as the function of orphanhood is concerned: the reception of facts in which we had little or no share of responsibility leaves us freer to interpret them.

If the orphan is the narrator and especially when there are several narratees, some or all of them being secondary or backgrounded characters, the subjective positions of reading are open. More or less sublimated social values and affects, such as "pity," can become salient; the adult reader may be invited to identify with different parental figures or substitutes: adoptive parents, tutors and governesses, protectors, sentimental partners of the orphan; he or she may even become a rival for the absent, regretted legitimate parent(s). Complexity increases again in the case of direct overt enunciation: the narrator, who is then one with the implied author, is in a position to control not only textual events but also the receiver's tempo of contact with the text, his attention, and, partly, his intellectual and emotional response. This affiliation of the audience can either make us reenact our need for parents together with the orphan's or detect the storyteller's vested interest in the ideological content of his tale and arouse our suspicion. (The explicitness of the *roman à thèse* has certainly contributed to its decline and exclusion from the literary canon, after the didactic epic, for similar reasons.)

But who could say that orphanhood is not a technique of liberation at the same time as it allows an easier appropriation of the character's significance by the implied author? The orphan goes where he pleases, he has adventures. Since there is nobody but himself to look after him, to look for him and take him back, he engages in a head-first fight (or collusion) with the world as-it-really-is, without the protective cushion of parental love and directives. Learning at his expense, by trial and error, he will perhaps learn faster and more profoundly than other young people. He is freed from the worn-out jaded world vision of his elders — as almost all major characters are freed from work during their textual existence. The abandoned child used to be the ambassador of humankind who maintained quasi-human relations with the nonhuman world (Romulus and Remus breast-fed by a she-wolf, Daphnis by a goat, Chloe by a ewe, Mowgli, Tarzan, and other "wild children"). He revealed the humanity (the divinity) of Nature in exchange for the release of nonhuman forces in him. A self-appointed Hermes or Iris, the child met with the gods, spirits, fairies, and other supernatural beings. But, in a different social milieu, liberated from the bonds and limits of decorum (*biensé-ance*), fearless because he has nothing to lose and is too weak to be attacked, he will take a dive into a sordid world that surrounds us but which we ignore for commodity's sake or do not dare to explore: abandoned and orphaned children can visit hell and come out of it alive, holding Truth by the hand (Hector Malot's Rémy and other heroes, David Copperfield and Oliver Twist, long after Lazarillo de Tormes). The peculiarity of the nineteenth-century (popular) novel will rather be to send adults as well (Rodolphe and Jean Valjean, for example) on these trips underground. The lonely child is a mutant or a monster, son of heaven and hell, of the forest and the city, of innocence and wisdom, whose real *Bildung* will be his reintegration into the human community founded on tradition and successive generations of fathers and mothers (omitting him, the child). As an obol to join the club, he takes back to society the memories and traces of experience gained elsewhere: the *Little Prince* and his narrator do just that.

The orphan is at the same time irresponsible (he does not have to account for his actions before the parental court) and supremely responsible (potentially guilty) because he interrupts the normal course of things (generations). He experimentally does away with intermediaries and hierarchies—as lunatics and court fools do—learning without masters, knowing God without priests, procuring his own food and inventing love without models. He could paradoxically set a precedent by advising the public to become self-taught. He is at the same time younger (more puerile) and older (more mature) than another child of his age: he brings "poetic" disturbance to the conventional order of biographical narrative, and this is perhaps the main component of his uncanny seductive power. Pedophilia is at root the projection onto a child of the educator's own orphanhood (his unending bereavement and his uncompleted liberation).

Orphans in books are great teachers because they prop up the old lure of parentlessness, of authorlessness; Milan Kundera, with his usual multitiered irony, gets to the core of the problem:

> Not to have parents is the primary condition of freedom. But do not misunderstand me, it is not a matter of losing one's parents. . . . Freedom does not begin when parents are rejected or buried, but where *they are not.*[16]

In fact, orphans are above all freer than others to idealize the dead or absent parents by inventing them, to look for parents everywhere, like Le Clézio's little Mondo who asks anyone in the street to "adopt" him—and people cannot know what he means by it. Marie Miguet shows in an excellent recent article that the authorial voice itself plays this role of sense giver denied to all but a few characters of *Mondo et autres histoires* in the parallel explicative text of *L'Inconnu sur la terre;*[17] if we followed her, most stories of orphans could appear as intertextual allegories. Orphans spend their time and ours (re)working filial relationships; they exalt and multiply parenthood; they make great unfaithful lovers even when they do not become Don Juans. They have to become acceptable and conform or seem to conform to the will of others, "God" and society, because there was no one who was *obliged* to accept them as they were. This tendency is clearly present in Dickensian didactics, notably in *Great Expectations*.

Whatever quest the orphan may embark on, it is thus a quest of fatherhood, not because actual fathers are necessary or good to have, I would suggest, but because the lack of an actual father, of a *pater certus* for the somehow posthumous child, deprives him of the possibility of murdering the right man and coming into his own. "The father's figurative murder by the son enables individual growth, health and normality; enables the son to enter as well into the social structures of lawful order by affirming the symbolic structure of the family as excluding incest," writes Dianne F. Sadoff,[18] commenting on Lacan and Freud, and she goes on to show, with reference to Dickens, that this rite of passage is taken when the son starts to repay the symbolic debt to his father after he has symbolically murdered him. Yet the particular narrative situation created by orphanhood, which results in the multiplication of father figures and attempted murders by the son, is awkward to explain by the author's biography and in particular by the economic inversion of roles that took place in the lives of John and Charles Dickens: I shall propose instead to determine the benefit obtaining from the crime, and to whom it goes. As the orphan is generally bound to recruit a small army of figurative fathers, he becomes their producer, a father of fathers, a supreme fathering deity who slips his feet into the absent old man's shoes and takes up his role even in the old man's failure to *have* a son. The orphan discovers that begetting is not good enough: you must also survive to take possession. At the same time, the figurative son of many figurative fathers becomes many sons, many selves, both successive and simultaneous, who, while transforming some of their values in the process, also transfer them from possible world to possible world, thus exemplifying and prefacing the process of generalization that constitutes the second face of any didactic construction of meaning.

Repetition, with varying degrees of displacement, is built into the structure of orphanhood, as we can see perfectly in Eugène Sue's *Arthur*. Moreover, it is not only or not essentially a pedagogical technique, as has been suggested about *The Little Prince*, but mainly the content of the lesson itself: the maxim "One must repeat," including death and procreation among its standard objects—figured by the intelligible use of language after others that we call grammaticality—is all in all the key signified of any narrative *qua* expression and artistic text, forever in competitive tension with its corollary and apparent contrary, "One must delay." Orphanhood, by making the symbolic murder of the actual father impossible, obliges the orphan to repeat it under the guise of unsatisfactory murders, sometimes actual, of figurative fathers, and this delays, perhaps indefinitely, the moment when, having no one behind us, we have no one between us and death, that moment that has indeed always been and will always be the present. Narrative delays more efficiently or more systematically than other discourses because it repeats death through the litote of "change," "passing," and "passing by" for "passing away," to the point of exhaustion, and orphans make better bearers of narrative than other characters because they also carry within their attributes this infinite incompleteness that is the law of all narrative even within its own temporal span.

Orphans need a spouse more than others. At the same time, the prohibition of incest is somewhat attenuated for them, since they could no longer dispossess their father or mother of his or her spouse, even if this character is still alive; or rather, the prohibition of incest is already displaced for them and its object blurred by circumstances; their choice of incestuous objects is much more open and "arbitrary" or, if you prefer, creative, than the ordinary child's. If actual brothers and sisters are not provided by the text or are impractical, or the desire for them is already too severely repressed to be able to surface, any cousins or indeed any ordinary partner, childhood friend, classmate or girl-next-door will do, as in "real life."

Orphanhood narratives, the *novelas rosas* in particular, cast a new light on the symbolic nature of the prohibition of incest, whose aim is not only to be literally obeyed but also to be symbolically transgressed after it is analogically constructed. If the mother, for instance, and, by extension, the sister, are forbidden sexual objects, all women must be "the same" so that the carnal knowledge of any of them will stand for that of the forbidden objects and infringe as required. By marrying a "woman-as-future-mother," a man procures a wife for the father he replaces, just as the hero of the film *Back to the Future* is obliged to procure his own mother for his father if he does not want to be retroactively destroyed. Marriage, significantly, makes our spouse's parents our parents-in-law, turning our spouse into our legal brother or sister, also as brother or sister of our brothers-and sisters-in-law. Not less significantly, we should infer that our own family is *out*lawed by our marriage, it is banned, locked out of wedlock; it becomes symbolically dead. In the *novela rosa*, the transference of the prohibition of incest onto an object that makes it more or less easily transgressible is realized by means of close or distant cousins, another child "adopted" by the same person, a brother's or sister's best friend, or sometimes an uncle-niece relationship. One late nineteenth-century *novela por entregas, Corona de azahar, corona de espinas*, by Luis de Val, goes as far as uniting half-brother and sister, but it is precisely the entire range of kinship used, from close blood relatives like these to totally unrelated people who fantasize an endogamic rapport, that makes the point.

It has been often noted that Estella is the daughter of Magwitch, Pip's benefactor and ghostly father, and the "adopted" daughter of Miss Havisham, Pip's supposed benefactress and ghostly virgin-mother; but these "facts" become (partly) known to Pip rather late in his textual career, long after his masochistic choice of object. Pip and Estella, though, have one thing in common: they are orphans. All parentless children are a big family, brothers and sisters attracted to each other, free to mate and consequently obliged to construct a prohibition whose transgression will make their union significant and rewarding, in order to exploit the subjacent function of the law, conform and maintain it, passing it on to their progeny, ourselves, readers, posterity of the text. A complex imaginary kinship is redundantly (repetitively) superimposed on the basic kinship of orphanhood just outlined, as the text of *Great Expectations* develops. Even Estella's contempt for Pip and his masochistic response should be interpreted in this light: her social elevation also stands for the age and superiority of a grown-up, an older sister, a mother.

This is why I do not share the general dissatisfaction of critics with the second ending of the novel and its tempting evocation of Estella's and Pip's final reunion. I want this "conventional fairy-tale ending,"[19] and it is truly necessary on many grounds: in the first place, to put an end to the lies born of "Estella's insistence on the apprentice-boy's commonness,"[20] that is, by extension, to Pip's narration of his life story. Narrative discourse is in itself a lie, a false representation of temporal discontinuity and ontological disjunction as continued identity of the subject and junction of the contraries, blurring the difference "between life and death." The final lie of definitive reunion, when it occurs, is, on the contrary, that which marks the beginning of eventless, "pure" unoriented time, antitime, the nonrepresentable that narrative has left hanging everywhere on its infinite margins, unable as it is to limit its proliferation or give it a shape. Narrative is all the more exemplary when it confesses its own weaknesses and tries to make amends for them.

Moreover, to criticize this ending amounts to preferring the "quiescence" of the Princesse de Clèves, the conformity of resignation or despondency to that of fulfilment, a choice perhaps wrongly motivated by the power of irony that modern artists have tried once the power of promise was taken away from them in the wake of the secularization of society and the related entry of symbolic goods into the economic market. In fact, "romantic" endings have their own irony: they reward the reader's intellectual and affective investment with a vicarious, spectacular satisfaction that can only be called an end and is provided by the inexplicable, aleatory magic that changes the indistinct form of absence into the indescribable signified of presence (not its inscription, as does the elegy). Pip has (almost) renounced Estella and it is also when he gladly finds himself reproduced by others (there is a little Pip, son of Joe and Biddy), it is at the very moment when he plays Magwitch to the shadow of Pip over his parents' tombstone and effaces or resorbs his entire life into a last minor repetition that makes it useless and takes all the drama out of it—it is just then that the dream comes true, as a supplement and a rest, equally sweet and discolored. *Great Expectations* relativizes our projects more efficiently in this fashion than if they were left pending for eternity. After all, the boojum was a snark, and the only long way to get hold of a snark is to discover that boojums *are* snarks (or vice versa, in reversible speech); this is the kind of lesson that only the best-wrought exemplary narratives—among them romances of successful orphanhoods—can teach.

Some twenty years ago, an American critic found a strange parallel between Pip's plot and the story of Telemachus in Homer.[21] Despite the farfetched attribution of such a "source" to the Dickensian novel, the resemblance is meaningful because it underscores other constants shared by the didactic epic and the didactic novel—or the epic and the novel when submitted to didactic reception. We could well wonder whether a wandering and blundering son, an orphaned son-of-something, away from a wandering and blundering remote father known by imagination rather than memory, is not our own image or, better, our prefigured, idealized image as readers: the authoritative, indisputable meaning obtained from an absolute father is always on its way back home and ever delayed. We read instead meanings furnished by professional tutors and those scrambled into a mixture of lies and truths by worldly appearances in general.

The exemplary didactic narrative tends to be "self-referential" insofar as it figures and inscribes in its key normative structures the ideal structures of its own reception and interpretation. This is really a device with a double function: it avoids, partly at least, the often vexing problem of verisimilitude and constitutes, particularly for the postmodernist reader, an index of specularity, a typical shifter of aestheticization. This is at the same time one source of the fourth objection against Fénelon's *Télémaque*, according to Ramsay's discourse that prefaces it:

> Some people believe that the author of Télémaque exhausts too much
> his topic, by the abundance and wealth of his genius. He says every-
> thing and does not leave anything for others to think.[22]

The reason given ("Like Homer, he [Fénelon] puts nature completely before your eyes") differs from my suggestion, but the polylogical structure of enunciation, in which the framing narrator, Telemachus, Mentor, Calypso, and others all have their share, undoubtedly contributes to this oppressive feeling by multiplying the narratees and attempting to control all of them. Mentor-Minerva manages in the process to displace Telemachus's choice of object from Calypso, a figurative mother, and Eucharis, a nymph, to Antiope, the daughter of King Idomeneus, a sister-figure that he receives from the hands of both Idomeneus ("Idoménée embraced Télémaque like his own son")[23] and Minerva. At the same time, a further delay is imposed: Télémaque must return to Ithaca at last and seek the approval of his reinstated father, Ulysses, before he can marry Antiope. Submissive to the wills of their respective fathers, who speak for the will of the gods, the young people can rest assured that absence and delay will not alter "their" common project:

> She will never promise herself to anyone; she will let herself be given
> away by her father; she will only take for her husband a man who
> respects the gods and fulfills all the requirements of decorum. (p. 551)

The *roman à thèse*, according to Suleiman, builds on realist foundations, defined, differently but not incompatibly with our views, as "the aesthetic of verisimilitude and representation."[24] I shall argue, in broader terms, that a heavy dependence on the Discourse of history (or myth, in olden times) is an essential contribution to the totalitarian exemplariness of fictionalized narratives that do not have to state either their own intepretation or its pragmatic transformation: "Even though the story occupies, in the hierarchy of levels, the lowest position . . . , it is the only element that a parable cannot 'omit' without becoming, by that very fact, something else."[25] Ramsay addresses himself to this question both in his *Discours de la poésie épique* and in the short preface to his own *Voyages de Cyrus*, subtitled *Histoire morale*. In the latter, he explicitly locates his didactic narrative in a blank of history, or rather in a historical spot in which possible events are found outlined only in dots:

I have made good of the silence of the Ancients on the youth of this
Prince in order to make him travel. . . . I have deviated as little as I
could from the most accurate Chronology.[26]

This apparent contradiction, like the justification of Fénelon's anachronisms ("in
remote Antiquity, whose annals are so uncertain . . . , it is permissible to adapt
[*accommoder*] the old tradition to one's topic"),[27] belies that history—God's own
work, His narrative whose characters are actual men and women—is the inexhaustible reservoir of authority in narrative form. Human action *is* an interpretation of the will of God, the secret Father, and the success or failure of human un-
dertakings *is* God's judgment on earth, His own intepretation of His Law. God's
orphans should just read comparatively attempts and denouements to reconstruct
God's syntax and make themselves—their lives and minds—into particular instances of it.

The Fable: Doxa *or Secrecy?*

Although the fable shares many characteristics of the exemplary narratives
evoked earlier in this chapter, it cannot be included in the same class without the
recognition of some important nuances. In chapter 9 I discussed the specificity
of short and incident narratives in general. While keeping these conclusions in
mind, I shall now place the emphasis on the relation between three elements—
metaphoricity, discourse articulation and didactic process—in the fable, taken in
its most banal sense: a short narrative with an explicit (that is, strongly marked)
educational aim.

Suleiman draws a distinction between "fables without a rule of action," which
she calls "non-exemplary," and those that "imply a value system or an ethic."[28]
Although she concedes that the former may "tell a story 'rich in lessons about
life,' " (ibid.), she considers them to be primarily descriptive of human nature and
the way things are, rather than prescriptive of a particular attitude or line of action
under determined circumstances. Having warned several times already that the
boundaries between cognitive and prescriptive contents are tenuous, I hope to see
it confirmed once more and perhaps, more important, to show why this is so in
terms of a communication theory of literature.

In his *Traité du poème épique* (1675), René Le Bossu defined the fable as "a
discourse invented in order to form the morals by means of instructions disguised
under the allegories of an action."[29] Since the word "allegory" is not used here
in its precise rhetorical sense, we may simply understand it as "trappings" or "outward aspect." There would be no need to insist on the cliché that truth cannot be
fully appreciated naked if, in the sentence quoted, "instructions" did not occupy
the usual place of "truth" and an "action," a story, that of poetic ornament: truth
is seen as imperative in itself, but, clad in an action, it can pass for something
else and, because this something cannot be a lie, which would be repulsive, it can

only be a fiction. In other words, fiction is the result of the superposition of an action on the truth that it espouses, and fictionality in a fable is only apparent. Three simultaneous transformations have taken place in the *discours inventé*: truth into fiction, timelessness of moral rule into time-bound action, and injunctive discourse into constative discourse. By detransforming (reducing) one of these transformations, we do the same *ipso facto* to the other two. But why should we start to detransform at all, if truth is less pleasant than the fable as it stands? This is where the semantic filling out of subjects (characters) and actional predicates comes into play:

> There are [for Le Bossu] three kinds of fables, differentiated according to the characters introduced into the narrative. The *Raisonnables* cast men and gods as actors; the *Moratae*, animals with certain superimposed human attributes, and the *Mixtes*, a combination of the other two.[30]

We now understand better Ramsay's complex position on the content of epic action, developed in a paragraph subtitled "L'action doit être merveilleuse," at the end of which he too quotes Le Bossu. The epic action must be marvelous without reaching the point of absurdity or extravagance. It will thus achieve two aims: be striking and attractive, and manifest the all-powerful presence of the god(s). I would like to add that the marvelous, together with a lack of truth—this time, in the sense of conformity to historical documents—and joining forces with probability or verisimilitude in the sequence of events and the appropriateness of acts and events to characters and settings, signals invention, the art of the poet; it delates the transformation accomplished and prompts the detransformations to be carried out in order to make the tale really *interesting*, that is, relevant to the reader's life experience as much as exciting to his sense of artistry. It is noteworthy that the actor is not man alone in any of the three categories of fables listed by Le Bossu: a cast of animals, in the Aesopic fable, gods and nymphs together with men in the epic, like a cast of anachronistic philosophers and heroes in a "Dialogue of the Dead" or a queer exotic setting in a philosophical tale, are all indexes of nonliterality, pointing to the detransformational decoding required to make full sense of the fable. The instructions of truth will be more valuable if they result from our labor of discovery, and the profitability of this labor is perhaps the major buried lesson of all fables: "Le laboureur et ses enfants" would then be the absolute paradigm of the genre.

But secrecy cannot be valued forever for its own sake; the veils repeatedly imposed on Truth have a counterpart: the unspeakable fascination of her nudity, the damp depths of her well, the skeleton that holds her alluring flesh in place. The fable is a cruel genre at heart. Sometimes its disguises are so exaggerated, so "loud" that they become grotesque; the grotesqueness of the disguise then transpires into the subjacent presented world—a world of pretenses—in such a way that we realize it is actually there.

When fabulous disguise mimics a worldly travesty like an inverted image in a looking glass, the fable is hardly different from satire: we could query its "exemplary" character, if the people criticized are not going to follow the advice, we can be sure, and the ordinary reader is not in the position of needing it. But in order that there be exemplariness, it suffices that we share experimentally the disguise, we must ourselves become temporary accomplices of the corruption of reality by misleading representation. We are forced to "buy the crap" in order to turn away from it in disgust: "Aunque se vista de seda / la Mona, Mona se queda" (Even clad in silk, the Monkey remains a Monkey) is the starter proverb of a late eighteenth-century Spanish political fable.[31] The theme of the lazy, rich captive animal, brought to the city, who escapes to the wilderness and wants to rule there, only to make a fool of himself and be nearly put to death by the brave, naive members of his species that he tried to impress, is a frequent one in the fable, perhaps because it is a metaphor of the risks we run when we read it and begin to like the disguise for itself, a symbol too of the fable's own condition.

Many fables, on the other hand, draw an unambiguous moral from the story, some piece of advice good for the audience of all times and all countries; they do not leave us anything to guess and make such use of redundancy that the anonymous tale that precedes the moral seems retrospectively to be a superfluous interchangeable appendix, betraying itself for the fruit of almost mechanical repetition that it is in fact: Why is it, ask the critics of the fable, that so many texts of this genre are translations and adaptations? Why is it so difficult to invent new fables, as if, after seven thousand years that beasts have existed and talked, nothing new could be said on the Animal Farm?

We shall find the answer in the fables themselves, in the conception of history that they conceal as much as they exhibit it. History, for the fable, is not mere repetition, though it is the combination of two series: a combination of regular events to be expected from the inescapable transmission of instinct by the will of God or the nature of Nature, who want people and things to be what they are, and an irregular series of accidents produced by the imperfect transmission of knowledge and belief inherent in human foolishness, which experience only, acquired with age, is able to modify. Wisdom fables try to supply an equivalent of this experience, an impossible shortcut to the benefits of seniority: what price will they make us pay for it? A comparative glance at La Fontaine's fable "The Wolf, the Goat, and the Kid" and at its fourteenth-century forerunners, the Ysopet I and Ysopet II collections, reveals the awful identity of the injunctor behind the benevolent protective voice of the fabulator. Even if its life is spared, the kid *will be sacrificed* on the altar of the Law; the Father was speaking under the sweet motherly goatskin. He will not go away and leave the kid alone:

Pour ce, vous dis qu'en l'enfant vient
Grant preu, quand il voit et retient
La bonne doctrine du père:
Et qui non fait, il le comère.[32]
[So I tell you that to the child comes
Great benefit [literally, price], when he sees and keeps
the father's good doctrine
And he who does not will pay for it]

The exemplary text trades promised power against the acceptance of castrating limitation; actual castration is the symbolic threat waved in our face, if we do not accept symbolic castration: Hold on a moment, says the woodcutter to death, and Hernani to his other father blowing the horn in the depths of the woods to claim his life, wait a moment, but in vain, the moment is gone when the tale closes. Is there, then, no lesson less pessimistic?

Self-Imitation, Self-Generation, Self-Destructive Teaching, and Other Related Problems for Further Investigation

In chapter 4, I had merely dabbed at allegory viewed as a genre of fictional reference among others, some of these, like utopia and rehearsal, being undoubtedly programmatic in outlook. It would be beyond the scope of this book, and the limits of the reader's patience, in our haste to give theorization a denouement, to now reconsider allegory thoroughly in the perspective of its function rather than its structure, but this possibility offers food for thought and deserves a few enigmatic lines, (like) a foot in the doorway of satisfaction, in order to keep it ajar from outside and prevent the final petrification of theorizing into theory.

Metaphor is not the arbitrary transference of certain properties (valences and particular combinations of semes) from one lexical item or sequence to another, but the selection of a signifier [b] instead of another signifier [a] when the lexical signified of [b] shares one or more sememes with the signified of [a], but archsememes A and B are not connected by relations of referential proximity or inclusion. Metaphor recenters interpretively the semantic aggregate subtended by constant reference, renders irrelevant some of the denotative elements of the "original" signified A (hypothetical in absentia), and reactivates as connotators some or all of the semantic elements of the "ex"-signified B now discarded as denotatively irrelevant or logically incompatible. Metaphor impoverishes denotation in extension and modifies connotation in various ways: sometimes it makes it richer, at other times it changes it or its value; at any rate it shifts connotative emphasis while leaving reference essentially unmodified. If I say "flame" instead of "love," I still refer to the mental and physical dispositions of a subject toward another being placed by the former in the object roles of such verbs as "desire," and "admire," but I denote something narrower than "love" in general and whose connotations are geared to spontaneity, expense, irrationality, violence, and so on. Metaphor, like other tropes, can be at the root of a narrative program, and an extended metaphor can carry narrative elements, but an allegory is *not* an extended metaphor, for several reasons: first, allegory is essentially narrative and bears on two levels of sequences at least—sequence of signs and sequence in the presented world(s)—while metaphor does not need to be narrative and is indifferent to sequence; second, allegory is based on the (ideally) perfect coincidence of two narrative sequences, the "literal" or concrete, and the conceptual, without the precedence of one over the other; third, allegory uses, whenever it can, the whole connotative and denotative range of the two signs it puts to work concurrently.

Therefore, allegory, which is akin to juxtalinear translation in structure, seeks its own completion and can develop on the assumption that such completion and closure is possible, whereas metaphor makes its efficiency rest on loose ends, incompletion, and uncertainty, even when it is extended. Although metaphor makes new riches glitter as it opens contrived depths in the moiré of connotation, and in spite of its frequent association with hyperbole, it is placed forever under the sign of want and serves the lyrical in close collaboration with the oxymoron: the surrealists have brought the ultimate proof of it. Allegory, in contrast, is a syllepsis of two narratives with exactly the same structures but two different sets of actors, typically one set of "human" actors and the other "abstract" or conceptual (as in the *Faerie Queene*), or one set "natural" and the other "abstract" or psychological (as in the poem by Jean-Baptiste Rousseau studied in chapter 4). The two narratives run parallel until they meet: this is the paradox of allegory.

In allegory the two narratives mirror each other; this is supposed to mutually reinforce the truth-value of individual plots brought by their rigorous semantic coherence and syntactic consistency. The final output is meant nevertheless, at least in the more orthodox Christian tradition, to bring to bear the stress of persuasion on a spiritual sense that it is difficult not to enroll on the side of the "abstract" and "conceptual," even when it should unify, effect a superior synthesis of the separate meanings of the two parallel stories. Edwin Honig, in his fundamental book on the topic, appropriately quotes Thomas Aquinas's *Summa*:

> The author of Holy Writ is God, in whose power it is to signify His meaning not by words only (as man can also do), but also by things themselves. . . . this science has the property that the things signified by the words have themselves also a signification.[33]

By the way, it is clear that the staple of allegory is *not* personification, as Samuel R. Levin would have it.[34] Personification is simply a remarkably efficient and economic device for "superposing" two stories; it has grossly the same function and effect as a grammatical plural and, to this effect, the subject bears a recognizable mark, that is, the capitalization of the initial. Instead of saying "I go and you go," one can say, "We go"; similarly, instead of saying "idleness is vicious and this woman is vicious," one can say, "Idleness is vicious." Allegories also tend to multiply bridges between their parallel narratives, the parallel being sometimes hypermotivated by apparently irrelevant coincidences, like the famous pun on which the Catholic Church is built. In fact, this insistence on motivation reveals the basic structural weakness of allegory and weakens it even more. Allegories, particularly the longer ones, tend to fail in their attempted transference of obviousness from their human-natural narratives to the abstract-conceptual ones and then on to the spiritual supranarrative, because protracted specularity (in Dällenbach's sense) becomes eventually valued for its own sake, within the closure of the Jakobsonian poetic function or, at best, of Mukarovsky's aesthetic function. The allegorical text has a structural tendency to become "allegorical of itself" and thus to teach a nonlesson, a lesson about art that remains internal to the realm of art and lacks any application or supportive evidence, once transported out of it.

Another self-defeating strategy can be seen in narratives that overplay their didactic tricks: melodrama, romance, edifying and children's literature, crime fiction, historical biographies, and many more kinds seem to fall easily into this trap. I shall give only one example.

In the classical petit-bourgeois love story whose reign lasted approximately a century in Europe, between the mid-nineteenth century and the 1960s, the overt ideology is generally conservative, reproductive, or reactionary, but propagandistic aims are unabashedly proclaimed by some authors and pressure groups in the network of literary communication. The best-selling novels of Spanish author Rafael Pérez y Pérez are virtually the most accomplished type of totalitarian fiction in this century. No sooner has a female character confessed her conservative, traditionalist proclivities to her diary bound in red leather like a missal, than she is taken by a dynamic young engineer on a tour of her grandfather's steelworks. As she advocates considerate treatment of the deserving Christian working class — who should be allowed to raise nondangerous, God-fearing, healthy, grateful families — her eyes meet those of the handsome young man, a self-made, born leader whose aristocratic family has lost their wealth due to the misguided, unchristian idleness or hazardous speculations of some ancestor. A few days later, she tries to help a dying young girl whose father, a communist criminal, wild and violent, will reluctantly discuss class struggle or class collaboration with his benefactor until he is at last touched by divine grace and realizes all the evil and misery that was caused by his foolish pride and envy . . .

Authoritarian, directly prescriptive Discourse is shared by the Σ narrator and a few privileged characters, not always fathers and traditional figures of authority but, on the contrary, young heroes and heroines who discover life with innocent eyes, or generous, forgiving old curates. Deliberative Discourse is held by the protagonists in their dialogues, oral or epistolary, and in their introspective interior monologues where passionate duty and passionate desire come to sit before the tribunal of their conscience. And exemplary behavior is carried out by the heroine whose good heart never fails in spite of all those irresponsible crazy phases she goes through during her protracted adolescence. Eventually, the deliberative and authoritarian modes are so opposed that they cancel each other, even if they did not suffer as they do from their internal contradictions. Aristotle already knew that truths that are supposed to be obvious and fundamental should not be proved—subjected to deliberation—but enforced, by legal violence if necessary.[35] If the assertion that one should love one's parents is both the object of pure injunctive discourse and a topic for deliberation, the first appears arbitrary and excessive, since the values concerned can be discussed, and the second appears superfluous, because authority should be sufficient to safeguard these values without summoning reason, dialogue, and other "democratic" gimmicks to the rescue. The exemplary technique itself relies on a promise of sexual satisfaction made by the text long before this satisfaction becomes legally possible, so that, when it is fulfilled in the end, any possible enjoyment *of* the law is replaced by a fundamentally unlawful desire that cheats the law by applying it in such a way that it conforms to its original aims. The Nationalist victory in the Spanish civil war and the taming of Masaniello's Neapolitan rebels in 1647 are, within their respective textual worlds, motivated by the *telos* of sexual enjoyment. And incest, once accomplished, retains its ambiguous meaning: it both reproduces the unity and at-oneness of the family and remains the symbolic transgression that some authority will now be "morally" obliged to sanctify.

Redundant and self-destructive didactic processes, often found in popular narratives, do not only reveal that there is no teaching without seduction and the risks entailed by making the values to be transmitted an object of transaction and exchange—since they need to be moved from sender to receiver. By making these values compensable, didacticism confirms once more the irreducible duality of narrative discourse itself, at once the secret fruit of condensation that seeks to conceal and contain, resolve and resorb the yes and the no that all things turned alive by our lives bear in them, and also a blatant unveiling of the instability and untrustworthiness of all nouns and all names, all potential subjects *to* changes of signification, even when they pass for subjects *of* change. The structuralist narratologies of the 1960s, following the Proppian quest for a universal schema of *actions*, were probably right, on their own terms, to favor the study of events: narrative predicates render very fragile indeed the subjects involved, but it is high time to develop approaches that would no longer take for granted or simply ignore the fate of the subject, its own transitive nature. Enough flowers have withered on the grave of that Unknown Soldier of History; a preoccupation with his functions must be central to the project of a communication theory of artistic acts.

Lyrical discourse will have to join in and make its own suggestion: the past and future beloved blind being in us will always be our next of kin, but the meaning of this blindness will never surpass its horror or the beauty of our desire, and its darkness will never authorize our present insight.

Notes

Notes

1. The Nature and Purpose of Narratology

1. Martin, *Recent Theories of Narrative*, p. 8.
2. Berthoud, "Narrative and Ideology," in Hawthorn, *Narrative*, p. 101.
3. Farcy, "De l'obstination narratologique," pp. 491–506.
4. See Mathieu-Colas, "Frontières de la narratologie," p. 106.
5. See Eagleton, *Literary Theory*, pp. 196–206.
6. See Ricoeur, *Temps et récit*, 3 vols.
7. Brooks, *Reading for the Plot*, p. 91.
8. Todorov, "Les Transformations narratives," p. 333, quoted by Brooks, *Reading for the Plot*, p. 91.
9. Brooks, Ibid., p. 56.
10. See Fromm, *The Forgotten Language*, p. 241–49.
11. See Coste, 1980.
12. Prince, *Narratology*, pp. 1, 2, 4, 4–5.
13. LaCapra, "History and Psychoanalysis."
14. Vann, "Louis Mink's Linguistic Turn," p. 8.
15. White, *Tropics of Discourse*, p. 31.
16. Mink, "Narrative Form," in Canary and Kozicky, *The Writing of History*, p. 142.
17. White, *Tropics of Discourse*, p. 61.
18. Greenblatt, "Splenditello," pp. 5–6.
19. Nowell-Smith, "Historical Facts," in Carr et al., *Philosophie de l'histoire*, p. 322.
20. DeCerteau, "L'Histoire, science et fiction," in Carr et al., *Philosophie de l'histoire*, p. 31.
21. Pompa, "Narrative Form, Significance, and Historical Knowledge," in Carr et al., *Philosophie de l'histoire*, pp. 145, 148, 149–50, 156.
22. Marrou, *De la connaissance historique*, pp. 26, 225.

23. See Ariès, *Le Temps de l'histoire*, p. 247.

24. Jameson, *The Political Unconscious*, p. 13.

25. See White, "The Question of Narrative in Contemporary Historical Theory," particularly pp. 22–25.

26. Jameson, *The Political Unconscious*, p. 25.

27. Frow, *Marxism and Literary History*, p. 118.

28. Ibid., p. 121.

2. The Structure and Formation of Narrative Meaning

1. Barthes, "Introduction à l'analyse structurale des récits," p. 3.

2. Ibid., p. 4.

3. See Coquet, *Sémiotique littéraire*, particularly chapter 3: "Problèmes de l'analyse structurale du récit: *L'Etranger* d'Albert Camus," pp. 51–65.

4. Halliday, *Language as Social Semiotic*, p. 35.

5. Foucault, *L'Archéologie du savoir*, pp. 53, 63.

6. See, for example, Iser, *Implied Reader*, p. 282; *Act of Reading*, pp. 123ff.; Genette, "Frontières du récit," in *Figures II*, p. 60: "But, from the point of view of the modes of representation, telling an event and describing an object are similar operations, which play on the same resources of language. The most significant difference might perhaps be that narration restores, in the temporal succession of its discourse, the equally temporal succession of events." See also Barthes, *S/Z*, pp. 35–36: "The space of the readerly text is in every respect comparable to a classical musical score."

7. Illustration in Uspensky, *Poetics of Composition*. The same analysis can be given of illustration 2 in the princeps edition of *Leander and Hero*, reproduced here, p. 39.

8. See Ricardou, *Le Nouveau Roman*, pp. 76 and 109–12.

9. Prince, *A Grammar of Stories*, p. 17.

10. Prince, *Narratology*, p. 62.

11. I should add that, like Richard Hudson, *Word Grammar*, pp. 130ff., I cannot see any clear boundary between semantic and pragmatic structures.

12. Prince, *Grammar*, p. 19.

13. Prince, *Narratology*, p. 4.

14. Foucault, *Archéologie*, pp. 16–17.

15. Greimas and Courtes, *Sémiotique: Dictionnaire raisonné de la théorie du langue*, p. 297.

16. Traugott and Pratt, *Linguistics for Students of Literature*, p. 248.

17. See R. Martin, *Pour une logique du sens*, p. 31.

18. See Banfield, "Ecriture, Narration and the Grammar of French," in Hawthorn, *Narrative*, p. 5.

19. See Weinrich, *Le Temps*, pp. 30–49.

20. See chapter 7, pp. 220–24; aspect, supported or not by tense shift, is decisive in this kind of sequence.

21. See McCawley, *Everything That Linguists Have Always Wanted to Know*, pp. 123–25; see also Quine, *Methods of Logic*, pp. 268ff.

22. Thomason, *Symbolic Logic*, mentioned by McCawley, *Everything*, p. 124.

23. Kress and Hodge, *Language as Ideology*, p. 120.

24. As a "poetic" truth; see Dante, *Vita nuova*, chapter 25.

25. Pérez y Pérez, *Palomita torcaz*, pp. 5–6 (my translation).

26. See Coste, 1987b.

27. Chatelain, "Récit itératif et concrétisation," p. 305.

28. Barthes, "Introduction à l'analyse," p. 26.

29. Bache, "Tense and Aspect in Fiction," p. 95.

30. That is, more or less amenable to the literary regime of reception (see chapter 3).

31. *Enfance III*. Original text in Rimbaud, *Illuminations*, in *Oeuvres complètes*, p. 123. I have used, among other English renderings, a translation by Enid Rhodes Peschel, *A Season in Hell. The Illuminations* (New York: Oxford University Press, 1973, p. 113).

32. See Wing, *Present Appearances*, pp. 68ff.

33. Jenny, "Le Poétique et le narratif."

34. See Coste, 1981.

35. See chapter 9, pp. 259–62 on the constraints of short forms.

36. Cohn, *Transparent Minds*, p. 34.

37. James, *In the Cage*, p. 367.

3. Narrative and Verbal Art: Literariness in Communication

1. Mukarovsky, *Aesthetic Function, Norm, and Value as Social Facts*.

2. In Sebeok, ed., *Style in Language*, pp. 350–77.

3. Mukarovsky, *Aesthetic Function*, p. 7.

4. Jakobson, "Closing Statement: Linguistics and Poetics," p. 371.

5. Mukarovsky, *Aesthetic Function*, p. 89.

6. To the extent that Henri Bonnard, author of a French textbook for senior high school students, can write that "most theorists of literature and poetry refer to [Jakobson's diagram of communication]" (*Procédés annexes d'expression* [Paris: Magnard, 1982], p. 14).

7. The word used in Russian by several theorists was *ustanovka*. Some of the equivalents offered by Russian-English dictionaries are "placing," "adjustment," "aim," "directive," and "precept." Peter Steiner writes: "The term is very resistant to translation or explanation. It has two common meanings in Russian . . . : 'intention' on the one hand, and 'orientation,' 'the idea of positioning oneself in relation to some given data,' on the other." Following Elmar Holenstein, Steiner also relates *ustanovka* to the idea of "goal-directed process" or "directive correlation," not introduced through a psychological subject. But the problem with eliminating psychological subjects is that they return surreptitiously, their functions being projected upon personified processes or institutions. See Steiner, "Three Metaphors of Russian Formalism," and Holenstein, "On Poetry," in Smith, *Structure and Gestalt*, pp. 1–43.

8. Jakobson, "Closing Statement: Linguistics and Poetics," p. 355.

9. Quoted by Erlich, *Russian Formalism*, p. 183.

10. Todorov, ed., *Théorie de la littérature*.

11. Coleridge, "The Nightingale," in Wordsworth and Coleridge, *Lyrical Ballads*, pp. 40–44.

12. See Tomachevski, *Teoría de la literatura*, p. 14.

13. See Compagnon, *La Seconde main*, particularly pp. 359ff.

14. See Coste, 1980.

15. See Riffaterre, *La Production du texte*, particularly p. 98.

16. Barsch and Hauptmeier, "Speculations about Jakobson," p. 553.

17. Waugh, "Poetic Function in the Theory of Roman Jakobson," p. 57.

18. Although my views have evolved considerably since I first read his book, I am permanently indebted to Mircea Marghescou's approach to the concept of literariness; see Marghescou, *Le Concept of littérarité*, particularly the first part: "Construction du concept."

19. This reading pretends to be guided by the phonic matter of the poem and its rhythm, but quotations from Mallarmé himself, who mentions the connotation of fecundity for the letter "b," and many other interpretations of individual "sounds" originate in fact in the shapes of letters associated with the meanings of certain French words in which they occur.

20. Sartre, *Les Mots*, p. 50.

21. Federman, *Take It or Leave It*, unpaginated.

22. See Roger, *Proust: Les Plaisirs et les noms*.

23. See Kerbrat-Orecchioni, *La Connotation*, pp. 114–16, 142–43, 251.

24. See Orlando, *Toward a Freudian Theory of Literature*, notably pp. 56 and 78.

25. Lyons, *Semantics*, vol. 2, p. 551.

4. A Manmade Universe? Or, The Question of Fictionality

1. Stendhal, *Le Rouge et le noir*, in *Romans et nouvelles*, vol. 1, p. 219. The following quotations are all from pp. 219–24 (my translation, as are all the quotations in this chapter).

2. Pavel, *Fictional Worlds*, p. 33.

3. See René Fonvieille, *Le Véritable Julien Sorel* (Paris: Arthaud, 1971). The critic Robert Kanters published a review of the book under the title: "Le Véritable Antoine Berthet," *Le Figaro*, December 3, 1971.

4. Pearson, "A la recherche du temps présent," p. 253.

5. The subtlety of Stendhal's handling of the traveler's device becomes very striking when we compare it with similar tricks in other novelistic beginnings chosen at random. I shall quote three:

"In the mountains of the Creuse region, toward the Bourbonnais and the Combraille country, in the middle of the poorest, saddest and most desolate part of France, the most unknown of industrialists and artists alike, you will oblige me if you notice, should you ever visit this place, a high barren hill, topped with some boulders which would not strike much your attention without the advice I am going to give you. Climb up the hill . . . " (George Sand, *Jeanne* [1844. Paris: Calmann-Lévy, 1881]).

"Nyon is the first town to be found between Geneva and Lausanne, at a point where the road follows closely the edge of the lake. Almost all the locality is built on the plateau that stretches behind, and, from the bottom, the traveler sees only the top of it. . . . The house on the right is my house, the parson's house, as the green and white striped shutters show" (Yves Velan, *Je* [Paris: Seuil, 1959]).

"If you know Starkfield, Massachusetts, you know the post-office. If you know the post-office you must have seen Ethan Frome drive up to it, drop the reins on his hollow-backed bay and drag himself across the brick pavement to the white colonnade; and you must have asked who he was" (Edith Wharton, *Ethan Frome*).

Compare: "If the traveler stops even a few moments in that main street of Verrières, which ascends from the bank of the Doubs to the top of the hill, you can bet a hundred to one that he will see a tall man who looks busy and important" (*Le Rouge*, p. 220).

6. Stendhal, *Le Rouge*, p. 224.

7. Stendhal, *Lucien Leuwen*, in *Romans et nouvelles*, vol. 1, pp. 1026, 1033, 1035, 1037.

8. Prince, "Ceci n'est pas l'inénarré," p. 4.

9. Ibid., p. 6.

10. Ibid., p. 8.

11. Stierle, "Réception et fiction," p. 313.

12. Maitre, *Literature and Possible Worlds*, p. 65.

13. Coste, "Le principe de réalité," in "Apologie de la non-prose, suivi de Poèmes recents."

14. Ohmann, "Literature as Act," quoted by Martin, *Recent Theories of Narrative*, p. 183.

15. Pavel, *Fictional Worlds*, p. 23.

16. Fontanier, *Les Figures du discours*, p. 49.

17. Ibid., p. 379.

18. Barthes, *S/Z*, trans. Miller, p. 65.

19. This idea is developed at length in my work in progress, *Absence and Becoming: A Theory of Lyrical Discourse*.

20. Maitre, *Literature and Possible Worlds*, p. 65.

21. See particularly Pavel, "*Possible Worlds in Literary Semantics*."

22. Doležel, "Pour une typologie des mondes fictionnels," in Parret and Ruprecht, *Exigences et perspectives de la sémiotique*, p. 8.

23. See Balzac, "Sarrasine," in Barthes, *S/Z*, trans. Miller, p. 234.

24. Freud, *Interpretation of Dreams*, pp. 182–95.

25. Roddenberry, *Star Trek*, p. 13.

26. Milza and Berstein, *Le Fascisme italien 1919–1945*, p. 35.

27. See Orlando, *Freudian Theory of Literature*, particularly pp. 137–88.

28. But not exclusively: the journal *Literary Onomastic Studies* is published yearly in the United States.

29. See, for example, various contributions to SEL, *Le Personnage en question*.

30. See Roger, *Proust: Les Plaisirs et les nous*.

31. Grivel, *Production de l'interêt romanesque*, p. 131.

32. Vonnegut, "Harrison Bergeron," in Allen, *Science Fiction*, p. 141.

33. Potocki, *La Duchesse d'Avila* (Manuscrit trouvé à Saragosse), p. 249.

34. An introductory pastiche of Duras's fans, in Coste, 1985b. p. 165.

35. Turner, "Process, Systems, and Symbols," p. 68. I am indebted to Ronald Judy III, now a Ph.D. student at the University of Minnesota, who attracted my attention to this invaluable concept in 1981.

36. Duras, *Le Ravissement de Lol V. Stein*, p. 9.

37. Duras, *Détruire dit-elle*, p. 13. For an interpretation of "rehearsal" in a different perspective, see Coste, "Rehearsal: An Alternative."

38. Duras, *L'Amour*, p. 11.

39. See, among other works, Márquez Rodríguez, *Lo barroco*.

40. Santa Teresa de Jesús, *Su vida*, p. 124.

41. See, for example, Hutcheon, *Narcissistic Narrative*, and Waugh, *Metafiction*.

42. See, for example, Dällenbach, *Le Récit spéculaire*, and Genette, *Palimpsestes*.

43. See Ricardou, *Problèmes du Nouveau Roman*, and *Pour une théorie du Nouveau Roman*.

44. Rubert de Ventós, *El arte ensimismado*, p. 87.

45. See, for example, Garvey, *Juan Marsé's Si te dicen que caí*, and Swearingen, *Reflexivity in Tristram Shandy*.

46. Sterne, *Tristram Shandy*, p. 41.

47. See Prince, "Narrative Pragmatics, Messages, and Point."

48. Sterne, *Tristram Shandy*, pp. 94–95.

49. Nabokov, *Speak, Memory*, p. 150.

50. In the 1985 edition, Part 2.

51. Jean-Baptiste Rousseau, quoted by Fontanier, *Les Figures du discours*, p. 117.

52. Fontanier, ibid., p. 114.

53. Todorov, *Introduction à la littérature fantastique*, p. 68–69.

54. Fontanier, *Figures*, p. 117.

55. Todorov, *Introduction*, p. 77.

56. Ségur, *Histoire de Blondine*, p. 16.

57. See, for example, the two stories commented on by Eco, *Lector in fabula*.

58. Charles, *Rhétorique de la lecture*, pp. 118ff.

59. Pavel, *Fictional Worlds*, p. 78.

60. Huizinga, *The Waning of the Middle Ages*, p. 254.

61. Marot, in Musée, *La Touchante Aventure*, p. 121.

5. Who's Who and Who Does What in the Tale Told

1. Greimas, *On Meaning*, pp. 106–07.

2. See Greimas and Courtés, *Sémiotique: Dictionnaire raisonné*, p. 3.

3. See Bremond, *Logique du récit*, pp. 131–241.

4. Hamon, "Pour un statut sémiologique du personnage," in Barthes et al., *Poétique du récit*, p. 129.

5. Cervantes, *Don Quixote*, trans., 1882, p. 148 (in the original, p. 125).

6. Galdós, *Zumalacarregui*, p. 791.

7. Gide, *Symphonie pastorale*, p. 80.

8. Galdós, *Los Apostólicos*, p. 581.

9. Zola, *Rome*, p. 43.

10. Zola, *Paris*, p. 41.

11. Florian, *Estelle*, p. 293.

12. Compton-Burnett, *The Last and the First*, p. 128.

13. Cervantes, *Don Quixote*, p. 530 (in the original, p. 469).

14. Volponi, *The Worldwide Machine*, p. 212.

15. Brautigan, *The Abortion*, p. 28.

16. Frow, "Spectacle Binding," p. 227.

17. Chatman, *Story and Discourse*, p. 139.

18. *Mayfair*, vol. 14, no. 11, p. 127.

19. Hamon, "Pour un statut sémiologique du personnage," pp. 150ff.

20. See Coste, 1979.

21. Frow, "Spectacle Binding," p. 239.

22. Fowles, *The Magus*, p. 15.

23. The phrase is the title to the third chapter of Couturier and Durand, *Donald Barthelme*.

24. Patricia Waugh (*Metafiction*, p. 79ff.) noted this, although genres other than the detective story and the thriller are simply listed.

25. Barthelme, *The Dead Father*, p. 104.

26. Zéraffa, *Personne et personnage*, p. 460.

27. Blanchot, *L'arrêt de mort*, p. 57.

28. Descombes, "Les Embarras du référent," p. 780.

29. Des Forêts, *Le Bavard*, p. 47–48.

30. See Mortimer, *Clôture narrative*, chapter 6.

6. Voices: Knowing, Telling, and Showing It or Not

1. Genette, *Nouveau Discours du récit*, pp. 68, 69.

2. Lintvelt, *Essai de typologie narrative*, pp. 24–25.

3. Tacca, *La voces de la novela*, p. 69.

4. See Prince, "Introduction à l'étude du narrataire," and Rousset, "La Question du narrataire."

5. *Epic of Gilgamesh*, ed. Sandars, p. 61.

6. See *Epic of Gilgamesh*, ed. Heidel, 1963.

7. In Maupassant, *La Main gauche*.

8. Potocki, *La Duchesse d'Avila (Manuscrit trouvé à Saragosse)*, p. 47.

9. Hawthorne, *The Scarlet Letter*, p. 42.

10. Duras, *Savannah Bay*, p. 110.

11. Greimas and Courtès, *Sémiotique: Dictionnaire raisonné*, p. 128.

12. See, for example, Altman, *Epistolarity*; Groupe μ: *Rhétorique de la poésie*; Renza, "The Veto of the Imagination."

13. Gaddis, *The Recognitions*, p. 510.

14. Rimmon-Kenan, *Narrative Fiction*, p. 90.

15. Valette, *Esthétique du roman moderne*, p. 34.

16. Genette, *Nouveau discours du récit*, p. 49.

17. Chatman, *Story and Discourse*, p. 154.

18. Lotman, "Point of view in a text," p. 339.

19. Wharton, *Ethan Frome*, p. 3.

20. Chatman, *Story and Discourse*, p. 153.

21. This short story by Balzac (1830), on the theme of cruel jealousy, has for its Σ narrator Dr. Bianchon, who tells it at the end of a party; his curiosity for the facts was prompted by the aspect of an abandoned castle, and he was told the truth by a former servant who witnessed the tragic events.

22. James, *The Europeans*, p. 128.

23. Genette, *Nouveau discours du récit*, p. 29.

24. Ségur, *Blondine*, pp. 27–30.

25. Bakhtine, *Esthétique et théorie du roman*, p. 181.

26. See, for example, this fragment:

she	*don't mention it*
he	*why can't you shut up*
she	*why can't you shut up*
he	*shut up*
she	*you shut up*
	(both together)
he	*shut up*
she	*shut up*

(Laing, *Do You Really Love Me?* p. 24).

27. Rulfo, *Pedro Páramo*, pp. 187–88.

28. González Boixo, "Introducción," in Rulfo, *Pedro Páramo*, p. 29.

29. Mairet, *Sylvie*, pp. 20–22, 27–28. Spelling slightly modernized.

30. Saint-Amant, "La Métamorphose de Lyrian et de Sylvie," in *Oeuvres complètes*, p. 72.

31. Compton-Burnett, *Manservant*, pp. 218–21.

7. Binding and Unfolding: On Narrative Syntax

1. Chomsky, *Syntactic Structures*, p. 11.

2. See, for example, Todorov, *Grammaire du Décaméron*, and Courtès, "Une Lecture sémiotique de 'Cendrillon,' " in *Introduction à la Sémiotique narrative*.

3. Genette, *Figures II*, p. 56.

4. See, for example, Ricardou, "Problèmes de la description," in *Problèmes du Nouveau Roman*, pp. 125–57; Ricardou, "Le Texte en conflit," in *Nouveaux problèmes du roman*, pp. 24ff.; Hamon, "Qu'est-ce qu'une description?" pp. 465–85; Hamon, *Introduction à l'analyse du descriptif*.

5. Hamon, *Analyse*, p. 7.

6. Contrary to Genette's affirmation in *Figures II*, p. 59 (English translation of this paper: "Boundaries of Narrative," *New Literary History*, 8 [1976], pp. 1–15).

7. Hamon, "Qu'est-ce qu'une description?" p. 466.

8. *Epic of Gilgamesh* (Sandars), p. 77.

9. Van Buuren, "L'Essence des choses."

10. Debray-Genette, "La Pierre Descriptive," p. 299.

11. Hamon, "Qu'est-ce qu'une description?" p. 484, n. 46.

12. Brooks, *Reading for the Plot*, p. xi.

13. Calvino, *Our Ancestors*, p. 70.

14. A phrase borrowed from Hamon, *Texte et idéologie*.

15. Sternberg, *Expositional Modes and Temporal Ordering in Fiction*, p. 8.

16. Morrissette, *Les Romans d'Alain Robbe-Grillet*.

17. *The Australian*, January 2, 1981.

18. Flaubert, *L'Education sentimentale*, p. 160.

19. In particular, by Chatelain, "Itération interne et scène classique," "Récit itératif et concretisa-tion," "Frontières de l'itératif."

20. Hesse, *Siddhartha*, p. 51.

21. Baquero Goyanes, *Estructuras de la novela actual*, pp. 63–65.

22. Genette, *Figures III*, pp. 122–23 and 141–44.

23. Chatman, *Story and Discourse*, pp. 75–76.

24. Rousset, *Leurs yeux se rencontrèrent*, p. 7.

25. Baquero Goyanes, *Estructuras*, p. 63, referring to Souvage, *An Introduction to the Study of the Novel*, p. 41.

26. Barthes, "Structural Analysis," in *Image-Music-Text*, p. 101.

27. I mean that initiated in the 1940s with Joseph Frank's essay in the *Sewanee Review*; see his "Answer to Critics," and Mitchell, "Spatial Form in Literature."

28. See Meyer, ed., *L'Interrogation*, and forthcoming Acts of Cerisy-La-Salle 1987: "Argumenta-tion et signification."

29. Wilson and Sperber, "Remarques," pp. 81–82.

30. See Barthes, *S/Z* (1976), p. 26.

31. Gaddis, *The Recognitions*, p. 298.

32. Zéraffa, "Fiction et répétition," in Passeron, *Création et répétition*, p. 121.

33. Dante, *Vita nuova*, chapter 21, p. 46.

34. Perry, "Literary Dynamics," p. 50.

35. Said, *Beginnings*, p. 76.

8. Narrative Economy

1. See Cros, *Théorie et pratique sociocritique*, and the journal *Sociocritique/Sociocriticism*, pub-lished since 1985.

2. Goldmann, *Structures mentales et création culturelle*, p. xiii.

3. See Hamon, *Texte et idéologie*, pp. 12ff.

4. See Macherey, *Pour une théorie de la production littéraire*, pp. 174ff.

5. See Coste, 1976 and 1977; see also Shell, *The Economy of Literature*.

6. See Leenhardt, *Lecture politique du roman*.

7. See Jameson, *The Political Unconscious*.

8. See Jameson, ibid., p. 85, for a definition.

9. In *Cuentos completos*, pp. 63–93.

10. Inoue, *The Hunting Gun*, p. 57.

11. Gaddis, *The Recognitions*, p. 960.

12. Sterne, *Tristram Shandy*, p. 615.

13. Eagleton, *Criticism and Ideology*, p. 98.

14. See Chambers, "Le Texte 'difficile' et son lecteur."

15. See Coste, 1985a.

9. Narrative within Genres and Media

1. Guillén, *Literature as System*, p. 108.
2. Genette et al., *Théorie des genres*, p. 7.
3. See Hambürger, *Logique des genres littéraires*.
4. See Hernadi, *Beyond Genre*, particularly p. 184.
5. See Jost, *Introduction to Comparative Literature*, pp. 129–33.
6. See Barat et al., *Théorie des genres et communication*, p. 7.
7. See Marino, "Toward a Definition of Literary Genres," in Strelka, *Theories of Literary Genres*.
8. See Todorov, "La Notion de littérature" and "L'Origine des genres," in *Les Genres du discours*, pp. 13–26 and 44–60, respectively.
9. Lanson, *Méthode de l'histoire littéraire*, p. 23.
10. Genette, *Nouveau discours du récit*, p. 12.
11. See, among others, Lejeune, *Le Pacte autobiographique*.
12. Freud, *Jokes*, pp. 118, 119.
13. A collection of recent short stories by an Argentinian writer, born in 1942, who lives in Madrid.
14. Sternberg, *Expositional Modes and Temporal Ordering in Fiction*, p. 1.
15. Sylvester, *La prima carnal*, p. 111.
16. Poe, *Complete Tales and Poems*, p. 465.
17. Sylvester, *La prima carnal*, p. 108.
18. See Dällenbach, *Le Récit spéculaire*, pp. 30, 84.
19. In *La prima carnal*, pp. 117–42.
20. In *Cuentos completos*, pp. 115–37.
21. See, for example, Coste, "Apologie de la non-prose." and and "Le Recours du vers et le sujet de la prose."
22. Fourier, *L'Attraction passionnée*, pp. 58–59.
23. Black, *Critical Thinking*, p. 147.
24. Marlowe and Chapman, *Héro et Léandre*, p. 80.
25. Hugo, *La Légende des siècles*, vol. 2, p. 190.
26. Voltaire, *La Henriade*, p. 556.
27. Taylor, in Voltaire, *La Henriade*, p. 227.
28. Poe, *Complete Tales and Poems*, pp. 951–54.
29. Dorchain, *L'Art des vers*, p. 364.
30. Lamb, *Tales from Shakespeare*, pp. 139–40.
31. See Rimmon-Kenan, *Narrative Fiction*, pp. 106ff.
32. See chapter 1, pp. 4–6.
33. Mathieu-Colas, "Frontières de la narratologie," pp. 106–7.
34. A satirical piece against a Minister and tyrant of the Eastern Roman Empire, who grew rich at the expense of the Arians, confiscating their property on the pretext of religious dissidence.
35. Lope de Vega, *El Nuevo Mundo descubierto por Cristobal Colón*, p. 351. It is remarkable and a clear sign of Prescott's irony that these lines are placed by Lope in the mouth of the allegorical character Idolatría. The same arguments against the Spaniards are given twice by the Devil himself; "No los lleva cristiandad / Sino el oro y la codicia" (p. 352) and "Estos, codiciando oro / De tus Indias, se hacen santos; / Fingen cristiano decoro / Mientras vienen otros tantos / Que lleven todo el tesoro" (p. 377). Lope's play itself, severely judged by a number of Spanish critics and not included in many anthologies of the *Comedias*, is a typical example of ideological overkill and contradiction between didactic methods.

36. Prescott, *Conquest of Peru*, p. 232.
37. Saintsbury, *A Short History of English Literature*, p. 626.
38. Lukács, *Historical Novel*, p. 45; see also pp. 230ff.
39. For a more complete version of part of this section, see Coste, 1987.
40. Blanchot, *L'Espace littéraire*, p. 115.
41. See chapter 2, pp. 59–60.
42. The horizontal face-to-face of Herod with Iaokannan's head, and that of Salome with Mannei are significant but less important; they link protagonists with secondary characters
43. A poem written by Wordsworth in 1798 or 1799, published in 1800; see it under the curiously inappropriate title "Song" in Stephen Gill (ed.), *William Wordsworth*, pp. 147–48.
44. Metz, *Essais sur la signification au cinéma*, p. 129.

10. What Tales Tell Us to Do and Think, and How

1. See O'Malley, "Content and Rhetorical Forms in Seventeenth-Century Treatises on Preaching," especially p. 242.
2. See Jolles, "La Légende," in *Formes simples*, pp. 27–54.
3. Struik, *Birth of the Communist Manifesto*, p. 58.
4. Engels, "Draft," in Marx and Engles, *Collected Works*, vol. 6, pp. 96ff.
5. Engels, "Principles of Communism," in ibid., pp. 341–57.
6. Quoted by Struik, *Birth of the Communist Manifesto*, p. 60.
7. Marx and Engels, "Manifesto," in Struik, ibid., p. 89.
8. Kaminskas, "*Le Petit Prince* ou la bonne pédagogie," p. 65.
9. See Chambers, "Violence du récit."
10. O'Malley, "Content and Rhetorical Forms," p. 240.
11. See Suleiman, *Authoritarian Fictions*, and Foulkes, *Literature and Propaganda*.
12. Freud, "Family Romances, in *Standard Edition*, vol. 9, p. 238.
13. Brooks, *Reading for the Plot*," p. 115.
14. See Coste, 1985c and 1987b
15. Freud, "Family Romances," pp. 239–40.
16. Kundera, *La Vie est ailleurs*, p. 176.
17. See Miguet, "Le Pacte allégorique de J.-M. G. Le Clézio."
18. Sadoff, "The Dead Father," p. 39.
19. Brooks, *Reading for the Plot*," p. 137.
20. See Sadoff, "The Dead Father," p. 55.
21. See Warner, "Dickens Looks at Homer."
22. Ramsay, "Discours," in Fénelon, *Télémaque*, p. xxxi.
23. Fénelon, *Télémaque*, iin *Oeuvres complètes*, vol. 6, p. 546.
24. Suleiman, *Authoritarian Fictions*, p. 22.
25. Ibid., p. 36.
26. From the prologue in the first edition consulted, p. i, not reproduced in some later editions.
27. Ramsay, "Discours," in Fénelon, *Télémaque*, p. xxix.
28. Suleiman, *Authoritarian Fictions*, p. 46.
29. Quoted by Noel, *Theories of the Fable in the Eighteenth Century*, p. 19.
30. Ibid.
31. Bosch and Cere, *Los fabulistas y su sentido histórico*, p. 19.
32. Published by Robert, *Fables inédites*, vol. 1, p. 279.
33. Honig, *Dark Conceit*, p. 59.
34. Levin, "Allegorical Language."
35. Aristotle, *Rhetoric*, pp. 11–12, 73, and 234.

Bibliography

Bibliography

1. Works mentioned and quoted

Altman, Janet Gurkin. *Epistolarity: Approaches to a Form*. Columbus: Ohio State University Press, 1982.

Ariès, Philippe. *Le Temps de l'histoire*. 1954. Paris: Seuil, 1986.

Aristotle. *The Rhetoric*. Trans. Lane Cooper. New York: Appleton-Century-Crofts, 1932.

Arlincourt, Vicomte d'. *Ismalie ou la Mort et l'Amour*. Vol. 1. Paris: Ponthieu, 1828.

Bache, Carl. "Tense and Aspect in Fiction." *Journal of Literary Semantics*, (August 1986), pp. 82–97.

Bakhtine, Mikhaïl. *Esthétique et théorie du roman*. Paris: Gallimard, 1978.

Banfield, Ann. "Ecriture, Narration, and the Grammar of French." In Hawthorn, *Narrative*, pp. 1–27.

Baquero Goyanes, Mariano. *Estructuras de la novela actual*. Barcelona: Planeta, 1970.

Barat, Jean-Claude, et al. *Théorie des genres et communication*. Bordeaux: Université de Bordeaux III, 1978.

Barsch, Achim, and Helmut Hauptmeier. "Speculations about Jakobson: Logical Reconstruction from a Literary Point of View." *Poetics*, 12 (1983), pp. 537–65.

Barthelme, Donald. *The Death Father*. New York: Quokka-Pocket Books, 1978.

Barthes, Roland. "Introduction à l'analyse structurale des récits." *Communications*, 8 (1966), pp. 1–27.

Barthes, Roland. "Introduction to the Structural Analysis of Narratives." In *Image-Music-Test*. Glasgow: Fontana/Collins, 1979, pp. 79–124.

Barthes, Roland. *S/Z*. Paris: Seuil: 1970.

Barthes, Roland. *S/Z*. Trans. Richard Miller. New York: Hill & Wang, 1974.

Berthoud, J. A. "Narrative and Ideology: A Critique of Fredric Jameson's *The Political Unconscious*." In Hawthorn, ed., *Narrative*, pp. 101–15.

Black, Max. *Critical Thinking: An Introduction to Logic and Scientific Method*. 2nd ed. Englewood Cliffs, N.J.: Prentice-Hall, 1959.

Blanchot, Maurice. *L'Arrêt de mort*. Paris: Gallimard, 1948.

Blanchot, Maurice. *L'Espace littértaire*. 1955. Paris: Gallimard, 1968.

Bosch, Rafael, and Ronald Cere. *Los fabulistas y su sentido histórico*. New York: Collección Iberia, 1969.

Brautigan, Richard. *The Abortion: An Historical Romance 1966*. New York: Simon & Schuster, 1971.

Bremond, Claude. *Logique du récit*. Paris: Seuil, 1973.

Brooks, Peter. *Reading for the Plot: Design and Intention in Narrative*. New York: Vintage Books, 1985.

Calvino, Italo. *Our Ancestors (The Cloven Viscount; Baron in the Trees; The Non-Existent Knight)*. London: Picador, n.d.

Canary, Robert H., and Henry Kozicki, eds. *The Writing of History: Literary Form and Historical Understanding*. Madison: University of Wisconsin Press, 1978.

Carpentier, Alejo. *Cuentos completos*. Barcelona: Bruguera, 1983.

Carr, David, et al., eds. *La Philosophie de l'histoire et la pratique historienne d'aujourd'hui*. Actes du Colloque d'Ottawa, April 18–20, 1980. Ottawa: University of Ottawa Press, 1982.

Certeau, Michel de. "L'Histoire, science et fiction." in Carr et al., *La Philosophie de l'histoire*, pp. 19–39.

Cervantes Saavedra, Miguel de. *The Ingenious Gentleman Don Quixote de la Mancha*. Translation based on that of Peter Anthony Motteux. Edited by Edward Bell. London: George Bell and Sons, 1882.

Cervantes Saavedra, Miguel de. *El Ingenioso Hidalgo Don Quijote de la Mancha*. 1605–15. Madrid: Ediciones Castilla, 1966.

Chambers, Ross. "Le Texte 'difficile' et son lecteur." In Colloque de Cerisy, *Problèmes actuels de la lecture*. Paris: Clancier-Guénaud, 1982, pp. 81–93.

Chambers, Ross. "Violence du récit: Boccace, Mérimée, Cortázar." *Revue Canadienne de Littérature Comparée*, 12 (June 1986), pp. 159–86.

Charles, Michel. *Rhétorique de la lecture*. Paris: Seuil, 1977.

Chatelain, Danièle. "Frontières de l'itératif." *Poétique*, 65 (1986), pp. 111–24.

Chatelain, Danièle. "Itération interne et scène classique." *Poétique*, 51 (1982), pp. 369–81.

Chatelain, Danièle. "Récit itératif et concrétisation." *Romance Review*, 72 (1981), pp. 304–16.

Chatman, Seymour. *Story and Discourse: Narrative Structure in Fiction and Film*. Ithaca: Cornell University Press, 1978.

Chomsky, Noam. *Syntactic Structures*. The Hague: Mouton, 1957.

Cohn, Dorrit. *Transparent Minds: Narrative Modes for Presenting Consciousness in Fiction*. Princeton, N.J.: Princeton University Press, 1978.

Compagnon, Antoine. *La Seconde main, ou le travail de la citation*. Paris: Seuil, 1979.

Compton-Burnett, Ivy. *The Last and the First*. New York: Knopf, 1971.

Compton-Burnett, Ivy. *Manservant and Maidservant*. 1947. Oxford: Oxford University Press, 1983.

Coquet, Jean-Claude. *Sémiotique littéraire: Contribution à l'analyse sémantique du discours*. Tours: Mame, 1973.

Coste, Didier. "Apologie de la non-prose, *suivi de* Poèmes récents." *Poésie*, 32 (1985), pp. 51–63.

Courtés, Joseph. *Introduction à la sémiotique narrative et discursive: Méthodologie et application*. Paris: Hachette, 1976.

Couturier, Maurice, and Régis Durand. *Donald Barthelme*. London: Methuen, 1982.

Cros, Edmond. *Théorie et pratique sociocritiques*. Montpellier: Université Paul Valéry, 1983.

Dällenbach, Lucien. *Le Récit spéculaire: Essai sur la mise en abyme*. Paris: Seuil, 1977.

Dante Alighieri. *Vita Nuova*. Milan: Rizzoli, 1952.

Debray-Genette, Raymonde. "La Pierre Descriptive." *Poétique*, 43 (1980), pp. 293–304.

Descombes, Vincent. "Les Embarras du référent." *MLN*, 101 (1986), pp. 765–80.

Doležel, Lubomir. "Pour une typologie des mondes fictionnels." In Herman Parret and Hans-Georg Ruprecht, eds., *Exigences et perspectives de la sémiotique: recueil d'hommages pour Algirdas Julien Greimas*. Amsterdam: Benjamins, 1985.

Dorchain, Auguste. *L'Art des vers*. Paris: Librairie Garnier, 1919.

Duras, Marguerite. *L'Amour*. Paris: Gallimard, 1971.

Duras, Marguerite. *Détruire dit-elle*. Paris: Minuit, 1969.

Duras, Marguerite. *Le Ravissement de Lol V. Stein*. Paris: Gallimard, 1964.

Duras, Marguerite. *Savannah Bay*. New ed. Paris: Minuit, 1983.

Eagleton, Terry. *Criticism and Ideology: A Study in Marxist Literary Theory*. London: NLB, 1976.

Eagleton, Terry. *Literary Theory: An Introduction*. Minneapolis: University of Minnesota Press, 1983.

Eco, Umberto. *Lector in fabula: La cooperación interpretativa en el texto narrativo*. Barcelona: Lumen, 1981.

Epic of Gilgamesh. English version and introduction by N. K. Sandars. Harmondsworth: Penguin Books, 1960.

[*Epic of Gilgamesh*]: *The Gilgamesh Epic and Old Testament Parallels*. 1949. By Alexander Heidel. Chicago: The University of Chicago Press, 1963.

Erlich, Victor. *Russian Formalism*. 3rd ed. New Haven, Conn.: Yale University Press, 1981.

Farcy, Gérard-Denis. "De l'obstination narratologique." *Poétique*, (1986), pp. 491–506.

Federman, Raymond. *Take It or Leave It*. New York: Fiction Collective, 1976.

Fénelon, François Salignac de la Mothe. *Les Avantures de Télémaque, fils d'Ulysse*. London: Tonson and Watts, 1719.

Fénelon, François Salignac de la Mothe. *De l'Education des filles*. 1689. In *Oeuvres Complètes*. Vol. 5. Geneva: Slatkine Reprints, 1971, pp. 563–603.

Flaubert, Gustave. *L'Education Sentimentale*. 1869. In *Oeuvres complètes*, vol. 2. Paris: Seuiul, 1964.

Florian, Jean-Pierre Claris de. *Estelle, roman pastoral*. 2nd ed. Paris: Imprimerie de Monsieur, 1787.

Fontanier, Pierre. *Les Figures du discours*. 1830. Paris: Flammarion, 1977.

Forêts, Louis-René des. *Le Bavard*. 1947. Paris: Gallimard, 1978.

Forêts, Louis-René des. *La Chambre des enfants*. 1960. Paris: Gallimard, 1983.

Foucault, Michel. *L'Archéologie du savoir*. Paris: Gallimard, 1969.

Foulkes, A. P. *Literature and Propaganda*. London: Methuen, 1983.

Fourier, Charles. *L'Attraction passionnée*. Paris: Jean-Jacques Pauvert, 1967.

Fowles, John. *The Magus*. Rev. ed. Frogmore-St. Albans: Triad Panther, 1977.

Frank, Joseph. "Spatial Form: An Answer to Critics." *Critical Inquiry*, 4 (1977), pp. 231–52.

Frank, Joseph. "Spatial Form in Modern Literature." *Sewanee Review*, 53 (1945), pp. 221–40, 433–56, 643–53.

Freud, Sigmund. "Family Romances" (1909). In *Standard Edition*, vol. 9. Ed. James Strachey (London: Hogarth Press,), pp. 237–41.

Freud, Sigmund. *The Interpretation of Dreams*. Harmondsworth: Penguin Books, 1976.

Freud, Sigmund. *Jokes and Their Relation to the Unconscious*. Harmondsworth: Penguin Books, 1976.

Fromm, Erich. *The Forgotten Language: An Introduction to the Understanding of Dreams, Fairy Tales and Myths*. New York: Rinehart, 1951.

Frow, John. *Marxism and Literary History*. Cambridge, Mass.: Harvard University Press, 1986.

Frow, John. "Spectacle Binding: On Character." *Poetics Today*, (1986), pp. 227–50.

Gaddis, William. *The Recognitions*. 1952. New York: Avon, 1974.

Garvey, Diane I. "Juan Marsé's *Si te dicen que caí*: The Self-reflexive Text and the Question of Referentiality." *MLN*, 95 (1980), pp. 376–87.

Genette, Gérard. *Figures II*. Paris: Seuil, 1969.

Genette, Gérard. *Figures III*. Paris: Seuil, 1972.

Genette, Gérard. *Nouveau discours du récit*. Paris: Seuil, 1983.

Genette, Gérard. *Palimpsestes: La Littérature au second degré*. Paris: Seuil, 1982.

Genette, Gérard, et al. *Théorie des genres*. Paris: Seuil, 1986.

Gide, André. *La Symphonie pastorale*. Paris: Lettres Modernes-Minard, 1970.

Gilgamesh. Translated from the Sîn-leqi-unninï version by John Gardner and John Maier with the assistance of Richard A. Henshaw. New York: Vintage Books, 1985.

Goldmann, Lucien. *Structures mentales et création culturelle*. Paris: Anthropos, 1970.

Goytisolo, Luis. *Las afueras*. 1958. Barcelona: Seix Barral, 1971.

Greenblatt, Stephen. "Splenditello." *London Review of Books*, June 19, 1986, pp. 5–6.

Greimas, Algirdas-Julien. *On Meaning: Selected Writings in Semiotic Theory*. Trans. Paul Perron and Frank Collins. Minneapolis: University of Minnesota Press, 1987.

Greimas, Algirdas Julien, and Joseph Courtès. *Sémiotique: Dictionnaire raisonné de la théorie du langage*. Paris: Hachette, 1979.

Grivel, Charles. *Production de l'intérêt romanesque: un état du texte (1870–1880). Un essai de constitution de sa théorie*. The Hague: Mouton, 1973.

Groupe µ. *Rhétorique de la poésie: Lecture linéaire, lecture tabulaire*. Brussels: Editions Complexe, 1977.

Guillén, Claudio. *Literature as System: Essays toward the Theory of Literary History*. Princeton, N.J.: Princeton University Press, 1971.

Halliday, M. A. K. *Language as Social Semiotic: The Social Interpretation of Language*. Baltimore: University Park Press, 1978.

Hamburger, Käte. *Logique des genres littéraires*. Paris: Seuil, 1986.

Hamon, Philippe. *Introduction à l'analyse du descriptif*. Paris: Hachette, 1981.

Hamon, Philippe. "Pour un statut sémiologique du personnage." In Roland Barthes et al., *Poétique du récit*. Paris: Seuil, 1977, pp. 115–180.

Hamon, Philippe. "Qu'est-ce qu'une description?" *Poétique*, 12 (1972), pp. 465–85.

Hamon, Philippe. *Texte et idéologie: Valeur, hiérarchies et évaluations dans l'oeuvre littéraire*. Paris: PUF, 1984.

Hawthorn, Jeremy, ed. *Narrative: From Malory to Motion Pictures*. London: Edward Arnold, 1985.

Hawthorne, Nathaniel. *The Scarlet Letter*. New York: New American Library, 1980.

Hernadi, Paul. *Beyond Genre: New Directions in Literary Classification*. Ithaca: Cornell University Press, 1972.

Hesse, Hermann. *Siddhartha*. 1922. London: Picador, 1973.

Holenstein, Elmar. "On the Poetry and the Plurifunctionality of Language." In Barry Smith, ed. *Structure and Gestalt: Philosophy and Literature in Austria-Hungary and Her Successor States*. Amsterdam: Benjamins, 1981.

Honig, Edwin. *Dark Conceit: The Making of Allegory*. Evanston, Ill.: Northwestern University Press, 1959.

Hudson, Robert. *Word Grammar*. Oxford, Basil Blackwwell, 1984.

Hugo, Victor. *La Légende des siècles*. 1859–83. Vol. 2. Paris: Classiques Garnier, 1955.

Huizinga, J. *The Waning of the Middle Ages*. Harmondsworth: Penguin Books, 1972.

Hutcheon, Linda. *Narcissistic Narrative: The Metafictional Paradox*. Waterloo, Ontario: Wilfrid Laurier University Press, 1980.

Inoue, Yasushi. *The Hunting Gun*. 1949. Tokyo: Charles E. Tuttle, 1961.

Iser, Wolfgang. *The Act of Reading: A Theory of Aesthetic Response*. London: Routledge and Kegan Paul, 1978.

Iser, Wolfgang. *The Implied Reader: Patterns of Communication in Prose Fiction from Bunyan to Beckett.* Baltimore: Johns Hopkins University Press, 1974.

Jakobson, Roman. "Closing Statement: Linguistics and Poetics." In Thomas A. Sebeok, ed., *Style in Language.* Cambridge, Mass.: MIT Press, 1960, pp. 350–77.

James, Henry. *The Europeans.* 1878. Harmondsworth: Penguin Books, 1976.

James, Henry. *In the Cage.* In *The New York Edition of Henry James.* New York: Charles Scribner's Sons, 1936. Vol. 11, pp. 367–507.

Jameson, Fredric. *The Political Unconscious: Narrative as a Socially Symbolic Act.* London: Methuen, 1981.

Jenny, Laurent. "Le Poétique et le narratif." *Poétique,* 28 (1976), pp. 440–49.

Jolles, André. *Formes simples.* 1930. Paris: Seuil, 1972.

Jost, François. *Introduction to Comparative Literature.* Indianapolis: Bobbs-Merrill, 1974.

Kaminskas, Jurate. "*Le Petit Prince* ou la bonne pédagogie: Une analyse sémiotique des structures didactiques." *Canadian Modern Language Review,* 40 (1983), pp. 61–69.

Kawin, Bruce F. *Telling It Again and Again: Repetition in Literature and Film.* Ithaca: Cornell University Press, 1972.

Kerbrat-Orecchioni, Catherine. *La Connotation.* Lyon: Presses Universitaires de Lyon, 1977.

Kierkegaard, Søren. *Repetition: An Essay in Experimental Psychology.* 1843. New York: Harper Torchbooks, 1964.

Kress, Gunther, and Robert Hodge. *Language as Ideology.* London: Routledge & Kegan Paul, 1979.

Kristeva, Julia. *La Révolution du langage poétique: L'avant-garde à la fin du XIXe siècle: Lautréamont et Mallarmé.* Paris: Seuil, 1974.

Kundera, Milan. *La Vie est ailleurs.* Paris: Gallimard, 1981.

LaCapra, Dominick. "History and Psychoanalysis." CHS Occasional Papers, no. 5. Center for Humanistic Studies, University of Minnesota, Minneapolis, 1985.

Laing, R. D. *Do You Love Me?* Harmondsworth: Penguin Books, 1976.

Lamb, Charles and Mary. *Tales from Shakespeare.* London: Dent-Dutton, 1956.

Lanson, Gustave. *Méthodes de l'histoire littéraire.* Paris: Les Belles Lettres, 1925.

Le Clézio, J. M. G. *Mondo et autres histoires.* Paris: Gallimard, 1982.

Leenhardt, Jacques. *Lecture politique du roman: La Jalousie d'Alain Robbe-Grillet.* Paris: Minuit, 1973.

Lejeune, Philippe. *Le Pacte autobiographique.* Paris: Seuil, 1975.

Levin, Samuel R. "Allegorical Language." in Morton W. Bloomfield, ed., *Allegory, Myth and Symbol.* Cambridge, Mass.: Harvard University Press, 1981.

Lintvelt, Jaap. *Essai de typologie narrative: le "point de vue."* Paris: José Corti, 1981.

Lotman, Juri M. "Point of View in a Text." *New Literary History,* 6 (1975), pp. 339–52.

Lukács, Georg. *The Historical Novel.* Trans. Hannah and Stanley Mitchell. London: Merlin Press, 1962.

Lyons, John. *Semantics.* 2 vols. Cambridge: Cambridge University Press, 1978.

McCawley, James D. *Everything That Linguists Have Always Wanted to Know about Logic* But Were Ashamed to Ask.* Oxford: Basil Blackwell, 1981.

Macherey. *Pour une théorie de la production littéraire.* Paris: Maspero, 1966.

Mairet, Jean. *Sylvie, tragi-comédie pastorale.* 1628. Critical edition by Jules Marsan. Paris: Droz, 1932.

Maitre, Doreen. *Literature and Possible Worlds.* London: Pembridge Press, 1983.

Marghescou, Mircea. *Le Concept de littérarité: Essai sur les possibilitiés théoriques d'une science de la littérature.* The Hague: Mouton, 1974.

Marino, Adrian. "Toward a Definition of Literary Genres." In Joseph P. Strelka, *Theories of Literary Genre.* Yearbook of Comparative Criticism, vol. 8. University Park: Pennsylvania State University Press, 1978, pp. 41–56.

Marlowe, Christopher, and George Chapman. *Héro et Léandre*. Paris: Aubier-Montaigne, 1950.

Marquez Rodríguez, Alexis. *Lo barroco y lo real-maravilloso en la obra de Alejo Carpentier*. Mexico City: Siglo Veintiuno Editores, 1982.

Marrou, Henri-Irénée. *De la connaissance historique*. 1954. Paris: Seuil, 1975.

Martin, Robert. *Pour une logique du sens*. Paris: PUF, 1983.

Martin, Wallace. *Recent Theories of Narrative*. Ithaca: Cornell University Press, 1986.

Marx, Karl, and Friedrich Engels. *The Communist Manifesto*. In Dirk J. Struik, *Birth of the Communist Manifesto*. New York: International, 1971.

Mathieu-Colas, Michel. "Fontières de la narratologie." *Poétique*, 65 (1986), pp. 91–113.

Maupassant, Guy de. *La Main gauche*. 1889. Paris: Hachette, 1973.

Metz, Christian. *Essais sur la signification au cinéma*. Vol. 1. Paris: Klincksieck, 1968.

Meyer, Michel, ed. *L'Interrogation. Langue Française*, no. 52. Paris: Larousse, 1981.

Miguet, Marie. "Le Pacte allégorique de J.-M. G. Le Clézio" (*Mondo et autres histoires, L'Inconnu sur la terre*). *Corps écrit*, no. 18, (June 1986), pp. 115–22.

Milza, Pierre, and Serge Berstein. *Le Fascisme italien, 1919–1945*. Paris: Seuil, 1980.

Mink, Louis O. "Narrative Form as a Cognitive Instrument." In Canary and Kozicki, eds., *The Writing of History*, pp. 129–49.

Mitchell, W. J. T. "Spatial Form in Literature: Toward a General Theory." *Critical Inquiry* (1980), pp. 539–67.

Morrissette, Bruce. *Les Romans de Robbe-Grillet*. Paris: Minuit, 1981.

Mortimer, Armine Kotin. *La Clôture narrative*. Paris: José Corti, 1985.

Mukarovsky, Jan. *Aesthetic Function, Norm and Value as Social Facts*. Ann Arbor: Michigan Slavic Publications, 1970.

Musée. *La Touchante Aventure de Héro et Léandre*, remise au jour, traduite en prose, by Thierry Sandre. Amiens: Edgar Malfère, 1924.

Nabokov, Vladimir. *Speak, Memory*. New York: Putnam's, 1966.

Noel, Thomas. *Theories of the Fable in the Eighteenth Century*. New York: Columbia University Press, 1975.

Nowell-Smith, P. H. "Historical Facts." In Carr, et al., *La Philosophie de l'histoire*, pp. 317–23.

Ohmann, Richard. "Literature as Act." In Seymour Chatman, ed., *Approaches to Poetics*. New York: Columbia University Press, 1973, pp. 81–107.

O'Malley, John W. "Content and Rhetorical Forms in Sixteenth-Century Treatises on Preaching." In James J. Murphy, ed., *Renaissance Eloquence: Studies in the Theory and Practice of Renaissance Rhetoric*. Berkeley: University of California Press, 1983, pp. 238–52.

Orlando, Francesco. *Toward a Freudian Theory of Literature, with an Analysis of Racine's Phèdre*. Baltimore: Johns Hopkins University Press, 1978.

Pavel, Thomas G. *Fictional Worlds*. Cambridge, Mass.: Harvard University Press, 1986.

Pavel, Thomas G. "Possible Worlds in Literary Semantics." *Journal of Aesthetics and Art Criticism*, (1975), pp. 319–32.

Pearson, Roger. "A la recherche du temps présent: quelques réflexions sur l'art de la chronique dans "Le Rouge et le Noir.' " *Stendhal Club*, 27 (1984–85), pp. 247–63.

Pérez Galdós, Benito. *Los Apostólicos*. In *Episodios nacionales*. Vol. 2. Madrid: Aguilar, 1979, pp. 567–676.

Pérez Galdós, Benito. *Zumalacarregui*. In *Episodios nacionales*. Vol. 2. Madrid: Aguilar, 1979, pp. 789–889.

Pérez y Pérez, Rafael. *Palomita torcaz*. Barcelona: Juventud, 1943.

Perry, Menakhem. "Literary Dynamics: How the Order of a Text Creates Its Meanings." *Poetics Today*, (1979), pp. 35–64.

Poe, Edgar Allen. *The Complete Tales and Poems*. Harmondsworth: Penguin Books, 1982.

Pompa, Leon. "Narrative Form, Significance and Historical Knowledge." In Carr et al., eds., *La Philosophie de l'histoire*, pp. 143–57.

Potocki, Jean. *La Duchesse d'Avila (Manuscrit trouvé à Saragosse)*. Paris: Gallimard, 1972.

Prescott, William H. *History of the Conquest of Peru, with a Preliminary View of the Civilization of the Incas*. Rev. ed. London: Swan Sonnenschein, 1889.

Prince, Gerald. "Ceci n'est pas l'inénarré." Paper presented at the 20th Century French Studies Colloquium, March 1987, Duke University, Durham, N.C.

Prince, Gerald. *A Grammar of Stories: An Introduction*. The Hague: Mouton, 1973.

Prince, Gerald. "Introduction á l'étude du narrataire." *Poétique*, 14 (1973), pp. 178–96.

Prince, Gerald. "Narrative Pragmatics, Message, and Point." *Poetics*, 12 (1983), pp. 527–36.

Prince, Gerald. *Narratology: The Form and Functioning of Narrative*. Berlin-New York-Amsterdam: Mouton, 1982.

Quine, W. W. *Methods of Logic*. 4th ed. Cambridge, Mass.: Harvard University Press, 1982.

Ramsay, Andrew Michael. *Les Voyages de Cyrus, avec un discours sur la théologie et la mythologie des païens*. Par M. de Ramsay, traduit par J. E. G. M. de la Grange. Philadelphia: James Rivington, 1796.

Ramsay, André Michel, chevalier de. "Discours de la poésie épique et de l'excellence du Poème de Télémaque." In Fénelon, *Les Avantures de Télémaque*. 1719, pp. i–xxxv.

Ramsay, André Michel, chevalier de. *Les Voyages de Cyrus, Histoire morale*. 1727. Nouvelle édition. La Haye: chez Nicolas van Daalen, 1768.

Renza, Louis A. "The Veto of the Imagination: A Theory of Autobiography." In James Olney, ed., *Autobiography: Essays Theoretical and Critical*. Princeton, N.J.: Princeton University Press, 1980, pp. 268–95.

Ricardou, Jean. *Nouveaux Problèmes du roman*. Paris: Seuil, 1978.

Ricardou, Jean. *Le Nouveau Roman*. Paris: Seuil, 1973.

Ricardou, Jean. *Pour une théorie du Nouveau Roman*. Paris: Seuil, 1971.

Ricardou, Jean. *Problèmes du Nouveau Roman*. Paris: Seuil, 1967.

Ricoeur, Paul. *Temps et récit*, 3 vols. Paris: Seuil, 1983–85.

Riffaterre, Michael. *La Production du texte*. Paris: Seuil, 1979.

Rimbaud, Arthur. *Oeuvres complètes*. Ed. Antoine Adam. Paris: Gallimard, 1972.

Rimmon-Kenan, Shlomith. *Narrative Fiction: Contemporary Poetics*. London: Methuen, 1983.

Robert, A. C. M. *Fables inédites des XIIe, XIIIe et XIVe siècles et fables de La Fontaine rapprochées de celles de tous auteurs qui avaient, avant lui, traité les mêmes sujets*. 2 vols. Paris: Etienne Cabin, 1825.

Roddenberry, Gene. *Star Trek: The Motion Picture*. London: Futura, 1979.

Roger, Alain. *Proust, Les Plaisirs et les noms*. Paris: Denoël, 1985.

Rousset, Jean. *Leurs yeux se rencontrèrent: La scène de première vue dans le roman*. Paris: José Corti, 1981.

Rousset, Jean. "La Question du narrataire." In Colloque de Cerisy: *Problèmes actuels de la lecture*. Paris: Clancier-Guénaud, 1982, pp. 23–34.

Rubert de Ventós, Xavier. *El arte ensimismado*. 1963. Barcelona: Ediciones Península, 1978.

Rulfo, Juan. *Pedro Páramo*. ed. José Carlos Gonzalez Boixo. Madrid: Cátedra, 1984.

Sadoff, Dianne F. "The Dead Father: *Barnaby Rudge*, *David Copperfield*, and *Great Expectations*." *Papers on Language and Literature*, 18 (1982), pp. 36–57.

Said, Edward W. *Beginnings: Intention and Method*. New York: Columbia University Press, 1985.

Saint-Amant (Marc-Antoine de Gérard). *Oeuvres complètes*. Ed Ch.-L. Livet. Vol. 1. Paris: Jannet, 1985.

Saint-Exupéry, Antoine de. *Le Petit Prince*. In *Oeuvres*. Paris: Gallimard, 1959.

Saintsbury, George. *A Short History of English Literature*. London: Macmillan, 1924.

Santa Teresa de Jesús. *Su vida*. Madrid: Espasa Calpe, 1943.

Sartre, Jean-Paul. *Les Mots*. Paris: Gallimard, 1964.

Ségur, Comtesse de. *Histoire de Blondine suivi de Ourson*. Paris: LGF 1982.

SEL (Séminaire d'études littéraires, IVe Congrès). *Le Personnage en question*. Toulouse: Université de Toulouse-le-Mirail, 1984.

Shakespeare, William. *King Lear*. Ed. H. H. Furness. "New Variorum Edition," vol. 5. Philadelphia: Lippincott, 1899.

Shell, Marc. *The Economy of Literature*. Baltimore: Johns Hopkins University Press, 1978.

Souvage, Jacques. *An Introduction to the Study of the Novel, with Special Reference to the English Novel*. Ghent: Story-Scientia, 1965.

Steiner, Peter. "Three Metaphors of Russian Formalism." *Poetics Today*, (Winter 1980–81), pp. 59–116.

Stendhal. *Romans et nouvelles*. Vol. 1. Paris: Gallimard, 1952.

Sternberg, Meir. *Expositional Modes and Temporal Ordering in Fiction*. Baltimore: Johns Hopkins University Press, 1978.

Sterne, Laurence. *The Life and Opinions of Tristram Shandy, Gentleman*. 1759–67. Harmondsworth: Penguin Books, 1978.

Stierle, Karlheinz. "Réception et fiction." *Poétique*, 39, (1979), pp. 299–320.

Struik, Dirk J. *Birth of the Communist Manifesto*. New York: International, 1971.

Suleiman, Susan Rubin. *Authoritarian Fictions: The Ideological Novel as a Literary Genre*. New York: Columbia University Press, 1983.

Swearingen, James E. *Reflexivity in Tristram Shandy: An Essay in Phenomenological Criticism*. New Haven, Conn.: Yale University Press, 1977.

Sylvester, Santiago. *La prima carnal*. Barcelona: Anagrama, 1986.

Tacca, Oscar. *Las voces de la novela*. 2nd ed. Madrid: Gredos, 1978.

Thomason, Richmond. *Symbolic Logic*. New York: Macmillan, 1970.

Todorov, Tzvetan. *Grammaire du Décaméron*. The Hague: Mouton, 1969.

Todorov, Tzvetan. *Les Genres du discours*. Paris: Seuil, 1978.

Todorov, Tzvetan. *Introduction à la littérature fantastique*. Paris: Seuil, 1970.

Todorov, Tzvetan, ed. *Théorie de la littérature: Textes des Formalistes russes*. Paris: Seuil, 1965.

Tomachevski, Boris. *Teoría de la literatura*. Madrid: Akal, 1982.

Traugott, Elizabeth Closs, and Mary Louise Pratt. *Linguistics for Students of Literature*. New York: Harcourt Brace Jovanovich, 1980.

Turner, Victor. "Process, System and Symbol: A New Anthropological Synthesis." *Daedalus*. 106 (1977), pp. 60–80.

Uspensky, Boris. *Poetics of Composition*. Berkeley: University of California Press, 1973.

Valette, Bernard. *Esthétique du roman moderne: Le Roman en France: XIXe et XXe siècles*. Paris: Nathan, 1985.

Van Buuren, Maarten. "L'Essence des choses: Etude de la description dans l'oeuvre de Claude Simon." *Poétique*, 43 (1980), pp. 324–33.

Vann, Richard T. "Louis Mink's Linguistic Turn." *History and Theory*, 26 (1987), pp. 1–14.

Vega Carpio, Lope Félix de. *El nuevo mundo descubierto por Cristobal Colón* (1614). In *Obras de Lope de Vega*. Vol. 11, pp. 341–80. Madrid: Rivadeneyra, 1900.

Volponi, Paolo. *The Worldwide Machine*. London: Calder & Boyars, 1969.

Voltaire. *La Henriade*. Critical edition by O. R. Taylor. 2nd ed. *The Complete Works of Voltaire*. Vol. 2. Geneva: Institut et Musée Voltaire, 1970.

Vonnegut, Kurt Jr. "Harrison Bergeron." 1950. In Dick Allen, *Science Fiction: The Future*. New York: Harcourt Brace Jovanovich, 1971.

Warner, John R. "Dickens Looks at Homer." *The Dickensian*, 60 (1964), pp. 52–54.

Waugh, Linda R. "The Poetic Function in the Theory of Roman Jakobson." *Poetics Today*, 2 (Autumn 1980), pp. 57–82.

Waugh, Patricia. *Metafiction: The Theory and Practice of Self-Conscious Fiction*. London: Methuen, 1984.

Weinrich, Harald. *Le Temps: Le Récit et le commentaire*. 1964. Paris: Seuil, 1973.

Wharton, Edith. *Ethan Frome*. New York: Charles Scribner's Sons, 1911.

White, Hayden. "The Question of Narrative in Contemporary Historical Theory." *History and Theory*, 23 (1984), pp. 1–33.

White, Hayden. *Tropics of Discourse: Essays in Cultural Criticism*. Baltimore: Johns Hopkins University Press, 1978.

Wilson, Deirdre, and Dan Sperber. "Remarques sur l'interprétation des énoncés selon Paul Grice." *Communications*, no. 30 (*La Conversation*), (1979), pp. 80–93.

Wing, Nathaniel. *Present Appearances: Aspects of Poetic Structure in Rimbaud's Illuminations*. Columbia: University of Missouri Press, 1974.

Wordsworth, William. [*Works*]. Edited by Stephen Gill. Oxford: Oxford University Press, 1984.

Wordsworth, W., and S. T. Coleridge. *Lyrical Ballads*. Ed. R. L. Brett and A. R. Jones. New York: Methuen, 1968.

Zéraffa, Michel. "Fiction et répétition." In René Passeron, ed., *Création et répétition*. Paris: Clancier-Guénaud, 1982, pp. 121–36.

Zéraffa, Michel. *Personne et personnage, le romanesque des années 1920 aux années 1950*. Paris: Klincksieck, 1971.

Zola, Emile. *Paris*. 1898. Lausanne: Editions Rencontre, n.d.

Zola, Emile. *Rome*. 1896. Lausanne: Editions Rencontre, n.d.

2. The Author's Research on Narrative Communication

1976. "Economie textuelle / économie colonialiste." *Cahiers Internationaux de Symbolisme*, 31–32, pp. 121–35.

1977. "Politextual Economy: In Defence of an Unborn Science." In S. Knight and M. Wilding, *The Radical Reader*. Sydney, Wild and Woolley, pp. 37–53.

1979. "Heroic Function and Interpretation of Narrative." *MLN*, 94, pp. 1176–88.

1980. "Trois Conceptions du lecteur et leur contribution à une théorie du texte littéraire." *Poétique*, 43, pp. 354–71.

1981. "Structures narratives d'un récit non narratif: *Les Espaces brûlés* de Pierre Silvain. *Australian Journal of French Studies*, 18, pp. 89–100.

1982a. "Instalments of the Heart: Periodical Narrative and Text Demarcation. *Sub-Stance*, 33–34, pp. 56–65.

1982b. "Autobiographie et autoanalyse, matrices du texte littéraire." In C. Delhez-Sarlet and M. Cattani, eds., *Autobiographie et individualisme en Occident* (Colloque de Cerisy-la-Salle). Brussels, Institut de Sociologie, Université Libre de Bruxelles, pp. 249–63.

1983a. "Rehearsal: An Alternative to Production/Reproduction in French Feminist Discourse." In Hassan, Ihab, and Sally, *Innovation/Renovation*. Madison, University of Wisconsin Press, pp. 243–62.

1983b. "Où Jules Verne montre son jeu: *Le Château des Carpathes* comme allégorie de la communication narrative." *Cahiers des Lettres Modernes*, série "Jules Verne," no. 4, pp. 161–78.

1983c. "Nabokov, la référence et ses doubles." *Fabula*, 2, pp. 29–47.

1984a. "Conscience du texte et texte de l'inconscient: pour une problématique de la littérature post-freudienne." *Littérature*, 54, pp. 20–38.

1984b. "Fonctions cardinales du personnage et cohérence du récit." In Colloque du SEL, *Le Personnage en question*. Toulouse, pp. 11–21.

1984c. With M. Zéraffa, ed., *Le Récit amoureux* (Colloque de Cerisy-la-Salle). Sessey-Paris. Champ

Vallon. My foreword, pp. 3–7, and paper, "Le Genre du roman rose et la dissidence amoureuse," pp. 297–307.

1985a. "Discours de l'essai et discours narratif dans *De l'Amour*. In Colloque de Cerisy-la-Salle, *Stendhal*, "Mélanges de la Bibliothèque de la Sorbonne." Paris, L'Amateur de Livres, pp. 179–91.

1985b. "S. Thala, capitale du possible." In Danielle Bajomée and Ralph Heyndels, *Ecrire, dit-elle: imaginaires de Marguerite Duras*. Brussels, Editions de l'U.L.B., pp. 165–78.

1985c. "Le Roman familial dans le roman rose." in CLESH, ed., *Le Roman familial, Cahiers de l'UPPA*, n.s. 5, pp. 110–33.

1985d. "Enonciation dialogique et communication narrative: quelques propositions pour la recherche." *Fabula*, 5, May, pp. 149–52.

1985e. "*Lector in figura*: fictionalité et rhétorique générale." In Jean Bessière, ed., *Lectures, systèmes de lectures*. Paris, PUF, pp. 13–28.

1986. "Narratividad limitada en *Pueblo* de Azorín." In *Azorín, Cahiers de l'UPPA*, n.s. 8, pp. 189–95.

1987a. "Salomé vue par: programmes narratifs et programmes visuels." In J. P. Guillerm, ed., *Des mots et des couleurs, II*. Lille, Presses Universitaires de Lille, pp. 69–87.

1987b. *Conformité et narrativité: travail de reproduction idéologique et discours du changement, d'après quelques romans de Rafael Pérez y Pérez*. Microform edition, Lille, ART 1987. Selected Spanish translation forthcoming as *Bodas de tinta*, Madrid, Hiperíon, 1989.

1987c. "La scène, l'éclipse et l'alternative (réflexions sur le sens narratif et ses valeurs chez Pierre Mertens). *Lendemains*, 12, pp. 57–64.

1988a. "Genografía: normas y tensiones en las provincias del discurso." *Eutopías*, 3, pp. 37–52.

1988b. "*Allouma*, ou ce que la main gauche n'a pas dit à la main droite." *French Forum*, 13, 2, May, pp. 229–42.

1988c. "Débat, ébats et cours fatal: fonctions dialogiques et rhétorique narrative dans *Sylvie* de Jean Mairet." In Y.-A. Favre, ed., *Mélanges Maurice Descotes* pp. 57–80. Also forthcoming in *Romanic Review* November 1989.

1988d. "Le Recours du vers et le sujet de la prose." Paper presented at the Twentieth-Century French Studies Colloquium, February 1988, Pomona College, CA, forthcoming.

1988e. "La Mecanización del deseo." Paper presented at the International Symposium on *Modernidad y modernización*. Valencia, July 1988. Forthcoming. Minneapolis, Prisma Institute, 1989.

[work in progress] *Absence and Becoming: The Polemic and Dialectics of Lyrical Discourse*. Chapter 3, "The Returns of Narrative."

Index

Index

Theory and History of Literature

Didier Coste is a professor of French at San Diego State University and a *Maître de Conférences* in Comparative Literature at the Université de Pau, France. He has also held visiting appointments at the University of Oregon, New York University, the University of Minnesota, and Louisiana State University. Coste earned his doctorates in French studies from the University of Sydney and in Romance studies at the Université de Provence. Editor of *Le Récit amoureux* and author of *Bodas de tinta* (1989), Coste has published novels, poetry, and literary translations since 1963. He serves as editor of *Noesis*, chairs the Noesis Foundation, and contributes to many journals.

Wlad Godzich is professor of comparative literature and French studies at the Université de Montréal. He serves, with Jochen Schulte-Sasse, as editor of the series Theory and History of Literature.